Bold Thinking on Investment Management

The FAJ 60th Anniversary Anthology

CFA INSTITUTE

ISBN 978-1-932495-45-4

Printed in the United States of America
22 September 2005

ACKNOWLEDGMENTS

We would like to gratefully acknowledge the support and assistance of CFA Institute and the Advisory Council and Editorial Board of the *Financial Analysts Journal*:

CFA INSTITUTE

This anthology is published in the spirit of furthering the mission of CFA Institute . . .

To lead the investment profession globally by setting the highest standards of ethics, education, and professional excellence.

CONTENTS

Lessons of the Market

Through the Years

Bridging Theory and Practice

FOREWORD

Over the past 60 years, the *Financial Analysts Journal* has played an important role in publishing some of the best thinking in the industry, positing new theories, and challenging established wisdom. In these Reflections pieces, this tradition continues.

The academic world of finance has spawned some truly brilliant theorists and theories. They cover a wide range:

- Harry Markowitz showing that mean–variance optimization can maximize return at any given risk level;
- Merton Miller and Franco Modigliani suggesting that valuation should be independent of capital structure, such as debt-to-equity ratios;
- William Sharpe, John Lintner, and Jack Treynor suggesting, in the capital asset pricing model, that expected return is singularly related to nondiversifiable risk associated with the market portfolio;
- Stephen Ross and Richard Roll introducing arbitrage pricing theory;
- Eugene Fama and Kenneth French observing the importance of more than one priced risk factor;
- Fischer Black and Myron Scholes identifying a precise means of valuing options;
- Daniel Kahneman and Amos Tversky's work in behavioral finance suggesting a behavioral basis for market inefficiencies;

and the list goes on.

These theories have a common denominator: They all seek to describe how the world *should* work. Many of the original architects of these brilliant theories readily acknowledge that the theories are based on an array of implausible assumptions. To rely on the theories as *fact*, one must accept all the assumptions as *fact*. The sheer brilliance of many of the theories often blinds us to their limitations.

This reaction is reminiscent of the scientific view described by Ptolemy and Aristotle, which prevailed for 1,500 years until the Renaissance. The assumptions they propounded—a flat earth; a terra-centric universe; the four elements of earth, air, fire, and water as the fundamental building blocks of the universe; and the notion that objects twice as heavy should fall twice as fast—were all quite sensible. They matched people's intuitive beliefs and were crudely supported by observation. All were accepted, largely unquestioned and unchallenged, as fact. Ptolemy and Aristotle were unequivocally brilliant, as were most of their theories. Some of the theories, however, were merely good approximations of reality (e.g., the earth *is* flat, to a first-order approximation, for the distances that one can travel on foot in a week).

The theses of Copernicus, Galileo, and Isaac Newton, which eclipsed the Ptolemaic/Aristotelian worldview, were merely better approximations of reality and were subsequently eclipsed by those of Albert Einstein and others—to be superseded by other theories, many as yet unknown. In short, accepting theory as fact may be pervasive enough to slow the evolution of our understanding of the world, but in time, new theories arrive that improve on prior knowledge.

We need to constantly test, challenge, and seek to advance our best theories. To paraphrase Newton, we see far only if we stand on the shoulders of giants. We see the world more clearly if we do not take the easy path of accepting our best, our most far-reaching, and our most insightful theories as fact. Today's theories are the strong base on which we build, but they are only theories.

Finance theory will continue to advance apace as long as the *FAJ* welcomes articles that propound improvements in the theoretical foundations of the world of finance *and* articles that challenge the bestowed wisdom of the giants who laid these foundations.

With that mission in mind, this volume presents the *current* reflections of some of the very best thinkers in today's investment community as their ideas were presented throughout this 60th Anniversary year of the *FAJ*. The articles draw from the practitioner and the academic communities. The reflections span the past evolution of our industry, the current key trends and crosscurrents, and speculations on future directions for both theory and practice. It has been an honor and a privilege to serve as *FAJ* editor during this anniversary year as we assembled this impressive array of writers and their thoughts. I hope and believe that this volume can serve as a useful reference to our industry for many years to come.

Robert D. Arnott
Editor
Financial Analysts Journal

PREFACE

In January 1945—60 years ago—the *Financial Analysts Journal* circulated its inaugural issue to about 700 subscribers. Published by the New York Society of Security Analysts, the journal (then called *The Analysts Journal*) and its board of editors, with remarkable foresight, embarked on an important mission that remains as relevant today as it was then: "to advance the interests of our profession [and] to encourage thoughtful discussion and debate on topics of current interest" (see www.cfapubs.org). As a result of deliberate and dedicated effort, the *FAJ* has carefully documented the flow of best investment thinking through time. A journey through its issues is like watching a motion picture of the thoughts behind the profession so many of us enjoy.

Since its launch, the *Financial Analysts Journal* has published thousands of articles by thousands of authors, including eight winners of the Nobel Prize in Economics. The works of many of the most prominent thinkers in the investment industry have appeared in the *FAJ*. Nobel Laureate William Sharpe, for instance, has had 12 articles printed in the *FAJ*. Other important contributors over the years include Benjamin Graham (sometimes writing under the pen name "Cogitator") with 19 articles, Fischer Black with 18, and Martin Leibowitz with an incredible 33 articles.

In my opinion, the most profound lesson to be gleaned from a perusal of *FAJ* issues is that, even after 60 years, we are still a relatively young industry compared with, for example, physics or law. As a result, conventional wisdom as to what is "normal" or "equilibrium" continues to evolve and must be time dependent. This revealing insight clarifies that investment management is about ideas and people, with all of their cognitive biases, not irrefutable physical laws. I wish someone had pointed this out to me as a young asset allocator decades ago.

The *Financial Analysts Journal* is an integral part of CFA Institute, although the *FAJ*'s editor and boards work with great autonomy—as a result of the wisdom of the New York Society when the journal was first established and decisions on *FAJ* governance made by successor publishers, the latest of which is CFA Institute. Despite differing governing bodies, however, the *FAJ* adheres to the same standards and principles as CFA Institute, as is evident in its processes and procedures (available at www.cfapubs.org). It represents CFA Institute and has filled that role admirably. Within the broad portfolio of activities involving the CFA charter, standards of practice, advocacy, and professional development, the *FAJ* stands as a beacon of independently generated, rigorous research that ultimately helps shape and define the CFA Institute Global Body of Knowledge. It is fair to say, then, that the *FAJ* is an important element in advancing the mission of CFA Institute "to lead the investment profession globally by setting the highest standards of ethics, education, and professional excellence."

The *FAJ* and CFA Institute are proud to commemorate the *FAJ*'s 60th Anniversary, and these special Reflections articles celebrate this exciting milestone. Among the oldest journals (if not the oldest journal) dedicated to the interests of financial professionals, the *FAJ* began with a vision to advance investment-practitioner knowledge. As the *FAJ* moves forward, it will remain true to that vision. The initial goal to "prove useful to the financial communities of the country" has been achieved. Indeed, now the "financial communities" include a global readership of more than 100,000! By pursuing the goal of publishing the finest practitioner-oriented thinking and research in the field, the *FAJ* continues its instrumental role in helping us serve the markets and our clients.

Jeffrey J. Diermeier, CFA
CFA Institute President and CEO

OVERVIEW

A Provocative Year of Reflections and Bold New Insights

Rodney N. Sullivan, CFA

In our 60th year of linking innovative researchers to the broad investment community, the *Financial Analysts Journal* has offered the reflections of the most influential thinkers in investment management. These articles steep us in an unparalleled discussion of the past, present, and future of our industry. Concurrent with this celebration year, CFA Institute held the *FAJ* 60th Anniversary conference entitled *Reflections and Insights: Provocative Thinking on Investment Management* in February 2005. Several articles in this anthology are based on the authors' presentations at that conference, and several presentations can be viewed in their entirety on the CD attached to the back cover of this anthology.

A number of themes are developed in the articles written for this celebration year, and we organized this anthology by these themes. This overview is not intended to be exhaustive but to capture the essence of each theme. A "Through the Years" section provides short time capsules written by people significant in the journal's history. Included with these perspectives is an annotated timeline that reveals many of the developing themes of finance over the years.

As we assimilate the wisdom of the remarkable gathering of minds in this volume into our own understanding of investment management, we benefit greatly from their experienced yet forward-looking perspectives. We hope that this wonderful collection of essays makes a positive, profound impression on your investment thinking and practice.

Responsibilities to the Profession

One of the most important issues in our industry today is our ethical responsibilities, and the majority of the authors in this anthology, no matter what their primary subject, reflect these responsibilities. In addition to fiduciary responsibilities and statutory/regulatory compliance, ethical issues arise in numerous contexts, including relationships between principals and agents, between superiors and subordinates, and between analysts and clients.

Marianne M. Jennings, preeminent ethics scholar, suggests that those involved in the financial markets take an introspective look at how their behavior matches or does not match their high-flying ethics talk. Recall Enron Corporation's 64-page award-winning code of ethics and the CEO of conglomerate Tyco International, Dennis Kozlowski, laughably suggesting, "We have no perks, not even parking spaces." I guess a $6,000 personal shower curtain and lavish parties held at shareholder expense are not considered perks. As Jennings points out, words and documents do not necessarily produce ethical behavior—or reduce hubris. Changing a company, profession, and industry requires true, heartfelt reform and individual ethical courage. Jennings wonders whether after the latest and all the previous well-known shenanigans, we really "get it." Are individuals *now* reformed and exercising ethical courage and leadership in their companies?

Governance visionary Dean LeBaron, CFA, identifies two classes of contributors to the recent corporate scandals: financial analysts and independent directors. Each clearly played an enabling role in the recent rounds of corporate malfeasance, but both have hardly been mentioned in the ensuing hangover. Before we can say that we are on the road to reform and that we get it, in Jennings' opus sense, each of us needs a true ethical compass and a method of ethical analysis to which we firmly stick. In the case of analysts and directors, therefore, considerably improved transparency and accountability are needed, according to LeBaron (see also Dobson 2003).

Jeffrey J. Diermeier, CFA, president and CEO of CFA Institute, joins the discussion with a call to action for leaders of investment firms to create a covenant with clients to treat them fairly and to put them first. We can succeed as a profession only by placing client interests above all else; it is the sine qua non of our profession. This tenacity of purpose allows a highly profitable business *and* allows firms to be true to basic ethical principles. Diermeier contends that firms that extend offerings beyond their investment staff's capabilities cannot deliver on that fundamental covenant upon which all trust is built. Investment management is about service and integrity. We cannot forget either.

Investor Interests: Sine Qua Non

The call to return to our ethical roots is clearly and closely related to the issue of agency theory, which deals with the alignment of the interests of principals (e.g., individual investors) and agents (e.g., investment organizations). Among leading industry thinkers, a critical mass seems to be building that we need to correct the conflicts in our principal–agent relationships.

Keith Ambachtsheer, a longtime leader in the unraveling of principal–agent conflicts, succinctly summarizes the primary challenge in agency theory: Organizational structure must lead to mission clarity and alignment of interests between principals and the agents acting on their behalf. In the case of the typical U.S. corporate pension plan, Ambachtsheer finds an unnecessary conflict between the company's pension fund managers and the company's stakeholders. Corporate pension plans are managed by the same corporate managers who are responsible for maximizing returns for *all* stakeholders, and plan beneficiaries are just one of many constituents. The United Air Lines bankruptcy saga provides a case in point. Months prior to declaring bankruptcy, UAL ceased making any contributions to its pension funds, which produced legal action from the Pension Benefit Guarantee Corporation for nonpayment of contributions. This action, in turn, produced continuing strains between stakeholder groups—specifically, employees and management.

The pension–management agency problem also frequently rears its head in the form of unrealistic assumptions for returns on pension assets. Ambachtsheer suggests that such conflicts easily disappear with the adoption of well-governed, arm's-length, private-sector pension organizations or the use of risk-sharing arrangements among the multiple stakeholder groups.

David I. Fisher, famous for his prescience in regard to the investment management business, comments that an excess of money managers who are more passionate about the business than the investment management process will inevitably lead to a wave of reform. The reform will turn the profession away from the current practice of asset gathering and toward the creation of small boutiques focused on investment fundamentals. Perhaps the turning point has already been reached.

Legendary investor and writer John C. Bogle also finds important principal–agent issues in the current investment environment, which he deems to be too favorable toward the agents. In one of two pieces developed especially for the *FAJ* anniversary year, he concludes that the changes that have occurred in the mutual fund industry in the past 60 years have "benefited mutual fund managers to the direct and commensurate detriment of mutual fund investors." The mutual fund industry too often strives to maximize its own profitability, putting its own interests ahead of those of the principals it serves.

In a second piece, based on his presentation to the *FAJ* 60th Anniversary conference, Bogle emphasizes that the industry has changed from a profession with aspects of a business to a business with aspects of a profession—that is, from stewardship to salesmanship. Bogle points out that investors have not benefited from the economies of scale in asset management. Mutual fund assets under management rose 3,600 times between 1945 and 2004, but average expense ratios more than doubled—from 0.76 percent to1.56 percent. He also believes that this imbalance will lead to a wave of reform, as investors respond by insisting that agents put investor interests first.

Investment guru Gary P. Brinson, CFA, notes that something is clearly amiss when we compare aggregate active management fees with the zero sum of aggregate value added in the financial markets. Yet, curiously, active management fees are several times those of passive management. He predicts that this discrepancy means change is on the horizon—again, a reform movement. As in the case of mutual fund investors, buyers of investment management services will become increasingly aware of this imbalance and refuse to accept the fee arrangements. Fees must come down. Brinson thus proposes a thoughtful performance-based fee structure in which, in general, the fee would align the investor's results with the manager's performance. Any fee larger than the passive fee would be tied to value added relative to a specified benchmark.

In another thoughtful piece, Richard M. Ennis, CFA, explores the issues underlying the paradox of high active management fees existing in the presence of low active management payoffs. Reflecting on the causes of increasing efficiency in the U.S. financial markets, he notes, among other causes, improved information flow and innovative low-cost derivative products, such as futures, options, and swaps. To answer the question of whether active management fees are too high, Ennis points out that the probability of earning positive alpha faces an increasingly steep challenge as fees rise. Consider the unlikely possibility that a manager imposing a 3.0 percent fee will add alpha. This manager would need remarkable forecast accuracy to have a mere 15 percent likelihood of success in the alpha hunt. Moreover, this same amazingly skilled manager with a much lower 1.5 percent fee *still* has only a 46 percent chance of adding alpha. Simply put, good managers must also have "good" fee structures.

In his analysis of agency problems between investors and investment managers, Ambachtsheer calls for integrating the tools and insights of modern portfolio theory with principal–agent theory. MPT and standard finance theory assume that the ultimate investor is making investment choices, but today, most investors actually delegate investment decisions to financial professionals. Clearly, given the issues discussed by Ambachtsheer, Fisher, Bogle, Brinson, and Ennis—and see also Cornell and Roll (2005)—agents may behave differently from what the principals expect.

On the Shoulders of Giants

Insightful market historian Peter L. Bernstein provides a wonderful documentary of the development of investment theory. He reminds us how amazing it is that an entire body of knowledge was created from scratch in the 21-year span from 1952 to 1973. We have gained tremendously from the efforts of the industry legends who accomplished this feat—Harry M. Markowitz, Fischer Black and Myron Scholes, Jack Treynor, Robert C. Merton, and William F. Sharpe. As Bernstein aptly puts it, before these giants, we had "only rules of thumb and folklore."

In many ways, investors are just beginning to understand and implement the insights from these ingenious inventors of MPT. For instance, researchers have empirically identified a few select variables that seem to add to the explanation of average returns provided by the capital asset pricing beta—such as size, certain price ratios, and momentum—but the CAPM construct is difficult to test empirically because the market portfolio is so elusive. Some suggest that empirical tests of the CAPM represent a measuring problem inherent in the false notion that the mean–variance market model is best represented by a capitalization-weighted framework (see, e.g, Arnott, Hsu, and Moore 2005; Treynor 2005). What we know is that adjusted, enhanced—even radically different—frameworks will continue to emerge, which advances our theory and understanding.

Meir Statman, the distinguished investigator into behavioral finance, believes that our mean–variance framework needs adjusting because people are not mean–variance oriented. They are simply not the rational investors of MPT; they are the normal investors they have always been. Classical economics and finance theory assume market participants are rational and act on the basis of perfect knowledge. Normal investors may be primarily rational, but they have the cognitive biases we all have, which may produce market inefficiencies.

For Nobel Laureate Harry Markowitz, the empirical problems related to the CAPM come as no surprise. He shows us that, in reality, expected returns are *not* likely to be linearly related to betas. Adding to this observation, he shows why only one portfolio (with the only differences among investors being the amount of cash borrowing or lending) may *not* be efficient for all investors. Consider his conclusion that the composition of the risky portfolio may, in practice, change as we move along the efficient frontier.

Despite challenges to the CAPM, all agree that it demonstrates that the vast majority of portfolio risk, beta, is systematic market risk; alpha, as captured in unsystematic risk, has a zero expected value (or, after fees, negative value). The CAPM, then, in its truest sense, prescribes Bogle's mantra: "Go indexing, investor!"

Unforced Errors

The amazingly articulate Bogle notes that with defined-benefit pension plans being replaced by defined-contribution (DC) plans, everybody in the future will be an investor. The question is: What do individuals need in order to achieve self-sufficient investment success? He offers some simple, intuitive rules. First, investors must save more than they do today. On average, today's DC retirement accounts—401(k) plans and IRAs—are underused savings instruments. Only 22 percent of U.S. workers use 401(k) plans; only 10 percent own an IRA. Even more troubling is that balances in these plans average around a modest $30,000. Shockingly, one-half of people receiving Social Security benefits today find it is their only source of income.

The second rule of investing success is to use reasonable return expectations, not the bloated expectations commonly in use by pension plans. And we must keep our costs low. Between 1983 and 2003, the average equity mutual fund captured only about 79 percent of the market return (as measured by the S&P 500 Index). The disconnect comes largely from the additional costs of active management over passive management.

Investment maven Charles D. Ellis, CFA, points out that "costs" are not only the direct costs captured by expense ratios. Large losses are almost always caused by trying to get too much and taking too much risk. He shakes his head over our propensity go for the Big Score—even though we know that a 50 percent loss requires a *double* the next time we're up at bat just to get even. In effect, "we have met the enemy and it is us!" Ellis suggests that successful investing rests on two pillars: (1) plan *your* game and play *your* game to win according to what you planned and (2) don't lose.

By choosing indexing over active management, investors reduce both direct and indirect costs associated with active management. Today's typical active manager has portfolio turnover of more than 100 percent a year, which invariably leads to what Ellis suggests, in that management costs so much because of errors in decisions. These errors include transaction costs, mistakes, and of course, management fees.

Bogle supports this argument. He notes that investors serve their long-term interests best by, first, doing no harm. As in the game of tennis, investors too often lose the game of investing by making unforced errors. Investors would do well to play the investment game not by attempting to hit investment winners, which on average, leads to disappointing results, but by sticking to a realistic game plan. Hopefully, we can learn such simple and intuitive investment truisms from the sages of investing before it's too late to achieve our long-term objectives.

Economics and finance author Henry Kaufman offers us many lessons from his lengthy and successful career. One notable message is that models based on the assumption that past patterns will repeat in the future are sure to miss the critical ingredient in making solid projections—identifying what *differs* from the past. Exacerbating our tendency to create rearview models is our clear bias against negative financial and economic predictions. We are inclined to be optimistic, and other forces in our profession reinforce that inclination.

Martin L. Leibowitz, a leading recipient of the prestigious *FAJ* Graham and Dodd Award, offers clear insights into the market efficiency debate at the core of our business. He agrees with the message of Bogle and Ellis: Play a consistent game and avoid miss hits. He adds, however, that certain anomalies—some structural, others behavioral—do exist that create opportunities for a few great alpha-seeking hunters to seize upon. The great players—in tennis and investing—are those who are able to seize opportunities and force a win. That is, they succeed in generating alpha. Leibowitz cautions us, however, that although some pockets of inefficiency are discernible and actionable, other inefficiencies are simply out of reach. Therefore, in the pursuit of active alpha, investors are floating on a "sea of ambiguity."

In a similar vein, noted bond investor William H. Gross, CFA, conveys his thoughts on exploiting market distortions, or what he terms "structural market inefficiencies." Gross provides practitioner context by summarizing specific examples of structural inefficiencies that by definition possess longevity. The long-standing idea of selling (unlevered!) volatility is an example. The strategy can be accomplished quite simply by, for instance, owning a large share of residential mortgages relative to an index. Other structures are also available for the opportunistic portfolio, but Gross advises investors to select such structures in concert with their long-term view of the economy and to "not overdo it."

Finally, in avoiding unforced errors while pursuing active management, noted authority in portfolio risk management Richard Grinold offers a road map for understanding and managing the three key forces of success: return, risk, and cost. As noted by Grinold and many others we have mentioned here, success is limited largely by costs, both opportunity (indirect) costs and implementation (direct) costs. Adding value thus requires a highly disciplined approach.

Lessons of the Market

The 60th anniversary of the *FAJ* comes on the heels of a great equity market bubble and bust. Can we reach new levels of understanding by combining the insights of MPT with the hard lessons learned from real market experience? The irrepressible Clifford S. Asness thinks so. He advises that we can garner a great deal of insight from a historical market perspective. Much as Jennings asks whether we "get" the moral lessons of recent years, Asness asks whether equity investors "get" return expectations in today's environment. For equity investors, a historical view of P/Es plainly suggests that higher prices relative to earnings today imply lower future returns relative to the median. In short, for the future, equity investor expectations must be ratcheted down. Asness warns investors not to take comfort in the false hope that stocks *always* win over the long run. In a world with a low risk premium, this "false lesson" must be unlearned.

Furthermore, the notion that stocks win over the long run is based on a study of the United States—a country that has dominated the equity returns race. The long-term study of *global* equity market returns by Dimson, Marsh, and Staunton (2004) concluded that, based on current market returns, believers in stocks for the long run are irrationally exuberant. They painted a more subdued picture of long-term *global* equity market returns, both historically and, by extension, for the future. They also found, however, that lower volatility accompanies the temperate global returns. Thus, considering returns and return volatility together, international diversification is an important ingredient in successfully positioning a portfolio on the efficient frontier. Most U.S. investors, however, seem to have too little international exposure. Perhaps another unforced error?

Renowned author and professor Jeremy J. Siegel offers his reflections on the equity risk premium. He tells us that, on a compound basis, the premium has measured about 4 percent against U.S. T-bills over the very long period from 1802 through 2004. It rose over the years from a low of 2.2 percent in the first half of the 20th century to 5.4 percent during the most recent half century. His narrative offers some sensible explanations for the existence of an upward bias in the historical level of the risk premium. Some of these explanations are survivorship bias (the United States turned out to be the strongest capitalist country ever), transaction costs, and investor ignorance about true equity risks and returns because of a lack of available data. These biases reasonably combine to lower the historical equity risk premium by 1–2 percentage points.

Bridging Theory and Practice

A series of reflections articles make available to readers keen insights into tools of our trade. These articles are sure to spark practitioner interest and imagination and develop investor knowledge, skills, and abilities. For example, investment maven Abby Joseph Cohen, CFA, provides practical, down-to-earth advice for understanding the many limitations of the economic data we use. And Frank J. Fabozzi, CFA, well-known expert in fixed-income investing, discusses practical issues related to the structured finance arena. Valuation guru Aswath Damodaran tells us how companies can turn risk from a threat to their financial health into an opportunity to get ahead of the competition.

Nobel Laureate Clive W.J. Granger describes the current state of financial theory and predicts three directions for future empirical research in finance: exploration of conditional distributions, reinvestigation of the "facts" accepted on the basis of linear models, and possibly complete redefinition of our theory based on research into "jump" diffusions.

Conclusion

Investment management is as much about ideas and people—with all their cognitive biases—as it is about scholarly treatises. We have learned from our past successes as well as our past failures in determining how to move our profession forward, and we have an amazing story to tell. As we witness the unfolding applications of MPT to real portfolios in daily practice, we must be mindful of one of the cornerstones of our profession—ethical leadership. True ethical and professional leadership means putting clients, investors, first. This simple concept must serve as a litmus test for our daily decision making. Can we return to our roots of a *profession* with elements of a business rather than a business with the elements of a profession?

References

Arnott, Robert D., Jason Hsu, and Philip Moore. 2005. "Fundamental Indexation." *Financial Analysts Journal*, vol. 61, no. 2 (March/April):83–99.

Cornell, Bradford, and Richard Roll. 2005. "A Delegated-Agent Asset-Pricing Model." *Financial Analysts Journal*, vol. 61, no. 1 (January/February):57–69.

Dimson, Elroy, Paul Marsh, and Mike Staunton. 2004. "Irrational Optimism." *Financial Analysts Journal*, vol. 60, no. 1 (January/February 2004):15–25.

Dobson, John. 2003. "Why Ethics Codes Don't Work." *Financial Analysts Journal*, vol. 59, no. 6 (November/December): 29–34.

Treynor, Jack. 2005. "Why Market-Valuation-Indifferent Indexing Works." *Financial Analysts Journal*, vol. 61, no. 6 (November/December).

Ethics and Investment Management: True Reform

Marianne M. Jennings

These are introspective times for those involved in the financial markets. Some feel a sense of renewal via reform. Others, who have come to the realization that Frank Quattrone, late Silicon Valley guru of Credit Suisse First Boston, will do about one month in prison for each word that he wrote in a hasty e-mail to his employees, feel fear, particularly of New York Attorney General Eliot Spitzer and e-mail.[1] Others wonder if we really "get it." That is, after all that we have witnessed, been involved with, and, sadly, in some cases, sanctioned, are we really renewed and reformed, or have we simply taken our lashes and moved on to find other circuitous ways to do what we were doing before?

The answer to the question of true reform requires exploration of three areas: (1) the crises that led to the current market and regulatory reforms, (2) the reforms themselves, and (3) what will bring about true reform.

In the era of Enron, WorldCom, and the rest, the lapses were great, the conflicts many, and the cost, in terms of investor trust, nearly unspeakable. More than the reforms we have seen is needed: True reform must come from leaders with a strong moral compass.

Crises That Led to Reforms

Taking stock of the types of conduct that led to indictments, reforms, settlements, and fines yields two groups of observations: (1) The practices and conduct of analysts that were sanctioned and reformed were not close calls. (2) We were engaged in repetitive behavior; we've been down this road before.

Not Close Calls. One of the common defenses offered by those accused of ethical or legal lapses is, "It's a gray area," "The law is unclear," "Interpretations vary," or "It depends." These are the phrases of the gray area and a seeming justification or explanation for conduct that is questioned. The notion of whether gray areas exist is a discussion for another time, however, because the crises that led to questions about analysts and reforms in the investment field were not gray areas. Indeed, the various forms of conduct were not even close calls. No one within the field looks at Jack Grubman (late of Salomon

Marianne M. Jennings is professor of legal and ethical studies at the W.P. Carey School of Business, Arizona State University, Tempe.

Smith Barney), the fee structures, the compensation systems, and the conflicts and frets, "These were very nuanced ethical issues. I never would have seen those coming." Those within the field and its outside stakeholders look at the conduct of analysts and conclude: Where were your minds and what were you thinking when you did that? The ethical (and often accompanying legal) breaches were head-turners in terms of their impact on trust, credibility, and perceptions of analysts in two broad areas—namely, conflicts of interest and giving or allowing false impressions/falsehoods/fraud.

- *Conflicts of interest: Research vs. deals.* The research side of the house is inherently conflicted with the deal-seeking underwriter side of the house. The Chinese Wall compromise was just that, a compromise on the inherent conflict that was, itself, bound to be compromised. As the old saying goes, "Three people can keep a secret if two are dead." The assumption that those on the deal side of the house could keep a secret was flawed. Not only did they not keep the secrets on their side of the Chinese Wall in their shops; they also encouraged those on the research side to keep the deal going or make it even sweeter with research findings and releases.

The structure defied human nature and was in no one's best interest, particularly those seeking to maximize returns. Strong evidence indicates that independent analysts provide better investment advice than analysts housed within investment banks. A 2004 study comparing the performance of independent analysts with in-house analysts (in the 1996–2003 time frame) concluded that following the advice of the independent analysts yielded a difference of 8 percentage points (pps) more in returns (Barber, Lehavy, and Trueman 2004). Furthermore, the independent analysts were particularly strong during bear markets. After March 2000, when the NASDAQ peaked, independent analysts were double-digit better (17–22 pps more) than their in-house counterparts because the independents were much quicker to downgrade stocks. During a bull market, the performance tends to be about the same because all stocks are buys. Still, virtually all of the large investment bankers were using these conflicts to gain business and ensure that the businesses' shares retained their value. The investment banks in the study were sanctioned for their conduct during this era, but follow-up work by Barber et al. found the same results for nonsanctioned investment bank analysts. Virtually all of the firms have settled with the U.S. SEC on charges that their analysts issued "buy" recommendations on the basis of their desire to retain investment banking clients. The firms and their fines were as follows:

Citigroup	$400 million
Merrill Lynch & Company	$200 million
Credit Suisse First Boston	$200 million
Morgan Stanley	$125 million
Goldman Sachs	$110 million
Deutsche Bank	$87.5 million
Bear Stearns	$80 million
J.P. Morgan	$80 million
Lehman Brothers	$80 million
UBS Warburg	$80 million
U.S. Bancorp Piper Jaffray	$32.5 million
Thomas Weisel Partners	$12.5 million.[2]

The problems that resulted from the stilted solution offered by the Chinese Wall were predictable and predicted. In 1998, I wrote in an article in the *Journal of Investment Consulting* about the need for a new vision on ethics, conflicts, and the structure of investment management research

(Jennings 1998). The article encouraged discussion and change regarding conflicts in investment management research.[3] Despite the warnings and the defiance of human nature on the issue of conflicts, the practices continued until they were brought to a regulatory and prosecutorial head, with resulting mandatory reforms (discussed in the next section). Those in the profession saw the issues, but few in the field were willing to tackle them voluntarily.

- *Conflicts of interest: Use of position/research for personal gain.* Beyond the systemic conflicts of interest, run-of-the-mill insider trading issues still involved analysts and still affected the stature of the profession. One of the more dramatic probes involved an investigation of Holly Becker, a former star analyst (for retail stocks) at both Salomon and Lehman. The drama-filled accusations involved issues of market-moving information being released that allowed Becker's husband, Michael Zimmerman, a hedge fund trader formerly at Omega Advisors and then SAC Capital Advisors, to trade on inside information. The investigation focused on whether Zimmerman was able to profit by having Becker's research reports in advance.[4]
- *Conflicts of interest: Soft dollars.* The previous two forms of conflicting interests were both transparent and perhaps not the most significant ones. The public understood that analysts work for, for example, Morgan Stanley and that Morgan Stanley handles underwriting for the very companies given green lights by its analysts. Layers of conflicts existed, however, that were not discoverable by the public or investors.

Percolating beneath the conflicts within the firms and the individual use of market-moving research was the industry practice of soft dollars. Although widely used, rationalized, justified, and touted, the practice of compensating advisors through soft dollars is a conflict of interest.[5] Rather than being paid for advice, the advisor is paid a portion of the trading commissions from the broker designated as the trader for the client. The more trades, the more the advisor earns. For example, on a pension fund, the significant trades made on the advice of the investment advisor could produce millions in compensation. Regardless of avowed integrity on everyone's part, a conflict exists and abuses have occurred. In many cases, the self-interests of those receiving commissions trumped the interests of the client. For example, the pension fund for city employees of Chattanooga, Tennessee, is involved in litigation with its former advisor, William Keith Phillips, and his firms, UBS Wealth Management USA (Paine Webber) and Morgan Stanley, over soft dollar payments (Morgenson and Walsh 2004). Other cities are following suit, as it were, with San Diego also involved in a dispute with its pension fund advisor and cities in Florida, Virginia, and Pennsylvania pursuing various complaints against their advisors. Given the $5 trillion in pension funds in the United States, the issue is neither remote nor over in terms of its fallout.

Nor is the issue new or surprising. In 1998, the SEC released a report on its one-year sweep investigation of 75 broker/dealers and 280 investment advisors (SEC 1998). Fully three years before the market drop caused intense scrutiny, the SEC issued a wake-up call, a warning, and a proposed solution.[6] The executive summary of the SEC investigation presented the investigators' conclusions that soft dollars were being used for inappropriate expenses and that disclosures to clients were inadequate:

> While most of the products acquired with soft dollars are research, we found that a significant number of broker-dealers (3%) and advisers (28%) provided and received non-research products and services in soft dollar arrangements. Although receipt of non-research (or non-brokerage) products for soft dollars can be lawful if adequate disclosure has been made, our sweep inspections revealed that virtually all of the advisers that obtained non-research products and

services had failed to provide meaningful disclosure of such practices to their clients. Examples of products acquired included: advisers using soft dollars to pay for office rent and equipment, cellular phone services and personal expenses; advisers using soft dollars to pay an employee's salary; an adviser using soft dollars to pay for advisory client referrals and marketing expenses; an adviser using soft dollars to pay legal expenses, hotel and rental car costs and to install a phone system; and an unregistered hedge fund adviser using soft dollars to pay for personal travel, entertainment, limousine, interior design and construction expenses.

We also found that, even with respect to research and brokerage products and services within the safe harbor, many advisers' disclosure of their soft dollar practices was inadequate, in that it did not appear to provide sufficient information to enable a client or potential client to understand the adviser's soft dollar policies and practices, as required under the law.[7] Nearly all of the advisers that we examined made some form of disclosure to clients regarding their brokerage and soft dollar practices. Most advisers, however, used boilerplate language to disclose that their receipt of research products and services was a factor that they considered when selecting brokers. In our assessment, only half of the advisers that we examined described in sufficient detail the products, research and services that they received for soft dollars such that clients or potential clients could understand the advisers' practices. (SEC)

The vigorous defenses by firms and advisors in the arbitration proceedings brought by clients over soft dollar use is that the pension plans are sophisticated parties who understand the fee arrangements and the trade-offs for independent advice and research versus commission-compensated advice and that the client benefits from a net savings. The SEC's findings from nearly seven years ago explain the disparate views: There is a disconnect in the resolution of the conflict in that the disclosure by advisors may not be as forthcoming as they believe it to be.[8] As the 30th anniversary of the safe harbor provision and the resulting soft dollar fees approaches, the SEC has created a task force to study the issue once again and make recommendations on the issues, problems, and abuses.

- *Giving or allowing false impressions, falsehoods, and frauds: The cheerleader vs. the analyst*. The discussion of conflicts in the industry also revealed the parallel nature of the issues of false impressions, falsehoods, and fraud. That is, false impressions, falsehoods, and fraud arise if there has not been full and complete disclosure about the nature of advisor fees. The façade of analyst independence is, in itself, a false impression, but egregious examples of far more damaging falsehoods occurred that bordered on or constituted market frauds.

For example, Citigroup's Salomon Smith Barney and Grubman, its star telecommunications analyst of the dot-com era, continued a marketwide false impression about WorldCom that lasted for years beyond the time when WorldCom had already begun accounting fraud to maintain a false rise to the heights of the market. In the month WorldCom collapsed with admissions of the need for $3 billion in earnings restatements (that amount would later balloon to $9 billion), Grubman's quote about WorldCom still appeared on the company's website, to wit: "If one were to find comparables to WorldCom . . . The list would be very short and would include the likes of Merck, Home Depot, Wal-Mart, Coke, Microsoft, Gillette and Disney" (Weinberg 2002). Grubman crossed the line from analyst to cheerleader early on in the WorldCom relationship: "The sycophantism of Grubman is difficult to describe because it seems almost parody" (Jennings, forthcoming 2005). Grubman attended WorldCom board meetings and offered advice, and he introduced Bernie Ebbers, WorldCom's CEO, at analyst meetings as "the smartest guy in the industry" (Smith and Solomon 2002, p. C1). Grubman and his firm were completely intertwined with WorldCom, Ebbers, and the success of both (Smith and Solomon; Backover and O'Donnell 2002). Grubman's evaluation included the following conclusion: "We do not think any other telco will be as fully integrated and growth-oriented as this combination [WorldCom plus Sprint]" (Smith and Solomon, p. C3).

Conflicts of interest were fueling this logic-defying support. Salomon stood to earn $21 million in fees if the WorldCom–Sprint merger was approved in 1999. WorldCom did indeed give the bulk of its investment banking business to Salomon Smith Barney, but the hook was far more personal because Grubman and others gave Ebbers (and other officers of client companies) the opportunity to be first purchasers of hot IPO stocks. The figures in Congressional records indicate that Ebbers made $11 million in profits from investments in 21 IPOs recommended to him by Grubman (Morgenson 2002a, 2002b, 2002c).

Salomon and others later faced charges of profiteering on the IPO allocations (Valdmanis and Backover 2002). All denied any *quid pro quo* arrangement, but the impression left on the market and investor trust was indelible.

Far more was at stake for Citicorp than simply the investment banking business from WorldCom. In fact, the loans were tied to the value of WorldCom stock (Pulliam, Solomon, and Mollenkamp 2002). WorldCom's biggest lender was Citicorp, and it served as personal lender for Ebbers. One expert noted:

> Looking back, it looks more and more like a pyramid scheme. The deals explain why people were not more diligent in making decisions about funding these small companies. If the money was spread all over the place and everyone who participated early was almost guaranteed a return because of the hype, they had no incentive to try and differentiate the technology. And in the end, all the technology turned out to be identical and commodity-like. (Backover 2002)

Only after WorldCom stock had lost 90 percent of its value, just six weeks before its collapse, did Grubman issue his first negative recommendation on WorldCom, despite having issued negative recommendations on other telecom companies. Grubman, however, had doubts about WorldCom that he expressed privately even as he continued to issue nothing but positive reports on WorldCom. In e-mails uncovered by an investigation of analysts conducted by Spitzer, Grubman complained privately that he was forced to continue his buy ratings on stocks that he considered "dogs" (Gasparino 2002).

But the e-mails revealed more than candor about Grubman's recommendations. Grubman, the father of twins, wanted to see them admitted to one of Manhattan's most prestigious preschools—92nd Street Y—as the following memo to Sanford Weill, the chairman of Citigroup, reveals:

> On another matter, as I alluded to you the other day, we are going through the ridiculous but necessary process of pre-school applications in Manhattan. For someone who grew up in a household with a father making $8,000 a year and for someone who attended public schools, I do find this process a bit strange, but there are no bounds for what you do for your children.
>
> Anything, anything you could do Sandy would be greatly appreciated. As I mentioned, I will keep you posted on the progress with AT&T which I think is going well.
>
> Thank you.

Citigroup pledged $1 million to the school at about the same time Grubman's children were admitted, and Weill asked Grubman to "take a fresh look" at AT&T, a major corporate client of

Citigroup on whose board Weill served (even as AT&T's CEO, C. Michael Armstrong, served on Citigroup's board). Weill was counting on Armstrong's support to oust John Reed as co-CEO of Citigroup. Grubman then sent the following in an e-mail to Carol Cutler, another New York analyst, which brings the preschool admissions full circle with market analysis and battles for board control:

> I used Sandy to get my kids in the 92nd Street Y pre-school (which is harder than Harvard) and Sandy needed Armstrong's vote on our board to nuke Reed in showdown. Once the coast was clear for both of us (i.e., Sandy clear victor and my kids confirmed) I went back to my normal self on AT&T.

Grubman had upgraded AT&T from a "hold" to a "strong buy." After Reed was ousted, Grubman downgraded AT&T again. Grubman said that he sent Cutler the e-mail "in an effort to inflate my professional importance."

These actions are not close calls. Reviewing these missteps of one of the financial market's premier analysts, we are numb. There is no room for disagreement and no space for comfort in the reassurance that these are gray areas. The ethical lapses were clear; the conduct was indefensible. False impressions, falsehoods, and fraud were the results of the deep conflicts that consumed both financial and ethical judgments.

A Well-Trodden Road. The significant legislative and regulatory reforms, many still ongoing, that followed the bursting of the dot-com bubble and the Enron, WorldCom, Tyco International, and Adelphia Communications debacles represent the third great regulatory reform involving financial markets since the 1980s.

In the late 1970s and early 1980s, in the first of the three events that led to great regulatory reforms, 525 savings and loan institutions went into bankruptcy. Not only did auditors give their imprimatur to questionable accounting used by the S&Ls, they often gave clean audit opinions to insolvent S&Ls. In California, of the 36 S&Ls that went bankrupt, 28 had received clean audit opinions.[9] The reaction of Judge Stanley Sporkin to this debacle remains the classic question in all corporate financial collapses: "Where were these professionals . . . when these clearly improper transactions were being consummated? Why didn't any of them speak up or disassociate themselves from the transactions?"[10] Judge Sporkin was indicting both the lawyers and the accountants for their complicity in the collapses of most S&Ls in the United States.

Then came the era of investment banking firms and analysts giving their seal of approval to the junk bond deals, mergers, and hostile takeovers. The collapses following the wild ride of the 1980s market meant losses for bondholders that left these conservative investors with nothing but bankruptcies, even of government entities. Running simultaneously with this speculative market was a spat of insider trading that yielded many prosecutions, including those of the infamous Ivan Boesky and Michael Milken.[11]

In the third wave of scandals, analysts of the 1990s lent their credibility to teetering dot-coms and telecoms. In the aftermath, the cover of *Fortune* for 14 May 2001, just after the bubble burst, featured analyst Mary Meeker and the caption "Can We Ever Trust Again?" One year later (10 June 2002), the cover of *Fortune* featured Sallie Krawcheck and the caption "In Search of the Last Honest Analyst."[12]

The pattern in the three periods of excess followed by severe reforms is the same.[13] We lose our minds, anchors, and rational thought in the exuberance of the boom. Lines are crossed—by auditors, analysts, investors, and companies. Each in its own way pushes the envelope in terms of legal and ethical behavior, and the result is oppressive regulations that affect all who are involved in the markets. Although we cannot blame analysts for all the problems in all three eras, we can see the patterns in the behavior of all professionals associated with the markets.

In this last era of excess, analysts played a more prominent role than in the two previous collapses. One research director explained the role of analysts in the latest round of market excesses as follows:

> Prior to the bubble, I never saw an instance of an analyst being so spineless that he supported a transaction he didn't believe in. It was reputational suicide. But during the bubble, that changed. (Nocera 2004, p. 112)

Analysts became an integral part of the investment banking divisions of their companies and took a share in the deals that were brought about, often because of their recommendations (Nocera). At Credit Suisse First Boston, a group of analysts actually reported to investment banker Quattrone, subsequently convicted of obstruction of justice.

We fear nonconformity and shun the basics of finance and economics. So long as the market is rising, no one is harmed by these attitudes; there is no bad analysis because rising tides lift all boats and the dogs in them. In fact, those who dare question the emperor's clothing are often mocked or, worse, fired.

Throughout the times of the market's and analysts' enthusiasm for the likes of the WorldComs and Enrons, however, some analysts, using basic tools, questioned whether the enthusiasm for the companies that would eventually collapse was misplaced. For example, Scott Cleland, founder of Precursor Group, a Washington, DC–based investment research firm, predicted that the WorldCom–Sprint merger would fail and that if the merger failed, WorldCom would be a "dead model walking." WorldCom CEO Ebbers promptly called Cleland an "idiot." Interestingly, Cleland has been a bit of a stickler on conflicts of interest and disclosure. He owns no individual stocks, and in his interview for *Fortune* magazine on his prescient call on WorldCom, he said, "I should tell you I'm a Republican" (Gasparino, p. C1).

Enron's climb and stellar status did not charm analyst John Olson. Olson gleaned his information on Enron from talking with former employees who described the company as doing everything "on the edge" ("Why John Olson . . ." 2002). When Olson issued cautions to clients about Enron, Kenneth Lay, at that time Enron's chairman, wrote a letter to Olson's employer complaining, "John Olson has been wrong about Enron for over 10 years and is still wrong. But he is consistant [*sic*]" (Schwartz 2002). When Olson's boss showed him the note from Lay, Olson responded, "You know that I'm old and worthless, but at least I can spell consistent." Olson was quoted (Schwartz, Note 204) after Enron's collapse as believing that too many Wall Street analysts were being "schnuckels," a Yiddish word for dupes. He believed that too few "kicked the tires" of the company.

Indeed, the obvious principles of finance and economics were being left by the wayside in analyses of these companies. For example, using basic financial analysis, Bethany McLean, a liberal arts undergraduate and *Fortune* reporter, ran a story that picked up on the obvious problems with Enron, such as phenomenal earnings and no cash, but her story ran and lay dormant until Enron's collapse.[14] Peter Eavis of TheStreet.com also raised questions about Enron, including the suggestion that Enron's profit may have been a result of constant asset transfers. He also wrote about

Chief Financial Officer Andrew Fastow's dual roles as CFO of Enron and principal in the companies taking title to Enron assets. No mainstream media outlets or analysts picked up on his observations or questions. Ironically, McLean has since noted that she relied on a short seller as a source of information and expertise for doing her story. So, the quality of scrutiny by those whose interests lie in the truth about a company contains a message.

In these manias that develop, there is a cycle. It begins with a lack of scrutiny that is fueled not simply by conflicted analysts but also by a media enamored of companies and stories that defy all odds. The quotations and media accolades in **Exhibit 1** are comical when examined in hindsight because they reflect an evaluation that is opposite to the failing reality of the companies involved. As we look at what we know about the companies now, we think, "Why didn't we realize the hype? Why were we so duped by the hyperbole?"

There is no substitute for solid, objective analysis that finds the Achilles heel, no matter how much resistance and no matter what the media reports and denials of the officers may say.

Exhibit 1. The Cycle Begins

Quote/Award Question	Answer
What company's CEO was named one of *Business Week*'s top managers for 2000 and 2001?	Dennis Kozlowski (Tyco)
What CFOs were named CFO of the Year for 1999, 2000, and 2001?	Andrew Fastow (Enron), Scott Sullivan (WorldCom), and Mark Swartz (Tyco)
What company was ranked #44, #24, and #22 by *Fortune* as one of the 100 best companies to work for in the 1990s?	Enron
What company was described in 2001 as having a delivery and marketing model that would change its industry?	HealthSouth
What CEO said in 2001, "We have no perks, not even parking spaces"?	Dennis Kozlowski (Tyco)
What CEO said, "We are the good guys. We are on the side of angels"?	Jeffrey Skilling (Enron)
What company had a 64-page, award-winning code of ethics?	Enron
Who said, "People have an obligation to dissent in this company. . . . I mean, I sit up there on the 50th floor, in the library. I have no idea what's going on down there, so if you've got a problem with it, speak up. And if you don't speak up, that's not good"?	Jeffrey Skilling (Enron)
What corporate founder said, "It's more than just money. You've got to give back to the community that supported you"?	John Rigas (Adelphia)
Who said, "You'll see people who in the early days . . . took their life savings and trusted this company with their money. And I have an awesome responsibility to those people to make sure that they're done right"?	Bernie Ebbers (WorldCom)
What CEO said, "Boards should be absolutely certain that the company is run properly from a fiduciary standpoint in every degree. I am a great believer in the audit committee having full access to the auditors in every way, shape, or form"?	"Chainsaw Al" Dunlap (Sunbeam's nemesis)

Note: The last three quotes are from *Fortune* (18 November 2002), p. 54. The other material and quotes were collected by the author from various sources, including interviews, company materials, and speeches.

Reforms the Crises Hath Wrought

We are on the upside of a dramatic regulatory swing. The reforms in the area of investment analysis and management are detailed and demanding. The micro level of regulation is staggering:

- independent research on the part of the 10 largest brokerage firms (negotiated as part of a $1.4 billion settlement) at a cost estimated to be $7.5 million to $75 million over the next five years;
- independent boards of directors required at mutual funds;
- disclosure of holdings;
- codes of ethics required of investment advisors;
- training in ethics required of investment advisors;
- compliance officers required of funds and investment advisors;
- compensation disclosure requirements;
- required proxy vote disclosure;
- required costs disclosure, including costs related to investment advisement;
- rules on timing of trades to eliminate post-4:00 p.m. trading;
- restrictions on analysts attending pitch meetings for underwriting business;
- blocked phone and e-mail access between analysts and investment bankers;
- certification on analysts' reports that "all the views in this research report accurately reflect our personal views."

In addition are the Sarbanes–Oxley reforms that apply to all publicly held companies, including those involved in investment banking and brokerage:

- independent boards;
- independent audit committees;
- codes of ethics and ethics training;
- officer certification of financial statements;
- increased penalties for false financial statements;
- increased penalties for securities fraud;
- increased penalties for obstruction of justice, conspiracy, and other crimes chargeable for activities such as shredding documents;
- complete regulation of the accounting and audit professions.

The reforms are not complete; pending rules are in all stages of development—from promulgation to comment to research.

Interestingly, however, even though the investment industry is under a microscope and regulations are heaped upon regulations, the spark of true reform is not present. As with the two previous cycles of regulatory reform, we have details as a proxy for change, dramatic sweeps as a substitute for true reform, and fear as an assumed impetus for ethical conversion. Also, as with the two previous reform cycles, there is the inevitable tendency for those in the regulated industry to assume that the rules are intended for "the other guys," the unethical ones in the business.

This year, both the National Association of Securities Dealers and the SEC have announced investigations of rebates and where those rebates are going:

> It's something that's talked about in the business. Some hedge funds don't put that rebate back into their funds, but rather keep it for themselves. If a rebate is going to the fund manager, and not the fund, that is a big deal. It's not the fund manager's money. (Pulliam and Zuckerman 2005)

At the heart of this practice is a lack of disclosure, dishonesty, and the basic ethical breach of taking something that does not belong to you, yet the issues have gone unaddressed despite an industry besieged not only by regulatory questions but by reputational questions and issues of trust. The firms may be in compliance with the new regulations and outfitted with compliance officers, but they have not grasped the picture of true reform. The spirit of ethics is missing even as the regulations descend and consume.

The missing spirit of ethics emerges in matters as simple as attitudes about Sarbanes–Oxley, regulators, and Spitzer. Critics of Spitzer "couple theories of his desire for a political future with theological discussions of his origins from somewhere in the bowels of hell" (Jennings 2005). There is little rationality left in the discussions about Spitzer and less recollection by many of the industry practices that led to the fury and settlements of Spitzer.

Recent studies indicate that 74 percent of us believe our ethics are higher than those of our peers and 83 percent of us say that at least one-half of the people we know would list us as one of the most ethical people they know. An amazing 92 percent of us are satisfied with our ethics and character. Now juxtapose these data with the most recent revelations about our young people and their perceptions of business and ethics. More than half of male high school students and 32 percent of the female students agree with the following statement: "In the real world, successful people do what they have to do to win, even if others consider it cheating."[15] A joint Deloitte/Junior Achievement study reveals that 82 percent of U.S. high school students believe business leaders are unethical or are not sure whether they are ethical. Among U.S. college students, cheating increased from 11 percent in 1963 to 75 percent in 2003.

Moreover, the list of companies experiencing ethical collapse doesn't end. We may have moved on from WorldCom and Enron, but the past year has brought us Parmalat, round two of restatements from Nortel, reserves overstatements from Royal Dutch/Shell, price fixing at Marsh & McLennan Companies, and the near collapse of Fannie Mae (Federal National Mortgage Association). These scandals are as large as the initial ones that began the market slide and all the reforms.

We suffer from a dependency on laws and regulations and from myopia when it comes to ethics. Until the law tells us a practice is wrong, we continue what we're doing, taking comfort in dotting the *i*'s and crossing the *t*'s to comply with detailed reforms. In focusing on the details of the reforms, we miss the big picture of industry practices that clearly cross ethical lines but continue because current regulations have not yet found them to be legally problematic.

Chairman William Donaldson of the SEC has noted that "rulemaking alone cannot reform an industry. An industry must be motivated and committed to reforming itself."[16] Paul F. Roye, former director of the SEC Division of Investment Management, recently noted:

> I hope that the recent effort to review compliance policies and procedures has been therapeutic and an opportunity to rethink practices and ways of doing business, and that you have addressed or eliminated conflicts of interest and practices that can compromise investor interests. The fund business was built on trust and integrity, and trust and integrity must again become funds' hallmarks, if they are to continue to serve as the primary investment vehicle of American investors. That is why I challenge you to work seriously to implement not just the letter, but the spirit of the Commission's new mutual fund reforms. (Roye 2004b)

Embracing the spirit of the law applies to individual action and industry leadership. In all three of the regulatory cycles, true reform did not come about; that is, there was always another scandal, another loophole, another area in which abuses occurred (obvious abuses, as noted). New statutes and regulations simply made the conduct illegal; it was always unethical. The reforms in structure and practice are designed to keep the uncovered abuses from happening again. But reforms are chasing tigers, trying to catch them by the tail. They are always one step behind and incapable of keeping the tigers under control, unless the tigers agree to self-imposed control.

For example, in 1999, the SEC required mutual funds to track the stock and bond trades of their fund managers because the commission was concerned that these managers were abusing their positions by trading ahead of their purchases and sales for the funds (the market-moving blocks). Mutual fund share trades were exempt because no one anticipated, with a 4:00 p.m. eastern time close and what is in the funds at the end of the day, that their situation allowed any room for abuse. The funds proved them wrong, and now the 4:00 p.m. deadline is under additional regulation. No matter which turn the regulation takes, the market finds a means around it.[17]

The layers of responsibility for ethics are depicted in **Figure 1**. True market reform requires self-imposed control in the top layer—individual action—where the issue is whether conduct is ethical, not whether it is legal. When all the *systems* are installed at each level, we are ultimately dependent on individuals to exercise ethical courage and leadership in their companies and in the industry. Big-name lawyers as compliance chiefs and management consulting firms creating ethics programs are not substitutes for individuals with ethical spines. In the words of Stephen Cutler, the SEC's director of enforcement, all regulations and all enforcement actions are undertaken with one purpose: "Ultimately, what we're really interested in changing is behavior" (Davis 2004, p. C4).

Cutler also expressed frustration with current investment industry attitudes and an interest in the application of ethical principles to industry conduct, not more regulations:

> Shed the blinder of "industry practice" that may have made it possible for you not to see the conflicts that surround you daily. Just because the industry has always done something "that way," don't assume it's acceptable. It won't be acceptable to your customers when they come to understand the conflicts involved. (Davis, p. C4)[18]

Figure 1. Layers of Responsibility for Ethics

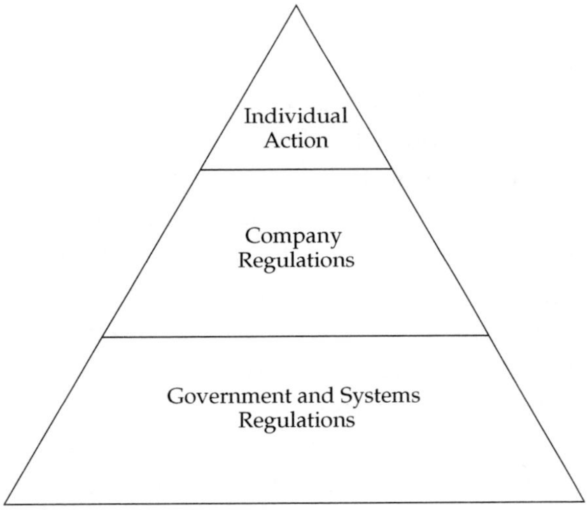

Achieving True Reforms

Now that this groundwork is in place—understanding that the missteps were not close calls and that true reform cannot come through regulation—the question is: How does the industry achieve true reform? The path is not quite a 12-step program, but critical elements do need attention, study, and work before reform can be realized. The following three steps were developed with the idea of changing people's mind-sets from regulatory fear and compliance to ethical leadership.

A Meaningful Ethical Compass. Moral relativism, the philosophical focus of liberal arts education from the 1960s forward, made its way into personal, business, and professional lives. The field of financial analysis was not exempt. The mantra of "there are no moral absolutes" has been used as a rationalization for inflated financial reports, commission rates for advisor fees, and favoritism for larger clients over others.

A look at the history of Merrill Lynch provides a glimpse of what was once a climate of absolutes. When Charles E. Merrill created his firm with Edmund Lynch, they had a motto: "Investigate, then invest." He formed his own firm because he was disgusted as a bond salesman for George H. Burr & Company when he realized he was pushing the bonds of companies that were near bankruptcy. As 1929 approached, Merrill told everyone that stocks were overpriced and to cash out. Perceived as a "nut," he sold his interest and left to run Safeway. Merrill was right; the rest lost their shirts. He reentered the business in 1940 with a new creation—an investment firm intended for the average person. He separated banking from research and paid analysts salaries, not commissions (Vickers 2004). His idea led to a small percentage of Americans with investments (16 percent) becoming today's figure of more than 50 percent. He did it running a business, at least through his passing in 1956, with moral absolutes. The questions we have now about analysts and investment firms are like those we had when Arthur Andersen collapsed: How do companies with such roots of absolute integrity drift so far from those founding principles? The answer lies in the word "absolute": They drift from their moral absolutes.

A moral absolute for analysts stems from the imperative to put clients first and is easily defined: Engage in no conduct that compromises reputation, integrity, or investors' perception of either. Put more simply: If you were the client, how would you react to this conduct? Or, perhaps more relevantly for investment managers, how would you react to this conduct by your analyst if you were the client when it was finally revealed to you?

There are two ways to manage a conflict of interest under this simple standard: (1) Do not do it (and the law has taken care of much of that approach through the reforms) or (2) disclose the conflict to those affected. And the disclosure requires that those affected truly understand the conflict and the degree of that conflict. In some situations, a conflict is so pervasive and controlling that the second resolution is not a workable option. Again, the post-Enron reforms have taken care of a number of such conflicts. But the second approach should apply for future relationships.

The lawsuits by various city pension funds indicate at least a misunderstanding by the pensions, if not a misrepresentation by the investment managers, about the commission arrangements and the costs associated with that compensation arrangement versus the costs of payment in hard dollars. Whether the investment professionals believe they did disclose the information properly is not the issue. If the client feels otherwise, perception and trust are at risk.

Perception and trust are not simply controlling factors in market research credibility; they are critical for the market's viability. It is stunning to read a quote such as the following from a Morgan Stanley spokesperson in response to the Chattanooga pension suit over fee disclosures:

> The Chattanooga Pension Board was a sophisticated and knowledgeable investor that was advised by its own counsel about all aspects of its relationship with us. (Morgenson and Walsh 2004, p. 13)

This statement illustrates how industry blinders have dimmed the bright ethical lines and how legal standards have become a substitute for ethical ones. Morgan Stanley had a fiduciary relationship with the pension board. The pension fund should not need its own separate counsel to explain its relationship and fee arrangements with its investment advisor, in whom trust is necessary and has been placed.

As the data on ethical opinions indicate, nearly all of us would swear that we adhere to ethical standards—such as making sure clients understand our disclosures. Yet the ethical lapses outlined here demonstrate that many have been operating without a moral compass. What happened?

The answer is that they were not engaged in ongoing introspection that forced examination of company and industry practices outside the comfort of groupthink. Analysts did not wake up one day and say, "Wait a minute! Conflicts of interest! Unfair IPO allocations! Lying about companies that are dogs! These are the ways to make real money!" Instead, there was a gradual degradation of reputation and integrity, a slow release of discomfort at crossing ethical lines until the bright lines so obviously crossed in the lapses discussed earlier were gone. "Everybody does it." "That's the way it has always been done." "This is done at the best firms." And "Who is really harmed by it anyway?" These attitudes became the basis for ethical analysis, and the discomfort of parting ways with an ethical compass was slowly whittled away by compensation and the commonality of an industry adrift. There was little introspection because everyone was wearing the industry blinders of rationalization. The city pension lawsuits are indicative of a loss of perspective; the advisors and their companies now battle their own clients for being sophisticated investors who should have known.

Retention of moral absolutes requires constant introspection, discussion of practices, and exploration of those practices from the perspective of clients and the market, not from industry practice. Presently, the SEC is examining new issues related to conflicts of interest. One is relationships between consultants and money managers and what fuels the recommendations consultants make to their clients about their fund managers. Another is industrywide practices involving fees, conferences, and soft dollars in the form of software or other perks (Solomon 2004). Many see the relationships, the conferences, and the fee arrangements as gray areas, but there are no gray areas, only rationalizations applied to conduct that, when viewed through absolute standards, is wrong. The conduct simply becomes more palatable when cushioned with the justification of industry practice or pressures of the moment.

Proper Ethical Analysis: Seeing the Issues and Avoiding Chicken-and-Egg Ethics.[19] In groups, industries, and companies where the ethical compass is askew, ethical analysis is also askew. Few things are more aggravating for a business ethicist than to watch debates on ethical issues in which the participants have missed the ethical issue altogether. The following excerpt from the audit field offers an example that induces such aggravation. It is taken from a Statement on Standards for Accounting and Review Services (SSARS) interpretation from the American Institute of Certified Public Accountants:

- Question (SSARS No. 1): When, during the performance of a compilation or a review engagement, the accountant suspects that a fraud or an illegal act may have occurred, what steps should be taken in performing the required communication?
- Interpretation: When an accountant suspects that a fraud or an illegal act may have occurred 1) the accountant communicates the matter, *unless clearly inconsequential*, to an appropriate level of management. If the suspected fraud or illegal act involves senior management, the matter should be communicated to an individual or group at the highest level within the entity, such as the manager (owner) or the board of directors. When the suspected fraud or illegal act involves an owner of the business, the accountant should consider resigning from the engagement. 2) Additionally, the accountant should consider consulting with his or her legal counsel and insurance provider whenever fraud or an illegal act is suspected. [Emphasis added.]

Focus on the term "unless clearly inconsequential" and recall that the question is whether the auditor must take steps to disclose illegal acts or fraud. When is illegality or fraud by an audit client inconsequential? The amount involved may be immaterial, but if the auditor has uncovered fraud or illegality by officers of a company, the future looks a bit foreboding.

Nonetheless, an analysis by a CPA of the problem offered the following:

> "We are asking management if they have knowledge of any fraud or suspected fraud involving management or others, *where fraud could have a material effect on the financial statements*," Cohen, an NYSSCPA [New York State Society of Certified Public Accountants] board member, said of the standard. "We are required to ask that question in the inquiries and then put it in the representation letter so management signs off on it. That's what the difference is, that was not there in the past." (Dismukes 2004) [Emphasis added.]

Again, focus on that phrase in italics and consider: When does fraud *not* have a material effect on the financial statements? When does the public *not* deserve to know that the officers of a company have engaged in just a teeny, tiny fraud? Lawyers once developed a similar standard excusing them from reporting the fraud of a client if it could prove embarrassing. To paraphrase the American Bar Association's rule on lawyer disclosure of such client misdeeds, fraud is almost always embarrassing, so an ethical analysis based on this standard would conclude that fraud need not be reported.

These issues and their resolutions are classically referred to as "sandbox" dilemmas and resolutions. The issues are resolved within the context of the industry, profession, or company's sandbox rules—the industry's way-we've-always-done-it rules—without reference to the ethics of virtue or moral absolutes. The resolution is inherently flawed because the blinders of the rules of play lead those affected to resolve the wrong dilemma. For example, one accounting profession ethical dilemma is as follows: What does the auditor do when he or she discovers through one client that purchases services from another client that the second client is about to lose that contract? The question is posed as "Does the auditor say anything to the other client?" This question shows that those in the auditing profession miss the ethical issue. The real issue is why the auditor took two companies with such conflicting interests as audit clients. The initial decision to handle both clients, with each possessing sensitive information about the other, was flawed, and the dilemma was bound to result.

Perhaps in the field of financial analysis, some of the initial decisions on industry practices, compensation, and structure were similarly flawed and the result was the misguided resolution of ethical dilemmas. The issue is not whether the Chinese Wall was breached. The issue is: Whatever made us think a Chinese Wall would work in the first place?

These types of dilemmas remind us of the great moral dilemmas and decline in the novel *A Simple Plan* by Scott Smith. Three friends come across millions in a crashed plane that has been buried in the snow. The plane was that of a drug runner, and the three friends remove the money, hide it, and plan to split it and then move to warmer climes once spring comes and the investigation of the plane and accident are completed. They will live elsewhere and spend their treasure trove without anyone noticing. From that moment on, the friends must lie, steal, and even backstab each other to keep their secret. They are even forced to resort to murder for the sake of preserving their money. The dilemmas they face in their concealment are what they debate and resolve, each time sinking farther into moral bankruptcy. They do not realize until it is too late that it was their initial decision to take the money that did not belong to them that was flawed. Every subsequent decision simply led them down a path of further corruption. Spotting and resolving ethical issues as they arise, not ignoring them until another crisis arises, is a key to the industry restoring its reputation and trust.

Heartfelt Reform and Individual Ethical Courage. A glance through the coverage of the industry in the financial press paints a picture of an industry besieged—but also resistant. Each speech by an SEC commissioner or regulator carries an overarching theme: Change yourselves or we will have to do it for you. Consider this example from Roye:

> I'd like to conclude my remarks by stating what should be obvious to all of us: Investors are asking whether they can trust the investment management industry. Winning back the trust of these investors will require effort and commitment—commitment to compliance, commitment to ethics, commitment to reform. As I have said before, the status quo is no longer acceptable to America's investors. Nor will they accept empty promises of reform. They are looking for action; they are looking for meaning behind the words; they expect a reinvigorated, investor-oriented investment management industry. (Roye 2004a)

Or consider a similar plea from another of his speeches:

> I further encourage you to commit the energy and resources that are necessary to fully implement the reforms so that they will foster an ethical atmosphere at fund firms and a focus on the needs and interests of fund investors. As the scandals revealed, many fund firms were not focused on their core responsibilities of serving their investors. Instead they were cutting unlawful quid pro quo deals to grow assets under management and maximize fund fees. Greed overtook integrity and a focus on profitability triumphed over firms' focus on fiduciary obligation and responsibility.
>
> All of us involved in managing, distributing and overseeing mutual funds must guard against these types of unhealthy attitudes from again infiltrating the fund business. When I asked one industry executive about the reason for the late trading and market timing abuses, he attributed the problem to the rapid growth of, and new entrants to, the fund business. But our enforcement docket is replete with names of old-line mutual fund organizations. (Roye 2004b)

The plea from the regulators—and, indeed, the plea I am making in this piece—is for individual ethical courage and organizational and individual ethical leadership. Dean Ned Hill of the Marriott School of Business at Brigham Young University has asked whether we have evolved from the point of simply having ethical knowledge to the point of acting on that knowledge through ethical courage and ethical leadership. His question can be formed into another pyramid that depicts what constitute the evolutionary keys necessary for true reform. The pyramid in **Figure 2** shows this ethical evolution. The pyramid in Figure 1 and the pyramid in Figure 2 meet, as they should, on the point of individual action born of individual courage and individual leadership within structural and systemic reforms.

As reforms are debated, opportunities arise that both analysts and investment firms can seize to position themselves as market leaders in the restoration of trust.[20] Far more is at stake than individual and company reputations. Markets do not function without trust. Capitalism depends on investor trust, and investor trust comes from the consistent, vigilant exercise of ethics by market participants, not from mere compliance. These past three years have been turbulent and trying times for investment firms. Embracing true reform, however—reform that consists of moral absolutes and vigilance in retaining the bright line between right and wrong—can restore the reputations that have been tarnished by years of ethical drift. Statutes, codes, and structural reforms cannot change an industry. Individual actions and ethical courage can.

Figure 2. Ethical Evolution

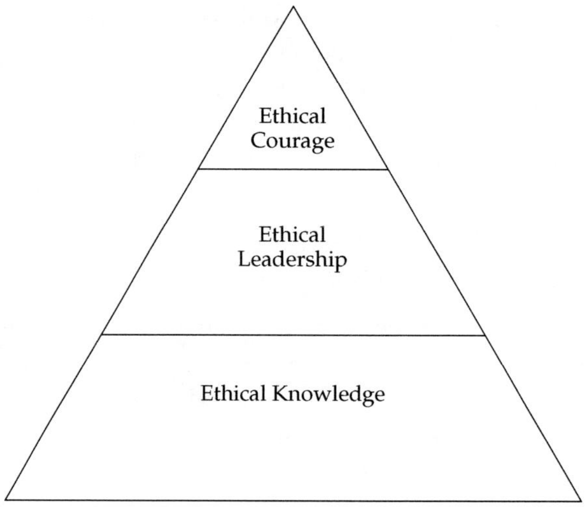

Source: Developed from thoughts by Dean Ned Hill, Marriott School of Management, Brigham Young University.

Notes

1. Quattrone forwarded a 22-word e-mail from his colleague, a lawyer, Richard Char, to his staff on 5 December 2000 that included a suggestion to his employees that they "clean-up those e-mails," a reference to the company's document retention and destruction policy, and the additional caveat, "I strongly advise you to follow these procedures." (See Sorkin 2004; portions of the quote were also found in Valdmanis 2004b.)
2. The settlement total was $1.4 billion from a series of cases brought by Spitzer, who detected the pattern of conflicts by sorting through e-mails from analysts that contained statements that were inconsistent with their recommendations and public statements about the stock (Valdmanis 2004a).
3. Interestingly, the review process for the 1998 article carried with it some tension when those reviewing the article objected to stating that there were conflicts of interest in the way analysts were employed and the structuring of their compensation. The article appeared only after language of appeasement was added to the piece.
4. Smith (2004). Becker resigned from Lehman while the investigations were pending.
5. The SEC (1998) described the conflict as follows: "Under traditional fiduciary principles, a fiduciary cannot use assets entrusted by clients to benefit itself. As the Commission has recognized, when an adviser uses client commissions to buy research from a broker-dealer, it receives a benefit because it is relieved from the need to produce or pay for the research itself. In addition, when transactions involving soft dollars involve the adviser 'paying up' or receiving executions at inferior prices, advisers using soft dollars face a conflict of interest between their need to obtain research and their clients' interest in paying the lowest commission rate available and obtaining the best possible execution."
6. The soft dollar phenomenon came into effect in May 1975 when the practice of fixed commissions was abandoned.
7. Section 28(e), known as the "safe harbor provision," was added to the Securities Exchange Act in 1975; among other things, it allows money managers to use the commission dollars of their advised accounts to obtain research and brokerage services. Also, it allows market forces to have more effect on commissions and analysis. CFA Institute standards on soft dollars may be found at www.cfainstitute. org/standards/ethics/soft_dollar/.
8. One survey found that 75 percent of respondents could not accurately define a fund expense ratio and 64 percent did not understand the impact of expenses on fund returns ("Investors Need to Bone Up on Bonds and Costs . . ." 2002).
9. For descriptions of the role of Charles Keating in the S&L scandal, see Stevenson (1991). For information on Keating's prison sentence, see Schine (1990).
10. Lincoln Savings & Loan Ass'n v. Wall, 743 F. Supp. 901, at 920 (D.D.C. 1990).
11. For background on Milken, Boesky, and junk bonds, see Smith (1997). See also Stewart (1991).
12. And beneath the caption was the stinging phrase, "Her analysts are paid for research, not deals."
13. The S&L collapse reforms are largely found in the Financial Institutions Reform, Recovery and Enforcement Act of 1989 (FIRREA), 12 U.S.C. § 191 *et seq.*, which required new minimum capital requirements for loans. The Boesky–Milken excesses brought us the Insider Trading Sanctions Act, 15 U.S.C. § 78u-1 (2002), which made it possible for the government to recover as a penalty three times the amount of profit made or loss avoided from the inside deal. Also, the Insider Trading and Securities Fraud Enforcement Act, 15 U.S.C. § 78ff (2002), upped the penalties for insider trading to 10 years and $1 million (now increased again as a result of the Sarbanes–Oxley Act).
14. Barringer (2002). In this story, *Fortune*'s managing editor, Rik Kirkland, said McLean's March 2001 story on Enron was "prescient, but it kind of went out and sank."
15. From the 2004 Josephson studies on character among youth: available at josephsoninstitute.org/Survey2004/.
16. Available at www.sec.gov/news/speech/spch120604pfr. htm.
17. In the accounting profession, the saying goes, "It takes the FASB four years to come up with a rule and the finance guys about four hours to find a way around it."
18. The areas of focus for the SEC's exploration of conflicts are expected to be hedge funds and client favoritism.

19. Chicken-and-egg ethics bogs down in the question of which comes first—personal or organizational ethics. According to Hamilton (2002), "Regardless of which comes first, personal or organizational ethics, both must move towards a higher ground."
20. A series of ads by TD Waterhouse contains the following language in large print: "'Objective, independent, third-party research.' Can your broker say that?" The copy in the ad emphasizes that the research does not come from "in-house research analysts."

References

Backover, Andrew. 2002. "WorldCom, Qwest Face SEC Scrutiny." *USA Today* (12 March):1B.

Backover, Andrew, and Jayne O'Donnell. 2002. "WorldCom Scrutiny Touches on E-mail." *USA Today* (8 July):1B.

Barber, Brad M., Reuven Lehavy, and Brett Trueman. 2004. "Comparing the Stock Recommendation Performance of Investment Banks and Independent Research Firms." Paper presented at the 15th Annual Conference on Financial Economics and Accounting (November).

Barringer, Felicity. 2002. "10 Months Ago, Questions on Enron Came and Went with Little Notice." *New York Times* (28 January):A11.

Davis, Ann. 2004. "Wall Street's 'Conflict Reviews': What's the Next Step?" *Wall Street Journal* (4 November):C1, C4.

Dismukes, Jay. 2004. "New Standards Add More Weight to Reviews." *The Trusted Professional*, New York Society of CPAs newsletter (August).

Gasparino, Charles. 2002. "Ghosts of E-Mails Continue to Haunt Wall Street." *Wall Street Journal* (18 November):C1, C13.

Hamilton, Jo. 2002. "The Chicken or the Egg . . . Which Comes First in Ethics?" *Ohio Investor* (November/December): www.cpimohio.org/newsletter/novdec/chickenegg.htm.

"Investors Need to Bone Up on Bonds and Costs According to Vanguard/MONEY Investor Literacy Test." 2002. Press release, Business Wire (25 September).

Jennings, Marianne M. 1998. "Ethics: Escaping the Either/Or Conundrum." *Journal of Investment Consulting*, vol. 1, no. 1 (December):viii–ix.

———. 2005. "The Ethical Lessons of Marsh & McLennan." *Corporate Finance Review*, vol. 9, no. 4 (January/February):43–48.

———. Forthcoming 2005. *Business Ethics: Case Studies and Selected Readings*. 5th ed. New York: Thomson.

Morgenson, Gretchen. 2002a. "Deals within Telecom Deals." *New York Times* (28 August):BU1, BU10.

———. 2002b. "Ebbers Got Million Shares in Hot Deals." *New York Times* (28 August):C1.

———. 2002c. "Ebbers Made $11 Million on 21 Stock Offerings." *New York Times* (31 August):B1.

Morgenson, Gretchen, and Mary Williams Walsh. 2004. "How Consultants Can Retire on Your Pension." *New York Times* (12 December):3-1, 3-13.

Nocera, Joseph. 2004. "Wall Street on the Run." *Fortune* (14 June):106–120.

Pulliam, Susan, and Gregory Zuckerman. 2005. "SEC Examines Rebates Paid to Large Funds." *Wall Street Journal* (6 January):C1, C4.

Pulliam, Susan, Deborah Solomon, and Carrick Mollenkamp. 2002. "Former WorldCom CEO Built an Empire on Mountain of Debt." *Wall Street Journal* (31 December):A1.

Roye, Paul F. 2004a. Remarks before the NAVA Regulatory Affairs Conference (14 June): www.sec.gov/news/speech/spch061404pfr.htm.

———. 2004b. Remarks before the ICI 2004 Securities Law Developments Conference (6 December): www.sec.gov/news/speech/spch120604pfr.htm.

Schine, Eric. 1990. "Charlie Keating Gets a Taste of L.A. Law." *Business Week* (8 October):46.

Schwartz, John. 2002. "Man Who Doubted Enron Enjoys New Recognition." *New York Times* (21 January):C8.

SEC. 1998. *Inspection Report on the Soft Dollar Practices of Broker-Dealers, Investment Advisers and Mutual Funds*, U.S. Securities and Exchange Commission (22 September): www.sec.gov/news/ studies/softdolr.htm.

Smith, Randall. 2004. "Retail Analyst Leaves Lehman amid Probe of Insider Trading." *Wall Street Journal* (23 June):C3.

Smith, Randall, and Deborah Solomon. 2002. "Ebbers's Exit Hurts WorldCom's Biggest Fan." *Wall Street Journal* (3 May):C1, C3.

Smith, Thomas A. 1997. "Institutions and Entrepreneurs in American Corporate Finance." *California Law Review*, vol. 85, no. 1 (January):1–78.

Solomon, Deborah. 2004. "SEC Examines Conflicts in Job of Consultants." *Wall Street Journal* (9 November):C1, C5.

Sorkin, Andrew Ross. 2004. "Ex-Banking Star Given 18 Months for Obstruction." *New York Times* (9 September):A1, C2.

Stevenson, Richard W. 1991. "The Justice Department's S. & L. Learning Curve." *New York Times* (15 December):E4.

Stewart, James B. 1991. *Den of Thieves*. New York: Simon and Schuster.

Valdmanis, Thor. 2004a. "Final 2 Banks Settle for $100 Million." *USA Today* (27 August):1B.

———. 2004b. "Quattrone Sentenced to Surprising 1 1/2 Years in Prison." *USA Today* (9 September):1B.

Valdmanis, Thor, and Andrew Backover. 2002. "Lawsuit Targets Telecom Execs' Stock Windfalls." *USA Today* (1 October):1B.

Vickers, Marcia. 2004. "Selling Stock to the Masses." *Business Week* (19 April):22.

Weinberg, Neil. 2002. "Wal-Mart Could Sue for Libel." *Forbes* (12 August):56.

"Why John Olson Wasn't Bullish on Enron." 2002. Special Report: Exploring the Enron Explosion, *Knowledge@Wharton* (21 February): knowledge.wharton.upenn.edu.

Our Role in Corporate Malfeasance

Dean LeBaron, CFA

Few of us have been surprised by the numerous and huge corporate scandals uncovered in the past five years. After all, such events invariably occur at the tail end of a bull market, and this market—which was, depending on your beliefs, either 10 years long or five decades long—has been no exception. History is replete with juicy tales of business malfeasance in every similar period, from the tulips in the 1600s to the hangover of the 1930s.

What is surprising this time is who we have selected for prosecution and who has escaped. Until the real culprits are identified and put away, reform cannot take place and is only a slogan.

We need to reform the performance we expect from ourselves as analysts and from independent directors before we can say we are "fixing the system."

We have seen our criminal justice system painfully, slowly bringing corporate officers to the bar of justice, often in public in handcuffs (presumably to prevent any last-minute looting of corporate bank accounts). And we have separated the interests of accountants and advisors from those of company officers so that the recipes for cooking the books must undergo inspection without the chefs—and with a little leavening from plea bargaining thrown into the pot.

It is the rare corporate officer, however, who actually serves a jail sentence. The CEO of ImClone Systems and his shareholder friends seem to be exceptions, although in the case of the friends, the wrongdoing was apparently not corporate behavior but deception with investigators. The few other groups of officers—those of WorldCom, Enron Corporation, Tyco International—are in varying stages of expensive legal maneuvering (the Enron case is notable because the top official, whose defense seems to be ignorance, has unusual federal political connections).

What are the crimes—inflating earnings by legal but misleading techniques, squandering corporate assets for personal use, failure to report significant events? In a climate of enormous egos and even more enormous stock options, we are not

Dean LeBaron, CFA, is president of Virtualquest, New London, New Hampshire.

surprised that, again, opportunity to exhibit greed would lead to these behaviors. In isolated incidents, most of us have seen these same circumstances, although not on this scale or accompanied by such deception, lead to ruin of employment and shareholder wealth. Such behavior results from weak internal ethical guidance of corporate officers, opportunity, a sense that everyone who is smart enough is doing it, and just plain, garden-variety greed. On top of the temptation provided by those features are the designs by regulatory bodies to illuminate only the most egregious of sins.

But when annual pay packets of more than $100 million are legally awarded to the CEO of the New York Stock Exchange, an organization that depends on public trust to work, something is amiss.

The two classes of culprits that are really to blame have not been touched or even mentioned as yet. And until they are, we are not likely to see any corrections other than a climate of more modest financial expectations for the executive workers caring for shareholder assets.

The first category is the most difficult for us, as financial analysts, to identify because it is *us*. We are at fault for not uncovering corporate misbehavior in its early stages and reporting it to our constituencies. We are at least 70,000 strong, and most of us study companies—in the United States and elsewhere. We ask questions, probe, and claim we independently assess the job corporate managers are doing. Yet, in the few cases I have mentioned, analysts were complicit in rather than preventive of corporate misbehavior.

And our excuse is that "we did not know" or "we accepted the numbers" (despite the fact that when I last looked at CFA exams, candidates were tested on their ability to ferret out unusual deviations from financial statements).

The second category is the independent directors who are elected and paid by shareholders to represent shareholder interests. This group has better access to information on an individual company than analysts do but is burdened by friendships with managers and the wish of directors to continue in their posts. To my knowledge, not a single independent director has been charged in the well-publicized corporate cases. Were they asleep? Did they fail to ask questions or not understand the answers? They must, even those with important political connections, be called to account for their dereliction of duty.

When we reform the performance we expect from these two groups—analysts and independent directors—we can say we are fixing the system. In both cases, transparency may be better than jail time or fines. Analysts should keep a public record of the companies they study and how they study them (visits, conference calls) so that those analysts who miss a corporate blowup will openly suffer for accepting the incorrect information. And directors need to be accountable for their individual votes on corporate actions, and in reelection campaigns, their claims to be working for shareholders should be challenged.

When we do these two things, then, and only then, can we talk about the good work we are doing for the capital markets we nurture.

Remember the Age and Purpose of Our Profession

Jeffrey J. Diermeier, CFA

We are a profession that began as honest, noble, and committed to fiduciary responsibilities. And we are a young profession that must not assume history is the norm.

What a wonderful treasure of thought and perspectives from some of our best this series of Reflections articles has been! The opportunity to have noted students of capital markets sit back and share with us their accumulated wisdom meets the test of the extraordinary. And I will share with you some inside information that guaranteed the success of the series: The authors enjoyed the effort.

I joined this profession 30 years ago, at the halfway point of the *Financial Analysts Journal*'s legacy. I was attracted by the application of economic principles in a free and open marketplace that assuredly would aid in higher standards of living for all, particularly those who did not know the capital markets. The notion that an open marketplace (rather than something like the feared military-industrial complex of my youth) dictated the many key decisions of capital and resource allocation put a rational face on a complex economic world.

Those who joined this profession knew a good living could be had in active management—but only by those fortunate enough and determined enough to deliver the goods. Back in the 1970s, rarely would you have to question whether a young apprentice's motivation was potentially one of greed.

Sadly, that circumstance has changed. And some of our newcomers are amazed to think that this profession was ever anything but "a money job." Without question, it is more difficult to hire individuals and investment managers today because of this attitude.

One of the most gratifying discoveries I made at my first job as I toiled away in the Trust Department at First Chicago was the degree to which the bank and, in fact, the whole Chicago investment community adhered to the concept of "fiduciary." The profession was honest and noble, and I did not have to compromise my rather idealistic values to be involved. This too has changed. As Jack Bogle has pointed out ("The

Jeffrey J. Diermeier, CFA, is president and CEO of CFA Institute, Charlottesville, Virginia.

Mutual Fund Industry 60 Years Later: For Better or Worse?" *FAJ*, January/February 2005), a business now stands where once stood a profession, and investor trust—and, therefore, investor confidence—hangs in the balance.

Unfortunately—and this is true of most CFA Institute activities, including the *FAJ*—the people who read these pages are largely in our choir. So, the question is: How do we get into the next church? For one thing, we need the help of readers like you. If you are a leader of an investment firm or function, I'm sure you take to heart that your business is at its root a service function in which you have a covenant with your clients to treat them fairly and to put them first. If you execute this basic philosophy well, you can generate a highly profitable business in the classic economic definition of profit *and* be true to basic principles. If you extend your offerings beyond your investment staff's capabilities, you cannot deliver on that fundamental covenant upon which all trust is built.

On another tack, 30 years ago, the profession was very young by any measure. In fact, when I was an asset allocator early in my career, the insight I would have found most valuable was that very fact: The profession is young. Therefore, supposedly normal equilibrium conditions were still in the formative phase. Conventional wisdom about the key relationships in the markets suffered from severe overconfidence. For example, the common view of the future long-term real rate of return on the so-called risk-free rate (proxied by 90-day U.S. T-bills) was 0.0 percent. It was driven by the Ibbotson–Sinquefield data (*Stocks, Bonds, Bills, and Inflation*), which showed nearly zero (0.1 percent) T-bill results for 1926–1980.

When I began my career, the history of our profession included only 12 years of the CFA designation and it had been only 50 years since Edgar Lawrence Smith argued (in *Common Stocks as Long Term Investments*, 1924) that equities were an investment, not a speculation. The explosion in financial theory and empirical research spawned by the database created and maintained by the Center for Research in Security Prices at the University of Chicago was only about a decade old. Indeed, the growth of CFA Institute and the CFA Program owes a great debt to the wave of thought and science put forth by the giants described by Peter Bernstein in his Reflections "Capital Ideas: From the Past to the Future" (*FAJ*, November/December 2005)—Franco Modigliani, Merton Miller, Harry Markowitz, William Sharpe, Jack Treynor, and others. This theory and this science, together with the pension explosion of the 1970s, were the grist for our mill.

So what are the lessons? First, historical relationships in markets that extend long enough to cover most of one's working age tend to become assumed as normal. Theories, under the scientific method, are created to support the data. Collective wisdom, supported by the surprising influence of the media, moves to premature closure and overconfidence. In a young market, rather than accepting that the supposed normal relationships are correct, highly profitable research is geared to why those relationships will change. Our profession is young, and we should not accept our history as the norm or as predictive of the future, and we should not close off debate about relationships in the markets. They will change, because after all, markets are largely about ideas and people.

Second, we can succeed as a profession only by placing client interests above all else. Investment management is about service and integrity. We cannot forget either.

Beyond Portfolio Theory: The Next Frontier

Keith Ambachtsheer

> The time has come to integrate the insights offered by information theory and principal–agent theory with the tools of portfolio management into a holistic, comprehensive theory of investing.

There is broad consensus among finance and investment academics about where investment theory's next frontier lies. For example, in his recent award-winning Perspectives article, Robert Merton (2003) reviewed "the rich set of tools" academia has bestowed on the practitioner community over the course of the last 50 years.[1] The challenge now, he opined, is to put these tools into practice. He concluded, "I see this as a tough engineering problem, not one of new science" (p. 23). Similarly, in their recent award-winning book on strategic asset allocation, John Campbell and Luis Viceira (2002) concluded:[2]

> One of the most interesting challenges of the 21st century will be the development of systems to help investors carry out the task of strategic asset allocation. (p. 225)

So, investment theory's next frontier seems to be about engineering systems to create better financial outcomes for investors. But is that really true?

Without doubt, the academic community can be proud of its intellectual achievements since the publication of Harry Markowitz's seminal 1952 treatise on portfolio selection.[3] The cited writings by Merton and by Campbell–Viceira offer important examples of how Markowitz's original version of portfolio theory has been extended:

- Most investment contexts require the consideration of multiple horizons rather than a single horizon. In some cases, short-horizon considerations dominate; in others, the primary focus should be on assessing long-horizon outcomes.
- Prospective future cash flows (and their purchasing power) typically offer a more useful perspective for assessing the reward and risk of long-horizon investment strategies than do future wealth prospects. Thus, in most cases, long-term inflation-linked bonds are the natural reference portfolio for assessing the reward and risk of alternative investment strategies.

Keith Ambachtsheer is a strategic advisor to major pension plans around the world and director of the Rotman International Centre for Pension Management, University of Toronto.

- For individuals, investment-related rewards and risks should be integrated with other considerations, such as human capital–related rewards and risks, longevity/mortality, real property, and education. Corporations also need to adopt this broad, integrative approach to managing investment-related rewards and risks (in their pension funds, for example). The same is true for endowments and foundations.
- Long-horizon prospects for equity and bond returns have time-variant, predictive components. Therefore, strategic asset allocation should always be a dynamic, rather than a static, process.

These four extensions of "old" portfolio theory represent major advances in investment theory, as it is broadly defined. However, does that reality logically make the "engineering of systems" to incorporate the extensions into practice the next frontier for investment theory?

Two More Considerations

Before we settle on what investment theory's next frontier really is, we should consider two additional (related) bodies of thought—information theory and principal–agent theory:

- *Information theory* addresses the question of whether economic actors (e.g., buyers and sellers of investment-related services) are in equivalent positions from an information perspective as they make decisions. It also addresses the economic consequences of informational asymmetry.
- *Principal–agent theory* addresses the question of whether or not the economic interests of principals (e.g., individuals) and agents making decisions on their behalf (e.g., investment organizations) are aligned. It also addresses the economic consequences of misalignment.

Both theories have rich academic histories of their own. For example, George Akerlof's (1970) classic article, "The Market for 'Lemons,'" was published more than 30 years ago.[4] In it, Akerlof asked why the prices of new cars plummet once their owners drive them off the lot. His answer is the informational asymmetry between the owner of the (now used) car and any future buyer. The sellers of used cars know whether or not their cars are lemons; the buyers do not. Used-car pricing reflects this reality.

What about the market for investment management services? In this market too, sellers typically know a great deal more about what they are selling than buyers know about what they are buying. In John Maynard Keynes' famous 1936 "beauty contest" analogy, the service sellers' challenge is to persuade buyers that the sellers are better than their competitors at forecasting which securities the participants in security markets will find most beautiful tomorrow.[5] The service buyers' challenge is to figure out whose claims to believe (a practically impossible challenge for nonexperts). In such a market, pricing (i.e., fee structure) does not determine market share; what determines market share is the persuasiveness of a seller's message.

The acute informational asymmetry characteristic of the financial services markets leads logically to principal–agent considerations. The classic treatise in this field is *The Modern Corporation and Private Property* by Adolf Berle and Gardiner Means (1933). They examined the implications of the separation of corporate ownership and control at a time when the robber baron era of capitalism had ended. In the new world, where owners were millions of remote, faceless shareholders rather than powerful individual owner/managers, Berle and Means wondered: Would boards of directors and managers continue to serve the financial interests of shareholders? Or would they use their power to serve their own interests?

The financial services arena today contains a clear parallel to these questions. Now, we ask: In a world where the clients/beneficiaries of various types of financial services organizations (e.g., pension funds, mutual funds, endowment funds, insurance providers) are millions of remote, faceless individuals, will the boards and managers of the organizations and the service providers they hire serve the financial interests of the clients/beneficiaries? Or will they use their power to serve their own interests?

Integrative Investment Theory

So, yes, practitioners should incorporate into old portfolio theory the cornucopia of conceptual and empirical jewels the academic finance and investment community has bestowed on them during the past 50 years. But that extension is not enough. We need more than simply the reengineering of investment decision systems. We must also integrate into our new investment model the profound issues raised by (1) the highly asymmetrical distribution of information in the financial services marketplace and (2) the fact that millions of ultimate beneficiaries at the bottom of the financial food chain rely on a mosaic of intermediary (agent) organizations to provide products and services that truly serve the beneficiaries' interests.

Imagine an investment theory that integrated old portfolio theory with post-1952 technical offerings of academia and also the economic concepts of asymmetrical information and potential misalignment of economic interests. Such a theory would recognize that client/beneficiary value creation is a function of the successful integration of five value drivers; that is,

$$\text{Client/beneficiary value creation} = f(A, G, R, IB, FE),$$

where:

A = agency issues

G = governance

R = risk issues

IB = investment beliefs

FE = financial engineering

From Better Theory to Better Outcomes

Would the implementation of a more holistic, integrative theory of investing produce better outcomes for the clients/beneficiaries of financial services organizations? I have no doubt that it would. Consider how the value drivers could be integrated.

Agency Issues. Agency issues can hinder client/beneficiary value creation in a number of ways, all of which lead to clients/beneficiaries being financially disadvantaged by their agents. Thinking what can be done to minimize agency problems can pay large dividends, however, for the clients/beneficiaries of financial services organizations.

In my judgment, the premier agency issue in the financial services industry continues to be the inherent conflict that results from for-profit organizations providing management services directly to millions of mutual fund investors. The combined forces of acute informational asymmetry and pronounced principal–agent problems logically lead to many clients paying too much for too little. These forces, and their adverse effects on clients, continue to be a major public policy issue today, despite being identified by Jack Bogle as early as 1950.[6] More than 50 years later, despite token efforts by securities regulators, this issue has yet to be addressed in the fundamental manner it deserves.

Variants on this same broad agency theme play out when for-profit organizations sponsor defined benefit (DB) or defined contribution (DC) pension plans. For example, within two years of the enactment of ERISA on Labor Day 1974, Jack Treynor, Patrick Regan, and William Priest (1976) showed that ERISA's requirement to manage corporate DB plans "for the sole benefit of the beneficiaries" is pure legal fiction. Corporate managers can also choose to have serious skin (their own and their shareholders') in the pensions game. In doing so, they create situations that lead to conflicting interests between themselves, plan members, and shareholders that are, at best, extremely difficult to resolve. In the end, arm's-length, not-for-profit co-ops with the necessary scale and scope to be cost-effective offer the best hope to rectify the "too little value at too high cost" outcomes that combinations of informational asymmetry and misalignment of economic interests continue to create for millions of clients/beneficiaries.[7]

Governance. Addressing agency issues is a necessary but not sufficient condition for enhancing client/beneficiary value creation. There is no guarantee that an arm's-length, not-for-profit co-op will be well managed. Just as an evolving body of thought constitutes finance/investment theory today, so an evolving body of thought constitutes governance and organization design theory. This theory provides the context for articulating an organization's mission, delegating strategic planning and implementation to a competent executive team, and regularly monitoring progress toward mission achievement.

Integrating elements of governance and organization design theory, I and my co-authors showed in 1998 that pension funds with strong governance and organization design characteristics have outperformed those with poor characteristics by a statistically significant 1 percent a year, net of operating costs and adjusted for differences in investment policy (Ambachtsheer, Capelle, and Scheibelhut 1998). Yet even today, seven years later (despite some notable exceptions), spanning the globe from Europe across North America to the Far East, issues of governance and organization design continue to receive only sporadic attention in organizations active in the financial services arena.

Risk Issues. The portfolio theory of the 1950s dealt with investment risk and risk tolerance in a creative but limited way. Academia has moved the yardsticks of relevant, practical risk definitions and measurement considerably since the early days. The challenge now is to move these new risk concepts into practice. This requires, for example, that the governors of pension and endowment funds insist that risk definitions and risk management be relevant to the specific contexts of their clients/beneficiaries.

As a specific example, DB pension plans undertaking balance sheet mismatch risk represent a complex web of contingent claims that various stakeholder groups have "issued" to/on each other. Yet despite the fact that the Black–Scholes principles for the valuation of contingent claims have been with us for 30 years now, the study of their implications for the establishment of risk tolerances for pension plan stakeholders, or for how DB balance sheets should be valued and disclosed, has barely begun. To their credit, Dutch academics and practitioners have taken the lead in developing these important ideas.[8]

Investment Beliefs. The degree to which an investment organization believes prospective return components are predictable over multiple horizons should be an important determinant of how its investment processes are structured. For example, if the expected equity risk premium is always equal to its historical 5 percent realization, "investing" for most pension and endowment funds boils down to taking on lots of equity market exposure to generate return and some bond market exposure to create a modest risk buffer. Attempting to produce a bit of net alpha by taking on a bit of additional risk becomes a justifiable sideshow. This simple investment paradigm logically leads to the common practice in pension and endowment funds of maintaining static policy portfolios over time.

This practice becomes dangerously simplistic, however, if the expected equity risk premium varies materially over time in at least a partially predictable manner, as in fact, appears to be the case.[9] Now, the proper management of risk leads to policy portfolios that vary in composition over time.

Similarly, today's definitions and measurement of "investment styles" do not stand up well when rigorously assessed in the light of defensible investment beliefs. For my money, Keynes' beauty contest analogy still offers the best model for genuine investment style differentiation. At the most fundamental level, he asserted, there are only two investment styles—the agency-driven beauty contest style and the principal-driven value-creation style. Almost 70 years ago, Keynes lamented that he saw too much beauty contest investing and too little investing that created genuine economic value for clients/beneficiaries. If Keynes were alive today, he would observe that there is not much new under the sun. Yet, the potential supply of value-creation investment services is as alive and well today as it was in Keynes' day. What remains in short supply is a genuine demand for such services.[10]

Financial Engineering. Integrating properly specified client/beneficiary risk tolerances with time-variant return expectations in a noisy, complex investment arena full of fees and transaction costs is no mean task. Here is where well-engineered, integrative investment systems can add significant value. As Merton noted in his 2003 Perspectives piece, the array of investment tools in the implementation toolkit continues to grow faster than institutions and investment professionals can devise ways to use them. My own modest contribution in the 1970s was to build and sell portfolio-rebalancing tools that measured and weighed the limited information content in analysts' alpha predictions against portfolio risk constraints and the certainty of transaction costs. Thus, the term "information coefficient," or IC for short, entered the financial engineering lexicon.[11] Today, Bob Litterman and his colleagues (2003) need a 626-page book to describe the tools in the current financial engineering toolkit.

Selecting the right tools out of the toolkit requires context, which is where the prior, effective integration of risk issues and investment beliefs is essential. But such effective integration requires, in turn, organizations that have aligned economic interests, mission clarity, and good governance. So, we arrive back where we started. The "Integrative Investment Theory" (IIT) circle is complete.

Evolution, not Revolution

Notwithstanding its logic, IIT will not change the world tomorrow. After all, it took the old portfolio theory 20 years to gain conceptual traction and another 20 years to work its way into investment practices. Fortunately, we are not at ground zero with IIT today. Bogle's 50 years of pioneering work in the mutual fund arena have already been acknowledged. In *The Unseen Revolution*, Peter Drucker (1976) anticipated many of the agency and governance challenges facing workplace pension funds as they struggle to become viable, cost-effective organizations that deliver predictable pension payments.[12] And here we are today, almost 30 years later, finally integrating these agency and governance elements with the basic elements of portfolio theory into a broader, more holistic theory of investing.

I shared an earlier conviction that the adoption of such a broader, more holistic theory would produce better outcomes for the millions of clients/beneficiaries of the financial services industry. Better outcomes in what way? The most direct, measurable outcome would be a material reduction in intermediation costs as financial services organizations were forced to move to a "value for money" philosophy in serving their clients/beneficiaries. But that is not all. IIT also holds the promise of a higher rate of societal wealth creation, as better-governed financial intermediaries reduce agency costs in the organizations they invest in and allocate financial capital more efficiently. That could be the biggest prize of all.

Notes

1. Merton's article received the Graham and Dodd Award for the Best Perspectives piece in the *Financial Analysts Journal* in 2003.
2. This book received the Paul A. Samuelson Award for Outstanding Scholarly Writing on Lifelong Financial Security from TIAA-CREF in 2002.
3. Markowitz (1952). Markowitz was the 1990 Nobel laureate in economics, together with Merton Miller and William Sharpe.
4. Akerlof received the 2001 Nobel Prize in Economics for his contributions to information theory.
5. In the kind of beauty contest Keynes was describing, contestants pick out the six prettiest faces from a hundred photos and the prize is awarded to the contestant whose choice most nearly corresponds to the *average preferences* of the group of contestants. See Chapter 12, "The State of Long-Term Expectation."
6. Bogle provided the historical perspective in a speech titled "Vanguard—Child of Princeton" delivered at Princeton University on 28 May 2004. A 30 September 2004 speech titled "The Convergence of Indexing and Active Management" provided data suggesting that the average mutual fund participant underperforms passive management not only by the annual 2 percent of incremental expenses paid but also by an additional 2 percent a year representing dysfunctional switching between funds. Both speeches can be found at the Bogle Financial Markets Research Center website (www.vanguard.com/bogle_site/sp20040528.htm), together with Bogle's many other speeches, articles, and books on the agency and informational asymmetry issues in the mutual fund industry. In a speech to the American Life Insurance Council (14 October 2002) titled "How We Can Profit from the Experience of Corporate America," Bogle argued that the same dysfunctional dynamics are also at work in the insurance industry.
7. See Ambachtsheer (1994). This article, winner of a Graham and Dodd Scroll Award, sets out the principles for measuring the cost-effectiveness of not-for-profit co-ops, such as co-op pension funds.
8. See Ponds (2003). Holland's two largest pension funds, ABP and PGGM, are funding a major research effort to develop practical methodologies to value pension promises related to both benefits and funding as contingent claims issued and held by various stakeholder groups.
9. See Arnott and Bernstein (2002). This work, winner of the 2002 Graham and Dodd Award for best article, revealed a strong positive correlation of 0.70 over the past two centuries between the expected equity risk premium (calculated by using a simple heuristic) and its subsequent 10-year realization.
10. To Keynes, value-creation investment services focus on generating healthy long-horizon cash flows, net of expenses, for patient investors. I think Keynes would agree that today's low-cost risk-control strategies would

qualify under this definition. So would low-cost index-matching strategies as long as they offered an adequate prospective risk premium. Integrative investment theory would suggest that, to minimize agency effects, active value-creating strategies should be implemented inside not-for-profit co-ops or outsourced to outside investment agents prepared to operate under economically fair, transparent reward- and risk-sharing arrangements.

11. Ambachtsheer and Farrell (1979). This Graham and Dodd Scroll Award–winning article was the last in a series of articles I wrote on measuring and using return predictions with limited information content that appeared in the *FAJ* and the *Journal of Portfolio Management* during the 1970s. The term "information coefficient" first appeared in 1974.
12. In the foreword to a reissue in 1996 of the original book, Drucker wrote, "No book of mine was ever more on target than *The Unseen Revolution,* first published in 1976. And no book of mine has ever been more totally ignored. . . ."

References

Akerlof, George. 1970. "The Market for 'Lemons': Quality, Uncertainty, and the Market Mechanism." *Quarterly Journal of Economics*, vol. 84, no. 3 (August):488–500.

Ambachtsheer, Keith. 1994. "The Economics of Pension Fund Management." *Financial Analysts Journal*, vol. 50, no. 6 (November/December):21–31.

Ambachtsheer, Keith, and James Farrell. 1979. "Can Active Management Add Value?" *Financial Analysts Journal*, vol. 35, no. 6 (November/December):39–57.

Ambachtsheer, Keith, Ronald Capelle, and Tom Scheibelhut. 1998. "Improving Pension Fund Performance." *Financial Analysts Journal*, vol. 54, no. 6 (November/December):15–21.

Arnott, Robert, and Peter Bernstein. 2002. "What Risk Premium Is 'Normal'?" *Financial Analysts Journal*, vol. 58, no. 2 (March/April):64–85.

Berle, Adolf, and Gardiner Means. 1933. *The Modern Corporation and Private Property*. Revised ed. New York: Harcourt, Brace, and World.

Campbell, John, and Luis Viceira. 2002. *Strategic Asset Allocation: Portfolio Choice for Long-Term Investors*. New York: Oxford University Press.

Drucker, Peter. 1976. *The Unseen Revolution: How Pension Fund Socialism Came to America*. New York: Harper & Row.

Keynes, John Maynard. 1936. *The General Theory of Employment, Interest, and Money*. New York: Harcourt, Brace.

Litterman, Robert B., and Quantitative Resources Group. 2003. *Modern Investment Management: An Equilibrium Approach*. New York: Wiley Finance.

Markowitz, Harry. 1952. "Portfolio Selection." *Journal of Finance*, vol. 7, no. 1 (March):77–91.

Merton, Robert. 2003. "Thoughts on the Future: Theory and Practice of Investment Management." *Financial Analysts Journal*, vol. 59, no. 1 (January/February):17–23.

Ponds, Eduard. 2003. "Pension Funds and Value-Based Intergenerational Accounting." *Journal of Pension Economics & Finance*, vol. 2, no. 3 (November): 295–325.

Treynor, Jack, Patrick Regan, and William Priest. 1976. *The Financial Reality of Pension Funding under ERISA*. Homewood, IL: Dow Jones–Irwin.

The Mutual Fund Industry 60 Years Later: For Better or Worse?

John C. Bogle

Over the course of the past 60 years, the mutual fund industry has undergone tremendous change. In 1945, it was a tiny industry offering a relative handful of funds—largely diversified equity and balanced funds. As 2005 begins, it is a multi-trillion-dollar titan offering thousands of funds with a dizzying array of investment policies and strategies. I have been actively engaged in this field since 1949—fully 55 years of the *Financial Analysts Journal*'s 60-year existence—when I researched and wrote my Princeton University senior thesis about mutual funds. I have spent my entire career in the mutual fund industry.

The staggering increase in the size of the industry and the huge expansion in the number and types of funds are but the obvious manifestations of the radical changes in the mutual fund industry. It has also undergone a multifaceted change in character. In 1945, it was an industry engaged primarily in the profession of serving investors and striving to meet the standards of the recently enacted Investment Company Act of 1940, which established the policy that funds must be "organized, operated, and managed" in the interests of their shareholders *rather than* in the interests of their managers and distributors. It was an industry that focused primarily on stewardship. Today, in contrast, the industry is a vast and highly successful marketing business, an industry focused primarily on salesmanship. As countless independent commentators have observed, asset gathering has become the fund industry's driving force.

Beneath the surface of this broad change lie numerous specific developments. This essay reviews 10 of the major

In the aggregate, the fundamental changes in the mutual fund industry during the past 60 years have benefited mutual fund managers, not mutual fund investors.

John C. Bogle is president of The Vanguard Group's Bogle Financial Markets Research Center.

Editor's Note: Mr. Bogle, whose Princeton University thesis was titled "The Economic Role of the Investment Company," joined Wellington Management Company in 1951 and led it from 1965 until 1974. He founded The Vanguard Group in 1974 and served as its CEO until 1996 and as senior chairman until 2000. The opinions expressed in this article do not necessarily represent the views of Vanguard's present management.

changes that have taken place in the mutual fund industry during the past 60 years, and then evaluates the impact of those changes, not only on the returns earned by the mutual funds themselves, but on the returns earned by their investors.

1. Bigger, More Varied, and More Numerous

The mutual fund industry has become a giant.[1] From a base of $882 million at the beginning of 1945, fund assets soared to $7.5 trillion in 2004, a compound annual growth rate of 16 percent. If the industry had merely matched the 7 percent nominal growth rate of our economy, assets would be only $50 billion today. (Such is the magic of compounding!) In 1945, 90 percent of industry assets were represented by stock funds and stock-oriented balanced funds. Today, such funds compose about 57 percent of industry assets. Bond funds now represent 17 percent of assets, and money market funds—dating back only to 1970—constitute the remaining 26 percent. So, what was once an equity fund industry now spans all three broad categories of marketable securities—stocks, bonds, and money market instruments. This change has been a boon to fund investors as well as to fund managers.

As **Table 1** shows, the number of funds has also exploded. The 68 mutual funds of yesteryear have multiplied to today's nearly 8,200 total, and they offer investment objectives and policies designed to meet almost any imaginable investment goal. As funds have become, overwhelmingly, the investment of choice for our nation's families, fund choice, fund selection, and asset allocation have become the watchwords of today's mutual fund industry.

The vehicles through which mutual funds are purchased have also changed. Funds are the underlying securities in variable annuities and, thanks to favorable federal tax legislation, are now held not only directly by investors but also in individual retirement accounts and in profit-sharing and employee savings plans. Assets in these tax-deferred plans today total $2.7 trillion, or nearly 40 percent of industry assets.[2]

2. Stock Funds: To the Four Corners of the Earth

Stock funds remain the industry's backbone and driving force and are the principal focus of this historical review. As their number soared, so did the variety of objectives and policies they follow. As **Table 2** shows, in 1945, the stock fund sector was dominated by funds that invested largely in highly diversified portfolios of U.S. corporations with large market capitalizations and with

Table 1. The Mutual Fund Industry: Growth in Funds and Assets

	1945		2004	
Type of Fund	Number of Funds	Assets (millions)[a]	Number of Funds	Assets (billions)
Stock/hybrid funds	49	$794.0	5,100	$4,266.9
Bond funds	19	88.0	2,100	1,246.8
Money market funds	0	—	970	1,962.2
Total	68	$882.0	8,170	$7,475.9

[a]Total assets of stock funds in 1945 estimated as 90 percent of industry total.

Sources: Wiesenberger and Investment Company Institute.

Table 2. Stock Funds: Number and Type

	1945		2004[a]	
Category	No. of Funds	% of Total	No. of Funds	% of Total
U.S. large-cap blend	38	77%	579	14%
Other U.S. diversified equity	0	—	2,484	59
Specialized	11	23	455	11
International	0	—	686	16
Total	49	100%	4,204	100%

[a]Includes all equity funds covered by Morningstar.

Sources: Wiesenberger and Morningstar.

volatility roughly commensurate with that of the stock market itself. Today, such middle-of-the-road funds are a distinct minority, and most other categories entail higher risks. Only 579 of the 4,200 stock funds measured by Morningstar now closely resemble their widely diversified blue-chip ancestors.[3]

What's more, the industry now also boasts 455 specialized funds focused on narrow industry segments—from technology to telecommunications (these two groups were particular favorites during the late stock market bubble). Some 686 international funds run the gamut from diversified funds owning shares of companies all over the globe to highly specialized funds focusing on particular nations, such as China, Russia, or Israel.

Sixty years ago, an investor could have thrown a dart at a broad listing of stock funds and had three chances out of four of picking a fund whose return was apt to closely parallel that of the U.S. stock market. Today, that investor has just one chance out of seven. For better or worse, the selection of mutual funds has become an art form. Indeed, it is fair to say that choosing a mutual fund has come to require the same assiduous analysis as selecting an individual common stock. Indeed, most investors now hold portfolios of *funds* rather than yesteryear's portfolios of *stocks*.[4]

One curious counterpoint to this trend is worth noting. Unmanaged index funds essentially representing the entire U.S. stock market (through the Wilshire Total Stock Market Index or the S&P Composite Stock Price Index) did not enter the field until 1975, but they have accounted for more than one-third of equity fund cash inflow since 2000 and now represent fully one-seventh of equity fund assets.[5] Such funds may be said to provide the *n*th degree of diversification.

3. Investment Committee to Portfolio Manager

The vast changes in fund objectives and policies have been accompanied by equally vast changes in how mutual funds are managed. In 1945, the major funds were managed almost entirely by investment committees. But the demonstrated wisdom of the collective was soon overwhelmed by the perceived brilliance of the individual. The Go-Go Era of the mid-1960s and the recent so-called New Economy bubble brought us hundreds of ferociously aggressive "performance funds," and the new game seemed to call for freewheeling individual talent. The term "investment committee" virtually vanished, and the "portfolio manager" gradually became the industry standard, the model for some 3,387 of the 4,194 stock funds currently listed in Morningstar, as **Table 3** reports. ("Management teams," often portfolios overseen by multiple managers, are said to run the other 807 funds.)

Table 3. Equity Fund Management Modes

Type	1945	2004
Committee	47	0
Single portfolio manager	2	3,387
Management team	0	807
Total	50	4,194

Note: No management form was listed for 10 funds in 2004.
Sources: Wiesenberger and Morningstar.

The coming of the age of the portfolio manager, whose tenure lasted only as long as the individual produced superior performance, moved fund management from the stodgy old consensus-oriented investment committee to a more entrepreneurial, free-form, aggressive (and less risk-averse) investment approach. Before long, moreover, the managers with the hottest short-term records were publicized by their firms and, with the cooperation of the media, turned into "stars." A full-fledged star system gradually came to pass. A few portfolio managers actually *were* stars—Fidelity Investments' Peter Lynch, Vanguard's John Neff, Legg Mason's Bill Miller, for example—but most proved to be comets, illuminating the fund firmament for but a moment before flaming out. Even after the devastation of the recent bear market and the stunning fact that the average manager now lasts for only five years, the portfolio manager system remains largely intact. The continuity provided by the earlier investment committee is but a memory.

4. Investment or Speculation?

Together, the coming of more aggressive funds, the burgeoning emphasis on short-term performance, and the move from investment committee to portfolio manager had a profound impact on mutual fund investment strategies, most obviously in soaring portfolio turnover—as shown in **Table 4**. In 1945, mutual fund managers did not *talk* about long-term investing; they simply *did* it. That's what trusteeship is all about. But over the next 60 years, that basic tenet was turned on its head and short-term speculation became the order of the day.

Not that the long-term focus did not resist change. Indeed, between 1945 and 1965, annual portfolio turnover averaged a steady 17 percent, suggesting that the average fund held its average stock for about six years. But turnover then rose steadily; fund managers now turn their portfolios over at an average rate of 110 percent annually. Result: Compared with the six-year standard that prevailed for some two decades, the average stock is now held by the average fund for an average of only 11 months.

Moreover, turnover rates do not tell the full story of the role of mutual funds in the financial markets. The dollars involved are enormous. For example, at a 100 percent rate, today's managers of $4 trillion in equity assets would sell $4 trillion of stocks in a single year and then reinvest that $4 trillion in other stocks, $8 trillion in all. Even though more competitive (and increasingly electronic) markets have slashed unit transaction costs, it is difficult to imagine that such turnover levels, in which trades often take place between two competing funds, can result in a net gain to fund shareholders collectively.

If a six-year holding period can be characterized as long-term investment, and if an 11-month holding period can be characterized as short-term speculation, mutual fund managers today are not investors. They are speculators. I do not use the word "speculation" lightly. Nearly 70 years ago, John Maynard Keynes contrasted *speculation* ("forecasting the psychology of the market") with *enterprise* ("forecasting the prospective yield of an asset") and predicted that the influence of speculation among professional investors would rise as they emulated the uninformed public—that is, seeking to anticipate changes in public opinion rather than focusing on earnings, dividends, and book values.

In my 1951 thesis on the mutual fund industry, I was bold enough to disagree with Keynes' baleful prediction. As funds grew, I opined, they would move away from speculation and move toward enterprise by focusing, not on the momentary, short-term price of the share, but on the long-term intrinsic value of the corporation. As a result, I concluded, fund managers would supply the stock market "with a demand for securities that is steady, sophisticated, enlightened, and analytic." I could not have been more wrong. Mutual funds, once stock *owners*, became stock *traders* and moved far away from what Warren Buffett describes as his favorite holding period: forever.

5. America's Largest Shareholders

In 1945, as **Table 5** shows, funds owned only slightly more than 1 percent of the shares of all U.S. corporations. Today, they own nearly 25 percent. They could wield a potent "big stick" but, with a few exceptions, have failed to do so. With their long record of passivity and lassitude about corporate governance issues, fund managers must accept a large share of the responsibility for the ethical failures in corporate governance and accounting oversight that were among the major forces creating the recent stock market bubble and the bear market that followed.

Table 4. Equity Fund Portfolio Turnover Rates

Year	Rate
1945	24% (est.)
1950	25
1955	14
1960	14
1965	20
1970	39
1975	36
1980	51
1985	83
1990	90
1995	77
2000	108
2003	110
2004[a]	112

Note: Turnover is the lesser of portfolio sources or sales as a percentage of fund assets.

[a]2004 data are for all funds that had reported as of 31 October.

Sources: For 1945–1987, Investment Company Institute, based on industry aggregates. For 1988–2004, Morningstar, based on turnover of average equity fund.

Table 5. Mutual Fund Ownership of U.S. Stocks

Year	Percent of Equities Owned
1945	1.4%
1950	3.1
1955	3.3
1960	4.8
1965	5.7
1970	6.2
1975	4.9
1980	3.0
1985	5.2
1990	8.1
1995	16.0
2000	22.4
2003	23.1
2004[a]	24.9

[a]2004 data are as of 30 June.

Sources: NYSE, Wilshire Associates, and Federal Reserve Flow of Funds Report.

It was not always this way. In the old days, when mutual funds were responsible owners, the December 1949 *Fortune* article that inspired my ancient thesis described them as

> the ideal champion of . . . the small stockholder in conversations with corporate management, needling corporations on dividend policies, blocking mergers, and pitching in on proxy fights. (p. 118)

Indeed, in 1940, the U.S. SEC called on mutual funds to serve in

> the useful role of representatives of the great number of inarticulate and ineffective individual investors in corporations in which funds are interested. ("Investment Trusts and Investment Companies," part 2, p. 371)

It was not to be. Once an own-a-stock industry, funds became a rent-a-stock industry. The change in the industry's focus from investment to speculation can hardly be unrelated to its failure to observe the responsibilities of corporate citizenship. A fund that acts as a trader, focusing on the price of a share and holding a stock for less than a year, may not even own a company's shares when the time comes to vote them at the corporation's next annual meeting. In contrast, a fund that acts as an owner, focusing on the long-term value of the enterprise, has little choice but to regard the governance of the corporation as of surpassing importance.

6. Compressed Investor Holding Periods

The change in the mutual fund industry's character has radically affected the behavior of the mutual fund shareholder. Sixty years ago, shareholders bought shares in broadly diversified funds and held them. As **Table 6** shows, in the 1950s and for a dozen years thereafter, fund redemptions (liquidations of fund shares) averaged 6 percent of assets annually, which suggests that the average fund investor held his or her shares for 16 years. Like the managers of the funds they owned, shareholders were investing for the long pull.

Table 6. Annual Turnover of Shares by Equity Fund Investors

Year	Shares Redeemed as Percent of Assets
1945	10.1%
1950	12.5
1955	6.4
1960	5.1
1965	6.1
1970	6.2
1975	9.7
1980	22.8
1985	36.5
1990	38.2
1995	29.3
2000	39.6
2002	41.0
2003	30.9
2004[a]	24.8

[a]2004 data are through September, annualized.

Sources: Wiesenberger and Investment Company Institute.

But as the industry introduced new funds that were more and more performance oriented, often speculative, specialized, and concentrated—funds that behaved increasingly like individual stocks—it attracted more and more investors for whom the long term didn't seem to be relevant. By 2002, the redemption rate had soared to 41 percent of assets, an average holding period of slightly more than three years. The time horizon for the typical fund investor had tumbled by fully 80 percent.

Much of this reduction in investor holding periods, we now know, resulted from investors' pervasive use of timing strategies based on such aspects as time-zone trading. Following the timing scandals that were revealed late in 2003, however, fund managers tightened up their controls designed to preclude excessive trading in fund shares, and the shareholder redemption rate has tumbled to about 25 percent; nonetheless, the resulting average holding period is just four years.

As the old buy-and-hold mantra turned to "pick and choose," *freedom of choice* became the industry watchword, and "fund supermarkets" with their "open architecture" made moving quickly from one fund to another easy. The cost of these transactions was hidden in the form of access fees for the shelf space offered by these supermarkets. Access fees are paid by the funds themselves, so swapping funds seems to be free, which tacitly encourages shareholders to trade from one fund to another. But although picking tomorrow's winners based on yesterday's performance is attractive in theory, there are no data that suggest the strategy works in practice. Quite the contrary!

7. New Funds Appear, Old Funds Vanish

Part of the astonishing telescoping of holding periods can be traced to opportunistic, gullible, and emotional fund investors as well as the change in the character of our financial markets (especially in the boom and bust of the stock market bubble during 1997–2002). But by departing from the industry's time-honored tenet of "we sell what we make" and jumping on the "we make what will sell" bandwagon—that is, creating new funds to match the market fads of the moment—this industry must also assume much responsibility for the soaring investment activity of fund investors.

As **Table 7** reports, the 1990s were a banner decade for fund formation; 1,600 new general equity funds alone came into existence, which was more than twice the number of funds in existence at the decade's outset. And the new funds typically carried higher risks than their predecessors. As New Economy stocks led the market upward in the latter part of the decade, mutual fund managers formed 494 new technology, telecom, and Internet funds and aggressive growth funds favoring these sectors.[6]

Table 7. Formation and Liquidation of Equity Funds

Decade	No. of New Funds	Fund Creation Rate	No. of Dying Funds	Fund Failure Rate
1950s	28 (est.)	80% (est.)	10 (est.)	13%
1960s	211	88	37	21
1970s	123	34	202	61
1980s	534	110	78	17
1990s	1,604	125	462	36
2000s[a]	980	52	1,045	56

Note: Creation and failure rates for each decade are summed annual rates.

[a]Figures for the 2000 "decade" represent the first four years annualized.

Sources: CRSP database and author's estimates.

Not only did the industry create such funds, it marketed them with unprecedented vigor and enthusiasm, both through stockbrokers and through advertising. At the market's peak in March 2000, the 44 mutual funds that advertised their performance in *Money* magazine bragged about amazing returns averaging +85.6 percent during the previous 12 months. During 1998–2000, equity funds took in $650 billion of new money—well over half a trillion dollars—overwhelmingly invested in the new breed of speculative, high-performance, aggressive growth funds.[7] Most of the money, of course, poured into those winners of yesteryear *after* they led the market upward. They would also soon lead the market on its subsequent downward leg, with their shareholders suffering losses of hundreds of billions of dollars.

After the fall, the formation of opportunistic new funds began to unwind and a record number of funds went out of business, usually merging into other, better-performing funds in the same family. During 1994–2003, fully 1,900 funds vanished—largely, the New Economy funds. The conservative equity funds of six decades ago were, as the saying goes, "built to last," whereas their aggressive new cousins seemed "born to die." The 10–20 percent failure rates that characterized the decades of the 1950s to the 1980s (except for the 1970s, following the 1973–74 bear market) reached 36 percent during the 1990s. Should present fund dissolution rates continue, some 2,800 of today's equity funds—more than one-half—will no longer exist a decade hence.

8. Cost of Fund Ownership

In 1945, as **Table 8** shows, the average expense ratio (total management fees and operating expenses as a percentage of fund assets) for the largest 25 funds,with aggregate assets of but $700 million, was 0.76 percent, generating aggregate costs of $4.7 million for fund investors. Six decades later, in 2004, the assets of the equity funds managed by the 25 largest fund complexes had soared to $2.5 trillion, but the average expense ratio had soared by 105 percent to 1.56 percent, generating costs of $31 *billion*.[8] In other words, while their assets were rising 3,600-fold, costs were rising 6,600-fold. (The dollar amount of direct fund expenses borne by shareholders of all equity funds has risen from an estimated $5 million annually in the 1940s to something like $35 billion in 2004, or 7,000-fold.) Despite the substantial economies of scale that exist in mutual fund management, fund investors have not only *not* shared in these economies, they have actually incurred higher costs of ownership.

Some of that enormous rise in the average expense ratio is a result of the inclusion of marketing expenses paid for by the fees allowed under Rule 12-b(1) of the Investment Company Act of 1940 adopted in 1980. These distribution fees have, in part, replaced traditional front-end sales charges. And although reductions in management fees that fully reflect the economies of scale are virtually nonexistent, investors have increasingly chosen no-load funds and low-cost funds. When portfolio transaction costs—an inseparable part of owning most funds—are added to expense ratios and

Table 8. Direct Costs of Fund Ownership: 25 Largest Fund Managers

Measure	1945	2004	Change
Total assets	$0.7 billion	$2,500 billion	3,600×
Fees and operating expenses (est.)[a]	$4.7 million	$31 billion	6,600×
Average expense ratio	0.76%	1.56%	+105%

[a]Excluding portfolio transaction costs, sales charges, and opportunity costs.

Sources: Wiesenberger and Strategic Insight.

sales charges, however (plus fees paid to financial advisors to select funds, which have also partly replaced earlier front-end loads), the costs of mutual fund ownership remain a substantial impediment to the ability of equity funds and their shareholders to capture the returns generated by the stock market.

9. Rise of Fund Entrepreneurship

Sixty years ago, the mutual fund industry placed its emphasis on fund management as a profession—the trusteeship of other people's money. Today, there is much evidence that salesmanship has superseded trusteeship as our industry's prime focus. What was it that caused this sea change? Perhaps trusteeship was essential for an industry whose birth in 1924 was quickly followed by tough times—the Depression and then World War II. Perhaps salesmanship became the winning strategy in the easy times thereafter, an era of almost unremitting economic prosperity. Probably, however, the most powerful force behind the change was that mutual fund management emerged as one of the most profitable businesses in our nation. Entrepreneurs could make big money managing mutual funds.

In 1958, only 13 years after the inaugural issue of the *FAJ*, the whole dynamic of entrepreneurship in the fund industry changed. Until then, a trustee could make a tidy profit by managing money but could not *capitalize* that profit by selling shares of the management company to outside investors. The SEC held that the sale of a management company represented payment for the sale of a fiduciary office, an illegal appropriation of fund assets. If such sales were allowed, the SEC feared, it would lead to "trafficking" in advisory contracts, a gross abuse of the trust of fund shareholders. But a California management company challenged the regulatory agency's position. The SEC went to court—and lost.

Thus, as 1958 ended, the gates that had prevented public ownership since the industry began 34 years earlier came tumbling down. A rush of initial public offerings followed, with the shares of a dozen management companies quickly brought to market. Investors bought management company shares for the same reasons that they bought shares of Microsoft Corporation and IBM Corporation and, for that matter, Enron: because they thought their earnings would grow and their stock prices would rise accordingly.

The IPOs were just the beginning. Publicly held and even privately held management companies were acquired by giant banks and insurance companies that were eager to take the new opportunity to buy into the burgeoning fund business at a healthy premium (averaging 10 times book value or more). The term "trafficking" was not far off the mark; there have been at least 40 such acquisitions during the past decade alone, and the ownership of some fund firms has been transferred numerous times. Today, among the fifty largest fund managers, only eight remain privately held (plus mutually owned Vanguard). Six firms are publicly held, and the remaining thirty-five management companies are owned by giant financial conglomerates—twenty-two by banks and insurance companies, six by major brokerage firms, and seven by foreign financial institutions.

Obviously, when a corporation buys a business, fund manager or not, it expects to earn a hurdle rate on its capital. So, if the cost of an acquisition is $1 billion and the hurdle rate is 12 percent, the acquirer will require at least $120 million of annual earnings. In a bull market, that goal may be easy for a mutual fund firm to achieve. But when the bear comes, we can expect a combination of (1) cutting management costs, (2) adding new types of fees (distribution fees, for example), (3) maintaining, or even increasing, management fee rates, and even (4) getting the buyer's capital back by selling the management firm to another owner (the SEC's trafficking in advisory contracts writ large).

It would be surprising if this shift in control of the mutual fund industry from private to public hands, largely those of giant financial conglomerates, had *not* accelerated the industry's change from profession to business. Such staggering aggregations of managed assets—often hundreds of billions of dollars under a single roof—surely serves both to facilitate the marketing of a fund complex's brand name in the consumer goods market and to build its market share. Conglomeration does not seem likely to make the money management process more effective, however, nor to drive investor costs down, nor to enhance the industry's original notion of stewardship and service.

10. Scandal

For 78 years—from its start back in 1924 through 2002—the mutual fund industry was free of major taint or scandal. But as asset gathering became the name of the game, as return on managers' capital challenged return on fund shareholders' capital as the preeminent goal, as conglomeration became the dominant structure, and as stewardship took a backseat to salesmanship, many fund managers were not only all too willing to accept substantial investments from short-term investors and allow those investors to capitalize on price differentials in international time zones (as well as engage in other unrelated but profitable activities); they were also willing to abet and even institutionalize these practices.

To improve their own earnings, managers put their own interests ahead of the interests of their fund shareholders. They allowed short-term traders in their funds to earn illicit higher returns at a direct, dollar-for-dollar cost to their fellow investors holding for the long term. Brought to light by New York Attorney General Eliot L. Spitzer in September 2003, the industry's first major scandal went well beyond a few bad apples. More than a score of firms, managing a total $1.6 trillion of fund assets, including some of the oldest, largest, and once most respected firms in the industry, have been implicated in wrongdoing. This scandal exemplifies the extent to which salesmanship has triumphed over stewardship.

For Better or Worse?

Clearly, the mutual fund industry of 2005 is different not only in degree but in kind from the industry of 60 years earlier—infinitely larger and more diverse, with more speculative funds focused on ever-shorter investment horizons. It is less aware of its responsibility for corporate citizenship; its funds are held by investors for shorter time periods; and it is far more focused on asset gathering and marketing. The fund industry is increasingly operated as a business rather than a profession and, despite the awesome increase in its asset base, has far higher unit costs. The culmination of these changes is a scandal that crystallizes the extent to which the interest of the managers has superseded the interest of fund shareholders. Way back in 1967, Nobel Laureate Paul Samuelson was smarter than he could have imagined when he concluded,

> there was only one place to make money in the mutual fund business—as there is only one place for a temperate man to be in a saloon, behind the bar and not in front of it . . . so I invested in a management company. (*Notre Dame Lawyer*, June 1969, p. 918)

Determining how well the investor—the intemperate customer on the other side of the bar in that saloon—has been served by the old industry versus by the new—is a fairly simple statistical matter. Although equity fund shareholders have, of course, made substantial profits during the industry's modern era, **Table 9** shows that the profits have been but a small fraction of what they could have captured simply by buying and holding a low-cost all-U.S.-equity index fund.

Table 9. Mutual Fund Returns vs. the Stock Market

Measure	1945–1965	1983–2003
Stock market return[a]	14.9%	13.0%
Average equity fund return	13.2%	10.3%
Shortfall	1.7 pps	2.7 pps
Fund share of market return	89%	79%

Note: Fund return in the second period was reduced by 0.3 percentage points as a minimal estimate of survivorship bias.

[a]S&P 500.

Source: Lipper.

- In 1945–1965, the average fund delivered 89 percent of the market's annual return. The small shortfall that did exist between the annual rate of return of the average equity fund and that of the S&P 500 Index was doubtless largely accounted for by the moderate costs of fund ownership in those two decades.
- In 1983–2003, with the shortfall at 2.7 percentage points, the average fund delivered only 79 percent of the market's annual return.

That a consistent gap exists between equity fund returns and stock market returns should not be a surprise, for in the long run, the record is clear: Equity mutual funds are commodities (and with relatively low survival rates, at that) that are differentiated largely by their costs. After all, with fund managers competing among themselves in selecting stocks, aggregate equity fund returns must inevitably parallel those of the equity market itself and thus fall short of those returns by the amount of their management, marketing, and turnover costs.

Although the data are lacking to account with precision for the gap between stock market returns and equity fund returns, the 20-year differentials between the return of the average fund and the index in both the old era and the new—as well as the increase in the spread—appear to be largely a result of fund costs. For example, in the 1945–65 period, equity fund expense ratios averaged about 0.8 percent and the cost of portfolio turnover (averaging about 16 percent a year) added perhaps another 0.8 percent, producing a 1.6 percent total, very close to the 1.7 pp lag shown in Table 9. In the 1983–2003 period, the average expense ratio was about 1.4 percent; portfolio turnover (90 percent annually on the average but at much lower unit trading costs than in the earlier period) added an estimated 1.0 percent, for a 2.4 percent cost, again very close to the 2.7 pp lag. (Because funds are rarely fully invested in stocks, opportunity costs may well account for the remaining differences between the cost and the shortfall.[9])

So, it is largely the increase in fund costs that led to the substantial reduction shown in Table 9 in the share of the stock market's return earned by the average equity *fund*.[10] But the average equity fund *shareholder* has fared far worse. Based on studies comparing traditional time-weighted (per share) returns and dollar-weighted (investor) returns over the past decade, the average fund investor earned an annual return fully 2.4 pps less than that of the average fund.

The change in the industry's character bears a heavy responsibility for the reduced earnings of the average fund shareholder. First, shareholders investing in equity funds have paid a heavy timing penalty: They invested too little of their savings in equity funds when stocks represented good values during the 1980s and early 1990s. Then, enticed by the great bull market and the wiles of mutual fund marketers as the bull market neared its peak, they invested too much of their savings in equity funds. Second, they have paid a *selection* penalty by pouring money into aggressive growth funds investing in the New Economy during the bubble while withdrawing money from value funds favoring the Old Economy.

While the stock market was providing an annual return of 13 percent during the past 20 years and the average equity fund was earning an annual return of 10.3 percent, the average fund *investor* (assuming that the 2.4 pp shortfall prevailed for the full period) was earning only 7.9 percent a year. Compounded over two decades, the 2.7 pp penalty of costs was huge. But the penalty of *character* was almost as large—another 2.4 pps. **Table 10** shows that $1.00 invested in the market and compounded at 13 percent grew to $11.50; the investor's $1.00 grew to $4.57, at best a modest reward for assuming the risks of equity investing during a period in which the stock market was providing returns well above long-term norms.

The point of this statistical examination of the returns earned by the stock market, the average fund, and the average fund owner is not precision, but direction. Whatever the precise data, the evidence is compelling that equity fund returns lag the stock market by a substantial amount, largely accounted for by cost, and that fund investor returns lag fund returns by a substantial amount, largely accounted for by counterproductive market timing and fund selection.

Where Do We Go from Here?

In the aggregate, the tens of millions of our citizens who have entrusted their hard-earned trillions to the care of mutual fund managers have not been well served by the myriad changes that have taken place in mutual funds during the past 60 years. What about mutual funds yet to come? My answer should not surprise you: It is time to go back to our roots; to put mutual fund shareholders back in the driver's seat, to return to the principles of the 1940 Investment Company Act and demand that funds be organized, operated, and managed in the interest of their shareholders rather than the interest of their managers and distributors.

Table 10. Comparison of Market Returns, Fund Returns, and Investor Returns, 1983–2003

Measure	Annual Return	Growth of $1.00
Stock market return	13.0%	$11.50
Average equity fund return	10.3%	$7.10
Gap between average fund and market	2.7 pps	$4.40
Estimated equity fund investor return[a]	7.9%	$4.57
Gap between average investor and average fund	2.4 pps	$2.53
Total gap between average investor and market	5.1 pps	$6.93

[a] Author's calculation based on a comparison of time-weighted returns with the dollar-weighted returns earned by the fund investors for 600 general equity funds during 1993–2003.

Some of the steps that must be taken would be relatively painless for fund managers—reducing turnover costs by, for example, bringing turnover rates down to reasonable levels. And some would be rather painful—reducing management fees and sales commissions and cutting operating and marketing costs. Because there is no reason to expect that today's $7.5 trillion fund industry can increase the portion of the market's returns earned by its funds by suddenly finding the ability to provide market-superior returns (after all, fund managers are essentially competing with one another), such cost reductions are the only realistic way to enhance the returns of the average fund.

To enhance the share of fund returns earned by fund *shareholders*, the industry needs to reorder its product strategies to focus once again on broadly diversified funds with sound objectives, prudent policies, and long-term strategies. The industry needs to take its foot off the marketing pedal and press down firmly on the stewardship pedal. At the same time, the industry must give investors better information about asset allocation, fund selection, risks, potential returns, and costs—all with complete candor. To do otherwise will doom the industry to a dismal future. For whatever the profession, finally, the client must be served. Whatever the business, finally, the customer must be served. As an article in a recent issue of *Fortune* (January 2003) quoted me as saying:

> Of course there's hope [the industry will change]. There's a guarantee it will get better. Investors won't act contrary to their own economic interests forever. (p. 113)

The need for change is obvious; the steps that must be taken equally obvious. It is high time for the mutual fund industry to return funds present to funds past, to restore the industry to its original character of stewardship and prudence. If funds come to refocus on serving shareholders—serving them "in the most efficient, honest, and economical way possible," as I wrote in my thesis 54 years ago—the future for this industry will be not simply bright but brilliant.

Notes

1. The term "mutual fund" refers to open-end investment companies, with redeemable shares, registered under the Investment Company Act of 1940 with the U.S. SEC.
2. These data are from the Investment Company Institute's *2004 Mutual Fund Fact Book.*
3. Today's accepted terminology for equity funds reflects this change. We have come to accept a nine-box matrix of funds arranged by market capitalization (large, medium, or small) on one axis and by investment style (growth, value, or a blend of the two) on the other. Yesterday's middle-of-the-road funds would today find themselves in the "large-cap blend" box, which now comprises only 14 percent of the equity funds in the Morningstar database.
4. Sign of the times: As the public interest moved from individual stocks to stock funds, the *New York Times* took appropriate action. On 30 June 1999, the daily mutual fund price listings were moved ahead of those of the NYSE and NASDAQ. Several years later, only the fund listings remained in the main financial section.
5. Strategic Insight Mutual Fund Research and Consulting.
6. Strategic Insight.
7. *2004 Mutual Fund Fact Book.*
8. Asset-weighted expense ratios were used in calculating total costs.
9. If stock returns average 12 percent and U.S. T-bills average 4 percent, the 8 percent spread on an average 5 percent cash position represents an opportunity cost of 40 bps. In any event, the fund returns exclude the impact of front-end sales charges and thus are overstated in both comparisons.
10. Federal and state income taxes represent yet a further toll on the returns earned by taxable fund shareholders. High portfolio turnover generates considerable tax inefficiency; during the past 15 years, equity fund after-tax returns lagged pretax returns by 2.2 pps a year—an additional burden that nearly *doubled* the confiscatory impact of the other fund costs.

A Step Backward Might Be a Good Thing

David I. Fisher

One of the things one does to prepare for a "reflections" speech is to review things that one has said in the past. In the process, I came across some comments I made about the business to an AIMR (now CFA Institute) conference in May of 2001.

I said the following:

> Let me begin with some thoughts on the consolidation of the financial services business that continues to reduce the number of independent money management firms. The rationale is always something like:
>
> - It will give us the scale required to compete.
> - Or it is required as the world goes global.
> - Or we need additional distribution.
> - Product diversification.
> - It enables us to keep our professional staff together while providing liquidity for senior people.
>
> Nobody says (or even whispers), "It's all about money." Wouldn't it be fun if someone in the future, when asked about selling out, said, "We couldn't resist the price"!
>
> I certainly don't make these comments out of envy but, rather, because I think it's important to focus on some of the secondary and tertiary effects of the process.
>
> - Money will be managed by people whose passions are more about the business than the investment management process.
> - The business will have increasing short-term pressures. It will be difficult for this not to impact the investment time horizon of organizations.
> - People will complain that our business just isn't as much fun as it used to be.
>
> That will bring us to the other side of the cycle, and we will see the very same folk reinventing themselves in newly formed boutiques and spreading the virtues of:
>
> - Independence.
> - Small is beautiful.
> - Focused organizations.
> - Equity participation for all the principals.
>
> This will happen as night follows day.

We need to reinstate what was good about the past and marry those concepts and methods to what's good about today.

David I. Fisher is chairman of Capital Group International, Inc., Los Angeles.

Editor's Note: This article was developed from Mr. Fisher's presentation to the *FAJ* 60th Anniversary conference titled *Reflections and Insights: Provocative Thinking on Investment Management* (February 2005).

If I had added the words "hedge funds" to the above list, I would have had it all right!

Last week, American Express announced that it was spinning off its investment management businesses. This is 20 years after the firm paid a billion dollars to buy IDS to get into the mutual fund business—which was 10 years after Capital took over the American Express Funds to get them *out of* the mutual fund business. This is the sort of thing I had in mind when I said that money will be managed by people whose passions are more about business than the investment management process. I believe that this phenomenon goes a long way toward explaining the reflections that follow.

The Good Old Days

Those who know me will quickly say that I have never been an "O, for the Good Old Days" sort of person. For me, what's always been most interesting is the future, and I have always had an optimistic bias. I am still this way, but as I reflect on my reflections, a good part of me is saying, "O, for the Good Old Days!" For me, the investment business has been about getting to know companies and trying to come to grips with their future prospects. That approach is easy to say but, as we all know, very difficult to execute.

It involves anticipating the future, which includes understanding the following:

- the company's management—their skill and their motivation,
- the regulatory environment,
- the strengths and weaknesses of the company's products and those of its competitors,
- the labor force and its cost structure,
- the balance sheet and its flexibility,
- dividend policy—

and the list goes on.

The next question is valuation. What are these future prospects worth? We have always used the "whole company" approach to investing: You multiply the price of the stock by the number of shares outstanding. The result is what the market currently thinks the company is worth. In our approach, the question that we must constantly answer is: Do we want to own the whole company at that valuation? If not, we shouldn't be willing to own less than the whole company. This is a daunting task—and when you get it right, it is a major high.

In the Good Old Days, most of our investment attention was directed toward making sure that our analysis of future prospects was correct. We would debate company issues endlessly and then do the same about the question of appropriate valuation. We still do all of this, but I am distressed and somewhat depressed by the notion that the rest of the world would prefer to talk more about the trading characteristics of the stock certificates in the portfolio than about the underlying fundamentals of the companies they represent. There is something wrong with this picture.

On the one hand, measures such as beta and tracking error are backward looking and quantifiable, so they are comfort producing. On the other hand, anticipating the future is anxiety producing. You may get it wrong—and sometimes badly wrong. I have long believed that the big money, however, is made in looking forward and correctly anticipating major change. It seldom happens by looking backward. The fall of the Berlin Wall, the end of the Cold War, the impact of the Internet, and the effect of China on the rest of the world were all difficult to figure out by looking in a rearview mirror. In most of these cases, you could get more insights about the future from the front section of the newspaper than from the business section.

And continuing this reflection on changes: How did mediocrity become an objective for a money manager? Some clients and consultants want to put tracking-error limits in the investment guidelines. Where did that notion come from? I was raised in this business with the concept that your objective was to *maximize* tracking error—it just had to be positive.

Also, in the Good Old Days, we thought of risk as the chances of losing money. *I still do!* Much of the rest of the world has come to think of risk as deviation from the benchmark. I think that, although it is important to know and even measure the degree to which your portfolio is different from the benchmark, when you call that deviation "risk," you are sending the wrong message: "It's OK to lose money as long as we do it somewhat slower than the benchmark."

We really are amazing products of the environment. Just a few years ago, all of the emphasis was on relative results. It didn't matter how much we were up; the question was where did we fit in the competitive universe. Just a few years and a bear market later, the focus is on absolute returns, with folks willing to pay enormous fees for relatively modest results.

Back to the definition of risk: If you asked a race car driver about the risk in what he does for a living, I think his answer would focus on the chances of crashing and burning. I doubt that he would say much about how far he was from the median car in the race. I guess I should just come out and say it: I identify more with a race driver's perception of risk than I do with that of modern portfolio theory (MPT).

With all that's great about the computer, there is some downside. Somehow, when we do a model in the computer (which we certainly should do), the answer takes on new meaning. Because the computer printed out the answer, it must be true. We are less focused on how fragile the end of the story is. Change the assumptions a little, and it can make a ton of difference in the conclusion.

The Good New Days

Having said all of this, there is a lot that has happened to make the investment business better now than when I started. Much of it has to do with the globalization process.

In the Good Old Days, we divided the world between the United States and the rest of the world (something only an American would do). We pretty much paid attention only to the U.S. markets. At Capital, all our assets were U.S. based and almost all our investments were in the United States. We might have owned Sony ADRs (American Depositary Receipts) or Royal Dutch/Shell, but that's about as exotic as we got. Now, something close to 40 percent of the assets we manage are international or global in objective and we have institutional clients in 47 different countries. That's a huge change.

The more important change is about people and the culture of organizations. Today, we have analysts and portfolio managers working for us who were born in 43 different countries. And I'll bet the direction, even if not to the same extent, is the same at most other investment organizations. This change affects the investment process in important and positive ways. An investment organization is less prone to judge everything through a U.S. filter when it has people who have grown up in a wide variety of circumstances and cultures. It makes the organization respectful of differences in culture and opinion.

When I joined Capital, I had never been out of the United States except for an afternoon in Tijuana, so it's safe to say that my resume at that time was a little light on international travel and exposure to cultural diversity. Today, we in the business see not only candidates who have traveled the globe but many candidates who have survived life-altering experiences. They come through our door bringing viewpoints and opinions that give us a broader understanding and deeper appreciation of what is happening in our world.

We now analyze companies through a global filter. Most investment management firms do, but not many years ago, you could have been a successful U.S. auto analyst without having insights into the prospects of Toyota or Honda. That is certainly not true today, and the investment world is better for the change. I could say the same thing about lots of other industries.

On another subject: I continue to be blown away by the quality of people who are attracted to this business. It's not us old guys that I am talking about. It's the kids. You might ask how I can be so critical of some aspects of MPT and be so positive about the kids who are products of that educational experience. The young folk I am talking about understand MPT, but they don't pray at its altar. Their passions are all about companies and the impact people can have on companies. They love figuring out how the future might be different from the past. They thrive on uncertainty and are comfortable with risk. They think a lot about the world and put most questions in a global perspective.

I do worry some that the current preoccupation with risk control will produce a fear-of-failure mentality. If that occurs, we will find ourselves attracting a greater number of technicians and a smaller number of creative thinkers. I doubt that the result would be a business that is more fun, and I know it wouldn't be as intellectually stimulating.

John Maynard Keynes best expressed my thoughts about the true challenge in the investment management business in *The General Theory of Employment, Interest and Money* when he wrote:

> Finally it is the long-term investor, he who most promotes the public interest, who will in practice come in for the most criticism, wherever investment funds are managed by committees or boards or banks. For it is in the essence of his behavior that he should be eccentric, unconventional and rash in the eyes of average opinion. If he is successful, that will only confirm the general belief in his rashness; and if in the short run he is unsuccessful, which is very likely, he will not receive much mercy. Worldly wisdom teaches that it is better for reputation to fail conventionally than to succeed unconventionally.

Final Reflection

Probably the most important reflection I want to share is that this business has given me the skill and the resources to give back to the world that has given me so much. That process has been among my greatest satisfactions. At Capital, we began a program about 22 years ago called "The Associates Program." We hire liberal arts graduates (whom I tell all the time are qualified for nothing except that they are bright, creative, self-starting, hard-working, ambitious folk) and give them six four-month assignments in different parts of the company in various locations. The program has been an enormous success.

A few years ago, we added a seventh assignment of four months, which is to make the world a better place. They can do almost anything—except tell me they want to go to work for their father-in-law. We will also give up to a year off to anyone who has been with us for seven years to go work for a not-for-profit organization of their choice. We pay them 75 percent of their compensation and give the other 25 percent to the not-for-profit. We are trying to send a message that giving back in whatever way they choose is a good deal. I think it has worked.

My encouragement to you is to remember that there is more to life than managing portfolios. Don't miss the chance to give something back. It's you who will benefit the most.

The Future of Investment Management

Gary P. Brinson, CFA

The reflections and conjectures I am going to share are grounded in my 35 years of experience in the field of investment management. These thoughts cover roughly six—sometimes related, sometimes not—topics. In preparing to launch these observations at the reader, I am mindful of Oscar Wilde's warning: "Experience is the name everyone gives to their mistakes."[1] I will leave it up to you to make your own judgment about whether my "experience" adds any value.

Reflection on 35 years in investment management and examination of the present lead to six observations and conjectures about portfolio management.

Global Portfolio Construction

The globalization of financial markets, which mirrors the conduct of businesses themselves, will continue to expand in breadth and scope. Constructing portfolios with a home-country bias will become increasingly suboptimal in terms of return and risk.

The process of building global portfolios will change markedly in the future. For example, equity asset allocation driven by country exposure will be replaced by allocation driven by global sectors and industries. Focusing on countries of origin makes no more sense for multinational companies than does emphasizing where in the United States a company is headquartered. More than 70 percent of world equity market capitalization is made up of companies conducting their business on a multinational platform. Does the country in which these multinational companies are headquartered matter? It matters about as much as Microsoft Corporation, for example, being headquartered in the State of Washington. The real issues are where the companies derive their revenues and incur their expenses across the globe and who their competitors are in the global markets. Any thoughtful analyst would be hard-pressed to name an industry in which global competition is absent. Thus, for an investment portfolio, sectors and industries will become the main building blocks of equity exposure.

Gary P. Brinson, CFA, is president of GP Brinson Investments and The Brinson Foundation, Chicago.

I do not mean to say that geography is not important to *all* companies. It may be particularly important for some—in small emerging markets, for example. Or if you are invested in a chain of hotdog stands located only in southern California, the geography and climate of southern California matter. For the large multinational companies, however, country is irrelevant.

Currency Exposure vs. Asset Exposure. Unfortunately, the movement to this global portfolio setting has been confused with the notion of currency exposure by some careless researchers. Currency exposure is an important but separate consideration in determining a desired global portfolio array. The attractiveness of an investment asset has nothing to do with its currency, and the attractiveness of a currency has nothing to do with a portfolio's asset holdings. An investor can have any currency focus or mix that is deemed optimal, irrespective of the underlying assets in the portfolio. Establishing and managing currency exposure is a straightforward process—no more daunting than the process for determining the asset allocation mix itself. It is a mystery to me why investors continue to confuse their determination of an appropriate asset mix with an appropriate currency mix. People still say, "Oh, well, I'm not going to (or I'm going to) invest in XYZ region or country because I don't like the currency (or I do like the currency)." To the contrary, successful global portfolios will be obtained, managed, and analyzed when asset mix and currency are seen as distinctly separate characteristics.

Return–Risk Relationships of Global Portfolios. An interesting characteristic of portfolios that span the asset allocation array across all of the global markets is that they display a return and risk relationship that dominates any individual asset class. In other words, their Sharpe ratios are decidedly better than anything an investor can achieve by using traditional techniques.

Investors with an appetite for low levels of risk and volatility can best maximize their results by owning a combination of a global portfolio and short-term cash equivalents rather than shifting their investments to asset classes with lower volatility. Similarly, investors with an appetite for high levels of risk can maximize their results by borrowing and leveraging up a global portfolio rather than shifting to asset classes with higher volatility. For example, over extended time periods, a global portfolio levered up to the volatility of equity markets provides returns significantly above the equity returns themselves. So, the notion of an optimal portfolio that is often discussed in the theory of finance does, in fact, exist in this global form, and leveraging this portfolio either upward or downward to a particular desired risk habitat will produce results clearly superior to traditional approaches for managing risk exposure that tilt portfolios toward higher- or lower-risk asset classes.

The Future: Continuous Markets? A final note on global investing is worth considering. In the future, asset markets will increasingly resemble currency markets, in that they will transact over 24-hour periods without defined opening and closing prices. Portfolio pricing will be set to an agreed Greenwich Mean Time to facilitate uniform reporting for clients, but the markets themselves will become continuous and globally available. Present discussions surrounding the "day of business" for the NYSE are only the beginning of this inevitable development.

Investing vs. Trading

Confusion abounds about the distinction between trading and investing. *Trading* is focused on short-term price changes that occur for any variety of reasons. *Investing* is a process focused on future economic cash flows from business activities that ultimately determine the value of an investment. Both activities merit attention to their respective risk and return characteristics—but with decidedly different time frames.

In the future, our profession will best serve all investors if the distinction between these two activities is clearly and forcefully made. The notion of "momentum investing" is an oxymoron. This momentum strategy is more aptly labeled "momentum trading," albeit with a somewhat longer time frame than arbitrage trading.

Bubbles in financial markets have existed for centuries and will not disappear, but perhaps investors' experiences will be less painful when they appreciate the distinction between trading and investing. The landscape is littered with failures from investors losing their way, thinking that their portfolios reflected an investment strategy when, in fact, the portfolios were nothing more than momentum-following trading vehicles.

Fundamental Expectations

In the future, investment analysis will become more rigorously grounded. Decision-making models have evolved nicely during the past 35 years, but unfortunately, inputs to the models have not. Careless assumptions, often not explicitly presented, have led investors to erroneous conclusions from model outputs. This condition is true for the markets in general and for individual companies in particular.

An example of this carelessness is associated with equity valuation models and their growth-rate inputs. Over a vast sweep of history dating from 1947 through 2004, the real (inflation-adjusted) growth trend rate of profits per share for the S&P 500 Index has been 1.8 percent annually. This finding is a simple empirical fact, and it holds equally well for full profit cycles within the 57-year span regardless of whether profits are defined as operating or reported. The dividend growth rate is somewhat lower, at a 1.2 percent annual real trend rate over the full period, although the rate is closer to the growth path of EPS when adjusted for share repurchases by companies in lieu of dividend payments.

If a typical model input is for a 7 percent nominal growth rate for EPS associated with the S&P 500, in an assumed inflation environment of 2.0–2.5 percent, then the implied real growth rate is in the range of 4.5 percent to 5.0 percent. This rate is far in excess of past experience, yet it reflects a fairly typical set of assumptions from analysts who should know better.

If one wishes to contend that 4.5–5.0 percent real EPS growth will be the obtained trend in the future, then one should be ready with a rigorous argument delineating what variables are changing and why they would cause the historical trend to leap from 1.8 percent to a much higher level. Such rigor is conspicuously absent. People may argue for any future growth rate they desire, but they need to defend their forecast in a rigorous fashion. Demands for this rigor in investment analysis will accelerate in the future as investors seek to explain disappointing results relative to model outputs achieved with careless input assumptions.

A brief comment is warranted here on the distinction between *reported* profits and *operating* profits. While operating profits *may* be appropriate for use with an individual company whose past record is devoid of the special write-offs and allowances depressing reported profits, they are totally inappropriate for a portfolio of companies, such as in the S&P 500. Quarter after quarter, year after year, the companies in this index have economic events that lower reported profits relative to operating profits. Which companies have write-offs changes from period to period, but the events for the index as a whole remain and are remarkable in their persistence. Why, then, would any reasonable analyst suggest using operating profits to guide them in their valuation of the S&P 500? Here we have the case of reported profits being, in fact, true operating profits because the write-offs are persistent and ongoing. If an individual company had persistent adjustments to reported profits, no analyst of any merit would insist on using the so-called operating profits as a guide to measuring the company's record or current valuation. The use of questionable operating profits is yet another example of where some investment professionals seem to have lost their focus in making distinctions important to credible analysis.

In addition, many pension plans and much promotional literature provided to individual investors make unreasonable assumptions about future expected investment returns. Historical returns from markets, unless properly calibrated, are not a sensible guide for setting future expectations. For example, from 1981 through the end of 2004, the annual return from a high-grade bond index was 10.0 percent; yet, not even an elementary student of finance would use that period of substantial declines in interest rates from an exceptionally high starting point as an indicator, given the level of interest rates today, of future returns. Claims made for stock market returns based solely on historical returns are analogous.

Today's investment market fundamentals and financial variables clearly suggest that future real returns from a mixed portfolio of stocks, bonds, and other assets (such as real estate) are unlikely to be greater than 4.5–5.0 percent. With an inflation assumption of 2.5 percent, nominal returns greater than 7.0–7.5 percent for these portfolios are unrealistic. Yet, many retirement plans continue to use much higher expectations for returns.

Fees

Investors will alter their acceptance of fees in the coming years. The future trend in fees, both institutional and retail, will almost certainly be downward. Fees cannot be avoided, but the level of fees associated with a given asset size will be influenced by increasingly aware buyers of investment management services. One need only measure the aggregate fees that are paid by investors as a group with the aggregate value added by their investment managers to see clearly that something is greatly amiss.

When high fees are the topic, the subject of hedge funds naturally comes to mind. Hedge funds are conceptually a great idea because they introduce the notion that active decisions can be made not only on the long side alone. When opportunities present themselves, investors need to consider what they can sell as well as what they can buy. So, the popularity and growth of hedge funds are understandable.

What cannot be explained is why people are willing to pay the considerable fees that hedge funds charge. Perhaps they are paying for historical returns, for hope, or out of desperation.

For the markets in total, the amount of value added, or alpha, must sum to zero. One person's positive alpha is someone else's negative alpha. Collectively, for the institutional, mutual fund, and private banking arenas, the aggregate alpha return will be zero or negative after transaction costs. Aggregate fees for the active managers should thus be, at most, the fees associated with passive management. Yet, these fees are several times larger than fees that would be associated with passive management. This illogical conundrum will ultimately have to end.

Active fee structures in the future will be bifurcated into one component for passive management and another component for alpha results. Properly structured, this approach will result in aggregate fees paid that are equal to passive management fees. The result will be sharply lower fees for the industry, with the fee savings passed on to investors in the form of higher net returns. A 25–50 bps a year increase in net returns to investors over a long horizon creates a large differential in net terminal wealth. In my mind, this change is not a question of "if" but "when."

Of course, performance-based fees are not a new concept, but the suggestion here is that they will become the norm and probably be applied in a more fitting fashion than we currently experience. Performance fees should be applied in a manner that conforms to the investor's length of time with the manager, not to some arbitrary time segment, such as a calendar year—unless reset or claw-back provisions (provisions for managers to cover past loses before paying themselves) align the investor's total time-period results with the manager's cumulative performance fee. Any fee larger than the agreed-upon passive fee should be either directly tied to value added relative to a specified benchmark or, for absolute-return strategies, applied to only the return in excess of an agreed-upon fixed-rate return that reflects market interest rates.

Lumpiness and Discontinuities

Successful investment management that seeks to provide value above appropriate benchmarks is a lumpy and discontinuous process. Market inefficiencies within any asset class and across all asset classes ebb and flow, and not in a nice smooth and predictable fashion. Managers and their clients need to do a much better job in the future of recognizing this characteristic of markets.

Successfully exploiting opportunities requires variable risk management—that is, varying a portfolio's normal risk appetite to be in alignment with opportunities. At times, perhaps long times, the opportunity set is devoid of value-adding characteristics. At other times, the opportunity set is rich and robust. The barren setting suggests a neutral, passive investment posture with lower risk exposure, whereas the fruitful setting calls for a large appetite for risk relative to the benchmark. My hypothesis, based on some 35 years of investment activity, is that substantial value can be added by active investment strategies but only over long time horizons that allow a manager to capture the relatively infrequent abnormalities when they present themselves.

Most investors and their clients avoid this type of adaptive behavior, however, because it appears unstable. The lumpy and discontinuous nature of this management style is uncomfortable for many. (Perhaps this intolerance by clients is one reason the strategy is not more widely embraced and why the reward for the few who follow it is so substantial.) But the markets themselves, with their lumpy and discontinuous opportunities for value-added exploitation, *are* unstable. Insisting on value-added investment results that are inconsistent with the reality of markets only leads to disappointing results.

Random Noise

Investment results are largely random noise. This statement is true even for extended time periods, but it has particular applicability in short-term intervals. By definition, random noise offers no predictive information, which is why past investment performance has no predictive value.

Therefore, the investment management field should ultimately evolve away from using past performance for anything other than its historical accounting value. Organizations that publish evaluations of past performance and imply a valuable predictive insight from such evaluations should be extinct in the not-far-distant future.

Many investors fail to appreciate the nature of random outcomes. For example, if 1,000 people in an auditorium are asked to predict a series of eight consecutive coin flips, two people will call all eight flips correctly and two other people will call all eight flips incorrectly. Neither duo has any particular ability or lack of ability to call coin flips, of course, nor is there any predictive value from the observed outcome. Both the "winning" pair and the "losing" pair have the same chance of predicting the next coin flip.

This exercise is much like the investment management business: Of the many thousands of managers, the appearance of success for some and failure for others is largely random. Furthermore, predictions of future success or failure based on past results are flawed. I hope that in the future, investors will spend more time and effort on an organization's investment philosophy, process, and people than on past results and, when analyzing past performance data, will apply statistically rigorous performance evaluation.

Coda

This article contains opinions and reflections gathered from my experiences in the investment management profession. Not all of these comments will resonate comfortably with everyone, but I hope some thoughts will inspire and assist the interested investment professional.

Note

1. From *Lady Windermere's Fan* (1892).

Are Active Management Fees Too High?

Richard M. Ennis, CFA

What are the prospects for alpha? Those of us who were launching our careers in the 1960s would never have believed a Greek letter would become the mantra of investment management. The money management establishment of that era dismissed the concept of "beta," which was just emerging from the grove of academe. Yet today, talk of "alpha"—beta's elusive companion, that precious portion of extra return—is everywhere. Managers say they harvest it, separate it from beta, and transport it about. Consultants and advisors tout their ability to pick "alpha-generating" managers of every stripe. Pension fund trustees hear they ought to stretch for alpha to meet hopeful actuarial assumptions. (Who couldn't use a little extra?) And the trade press and sponsors of commercial conferences avidly sustain the buzz. Pursuit of alpha, it seems, has become the Zeitgeist of our times.

Is alpha potential on the rise? Let's begin with a historical perspective.

If the potential payoff from active management has waned since 1960, why is the price of active management at or near its all-time high?

Market Efficiency

The 1950s saw the beginning of a sustained effort to evaluate the efficient market hypothesis (EMH). By 1970, the academic consensus was that the market was quite efficient.[1] At least one prominent practitioner of that era also threw his lot in with the academics. In 1976, Benjamin Graham said:

> I am no longer an advocate of elaborate techniques of security analysis in order to find superior value opportunities. This was a rewarding activity, say, 40 years ago, when our textbook "Graham and Dodd" was first published [1934]; but the situation has changed a good deal since then. In the old days any well-trained security analyst could do a good professional job of selecting undervalued issues through detailed studies; but in the light of the enormous amount of research now being carried on, I doubt whether in most cases such extensive efforts will generate sufficiently superior selections to justify their cost. To that very limited extent I'm on the side of the "efficient market" school of thought now generally accepted by the professors. (p. 22)

Richard M. Ennis, CFA, is a principal at Ennis, Knupp & Associates, Chicago.

Consider now the conditions that give rise to market efficiency. Is there reason to believe, *a priori*, that the market has become more or less efficient in the past 30 years?

Information. At the heart of an efficient market is freely available information. In the past 30 years, we have experienced what may be the greatest period of innovation in information technology in the history of humankind. The personal computer arrived on the scene in the mid-1970s. Before its coming, analysts relied on hand-held calculators, and those of us analyzing balance sheets in the 1960s used a slide rule for compound interest and present value calculations. Leveraging the abundant and versatile computing power we obtained are the Internet—a development of staggering proportions in its own right—and the creation of vast electronic databases. Within our industry, information technology has its own distinctive manifestations, such as the cornucopian Bloomberg system.

Communication. Fiber optics and satellite-based systems have revolutionized communication in the past 30 years. In days of old, we had no fax, no cable news, no cell phone, no e-mail, no Blackberry. International calling was crude and prohibitively expensive. Today, inexpensive and instantaneous global communication is pervasive.

Frictions. The EMH is predicated on the absence of frictions that might preclude trading, which eliminates mispricing. The advent and refinement of derivatives during the past 30 years have had a profound effect on reducing market frictions of various types. Contractual innovations such as futures, options, and swaps have reduced transaction costs and enabled risk sharing in entirely new ways.

Transaction costs for common stock trades have fallen significantly and steadily since the NYSE eliminated fixed minimum commission rates in May of 1975. **Figure 1** presents an estimate of one-way trading costs for U.S. equities from 1975 through 2004. Trading costs at the end of 2004 were roughly 10 percent of their level prior to the advent of negotiated rates. The merger now occurring of traditional trading venues with electronic ones promises further reductions in transaction costs.

Figure 1. One-Way U.S. Equity Trading Costs as a Percentage of Trade Value, 1975–2004

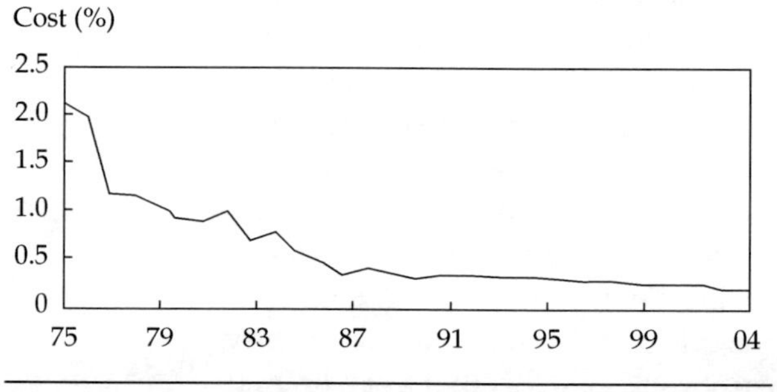

Sources: The data for 1975–1994 are from Wermers (2000), Table V, p. 1683, for converting transaction costs as a percentage of fund value to one-way costs, with turnover data provided by the author. Subsequent to 1994, the series was extrapolated by using per share agency commission rates provided by Greenwich Associates.

Institutional Ownership and the Rise of Arbitrage. Research has shown that the prevalence of security mispricing is inversely related to institutional ownership of shares.[2] Thus, the extent of institutional ownership is itself an index of market efficiency. According to the NYSE, 7 percent of the outstanding shares of common stock were held by institutions in 1950. The figure rose to 28 percent in 1970 and today stands at fully 50 percent.[3]

More than 7,000 hedge funds represent a new class of institutional investor. Hedge funds are highly opportunistic traders, often using leverage to maximally exploit mispricing. Many operate in a different dimension from the world of traditional long-only managers, with arbitrage-like (long–short) trading as the focal point. There can be little doubt that the accumulation of close to $1 trillion by hedge funds in the past 15 years has contributed to making markets more efficient.

Extraordinary advances in information and communication technology, dramatic reductions in transaction costs and other market frictions, and a sizable increase in institutional ownership, including a new breed of opportunistic trader and arbitrageur—all suggest that today's U.S. equity market has an even greater degree of market efficiency than the efficiency we posited 30 years ago. What does the empirical evidence say?

The Facts on Active Management. Many authors have examined whether active management successfully exploits whatever security mispricing might exist. Central to this literature are the persistence studies, which seek to identify a correlation of fund performance in one period with that of a prior period. These studies have been conducted by scholars all over the world.[4] The preponderance of this literature finds no evidence that top-performing funds in one period repeat their success in the next.

Cost-recovery studies have examined how management fees and transaction costs affect fund performance. Beginning with Jensen (1968), authors have consistently demonstrated that, on average, active investment managers underperform their benchmarks by an amount approximately equal to their fees. Indeed, recent studies have indicated that management expenses hurt average fund performance *more than* dollar for dollar (Carhart 1997; Bogle 1999).

Therefore, despite today's alpha mania, we have every indication that it has become harder, not easier, to beat the market in the past 30 years.

And Yet the Price Rises

Since about 1975, however, we have witnessed another pronounced trend, one that at first blush appears to be at odds with vigorously efficient markets and with the evidence on manager performance—namely, the steady rise of the price of active investment products. **Figure 2** illustrates the point. Since 1980, the average equity mutual fund expense ratio has risen from 0.96 percent to 1.56 percent.

Just as striking is the fact that a price increase of this magnitude would occur while revenue soared in an industry characterized by ease of entry and minuscule marginal costs. (The dollar-weighted average expense ratio also rose during this period but by a somewhat smaller margin, from 0.64 percent to 0.86 percent.)

A contributor to this rise in prices is the phenomenal growth during the past 15 years of the priciest form of money management—the hedge fund. In this type of fund, management fees are typically 1.5 percent on top of expense reimbursement, and all before the manager takes a sizable share of the profits. Ineichen (2005) estimated that the revenue of the hedge fund industry (including funds of funds) has averaged an astounding 5.9 percent of the value of assets, annually, since 1991.

Figure 2. Average Equity Fund Expense Ratio (Equal Weighted), 1980–2004

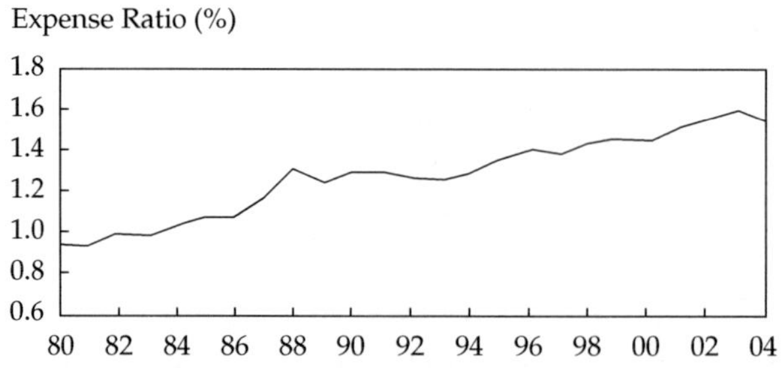

Source: Lipper Analytical Services.

As a product or service becomes less valuable over time, its price ordinarily declines. But even as efficient capital markets have become arguably more efficient, we have witnessed no downward pressure on the pricing of active management. Why not? I believe the answer lies in the phenomenal growth in the value of "assets-to-be-managed" in the past 25 years. In 1980, the aggregate value of investable capital markets *worldwide* stood at $7.5 trillion. By 2004, the figure had ballooned to $87.2 trillion.[5] This is an increase of more than 1,100 percent and represents *real* growth of more than 7 percent a year over the entire 24-year period. Accounting in part for this spectacular growth is that interest rates in the early 1980s were hitting their all-time high whereas stocks were extremely cheap. And the extraordinary prosperity of the 1980s and 1990s lay just around the corner. No doubt, this period will go down in the annals of money management as The Great Era of Asset Gathering.

Today, with interest rates near 4 percent and stocks yielding less than 2 percent, few among us expect double-digit investment returns for any extended period in the near future. In other words, the investment management industry is unlikely to benefit from the wind of extraordinary asset growth at its back as it did throughout the 1980s and 1990s. Yet, we live with a legacy of that era: historically high fee structures brought on by trillions upon trillions of dollars seeking growth during the boom and shelter in its aftermath.

When Are Management Fees Too High?

The economist in me avers that freely set prices are never too high (or too low); prices merely convey information. With that bow to economic theory made, I also believe that the higher the price of investment management, all else being the same, the harder it is to deliver a product that will satisfy the investor seeking a *net* gain from active management. Thus, the very *plausibility* of each active investment product varies inversely with the price that attaches to it.

My colleagues and I have devised a simple model to assess the plausibility of investment management fees.[6] Assume that active investment risk is normally distributed. Also assume that an investor has a horizon of at least 10 years, not an unreasonable assumption for most defined-benefit pension funds and certainly reasonable for the vast majority of endowments and foundations, which generally consider themselves perpetual in nature. Indeed, it is a reasonable assumption for most individual investors.

In the model, *manager skill* is represented by the *ex ante* probability that a manager will produce a positive cumulative alpha, after transaction costs but before management fees, over the course of 10 years. *Investor success* occurs when the investor, employing a particular manager, realizes a positive alpha after fees. In this model, skill translates directly into success; it is transformed only by assessment of a constant, namely, management expense. As in the real world, cost alone separates manager skill and investor success. (See Appendix A for model particulars.)

Figure 3 illustrates how the cost of active management affects the *ex ante* probability of investor success (vertical axis) for a particular degree of manager skill (horizontal axis). The active risk of 5 percent in this illustration is typical of an equity portfolio. The diagonal describes a truly hypothetical case in which the manager charges no fee. In the no-fee case, the *ex ante* probability that the manager of a portfolio with active risk of 5 percent will produce a positive alpha over 10 years is identical to the probability that the investor will realize a positive alpha. In other words, in the absence of fees, the investor realizes whatever alpha the manager earns.

The three curves in Figure 3 describe how imposition annually of three fee levels—0.5 percent, 1.5 percent, and 3.0 percent of the value of assets—affects the relationship, annually, of before- and after-fee probabilities.[7] At a higher level of cost, a greater level of skill is required to sustain a given probability of investor success. **Table 1** summarizes these relationships numerically.

The first column of Table 1 indicates that for an investor to enjoy an even chance of realizing a positive alpha when paying 0.5 percent, the manager's required skill level is 0.62. At 3.0 percent per year, the manager's required skill level rises to an inconceivable 0.97.

The second column of Table 1 turns the proposition around to show the probability that an investor will realize a positive alpha over a decade at various fee levels by employing a manager with skill equivalent to a 0.80 probability of producing a positive alpha, before fees. Despite investing with such an extraordinarily skillful manager, the probability that *the investor* can benefit from that skill drops from 0.70 at a fee of 0.5 percent to a mere 0.15 at 3.0 percent.

Figure 3. Plausibility: Probability of Investor Success for Various Fee Levels
(active risk = 5 percent; time horizon = 10 years)

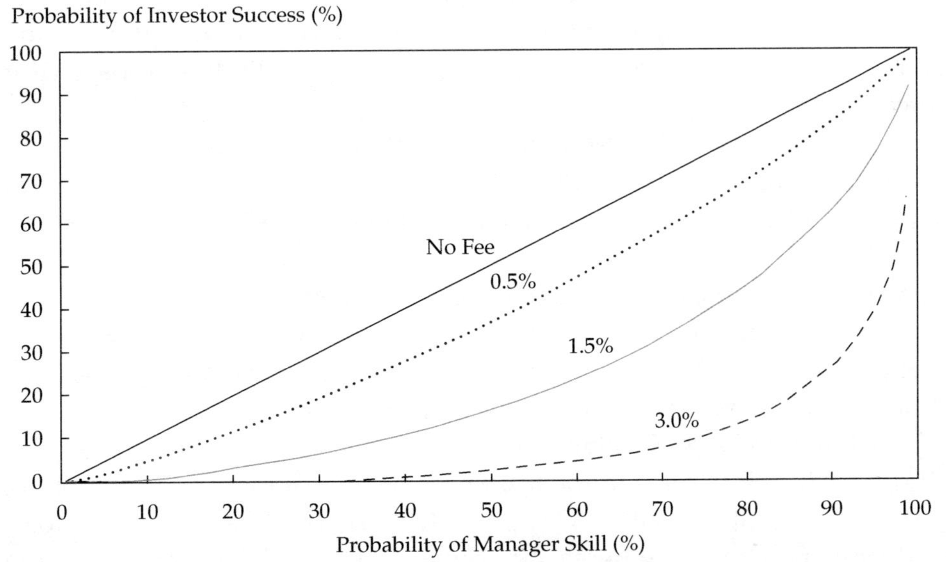

Table 1. Likelihood of Success under Various Fee Rates

Fee	Manager Skill Required for Investor to Have at Least a 50/50 Chance of Earning a Positive Alpha	Investor's Probability of Earning a Positive Alpha When Manager Skill Is 0.80
0.5%	0.62	0.70
1.5	0.83	0.46
3.0	0.97	0.15

Figure 3 and Table 1 illustrate what by now must be obvious: *A good manager cannot be "good" irrespective of cost.* And a management fee is too high when, despite the manager's ability to earn a positive alpha, the fee level drives the likelihood of investor success to be unacceptably low.

I do not claim that *all* active investment management services are overpriced. A number of fine equity mutual funds have expense ratios in the vicinity of 50 bps. And large institutional investors can establish separate equity portfolios with leading managers for less than 40 bps. Some successful hedge funds even have management (base) fees of 50 bps or less. For every such opportunity, however, dozens of other active managers use pricing that, in my judgment, is beyond the pale of plausibility.

The Future

Looking ahead, I see four trends:

First, markets will become even more efficient as frictions continue to disappear. The markets will approach the economist's efficient market ideal while never quite reaching it, which is to say that imperfections of some type will always be with us. And as long as imperfections persist, the prospect of trading profits will beckon. Actual gains from active management, however, will be as elusive as ever.

Second, facing the dual challenge of market efficiency and high costs, investors will continue to shift assets from active to passive management. Although indexing got its start in the early 1970s, passive investment before 1980 accounted for a negligible percentage of institutional assets. In the past 25 years, passive management of U.S. pension and endowment fund domestic equity assets has steadily risen to 44 percent of the total. Among public funds, passive investing has gained a 55 percent market share.[8]

Mutual fund investors have also responded to the challenges of attempting to beat the market by investing passively. According to Bogle (2005), index funds "have accounted for more than one-third of equity fund cash inflow since 2000 and now represent fully one-seventh of equity fund assets" (p. 17).

Third, some of active management's true believers will shift assets from expensive products to more reasonably priced products. Impetus for this move will be the growing realization that high fees sap the performance potential of even skillful managers. Signs of greater price sensitivity are appearing now. **Table 2** summarizes recent years' net cash flow data, sorted into quintiles by expense ratio (ER), for *active* large-capitalization domestic equity mutual funds

As Table 2 shows, in 1999, funds in the top two quintiles of ER took in $46 billion in net cash inflows; the bottom two quintiles took in $30 billion. In 2001, a shift occurred: The top two quintiles had net cash *outflows* of $6 billion, whereas the two lowest had *inflows* of $10 billion. In 2002, all

Table 2. Net Cash Flows to Active Large-Cap Domestic Equity Mutual Funds ($ billions)

ER Quintile	Typical ER Range	1999	2000	2001	2002	2003	2004
1 (highest)	> 2.00%	$21.1	$16.4	–$4.4	–$ 8.3	–$ 4.4	–$ 6.2
2	1.61–2.00	25.0	13.0	–1.3	–17.9	–8.0	–11.7
3	1.26–1.60	3.2	0.3	–2.5	–5.9	4.6	2.1
4	1.00–1.25	0.4	11.2	5.7	–4.9	0.2	0.2
5 (lowest)	< 1.00	29.8	–1.3	4.7	–0.3	32.0	28.4
Total net flow		$79.5	$39.6	$2.2	–$37.3	$24.4	$12.8

Source: Data from the Simfund mutual fund database of Strategic Insight Mutual Fund Research and Consulting, LLC.

flows were outflows. Years 2003 and 2004 are similar to one another in that the two most expensive quintiles experienced sizable net cash outflows whereas the least expensive garnered even larger net inflows.

Table B1 and **Table B2** in Appendix B show less pronounced patterns of price-conscious cash flows for, respectively, small-cap funds and non-U.S. equity funds.

A final prediction relates to the influence of hedge funds, whose sustained popularity has surprised many. The traditional investment management business and hedge funds have largely stood apart, separated by a cultural divide. Yet, traditional management funds and hedge funds have the same sole purpose: to make money by exploiting security mispricing. And as hedge funds seek to enlarge their market share while traditional managers defend their share, it will become increasingly clear that they are competitors.

The competition can be seen as a Hegelian dialectic, advancing from thesis to antithesis to synthesis. The traditional business represents the portfolio management thesis: (1) diversified and stylistic, (2) long only, (3) unleveraged, and (4) relatively transparent, with (5) fixed (guaranteed) compensation arrangements and (6) liquidity for investors. Hedge funds are the antithesis: (1) undiversified and opportunistic, (2) long–short (arbitrage) oriented, (3) leveraged, and (4) opaque, with (5) performance-based compensation and (6) lock-ups for investors.

Synthesis will bring about adaptations in both approaches. Some traditional money managers already are focusing on realizing alpha without regard to conventional notions of style; more will follow suit. Some are incorporating long–short techniques or expanded use of derivatives. And lockups might turn up in the traditional discipline in view of the vagaries of arbitrage (the spread on even a good trade can widen before it narrows) and the patience required to invest in the less-liquid sectors. Significant leverage, however, may not lend itself to money management for institutional clients, most of whom are fiduciaries acting on behalf of others. Only time will tell.

The synthesis of investment approaches will produce a new generation of institutional investment vehicles. They will have some key features of hedge funds, but these vehicles will have more the *feel* of conventional institutional investments, particularly in two areas—transparency and pricing. Transparency will present both cultural and reporting challenges for some managers. Pricing, whether fixed or contingent, will have to be *plausible*, which to me means that base fees must be a small fraction of those of most hedge fund managers.

Thus, the traditional business faces competition on two sides. On one side, indexing continues to erode traditional management's market share and will exert downward pressure on pricing for the first time in history. On the other side, hedge funds have introduced innovations in value-added investing that are difficult to ignore. Hedge funds might begin to provide greater transparency and a more judicious use of leverage as they strive to gain broad acceptance, but it remains to be seen whether dyed-in-the-wool hedge fund managers will—or even can, at this juncture—reduce charges enough to become plausible choices for the long run.

Interesting times lie ahead.

I thank Mike Sebastian for important contributions; Sudhakar Attaluri, Max Kotary, and Kevin Laughlin provided valuable research assistance.

Appendix A. Fee Plausibility Model

The plausibility model is designed to assess the economic reasonableness of investment management costs.[9] If a manager's fee is consistent with an acceptable probability of success to the investor, conditioned on the investor's estimate of the manager's likelihood of success (skill), the fee is said to be plausible.

We assume a normal distribution of manager alpha and assume that the information ratio is constant across levels of active risk. The inputs to the model are specified as follows:

T = investor's time horizon (in years)

σ = active risk of the manager

F = investment management fee

P_B = investor's estimate of the probability that the manager will produce a positive alpha *before fees* over the investor's chosen time horizon

The model's output is the probability that the investor will realize a positive alpha *after fees*, P_A, over the investor's chosen time horizon.

Given the investor's estimate of the probability the manager will produce a positive alpha before fees and the investor's chosen time horizon, we forecast the implied information ratio (IR) before fees as a numerical approximation of the integral:

$$P_B = \int_{-\infty}^{\text{Implied IR (before fees)}} \left[\frac{1}{\sqrt{2\pi}} e^{-\left(z^2/2\right)}\right], \tag{A1}$$

where z is the value for which we want the distribution.

Essentially, the model takes the probability and solves for the z-value (from a normal distribution with that portion below it) that attains the probability. The math can be done in Microsoft Excel by using the function NORMSINV. The syntax for the function is NORMSINV(P_B) = z-value.

We divide the z-value we obtained by the square root of the investor's time horizon to take into account the "square root of time" rule:

$$\text{Implied IR (before fees)} = \frac{z\text{-value}}{\sqrt{T}}. \tag{A2}$$

We translate the implied information ratio *before fees* to an implied information ratio *after fees* as follows:

$$\text{Implied IR (after fees)} = \frac{\left[\text{Implied IR (before fees)}\,\sigma\right] - F}{\sigma}\sqrt{T}. \quad \text{(A3)}$$

We then determine the probability that the investor will realize a positive alpha after fees over the investor's chosen time horizon by finding a numerical approximation of the following integral (finding the portion of the distribution of the information ratio to the left of the implied information ratio after fees):

$$P_A = \int_{-\infty}^{\text{Implied IR (after fees)}} \left[\frac{1}{\sqrt{2\pi}} e^{-\left(z^2/2\right)}\right], \quad \text{(A4)}$$

where z is the value for which we want the distribution.

The model solves for the probability that attains the z-value in Microsoft Excel using the function NORMSDIST. The syntax for the function is NORMSDIST(z-value) = P_A.

Appendix B. Cash Flows to Small-Cap and Non-U.S. Mutual Funds

Table B1. Net Cash Flows to Active Small-Cap Domestic Equity Mutual Funds ($ billions)

ER Quintile	Typical ER Range	1999	2000	2001	2002	2003	2004
1 (highest)	> 2.17%	$0.0	$ 1.2	$ 0.3	$ 0.5	$ 0.3	–$ 0.3
2	1.70–2.17	0.0	0.4	3.5	1.8	1.5	–0.1
3	1.40–1.69	1.9	9.3	4.9	4.0	4.7	1.8
4	1.15–1.39	0.0	1.8	5.3	5.1	7.7	4.1
5 (lowest)	< 1.15	–7.7	2.6	10.2	10.0	13.8	14.0
Total net flow		–$5.8	$15.3	$24.2	$21.4	$28.0	$19.5

Source: Strategic Insight.

Table B2. Net Cash Flows to Active Non-U.S Equity Mutual Funds ($ billions)

ER Quintile	Typical ER Range	1999	2000	2001	2002	2003	2004
1 (highest)	> 2.35%	$0.2	$ 1.1	–$0.7	–$ 0.5	–$ 0.2	–$ 0.2
2	1.92–2.35	0.3	3.3	–1.0	–0.1	0.3	1.4
3	1.51–1.91	0.8	3.6	–0.2	–0.1	0.7	3.6
4	1.23–1.50	1.0	4.1	1.4	3.7	7.2	10.4
5 (lowest)	< 1.23	3.3	9.4	–2.5	8.5	10.2	29.0
Total net flow		$5.6	$21.5	–$3.0	$11.5	$18.2	$44.2

Source: Strategic Insight.

Notes

1. For example, Roberts (1959), Osborne (1959), Cootner (1964), and Fama (1970).
2. See Bartov, Radhakrishnan, and Krinsky (2000); Dennis and Weston (2001); Sias, Starks, and Titman (2002); Phalippou (2004).
3. *NYSE Fact Book*, "Holdings of Corporate Equities in the U.S. by Type of Institution" (www.nysedata.com/factbook).
4. See, for example, Allen, Brailsford, Byrd, and Faff (2002) for a survey of the literature.
5. This information is from UBS Global Asset Management.
6. I am indebted to Mike Sebastian and Sudhakar Attaluri for their assistance in devising the model.
7. The shapes of the curves shift, of course, if you shorten the time horizon. But chopping the measurement periods into shorter segments does not alter the outcome for an investor that expects to operate for at least 10 years because all the 1- or 5-year probability distributions must combine to form the same 10-year distribution. Thus, as to time period, what matters is the investor's expected time horizon.
8. Greenwich Associates, "2004 Greenwich Associates' Market Data Trends," Greenwich report.
9. This model is also available as an electronic spreadsheet from the author (rennis@ennisknupp.com).

References

Allen, David, Tim Brailsford, Ron Byrd, and Robert Faff. 2002; revised June 2003. *A Review of the Research on the Past Performance of Managed Funds*. Fund Management Research Centre of the Securities Industry Research Centre of the Asian Pacific.

Bartov, E., S. Radhakrishnan, and I. Krinsky. 2000. "Investor Sophistication and Patterns in Stock Returns after Earnings Announcements." *Accounting Review*, vol. 75, no. 1 (January): 43–63.

Bogle, John C. 1999. *Common Sense on Mutual Funds*. New York: John Wiley & Sons.

———. 2005. "The Mutual Fund Industry 60 Years Later: For Better or Worse?" *Financial Analysts Journal*, vol. 61, no. 1 (January/February):15–24.

Carhart, Mark M. 1997. "On Persistence in Mutual Fund Performance." *Journal of Finance*, vol. 52, no. 1 (March):57–82.

Cootner, Paul, ed. 1964. *The Random Character of Stock Market Prices*. Cambridge, MA: MIT Press.

Dennis, P., and J. Weston. 2001. "Who's Informed? An Analysis of Stock Ownership and Informed Trading." Working paper, University of Virginia and Rice University.

Fama, Eugene F. 1970. "Efficient Capital Markets: A Review of Theory and Empirical Work." *Journal of Finance*, vol. 25, no. 2 (May):383–417.

Graham, Benjamin. 1976. "A Conversation with Benjamin Graham." *Financial Analysts Journal*, vol. 32, no. 5 (September/October):20–23.

Graham, Benjamin, and David Dodd. 1934. *Security Analysis*. New York: McGraw-Hill. (Various editions of this book are available, including the classic 2nd edition, 1940.)

Ineichen, Alexander M. 2005. "The Critique of Pure Alpha." UBS Global Equity Research (March).

Jensen, Michael C. 1968. "The Performance of Mutual Funds in the Period 1945–64." *Journal of Finance*, vol. 23, no. 2 (May): 389–416.

Osborne, M.F.M. 1959. "Brownian Motion in the Stock Market." *Operations Research*, vol. 7, no. 2 (March/April):145–173.

Phalippou, Ludovic. 2004. "What Drives the Value Premium?" EFA 2004 Maastricht Meetings Paper No. 3804; INSEAD Working Paper (May).

Roberts, Harry V. 1959. "Stock Market 'Patterns' and Financial Analysis: Methodological Suggestions." *Journal of Finance*, vol. 14, no. 1 (March):1–10.

Sias R., L. Starks, and S. Titman. 2002. "The Price Impact of Institutional Trading." Working paper, University of Texas and Washington State University.

Wermers, Russ. 2000. "Mutual Fund Performance: An Empirical Decomposition into Stock-Picking Talent, Style, Transaction Costs, and Expenses." *Journal of Finance*, vol. 55, no. 4 (August):1655–1703.

Capital Ideas: From the Past to the Future

Peter L. Bernstein

The body of thought that we consider modern finance theory is extraordinarily important. It permeates most of what investment analysts and managers do and influences how we think, whether we think about it positively or negatively. I am working on a revision of *Capital Ideas* (1992), but the basic 11 chapters—from Harry Markowitz to Black–Scholes option pricing—are going to remain exactly as they were in the original edition.

It is a remarkable story: In the space of 21 years, from 1952 to 1973, an entire body of knowledge was created essentially from scratch, with only a few scattered roots in the past. Nothing in the history of ideas can compare with this cascade of ideas in such a short period of time. Centuries came between Euclid, Newton, and Einstein. In economic theory, 160 years came between Adam Smith and John Maynard Keynes. When I started to work on *Capital Ideas*, one of the inspirations was that all of the heroes were still alive. It was an amazing opportunity.

Modern finance theory, modern portfolio theory, neoclassical economics—the ideas bestowed on us in two amazing decades by the giants in our field—are alive and well.

Modern Finance

Essentially, the assumptions, the simplifications, and the necessary conditions of neoclassical economics do not exist in today's complex world. Eugene Fama recently wrote that the capital asset pricing model (CAPM) is a theoretical triumph and an empirical disaster. In the summer 2004 issue of the *Journal of Economic Perspectives*, André Perold provided a beautiful description of the CAPM that is like reading a brilliant, clear light. And in the same issue, Fama and Kenneth French took up their cudgels against the model.

Noted innovator of behavioral finance Daniel Kahneman of Princeton University has won a Nobel Prize, which tells you that the exceptions to neoclassical finance theory are very important. We have bubble-and-bust markets, which suggests occasional irrational behavior in the markets in a macro sense.

Peter L. Bernstein is president of Peter L. Bernstein, Inc., New York City.

Editor's Note: This article was developed from Mr. Bernstein's presentation to the *FAJ* 60th Anniversary conference titled *Reflections and Insights: Provocative Thinking on Investment Management* (February 2005).

There are also many manifestations of violations of the classical model of investor behavior that create "mispricings" in the daily markets. So, what is the theoretical triumph? Why does it matter to us as practitioners to know, to understand, and to appreciate this body of knowledge?

What I am going to tell you seems amazing now; it is an extraordinary leap in human thinking. Before Markowitz, we had no genuine *theory* of portfolio construction, only rules of thumb and folklore. Before Bill Sharpe and Jack Treynor, we had no genuine *theory* of asset pricing, only rules of thumb and folklore. Before Merton Miller and Franco Modigliani, we had no general *theory* of corporate finance, only rules of thumb and folklore, and no recognition of the overwhelmingly powerful concept of arbitrage.

M&M (1958, 1963), although not much discussed, may have had the most influence of all—exceeding even the importance of option theory—for it was they who declared that any investment project and its associated financing plan must pass only one test—whether the project as financed will raise the market value of the company's shares. The market knows all. Only when the price of the stock goes up is the company earning its cost of capital. The theory was diverted into all kinds of unfortunate directions, but the idea that the stock price is all—the stock price is in our face every day, every minute—has had an enormous influence.

Before Fama and others, we had no *theory* to explain why the market was so hard to beat. I tell the story in *Capital Ideas* of the editor at Random House in the late 1960s, when I was working at Bernstein-Macaulay, who said there was a young fellow in finance, a very, very bright guy, whom she wanted me to meet. It turned out to be Bill Sharpe. When we first sat down to lunch, he turned to me and asked, with his wonderful charm, "Do you beat the market?" I was flabbergasted. How could anybody dare ask me such a question! The notion did not even exist that beating the market was a problem.

Before Black, Myron Scholes, and Robert Merton, we had no *theory* of option pricing, only rules of thumb and folklore.[1] We did not know what the notion of contingent claims could accomplish for understanding the corporation, in valuation, or hedging risks, or in opening new areas for investment managers to pursue.

An interesting example of how thinking about option theory can provide a new perspective is the recent NASDAQ "bubble." It was supposedly a bubble, but think about it in terms of options. NASDAQ is an index of a bunch of very young companies with more or less unlimited futures. Nobody knows which ones will succeed, but in the 1990s, a great deal of ferment was going on and big possibilities existed. If we look at those shares as options, it makes perfectly good sense that the downside was limited, the upside unlimited, and the index contained a great deal of uncertainty. As options, those shares may have been fairly valued in 1999. Before 1973, nobody would have even raised the question.

The academic creators of all these models knew that the real world is different from the models, but they were in search of a process, a systematic understanding of how markets work, how investors interact, and how portfolios should be composed. They understood that financial markets are about *capitalism*, a word we mention much too infrequently. Capitalism is a dynamic, complex, rough-and-tumble system in which there are always winners and losers, and we do not know in advance who is going to win and who is going to lose.

Merton said in 1987 that the traditional approach of modern economic theory is to divide the positive theories of *how* we behave almost completely from the normative theories of how we *should* behave. Despite all the controversy in the early days about the empirical tests, the design was not a finished work. It was a jumping-off point, a beginning of exploration, an integrative structure from which to make comparisons and to gain insights. And it has been very rich indeed.

The way people talked about the market before the 1950s was another world. The only people discussing any kind of theory were Benjamin Graham and John Burr Williams. Williams' work (1938) contained a kind of theory, but the discount rate was in the eye of the beholder. Graham's work was powerful, but it was normative, not positive. It told you what you should do, not how the market works. Both authors proposed theories of asset pricing; they did not develop the larger idea of the portfolio.

Then came Markowitz (1952). When I interviewed him for *Capital Ideas*, he told me how a chance meeting with a broker one day persuaded him to pursue his interest in operations research by investigating the stock market. Markowitz didn't know anything about the stock market, so he went to his professor. The professor also didn't know anything about the stock market but told Markowitz to read Williams. Now, Williams says you should buy the single stock with the greatest expected return. Markowitz thought, "But, you know, you have to think about risk as well as return."

By making risk the centerpiece of his ideas, Markowitz directed his attention to the essence of what investing is all about: Investing is a bet on an unknown future.

Challenging the Theory

The only competing doctrine to modern finance theory is in the behavioral finance literature. Behavioral finance is where alpha flourishes. I sat next to a famous hedge fund manager at dinner the other night, and I said, "How much of modern portfolio theory is involved in what you do?" He said, "It's tremendously important. Those are the guys we pick off every day." So, it is useful even to them.

The behavioral literature is so enormous and diverse that it is hard to pin down. The key question is whether the flaws that it reveals in modern portfolio theory imply that MPT is irrelevant or whether behavioral finance provides fresh insights. Is behavioral finance the new paradigm? Much of it is not really theory, not a set of generalizations but a collection of anecdotes. Many of the findings are ephemeral and, under no-arbitrage conditions, will be or have been competed away. Other features in the behavioral literature seem to be more deeply embedded. Robert Shiller pointed out back in the early 1980s that stock prices are too volatile relative to changes in the underlying fundamentals and saw this circumstance as a serious sign of lack of rationality among investors (Shiller 1981).

Others have attacked theories that assume the normal distribution in the market as not being the way the world works—for example, *The Misbehavior of Markets* (Mandelbrot and Hudson 2004). From prospect theory, the centerpiece of Kahneman and Amos Tversky's behavioral work (1974, 1979), we have learned that we are asymmetrical in our views of profits and losses: We are risk takers when we have losses and risk averse when we have profits. In addition, we tend to emphasize recent news rather than long-term trends. We yield to powerful, mysterious phenomena—herding and a taste for momentum.

All of these phenomena add up to insufficient and inadequate processing of information. Investors are not always and everywhere rational. Priors are usually mistaken about the right price. Indeed, even the notion in the efficient market hypothesis that there exists an equilibrium price, a correct price, is false. The world is moving so fast that the equilibrium price today will not be the same equilibrium price tomorrow.

Behavioral finance's impact on the market can be looked at also from other and different perspectives. Merton, in a speech given at the CFA Institute (at the time, AIMR) Annual Meeting of 2004, stated that he believes behavioral finance cannot be understood without understanding the institutions in which we work and under which we live. He believes that many of the anomalies pointed out in behavioral finance will change, will be altered (and in some cases overcome) by changing institutional arrangements. He may be excessively optimistic about some of these things, but it's important to understand what he is talking about. For example, Merton pointed out that more decisions are made by institutions, such as mutual funds, than by individuals for themselves, which changes the patterns in the marketplace. Our institutional framework has been changed by derivatives, by hedge funds, by falling transaction costs, by the end of the Glass–Steagall Act of 1930, by globalization of financial markets, and by the continual drive to a no-arbitrage condition. Merton also thinks investment committees make a difference. Those of us who have been involved with investment committees might wonder about this judgment, but the point is that as the institutional framework changes, the behavioral anomalies change because different forces are affecting them.

A strange two-way feedback process goes on between theory and behavior. Sociologists use a terrible but apt word to describe the relationship of theory to behavior—"performativity." It is akin to "self-fulfilling prophecy." When people read about a theory and believe in it, they begin to act in conformity to it. So, as we learn MPT ideas—we sit down and read Markowitz and Fama and so on—we begin to act that way. If we say the market is substantially efficient, we then have to rearrange portfolios in a particular way and worry whether we can beat the market. We even index our assets. So, we begin to prove the theory. If we find a new set of models that we believe in, we will begin to make those models work by reflecting them in our decision making.

Andrew Lo has written about the markets being evolutionary, Darwinian. As markets change and evolutionary forces come to play a role, the winners and losers of today are not the same as the winners and losers of yesterday or tomorrow. Having come into this business in 1951, I can attest to that truism. So, although behavioral finance is extremely important in trying to understand what is going on, we have to keep in mind that what look like anomalies today will not necessarily be anomalies tomorrow. Behavioral anomalies are where alphas lurk, but nobody would claim that finding alpha with any degree of consistency and skill is easy.

Status of Capital Ideas Today

With all the anomalies and all the manifestations of a lack of rationality in the markets, and with individualistic, Darwinian markets, how can anyone assert that capital ideas are alive and well? First, MPT is the root of all risk management theories today. MPT defines risk as volatility. The definition has a lot of problems because volatility is essentially a short-term phenomenon. But it has many advantages. Volatility reflects surprise; what happens is different from what was expected, which reminds us that investing is a risky business. Volatility is mathematically malleable, which may be why it has been a focus of theory. But for long-term investors, volatility has a different meaning. It is for them, in many ways, not risk but opportunity. Despite its shortcomings as a measure of risk, volatility is the only measure of risk that runs through all of the MPT body of thought.

I define risk as meaning that more things can happen than will happen. If there were no risk, we would know exactly what was going to happen, and vice versa. All "risk" really means is that the future is uncertain, the future is unknown. So, whether prices are going up or down, volatility is scary. In a period like 2001, you wonder what is going on. Today things look good; tomorrow they look bad. What is going on? If this is going up when I think things are bad, somebody must know more than I do! It's scary. So, although volatility in a strict sense is an incomplete measure of risk, in a psychological (gut) sense, it is a powerful measure of risk. Volatility makes us act differently from the way we would act if the market were calm all the time. Shiller, who is one of the most articulate, interesting, and powerful critics of MPT, nevertheless places overwhelming importance on risk and volatility and asserts that this contribution of portfolio theory towers over the whole field.

Furthermore, we know that capital ideas are alive and well because you cannot improve a theory until you have attacked it, and the attack does not have to be negative. It can be positive. Many applications of the techniques of risk management are as yet unexplored. Shiller and Merton are working in positive ways to develop new forms of risk management that will benefit people as citizens and workers as well as investors.

The efficient market hypothesis may not be an accurate description of reality. The market, in itself, is not truly efficient. Yet, it is the standard by which we judge market behavior and the standard by which we measure manager performance. No one has found important cases of lagged variables that consistently and forever explain stock price returns. Only a tiny number of investors consistently beat the market year after year on a risk-adjusted basis, even though the market itself is not fully efficient in the classical sense that all information is immediately known, understood, and reflected in asset prices without any lag. Yet, the idea of efficiency is spreading way beyond the United States, and markets abroad that were once considered very inefficient are becoming more efficient all the time. Lo is right: It's Darwinian out there.

Mean–variance efficiency requires assumptions we cannot make, especially relating to the role of time and the normal distribution, but the risk–return trade-off is central to portfolio selection and professional money management. Modern diversification takes many forms—not necessarily Markowitz's paradigm but, philosophically, still the Markowitz idea.

The capital asset pricing model is an empirical failure, and the CAPM beta is certainly no longer the single measure of risk. Yet, the notion of systematic versus specific risk infuses portfolio management. Meanwhile, today's concept of portable alpha as separate from beta is a big idea and a wonderful concept. All of the tools it uses come out of MPT.

Cliff Asness has pointed out that many hedge fund strategies change from alpha to beta as they become accepted and copied through the hedge fund population. Beta means "risk that cannot be diversified away," so as hedge funds begin to do the same things, hedge fund risk becomes beta risk. No alpha remains.

Finally, the ultimate offshoot of the CAPM is indexing. The market portfolio is the only mean–variance portfolio. This huge idea dominates everything that we do. Indexing is alive and well despite the foolishness of the bubble years and variations on the theme.

In addition to the powerful and deeply pervasive idea that market value is all that matters, M&M taught us something else—something we often forget—namely, the right side of the balance sheet and the left side of the balance sheet add up to the same number on the bottom. They are only opposite sides of the same things, despite all kinds of new ways to dice and splice the liabilities and the risks. We are finally beginning to learn Marty Leibowitz's lesson (1986) that pension funds have liabilities as well as assets and that there is a relationship between the two.

Along these lines, Merton has always considered the corporation to be a set of contingent claims in which corporate equity is really a put option that the stockholders have. The stockholders can always put the assets to the creditors—"Here, you take them." The strike price is the debt, the bond yield is the interest rate, and corporate volatility is the implied volatility that prices the equity's worth. To think about a company, the complex system we know as a corporation, in terms of these contingent claims offers important insights.

Finally, derivatives influence almost everything we do. Every aspect of investing, every strategy is in one way or another involved in hedging risks. Exciting work of many different forms is going on in this field.

Conclusion

If we say that the theories in *Capital Ideas* are obsolete, then in the same breath, we must say that Aristotle and Euclid are obsolete. Merton's father, Robert K. Merton, acknowledged, as Newton did, that we stand on the shoulders of giants. We cannot understand the investment process in the present unless we know where it came from, and it came from these ideas, one of the great intellectual leaps in history.

Note

1. Keith Ambachtsheer has important things to say about this area of theory in his wonderful article in the January/February 2005 *FAJ*.

References

Ambachtsheer, Keith. 2005. "Beyond Portfolio Theory: The Next Frontier." *Financial Analysts Journal*, vol. 61, no. 1 (January/February):29–33.

Bernstein, Peter L. 1992. *Capital Ideas: The Improbable Origins of Modern Wall Street*. New York: Free Press.

Cornell, Bradford, and Richard Roll. 2005. "A Delegated-Agent Asset-Pricing Model." *Financial Analysts Journal*, vol. 61, no. 1 (January/February):57–69.

Fama, Eugene, and Kenneth R. French. 2004. "The CAPM: Theory and Evidence." *Journal of Economic Perspectives*, vol. 18, no. 3 (Summer):25–46.

Kahneman, D., and A. Tversky. 1974. "Judgment under Uncertainty: Heuristics and Biases." *Science*, vol. 185:1124–31.

———. 1979. "Prospect Theory: An Analysis of Decisions under Risk." *Econometrica*, vol. 47, no. 2:313–327.

Leibowitz, Martin L. 1986. "Total Portfolio Duration: A New Perspective on Asset Allocation." *Financial Analysts Journal*, vol. 42, no. 5 (September/October):18–29, 77; reprinted in *Financial Analysts Journal*, vol. 51, no. 1 (January/February 1995 50th Anniversary Issue):139–148.

Mandelbrot, Benoit, and Richard L. Hudson. 2004. *The Misbehavior of Markets*. New York: Basic Books.

Markowitz, Harry M. 1952. "Portfolio Selection." *Journal of Finance*, vol. 7, no. 1 (March):77–91.

Merton, Robert C. 1987. "On the Current State of the Stock Market Rationality Hypothesis." In *Macroeconomics and Finance: Essays in Honor of Franco Modigliani*. Edited by Rudiger Dornbusch, Stanley Fischer, and John Bossons. Cambridge, MA: MIT Press.

Modigliani, Franco, and Merton Miller. 1958. "The Cost of Capital, Corporation Finance and the Theory of Investment." *American Economic Review*, vol. 48 (June):261–297.

———. 1963. "Corporate Income Taxes and the Cost of Capital: A Correction." *American Economic Review*, vol. 53 (June):433–443.

Perold, André F. 2004. "The Capital Asset Pricing Model." *Journal of Economic Perspectives*, vol. 18, no. 3 (Summer):3–24.

Shiller, Robert. 1981. "Do Stock Prices Move Too Much to Be Justified by Subsequent Changes in Dividends?" *American Economic Review*, vol. 71, no. 3 (June):421–436. Reprinted in *Economic Policy* (1996, Edward Elgar Publishing) and in *The History of Management Thought* (1997, Dartmouth Publishing).

Williams, John Burr. 1938. *The Theory of Investment Value*. Cambridge, MA: Harvard University Press (1997 edition available from Fraser Publishing, Burlington, VT).

Normal Investors, Then and Now

Meir Statman

The 1960 volume of the *Financial Analysts Journal* contains a pair of remarkable articles. In the first, "The Case for an Unmanaged Investment Company," Edward Renshaw and Paul Feldstein compared the returns of mutual funds with those of the DJIA and found that only 11 of 89 diversified common stock and balanced funds had returns higher than those of the DJIA. This and similar evidence led them to propose the creation of what we know today as an index fund:

> a new investment institution, what we have chosen to call an "unmanaged investment company"—in other words, a company dedicated to the task of following a representative average. (p. 43)

In the second article, "The Case for Mutual Fund Management," John B. Armstrong argued against the idea of an index fund, "[f]irst and foremost," because it

> ignores the fact . . . that the Dow Jones Industrial Average has not in fact matched common stock mutual funds with comparable volatility in performance results. (p. 37)

"John B. Armstrong" was the pen name of a man who had spent many years in the securities field and in the study and analysis of mutual funds. He was a graduate of Princeton University, and the title of his AB thesis was "Economic Role of the Investment Company." The real "John B. Armstrong" is John C. Bogle, the founder of The Vanguard Group, who introduced the first of many index mutual funds in 1976 and remains their foremost advocate.

Bogle reflected on index funds and changed his mind.[1] This 60th anniversary of the *FAJ* is an opportunity for all of us to reflect on past changes of mind and perhaps contemplate future ones.

The year 1960 was the middle of an extraordinary time when academics and practitioners of finance were changing

Investors were never "rational" as defined by standard finance. They were "normal" in 1945, and they remain normal today.

Meir Statman is Glenn Klimek Professor of Finance at the Leavey School of Business, Santa Clara University, California.

their minds, switching from a framework in which investors are "normal" to one in which investors are "rational." Normal investors are affected by cognitive biases and emotions; rational investors are not. Rational investors care only about the risk and expected return of their overall portfolios; normal investors care about more than that.

The portrait of investors as rational is the first foundation block of standard finance. Other foundation blocks are mean–variance portfolio theory, the capital asset pricing model (CAPM), and market efficiency. I describe normal investors as they were portrayed in the *FAJ* and other finance journals before standard finance was introduced and as they have emerged recently in behavioral finance.

Rational Investors

Merton Miller and Franco Modigliani described investors as rational in their classic 1961 *Journal of Business* article on dividend policy. Rational investors

> always prefer more wealth to less and are indifferent as to whether a given increment to their wealth takes the form of cash payments or an increase in the market value of their holdings of shares. (p. 412)

Rational investors are indifferent to dividend policy because an increment to their wealth in the form of dividends is different only in form, not in substance, from an increment in wealth in the form of capital gains. Miller and Modigliani wrote that the indifference of rational investors to dividend policy is

> obvious, once you think of it. . . . Obvious as the proposition may be, however, one finds few references to it in the extensive literature on the [dividend] problem. (p. 414)

Form, label, or packaging does not affect stock prices, according to Miller and Modigliani, because of the power of arbitrage. If the value of a company that pays generous dividends is higher than the value of an otherwise identical company that pays no dividends, rational investors will engage in arbitrage—selling shares of the first and buying shares of the second—until the values of the two companies converge. Indeed, arbitrage will do its work even if most investors are normal—that is, *are* affected by form, label, or packaging—as long as there are some rational investors who engage in arbitrage.

Recognition of the power of arbitrage led Miller to argue not only that security prices are affected by the "real considerations" of the earning power of the company's assets and its investment policy but also that exploration of considerations other than "real considerations" is a harmful distraction. As Miller wrote in 1986, in response to the behavioral approach to the dividend question proposed by Hersh Shefrin and me (1984):

> Behind each holding may be a story of family business, family quarrels, legacies received, divorce settlements, and a host of other considerations. . . . That we abstract from all these stories in building our models is not because the stories are uninteresting but because they may be too interesting and thereby distract us from pervasive market forces that should be our principal concern. (p. S467)

The preference of rational investors for more rather than less and the power of arbitrage also underlie the efficient market hypothesis (EMH), the second foundation block of standard finance. An efficient market is a market where prices are always equal to fundamental values. As Eugene Fama (1965) said in the *FAJ*, "in an efficient market at any point in time the actual price of a security will be a good estimate of its intrinsic value" (p. 56). Any deviation of price from value invites rational investors to engage in arbitrage, sometimes risk free and sometimes risky, and their trades drive price toward value.

The labels of "weak," "semistrong," and "strong" for the forms of the EMH would come only later, but Alfred Cowles noted in 1960 that the power of arbitrage would make markets efficient in the weak form, where prices follow a random walk. Citing Tjalling C. Koopmans, Cowles wrote that

> if the persistence in stock price movements were sufficient to provide capital gains appreciably in excess of brokerage costs, professional traders would presumably be aware of this situation and through their market operations would inadvertently wipe out the persistence in price movements from which they were attempting to profit. (p. 915)

Cowles published his first article on random walk in 1933; in 1998, Stephen Brown, William Goetzmann, and Alok Kumar argued that Cowles' article "is a watershed study that led to the random walk hypothesis and thus played a key role in the development of the efficient market theory" (p. 1330). But the real push for the random walk hypothesis had to wait until Harry Roberts' 1959 article and, especially, Fama's 1965 and other articles. Neither Roberts nor Fama cited Cowles' 1933 article.

Roberts wrote that many financial analysts "believe that the history of the market itself contains 'patterns' that give clues to the future, if only these patterns can be properly understood" (p. 1). He went on to examine the patterns of stock prices and found that they are no more than "statistical artifacts" that would arise by chance.

Fama titled his *FAJ* article "Random Walks in Stock Market Prices." Because stock prices move in a random walk, he wrote, "[a] simple policy of buying and holding a security will be as good as any more complicated mechanical procedure for timing purchases and sales" (p. 56).

The weak form of the EMH states that all securities prices are fully reflected in current securities prices; therefore, investors cannot gain abnormal returns through technical analysis—that is, by uncovering patterns in stock prices. The semistrong form states that all publicly available information is fully reflected in current securities prices; therefore, investors can gain abnormal returns neither through technical analysis nor through fundamental analysis, by which they uncover insights in public information. Tests of the semistrong hypothesis often require adjustment for differences in risk among stocks, and such tests did not come to full function until the mid-1960s when William Sharpe introduced the CAPM, in which beta measures the only risk that affects expected returns (see Sharpe 1964). The CAPM, in turn, had to await Harry Markowitz's development of mean–variance portfolio theory in the 1950s (see Markowitz 1999).

Markowitz recollected in his 1999 *FAJ* review of portfolio theory:

> Diversification of investments was a well-established practice long before I published my paper on portfolio selection in 1952. For example, A. Wiesenberger's annual reports in *Investment Companies* prior to 1952 (beginning 1941) showed that these firms held large numbers of securities. . . . What was lacking prior to 1952 was an adequate *theory* of investment that covered the effects of diversification when risks are correlated, distinguished between efficient and inefficient portfolios, and analyzed risk–return trade-offs on the portfolios as a whole. (p. 5)

Markowitz provided that theory in his mean– variance portfolio theory.

Markowitz wrote in his 1999 review of the 1952 article, however, that it "should be considered only as a historical document" (p. 6), that what represents his views is his 1959 book. Investors in the mean–variance portfolios Markowitz described are the rational investors of Miller and Modigliani. They care only about the expected return and risk of their overall portfolios. So, mean–variance investors are never reluctant to realize losses on individual stocks when tax savings add to their wealth. And mean–variance investors do not care about such characteristics as the dividend yield of stocks or the social responsibility of their companies, unless those characteristics affect the risk and expected return of their overall portfolios.

Markowitz's mean–variance portfolio theory is the third foundation block of standard finance, and Sharpe's CAPM is the fourth. Markowitz described the day when Sharpe started his CAPM work as follows:

> One day in 1960, having said what I had to say about portfolio theory in my 1959 book, I was sitting in my office . . . working on something quite different, when a young man presented himself at my door, introduced himself as Bill Sharpe, and said that he was . . . looking for a thesis topic. . . . We talked about the need for models of covariance. This conversation started Sharpe out on the first of his (ultimately many) lines of research, which resulted in [the CAPM]. (1999, p. 14)

Markowitz's mean–variance portfolio theory is prescriptive, recommending the mean–variance algorithm to investors who care only about the risk and expected return of their portfolios, but the CAPM is descriptive, describing investors who build mean–variance portfolios.

Finally, in 1968, Michael Jensen introduced "Jensen's alpha," based on the CAPM, and offered evidence supporting the semistrong EMH. He found that the risk-adjusted returns of mutual funds were lower, on average, than the return of the stock market as a whole. The foundation blocks of standard finance were now in place, supporting one another. Investors are to be considered rational, prices are efficient, risk is measured by beta, and investors form portfolios by the rules of mean–variance portfolio theory.

Normal Investors

Investors were normal before Miller and Modigliani described them as rational, and they remain normal today. In an *FAJ* article in 1957, before the introduction of standard finance, Howard Snyder tried to teach normal investors "how to take a loss and like it." Explaining that realizing losses increases wealth by reducing taxes, he wrote, "There is no loss without collateral compensation." He went on to note, however, that normal investors are reluctant to realize losses:

> Human nature being what it is, we are loath to take a loss until we are forced into it. Too often we believe that by ignoring a loss we will some day glance at the asset to find it has not only recovered its original value but has shown some appreciation. (p. 116)

Investors who exhibit the normal "human nature" behavior described by Snyder would have been branded irrational by Miller and Modigliani. Snyder's normal investors deviate from rational behavior in two ways. First, they do not always prefer more wealth to less, as rational investors do, because they forgo the increment to their wealth brought by tax savings. Second, unlike rational investors, they are not indifferent to whether a loss is labeled a paper loss or a realized loss.

Snyder's 1957 observation about the reluctance of normal investors to realize losses was reintroduced by Shefrin and me as the "disposition effect" in 1985, during the early period of behavioral finance. Shefrin and I analyzed the disposition of investors to sell winners too early and ride losers too long; our framework was a behavioral framework in which investors—normal investors—are affected by cognitive biases and emotions. A cognitive bias leads normal investors to consider their stocks one by one, in mental accounts distinct from their overall portfolios, and to distinguish paper losses from realized losses. Normal investors are reluctant to realize losses because realization closes mental accounts at a loss, thereby extinguishing all hope of recovery and inflicting the emotional pain of regret.

Investor attitudes toward dividends were the direct target of Miller and Modigliani in their 1961 article, which labeled as irrational any preference for dividends or for capital gains. One of the objects of their criticism was John Clendenin, who explored the preference for dividends and capital gains in a 1958 article. Clendenin wrote:

> Back in 1951, with the uncertainties of depression and war still uppermost in their minds, stockholders expressed strong preferences for conservative stocks, cash dividends, and safety above all. In 1958, after seven years of prosperity and stock-market boom, a majority of the answers indicate a willingness to own speculative as well as conservative stocks, a less positive emphasis on cash dividends, and an interest in market profits which is almost as great as that in income and safety. (p 48)

Attitudes toward dividends and capital gains continue to change as generations of investors come and go. Shefrin and I (1984) wrote that in 1974, some Consolidated Edison shareholders considered dividend checks the equivalent of Social Security checks and were extremely distressed when the company eliminated its dividend. We quoted from the transcript of Con Edison's shareholders' meeting of that year:

> A lady came over to me a minute ago and she said to me, "Please say a word for the senior citizens." And she had a tear in her eyes. And I really know what she means by that. She simply means that now she will only get one check a month, and that will be her Social Security, and she's not going to make it, because you have denied her that dividend. (p. 277)

The generation that followed the senior citizen investors in Con Edison did not care much about dividends, and by the peak of the 1990s boom, dividend yields were approaching zero. But the bust of the early 2000s might renew interest in dividends in the generation that follows.

The EMH was new and threatening in 1965, when Fama introduced it to the readers of the *FAJ*. In the efficient stock market world Fama described, there are no overpriced securities or underpriced ones. But analysts and investors believed there were. In 1957, Robert Tucker wrote in the *FAJ*:

> Security Analysts owe their very existence to the concept that value and price do not coincide. "Overpriced" and "underpriced" are adjectives repeatedly used in an analytical description of a security. (p. 93)

Security analysts continue to challenge the EMH in their daily work. Stanley Block (1999) reported in the *FAJ* that only 2.7 percent of security analysts agree strongly with the semistrong form of the EMH. Similarly, investors challenge the EMH in their daily investment behavior. Investors continue to allocate almost all their mutual fund money to active mutual funds that try to beat the market rather than to index funds that try to match it.

Academics took longer to challenge the EMH, but even some academics protested the increasing acceptance of the EMH in the early 1960s. Robert Weintraub (1963) wrote:

> In the past few years a number of academic papers have concluded that speculative price movements are random walks. . . . I shall argue that the random-walk hypothesis flies in the face of common sense and the facts and, moreover, suggests a degree of naïveté on the part of its advocates as to the rules of the game which professional speculators are playing. . . . It is a fact that there are professional traders who earn incomes from speculating on price movements. . . . These men, in effect, earn their incomes by betting against the applicability of the random-walk hypothesis. (pp. 59–61)

In the late 1970s and early 1980s, a series of return anomalies, such as those associated with size and book value to market value, were uncovered that gave academics additional pause. The anomalies might indicate that markets are inefficient. Alternatively, they might indicate that the CAPM is a bad asset-pricing model. In 1992, Eugene Fama and Kenneth French concluded that anomalies are reflections of a bad asset-pricing model rather than an inefficient market and created the three-factor model, in which size and book to market are factors rather than anomalies. The number of factors in asset-pricing models keeps growing; now, momentum and liquidity are often included. Perhaps, it's time for an asset-pricing model to include factors that reflect other preferences of normal investors.

Much of the distinction between rationality and normality in the investment context is a distinction between *utilitarian* and *expressive* characteristics. Expressive characteristics are those that enable normal people to identify their values, social class, and life style and to communicate them to others. For example, a Timex watch and a Rolex watch have identical utilitarian characteristics: They show the same hour. But they have different expressive characteristics. A Timex conveys reliability and thrift; a Rolex conveys riches and ostentation. As I have described in the *FAJ* (Statman 1999), value stocks can be considered the equivalent of Timex watches and growth stocks the equivalent of Rolex watches.

Behavioral asset-pricing theory (Shefrin and Statman 1994) offers a model that recognizes that the cognitive biases of investors cause the mean–variance-efficient portfolio to deviate from the market portfolio and cause the resulting behavioral betas, calculated relative to the mean–variance-efficient portfolio, to deviate from market betas. Recently, Fama and French (2004) presented similar ideas. Investors are interested in more than money payoffs, they stated; investors also want the pleasure of holding growth stocks or the virtue of holding socially responsible stocks, and their tastes may affect stock prices. So, expressive characteristics, such as those associated with growth or social responsibility, have a place in asset-pricing models.

Fama and French's 2004 article shows how great the change of mind has been since 1986, when Miller urged academics to stay away from "family business, family quarrels, legacies received, divorce settlements, and a host of other considerations," which he called distracting. We are moving toward asset-pricing models that combine utilitarian and expressive characteristics and toward a better understanding of market efficiency.

Markowitz wrote in his 1999 *FAJ* review that, although the benefits of diversification were known before he introduced mean–variance portfolio theory, no theory along the lines of mean–variance portfolio theory existed before his. But portfolio theory along the lines of *behavioral portfolio theory* (Shefrin and Statman 2000) did exist. In behavioral portfolio theory, investors build their portfolios as layered pyramids in which different assets, corresponding to different goals and different attitudes toward risk, fill the different layers. This concept of a layered portfolio goes back many years. In 1952, Arthur Wiesenberger listed the layers of portfolios from bottom to top as income, balanced, growth, and aggressive growth. Bonds were the right securities for the income layer; stocks with generous dividends, such as utility stocks, were right for the balanced layer; stocks that paid modest dividends were right for the growth layer; and stocks that paid no dividends were right for the aggressive growth layer.

In a similar approach, a 1929 article in the *Literary Digest* stated:

> The first step in a safe and sane financial program is insurance. . . . After insurance, the next requirement is to build up a cash reserve of at least $1,000 in the savings bank. After that, automatic thrift should be contracted for through installment savings plans, such as building-and-loan associations offer. When these fundamental steps have been taken, the investor is in position to acquire high-grade bonds and guaranteed first mortgages on real-estate. The next advance can be toward diversified preferred stocks, which offer a somewhat higher return. . . . The last step should be outright purchase of the best grade of diversified common stock. ("No Royal Road. . ." 1929, p. 55)

Some investors continue to pretend that they use mean–variance portfolio theory, perhaps because they want to present themselves as rational investors. Such investors feed into the mean–variance optimizer expected returns, standard deviations, and correlations, and the optimizer spits out asset allocations on the mean–variance-efficient frontier. But the optimizer is no more than a prop. The important asset allocation choices are made through constraints—such as "no more than 10 percent allocation to alternative investments." In short, the true (but unspoken) framework for normal investors' portfolios is behavioral portfolio theory.

Conclusion

Investors were normal before they were described as rational in the early 1960s, and they remain normal today. Normal investors are affected by cognitive biases and emotions, whereas rational investors are not. Rational investors care only about the risk and expected return of their overall portfolios, whereas normal investors care about more.

Wilford Eiteman sought to educate normal investors about dividend yield in a 1957 *FAJ* article: "The danger of current yield data lies in a tendency of uninformed investors to accept current yields as indicating the rate of return which they may expect" (p. 13). Harry Comer sought to educate normal investors about stock splits in a 1958 *FAJ* article:

> Recently a client asked if Bethlehem Steel did not look cheap "at 40." On being reminded that Bethlehem stock had been split 12-for-1 since the war, and that a price of $40 now is equivalent to $480 per share for the stock which was priced around $75 at the end of the war, he said he had forgotten about the splits. (p. 79)

More recently, some *FAJ* authors have been seeking to teach normal investors that

- stock prices move in patterns, not in a random walk (Zhou and Dong 2004),
- sentiment associated with St. Patrick's Day and the Jewish High Holy Days affects stock prices (Frieder and Subrahmanyam 2004),
- even professional traders are reluctant to realize losses (Garvey and Murphy 2004), and
- investors form portfolios by the rules of behavioral portfolio theory rather than those of mean–variance portfolio theory (Statman (2004).

Many years ago, in an early session of my economics studies, a professor asked if speculators stabilize prices or destabilize them. "Speculators are greedy profiteers," said one student. "Speculators jump on price bandwagons and destabilize prices," said a second student. Then came my turn. I said that speculators always stabilize prices. Speculators are smart, and they know when prices are too high or too low. They buy when prices are too low and sell when prices are too high, and in the process, they stabilize prices. "That is right!" said the professor; "What is your name?" I said my name, and I was proud, and I knew then and there that I would be an economist. But now I know that my answer was wrong. Facts I did not know then but do know now show that speculators stabilize prices at some times but destabilize them at others. I have changed my mind as the facts I know have changed.[2]

Much of finance has changed since the *FAJ* was founded in 1945, but the drive to uncover facts and make sense of them remains. Change of mind is an integral part of the process. As Keynes famously said, "When the facts change, I change my mind. What do you do, sir?"

Notes

1. The *Wall Street Journal* ("Bids & Offers" 2004) wrote, "Mr. Bogle, now 75, says he wrote the 1960 article under a pen name at the suggestion of Wellington's regulators and isn't embarrassed to acknowledge his authorship. The fund business in its early days did a better job of serving investors than now, he says" (p. C5).
2. For example, Markus Brunnermeier and Stefan Nagel (2004) found that hedge funds chose to ride the technology bubble of the late 1990s rather than counter it. They wrote, "Our findings question the efficient markets notion that rational speculators always stabilize prices. They are consistent with models in which rational investors may prefer to ride bubbles because of predictable investor sentiment and limits to arbitrage" (p. 2013).

References

Armstrong, John B. 1960. "The Case for Mutual Fund Management." *Financial Analysts Journal*, vol. 16, no. 3 (May/June):33–38.

"Bids & Offers: Heresy." 2004. *Wall Street Journal* (24 September):C5.

Block, Stanley. 1999. "A Study of Financial Analysts: Practice and Theory." *Financial Analysts Journal*, vol. 55, no. 4 (July/August):86–95.

Brown, Stephen J., William N. Goetzmann, and Alok Kumar. 1998. "The Dow Theory: William Peter Hamilton's Track Record Reconsidered." *Journal of Finance*, vol. 53, no. 4 (August):1311–33.

Brunnermeier, Markus K., and Stefan Nagel. 2004. "Hedge Funds and the Technology Bubble." *Journal of Finance*, vol. 59, no. 5 (October):2013–40.

Clendenin, John. 1958. "What Do Stockholders Like?" *California Management Review*, vol. 1, no. 1 (Fall):47–55.

Comer, Harry D. 1958. "High Prices Hidden by Stock Splits." *Financial Analysts Journal*, vol. 14, no. 1 (February):79–80.

Cowles, Alfred. 1933. "Can Stock Market Forecasters Forecast?" *Econometrica*, vol. 1, no. 3 (July):309–324.

———. 1960. "A Revision of Previous Conclusions Regarding Stock Price Behavior." *Econometrica*, vol. 28, no. 4 (October):909–915.

Eiteman, Wilford J. 1957. "Yield on Common Stock Investments." *Financial Analysts Journal*, vol. 13, no. 1 (February):13–14.

Fama, Eugene F. 1965. "Random Walks in Stock Market Prices." *Financial Analysts Journal*, vol. 21, no. 5 (September/October):55–59.

Fama, Eugene F., and Kenneth R. French. 1992. "The Cross-Section of Expected Stock Returns." *Journal of Finance*, vol. 47, no. 2 (June):427–465.

———. 2004. "Disagreement, Tastes, and Asset Prices." Working paper, University of Chicago.

Frieder, Laura, and Avanidhar Subrahmanyam. 2004. "Nonsecular Regularities in Returns and Volume." *Financial Analysts Journal*, vol. 60, no. 4 (July/August):29–34.

Friedman, Martin, and Leonard Savage. 1948. "The Utility Analysis of Choices Involving Risk." *Journal of Political Economy*, vol. 56, no. 4 (August):279–304.

Garvey, Ryan, and Anthony Murphy. 2004. "Are Professional Traders Too Slow to Realize Their Losses?" *Financial Analysts Journal*, vol. 60, no. 4 (July/August): 35–43.

Jensen, Michael. 1968. "The Problem of Mutual Funds in the Period 1945–1968." *Journal of Finance*, vol. 23, no. 2 (May):389–416.

Markowitz, Harry M. 1952. "Portfolio Selection." *Journal of Finance*, vol. 7, no. 1 (March):77–91.

———. 1959. *Portfolio Selection: Diversification of Investments*. New York: John Wiley & Sons.

———. 1999. "The Early History of Portfolio Theory: 1600–1960." *Financial Analysts Journal*, vol. 55, no. 4 (July/August):5–15.

Miller, Merton. 1986. "Behavioral Rationality in Finance: The Case of Dividends." *Journal of Business*, vol. 59, no. 4 (October):S451–S468.

Miller, Merton, and Franco Modigliani. 1961. "Dividend Policy, Growth, and the Valuation of Shares." *Journal of Business*, vol. 34, no. 4 (October):411–433.

"No Royal Road for the Small Investor." 1929. *Literary Digest*, vol. 103, no. 11 (14 December):52–55.

Renshaw, Edward F., and Paul J. Feldstein. 1960. "The Case for an Unmanaged Investment Company." *Financial Analysts Journal*, vol. 16, no. 1 (January/February):43–46.

Roberts, Harry. 1959. "Stock-Market 'Patterns' and Financial Analysis: Methodological Suggestions." *Journal of Finance*, vol. 12, no. 1 (March):1–10.

Sharpe, William F. 1964. "Capital Asset Prices—A Theory of Market Equilibrium under Conditions of Risk." *Journal of Finance*, vol. 19, no. 3 (September): 425–442.

Shefrin, Hersh M., and Meir Statman. 1984. "Explaining Investor Preference for Cash Dividends." *Journal of Financial Economics*, vol. 13, no. 2 (June):253–282.

______. 1985. "The Disposition to Sell Winners Too Early and Ride Losers Too Long: Theory and Evidence." *Journal of Finance*, vol. 40, no. 3 (July):777–790.

———. 1994. "Behavioral Capital Asset Pricing Theory." *Journal of Financial and Quantitative Analysis*, vol. 29, no. 3 (September):323–349.

———. 2000. "Behavioral Portfolio Theory." *Journal of Financial and Quantitative Analysis*, vol. 35, no. 2 (June):127–151.

Snyder, W. Howard T. 1957. "How to Take a Loss and Like It." *Financial Analysts Journal*, vol. 13, no. 2 (May):115–116.

Statman, Meir. 1999. "Behavioral Finance: Past Battles and Future Engagements." *Financial Analysts Journal*, vol. 55, no. 6 (November/December):18–27.

______. 2004. "The Diversification Puzzle." *Financial Analysts Journal*, vol. 60, no. 4 (July/August):44–53.

Tucker, Robert D. 1957. "A Discussion of Benjamin Graham's Central Value Concept." *Financial Analysts Journal*, vol. 13, no. 2 (May):93–95.

Weintraub, Robert E. 1963. "On Speculative Prices and Random Walks: A Denial." *Journal of Finance*, vol. 18, no. 1 (March):59–66.

Wiesenberger, Arthur. 1952. *Investment Companies*. New York: Arthur Wiesenberger and Company.

Zhou, Xu-Shen, and Ming Dong. "Can Fuzzy Logic Make Technical Analysis 20/20?" *Financial Analysts Journal*, vol. 60, no. 4 (July/August):54–75.

Market Efficiency: A Theoretical Distinction and So What?

Harry M. Markowitz

When one clearly unrealistic assumption of the capital asset pricing model is replaced by a real-world version, some of the dramatic CAPM conclusions no longer follow.

The capital asset pricing model (CAPM) is an elegant theory. With the aid of some simplifying assumptions, it comes to dramatic conclusions about practical matters, such as how to choose an investment portfolio, how to forecast the expected return of a security or asset class, how to price a new security, or how to price risky assets in a merger or acquisition.

The CAPM starts with some assumptions about investors and markets and deduces its dramatic conclusions from these assumptions. First, it assumes that investors seek mean–variance efficient portfolios; in other words, it assumes that investors seek low volatility and high return on average. Different investors may have different trade-offs between these two, depending on their aversion to risk. Second, the CAPM assumes that taxes, transaction costs, and other illiquidities can be ignored for the purposes of this analysis. In effect, it assumes that such illiquidities may impede the market's approach to the CAPM solution but do not change the general tendency of the market. A third CAPM assumption is that all investors have the same predictions for the expected returns, volatilities, and correlations of securities. This assumption is usually not critical.[1] Finally, the CAPM makes assumptions about what portfolios the investor can select. The original Sharpe (1964)–Lintner (1965) CAPM considered long positions only and assumed that the investor could borrow without limit at the risk-free rate. From this assumption, and the three preceding assumptions, one can deduce conclusions of the sort outlined in the first paragraph.

The assumption that the investor can borrow without limit is crucial to the Sharpe–Lintner model's conclusions. As illustrated later in this article, if we accept the other three CAPM assumptions but assume limited (or no) borrowing, the Sharpe–Lintner conclusions no longer follow. For example, if the four

Harry M. Markowitz is president of Harry Markowitz Company, San Diego, California.

premises of the Sharpe–Lintner original CAPM were true, then the "market portfolio"—a portfolio whose amounts invested are proportional to each security's market capitalization—would be an efficient portfolio. We could not find a portfolio with greater return (on average) without greater volatility. In fact, if the four premises of the Sharpe–Lintner original CAPM were true, the market portfolio, plus perhaps borrowing and lending, would be the *only* efficient portfolio. If, however, we assume the first three premises of the Sharpe–Lintner CAPM but take into account the fact that investors have limited borrowing capacity, then it no longer follows that the market portfolio is efficient. As this article will illustrate, this inefficiency of the market portfolio could be substantial and it would not be arbitraged away even if some investors could borrow without limit.

Before the CAPM, conventional wisdom was that some investments were suitable for widows and orphans whereas others were suitable only for those prepared to take on "a businessman's risk." The CAPM convinced many that this conventional wisdom was wrong; the market portfolio is the proper mix among risky securities for everyone. The portfolios of the widow and businessman should differ only in the amount of cash or leverage used. As we will see, however, an analysis that takes into account limited borrowing capacity implies that the pre-CAPM conventional wisdom is probably correct.

An alternate version of the CAPM speaks of investors holding short as well as long positions. But the portfolios this alternate CAPM permits are as unrealistic as those of the Sharpe–Lintner CAPM with unlimited borrowing. The alternate CAPM assumes that the proceeds of a short sale can be used, without limit, to buy securities long. For example, the alternate CAPM assumes that an investor could deposit $1,000 with a broker, short $1,000,000 worth of Stock A, then use the proceeds and the original deposit to buy $1,001,000 of Stock B. The world does not work this way.

Like the original CAPM, the alternate CAPM implies that the market portfolio is an efficient portfolio, although not the only one (as in the original CAPM). If one takes into account real-world constraints on the holding of short and long positions, however, the efficiency of the market portfolio no longer follows, as will be illustrated.

Both the original CAPM, with unlimited borrowing, and the alternate CAPM, with unrealistic short rules, imply that the expected return of a stock depends in a simple (linear) way on its beta, and only on its beta. This conclusion has been used for estimating expected returns, but it has lost favor for this use because of poor predictive results. It is still used routinely in "risk adjustment," however, for valuing assets and analyzing investment strategies on a "risk-adjusted basis." I will show here that the conclusion that expected returns are linear functions of beta does not hold when real-world limits on permitted portfolio holdings are introduced into the CAPM. This discussion will call into question the frequent use of beta in risk adjustment.

I will discuss the assumptions and conclusions of the CAPM formally and then illustrate the effect on CAPM conclusions of varying the CAPM assumptions concerning the investor's constraint set. Afterward, I will sketch how the points illustrated in the simple examples generalize to more complex cases. Finally, I will discuss the implications of the analysis for financial theory, practice, and pedagogy.

A Distinction

We should distinguish between the statement that "the market is efficient," in the sense that market participants have accurate information and use it correctly to their benefit, and the statement that "the market portfolio is an efficient portfolio." Under some conditions, the former implies the latter. In particular, if one makes the following assumptions,

A1. transaction costs and other illiquidities can be ignored (as I will do throughout this article),

A2. all investors hold mean–variance efficient portfolios,

A3. all investors hold the same (correct) beliefs about means, variances, and covariances of securities, and—*in addition*—

A4. every investor can lend all she or he has or can borrow all she or he wants at the risk-free rate,

then Conclusion 1 follows:

C1. The market portfolio is a mean–variance efficient portfolio.

C1 also follows if A4 is replaced by A4′:

A4′. investors can sell short without limit and use the proceeds of the sale to buy long positions.

In particular, A4′ says that any investor can deposit $1,000 with a broker, short $1,000,000 worth of one security, and buy long $1,001,000 worth of another security.

Neither A4 nor A4′ is realistic. Regarding A4, when an investor borrows, not only does the investor pay more than when the U.S. government borrows, but (a point of equal or greater importance here) the amount of credit extended is limited to what the lender believes the borrower has a reasonable probability of repaying. Regarding A4′, if the investor deposits $1,000 with a broker, Federal Reserve Regulation T permits the investor to buy a $2,000 long position *or* take on a $2,000 short position *or* take on a $1,000 long and a $1,000 short position, but it does not allow an unlimited amount short plus the same unlimited amount long, as assumed in A4′.

If one replaces A4 or A4′ with a more realistic description of the investor's investment constraints, then C1 usually no longer follows; even though all investors share the same beliefs and each holds a mean–variance efficient portfolio, the market portfolio need not be an efficient portfolio. This departure from efficiency can be quite substantial. In fact, the market portfolio can have almost *maximum* variance among feasible portfolios with the same expected value rather than *minimum* such variance; that is, the market portfolio can be about as *in*efficient as a feasible portfolio can get (see Chapter 11 of Markowitz 1987 or Markowitz and Todd 2000).

In addition to C1, A1 through A4 (or A1 through A4′) imply

C2. In equilibrium, the expected return for each security depends only on its beta (the regression of its returns against the return on the market). This relationship between the security's expected return and its beta is a simple, linear relationship.

C2 is the basis for the CAPM's prescriptions for risk adjustment and asset valuation. Like the first conclusion, C2 does not follow from assumptions A1 through A3 if A4 (or A4′) is replaced by a more realistic description of the investor's investment constraints.

Often, financial research attempts to determine "market efficiency" by testing whether C2 holds. But the failure of C2 to hold empirically does not prove that the market is not efficient in the general sense of possessing correct information and using it advantageously. Nor does the failure of C2 to hold empirically prove that the market is not efficient in the narrower sense of A2 and A3—namely, that participants hold mean–variance efficient portfolios in terms of commonly held correct beliefs. I will not argue here that A2 and A3 are true—or argue that they are false. I argue only that, in the absence of either A4 or A4′, the empirical refutation of C2 is not an empirical refutation of A1 through A3.[2]

Example. In this first example, I assume that investors cannot sell short or borrow (but I note subsequently that the same results hold if investors *can* borrow limited amounts or *can* sell short but are subject to Reg T or some similar constraint). The example assumes A1 through A3; that is, it ignores taxes, transaction costs, and other illiquidities; it assumes that all investors have the same beliefs about the means, variances, and covariances of security returns; and it assumes that each investor holds a portfolio that is mean–variance efficient in terms of these beliefs.

This example consists of long positions in three risky securities with the expected returns and standard deviations shown in **Table 1**. To keep things simple, we will assume that returns are uncorrelated. However, the results also hold for correlated returns.

Let X_1, X_2, and X_3 represent the fraction of her wealth that some investor invests in, respectively, Securities 1, 2, and 3. Assume that the investor can choose any portfolio that meets the following constraints:

$$X_1 + X_2 + X_3 = 1.0 \tag{1}$$

and

$$X_1 \geq 0,\ X_2 \geq 0,\ X_3 \geq 0. \tag{2}$$

The first of these is a budget equation; the second is a requirement that none of the investments be negative. We will contrast the efficient set and market portfolio we get with Budget Equation 1 and Nonnegativity Requirement 2 as constraints with the set and portfolio we get if we assume A4′ (that is, if we assume that Budget Equation 1 is the only constraint). In **Figure 1**, X_1—the fraction invested in Security 1—is plotted on the horizontal axis; X_2—the fraction in Security 2—is plotted on the vertical axis; and X_3—the fraction invested in the third security—is given implicitly by the relationship

$$X_3 = 1 - X_1 - X_2. \tag{3}$$

Figure 1 should be thought of as extended without limits in all directions. Every point (portfolio) on this extended page is feasible according to assumption A4′. For example, the point with X_1 = 93 and X_2 = –106 (therefore, X_3 = 14 according to Equation 3) is feasible according to assumption A4′ because it satisfies Equation 1. It is not feasible when Budget Equation 1 *and* Nonnegativity Requirement 2 are required because it does not satisfy $X_2 \geq 0$.

The only points (portfolios) in Figure 1 that satisfy Budget Equation 1 and Nonnegativity Requirement 2 are on and in the triangle whose vertices are the points (1,0), (0,1), and (0,0). The first of these points represents an undiversified portfolio with 100 percent invested in Security 1 (X_1 = 1.0); the second, a 100 percent investment in Security 2 (X_2 = 1.0); the third, a 100 percent investment in Security 3 (X_3 = 1.0). The diagonal side of the triangle connecting points (1,0) and (0,1) includes investments in Securities 1 and 2 but not Security 3; the horizontal side connecting (0,0) and (1,0) has investments in Securities 1 and 3 but not in Security 2; the side connecting (0,0) and (0,1) has X_1 = 0. Points within the triangle represent portfolios with positive investments in all three securities. The vertices, sides, and interior of the triangle all meet Budget Equation 1 and Nonnegativity Requirement 2.

Table 1. Expected Returns and Standard Deviations of Three Risky Securities

Security	Expected Return	Standard Deviation
1	0.15%	0.18%
2	0.10	0.12
3	0.20	0.30

Figure 1. Efficient Sets with and without Nonnegativity Constraints

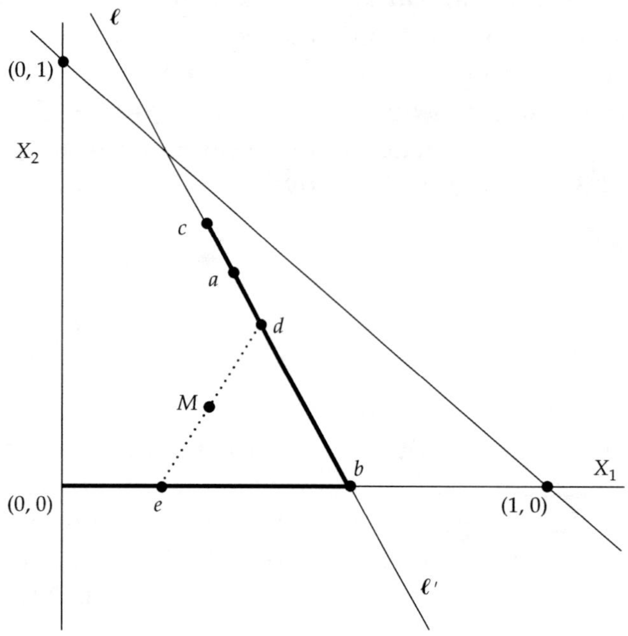

If assumption A4′ holds (therefore, Budget Equation 1 is the only constraint), then all the portfolios with the least standard deviation for various levels of expected return lie on the straight line labeled $\ell\ell'$ in Figure 1. Because two points determine a line, we know the whole line if we know two points on it. One point on the line is the portfolio that minimizes standard deviation among all portfolios on the extended page (i.e., among all portfolios that satisfy Equation 1). When returns are uncorrelated, this risk-minimizing portfolio satisfies

$$X_1 = \frac{K_c}{V_1}, \tag{4a}$$

$$X_2 = \frac{K_c}{V_2}, \tag{4b}$$

and

$$X_3 = \frac{K_c}{V_3}, \tag{4c}$$

where V_1, V_2, V_3 are the variances (standard deviations squared) of the three securities and K_c is chosen so that Equation 1 is satisfied; that is,

$$K_c = \frac{1}{(1/V_1)+(1/V_2)+(1/V_3)}. \tag{5}$$

Thus, when returns are uncorrelated, the variance-minimizing portfolio is always within the triangle. For the current example,

$X_1 = 0.28,$

$X_2 = 0.62,$

and

$X_3 = 0.10.$

This point is the point labeled "c" in Figure 1.

When returns are uncorrelated, another point on the line that minimizes portfolio variance for various levels of portfolio expected return is

$$X_1 = \frac{K_a E_1}{V_1}, \tag{6a}$$

$$X_2 = \frac{K_a E_2}{V_2}, \tag{6b}$$

and

$$X_3 = \frac{K_a E_3}{V_3}, \tag{6c}$$

where E_1, E_2, and E_3 are the expected returns of the three securities and K_a is chosen to satisfy Equation 1. In our example, this is the portfolio

$X_1 = 0.34,$

$X_2 = 0.50,$

and

$X_3 = 0.16.$

It is the point labeled "a" in Figure 1.

If we continue to assume Budget Equation 1 as the only constraint, all points on the straight line through a and c minimize portfolio variance for various levels of portfolio expected return. However, not all these points are *efficient* portfolios. Efficient portfolios are those encountered if we start at c and move continuously in the direction of a, and beyond, without stop. As we move away from c in this direction, portfolio expected return, E_P, and portfolio variance, V_P, increase. All portfolios encountered provide minimum V_P for the given E_P—*or greater* E_P—among all portfolios that satisfy Budget Equation 1. In contrast, if we start at c and move in the other direction, we do not encounter efficient portfolios (other than c) because V_P increases but E_P decreases. The same V_P but greater E_P can be found elsewhere on $\ell\ell'$.

Thus, in this example, if Budget Equation 1 is the only constraint, the set of efficient portfolios is the "ray" that starts at c and moves in a straight line through a and beyond.

As one moves on the line $\ell\ell'$ in the direction of a and beyond, at some point the line $\ell\ell'$ leaves the triangle. In the present example, this is the point labeled "b" in Figure 1, with

$X_1 = 0.58,$

$X_2 = 0.00,$

and

$X_3 = 0.42.$

Portfolio b still satisfies the constraints (Budget Equation 1 and Nonnegativity Requirement 2), but points beyond b on the line $\ell\ell'$ no longer satisfy Nonnegativity Requirement 2 because they violate the requirement that $X_2 \geq 0$. Beyond point b, therefore, the efficient set when Budget Equation 1 *and* Nonnegativity Requirement 2 are required departs from the efficient set when Budget Equation 1 only is required.

At point b, investment in Security 2 is zero ($X_2 = 0$). For efficient portfolios with higher expected return, the efficient set moves along the horizontal edge of the triangle, from b to (0,0), where an undiversified portfolio is invested only in Security 3 ($X_3 = 1$), the security with the highest expected return in the example.

We will see that, quite generally, a set of mean–variance efficient portfolios is "piecewise linear"; that is, it is made up of one or more straight-line segments that meet at points called "corner portfolios." When Equation 1 is the only constraint, the efficient set contains only one corner portfolio—namely, point c in Figure 1—and only one line "segment"—namely, the segment that starts at c and moves without end in the direction of increasing E_p. When nonnegativity constraints are imposed, the set of efficient portfolios typically has more than one segment and more than one corner portfolio. In Figure 1, this set of efficient portfolios consists of two line segments connecting three corner portfolios—c, b, and (0,0).

The Two-Fund Separation Theorem. The fact that two points determine a line is known in financial theory as the "two-fund separation theorem." In particular, all the portfolios on $\ell\ell'$ in Figure 1 can be obtained by (positive or negative) investments in portfolios a and c subject only to the constraint

$$X_a + X_c = 1, \tag{7}$$

where X_a and X_c are the "fractions" of the portfolio allocated to, respectively, subportfolios a and c. Note that Equation 7 permits the investor to short one portfolio and use the proceeds to invest more than 100 percent in the other portfolio. If both X_a and X_c are positive, then the resulting portfolio lies within the interval connecting a and c in Figure 1. If X_c is negative, then $X_a > 1$ and the resulting portfolio lies outside the interval, beyond a. Similarly, if $X_a < 0$ and $X_c > 1$, the portfolio lies outside the interval beyond c.

What is true in particular on $\ell\ell'$ is true in general for any two distinct points on any line in portfolio space. All points on the line can be represented by investments X_a and X_c in two distinct subportfolios on the line, where X_a and X_c satisfy Equation 7. I will use this relationship between points and lines several times.

The Market Portfolio. Consider a market in which investors must satisfy Budget Equation 1 and Nonnegativity Requirement 2. I show in the next section and in Appendix A that—in this case—beliefs about means, variances, and covariances that imply the efficient set in Figure 1 are consistent with market equilibrium.

Assume there are two types of investors in this market: cautious investors who select the portfolio at d = (0.40, 0.37) in Figure 1 and aggressive investors who select the portfolio at e = (0.20, 0.00). Similar conclusions would be reached if we specified two other portfolios as long as one of the portfolios were on one of the segments and the other portfolio were on the other segment of the efficient set. Similar conclusions would also be reached if there were more than two types of investors as long as some were on one segment and some on the other.

According to the two-fund separation theorem, the market portfolio lies on the straight line connecting d and e [for example, at M = (0.30, 0.19)]. The market is efficient, in that each participant holds an efficient portfolio, but note that the *market portfolio*, M, is not an efficient portfolio. It is not on either segment of the efficient set when Budget Equation 1 and Nonnegativity Requirement 2 are the constraints (nor is it, incidentally, on the ray that is the efficient set when Budget Equation 1 only is the constraint).

A Simple Market. The preceding shows that if investors selected portfolios subject to the constraints of Budget Equation 1 and Nonnegativity Requirement 2, all held the beliefs in Table 1, and some preferred portfolios on one segment of the efficient set and others preferred a portfolio on the other, then the market portfolio would not be a mean–variance efficient portfolio. This section shows that means, variances, and covariances that imply Figure 1 are consistent with economic equilibrium when shorting and borrowing are unavailable.

Imagine an economy in which the inhabitants live on coconuts and the produce of their own gardens. The economy has three enterprises, namely, three coconut farms. Once a year, a market convenes to trade the shares of the three coconut farms. Each year, the resulting prices of shares turn out to be the same as those of preceding years because the number of people with given endowments and risk aversion is the same each year (perhaps because of overlapping generations rather than immortal participants). Thus, the only source of uncertainty of return is the dividend each stock pays during the year—which is the stock's pro rata share of the farm's production.

It is shown in Appendix A that means, variances, and covariances of coconut production exist that imply the efficient set in Figure 1—or any other three-security efficient set that we cite. If we insist that coconut production be nonnegative, it may be necessary to add a constant to all expected returns (the same constant to each). Doing so will increase the expected returns of each portfolio but not change the set of efficient portfolios. It is then possible to find a probability distribution of coconut production, with production always nonnegative, for the given (slightly modified) means, variances, and covariances and, therefore, for the given set of efficient portfolios.

With such a probability distribution of returns, the market is rational, in the sense that each participant knows the true probability distribution of returns and each seeks and achieves mean–variance efficiency. Nevertheless, in contrast to the usual CAPM conclusion, the market portfolio is not an efficient portfolio. It follows that there is no representative investor, because no investor wants to hold the market portfolio. Also, as we will see in a subsequent section, expected returns are not linearly related to betas.

Arbitrage. Suppose that most investors are subject to Nonnegativity Requirement 2 but that one investor can short, in the CAPM sense—that is, is subject only to Budget Equation 1. (Perhaps the CAPM investor has surreptitious access to a vault containing stock certificates that he or she can "borrow" temporarily without posting collateral.) Would this CAPM investor arbitrage away the inefficiency in the market portfolio?

If there were a Portfolio P on $\ell\ell'$ that beat Market Portfolio M with certainty, then the CAPM investor could short any amount of M, use the proceeds to buy P, and make an arbitrarily large gain with certainty. But P does not beat M with certainty; it simply offers a better probability distribution. In fact, the investor with Equation 1 as the only constraint is better off picking a point on $\ell\ell'$ and ignoring M. **Figure 2** illustrates this idea. If P is any point *on* the line $\ell\ell'$ and M is any point *off* the line $\ell\ell'$, then according to the two-fund separation theorem, the portfolio produced by shorting M and using the proceeds (plus the original "$1") to buy P lies on the straight line connecting M and P. Specifically, it lies on the far side from M, beyond P, such as Q in Figure 2. But Portfolio Q is not efficient for the investor with Equation 1 as the only constraint. Some Portfolio R on $\ell\ell'$ (not shown in Figure 2) supplies a higher mean and lower variance.

Figure 2. Effect of Trying to Arbitrage an Inefficient Market Portfolio

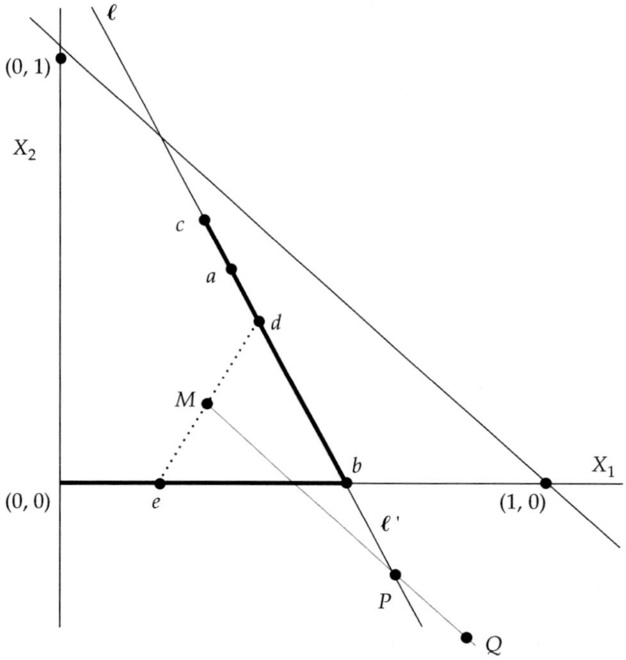

Now that we have seen that an investor subject only to Equation 1 will choose a portfolio from $\ell\ell'$ without regard to the market portfolio, let us consider market equilibrium when some investors are subject to Equation 1 only and some to Equation 1 and Nonnegativity Requirement 2. Suppose that, as in Figure 1, the average holdings (weighted by investor wealth) of investors subject to Budget Equation 1 and Nonnegativity Requirement 2 is the point *M*. It would be the market portfolio if these were the only investors. Suppose further that the wealth-weighted average of the one or more investors subject only to Equation 1 is point *P* in **Figure 3**. As in Figure 2, *P* must lie on $\ell\ell'$, whereas *M* typically lies off $\ell\ell'$. When both types of investors are present, the market portfolio lies on the straight line between the two averages, *M* and *P*, such as point M^a in Figure 3. The position of M^a depends on the relative wealth of the two types of investors, but in any case, it is off $\ell\ell'$; therefore, it is not efficient for investors subject to Equation 1 only.

Whether it is efficient for investors subject to both Budget Equation 1 and Nonnegativity Requirement 2 is a more complicated story. The portfolios M^a, M^b, and M^c lie on the straight line connecting *P* and *M*. Portfolio M^c cannot be a market equilibrium because it implies a negative total demand for Security 2. If M^b is the market portfolio, then the market portfolio is efficient for investors with Budget Equation 1 and Nonnegativity Requirement 2 as constraints but there is zero net demand for shares of Security 2. For an equilibrium with positive net demand for all three securities, the market must be within the constraint triangle, as M^a is in Figure 3. But such a combination of *M* and *P* is inefficient for investors subject to Budget Equation 1 and Nonnegativity Requirement 2, as well as for those subject only to Budget Equation 1.

Figure 3. Market Portfolios with and without Nonnegativity Constraints

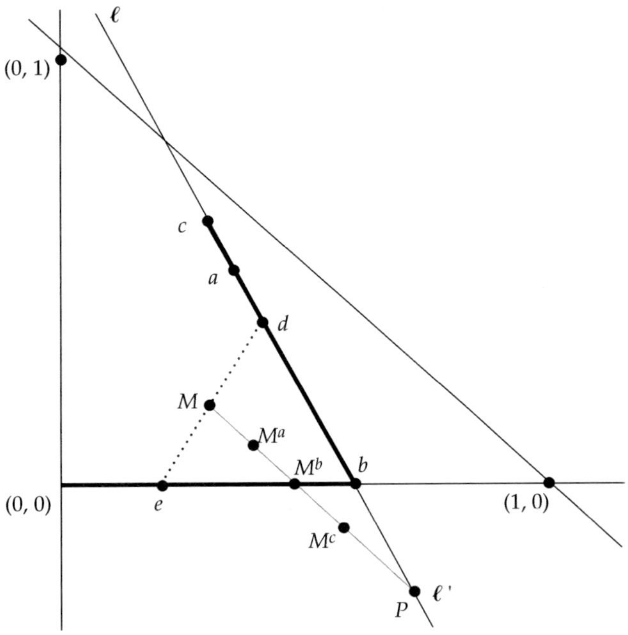

Expected Returns and Betas. If Assumptions 1–4 or 1–4′ are true, then Conclusion 2 follows: Expected returns are linearly related to the betas of each security. That is, for some choice of numbers a and b, the following three equations hold:

$$E_1 = a + b\beta_1, \tag{8a}$$

$$E_2 = a + b\beta_2, \tag{8b}$$

and

$$E_3 = a + b\beta_3, \tag{8c}$$

where β_i is the coefficient of regression of the return on the ith security against the return on the market. But these equations do not necessarily hold if A1–A3 are true but neither A4 nor A4′ is true.

In particular, C2 will typically not be true if investors satisfy A1–A3 but are subject to Equation 1 and Nonnegativity Requirement 2 as constraints. I will illustrate this statement in terms of the three-security example in Figure 3.

The first column of **Table 2** shows the fraction P_i of security i in Portfolio P on the $\ell\ell'$ line in Figure 3. The second column states the covariance between each security and P. Given our current assumption that the returns on the three securities are uncorrelated, the covariance between security i and Portfolio P depends only on how much of the security is in the portfolio, and it is given by the formula

$$\text{cov}(R_i,P) = P_iV_i, \text{ for } i = 1, 2, 3. \tag{9}$$

The beta of any security return regressed against any Portfolio P is defined to be

$$\beta_{i,P} = \frac{\text{cov}_{i,P}}{\text{var}(P)}. \tag{10}$$

These betas are listed in the last column of Table 2.

Table 2. Three Risky Securities in Portfolio *P* of Figure 3

Security	Percent in P	$\text{cov}_{i,P} = P_i V_i$	$\beta_{i,P}$
1	0.70%	0.0227	0.52
2	–0.25	–0.0036	–0.08
3	0.55	0.0495	1.12

Note: $\text{var}(P) = 0.0440$; $\beta_{i,P} = \text{cov}_{i,P}/\text{var}(P)$.

Similarly, **Table 3** shows the fraction held in Market Portfolio M, the covariance between each security and Portfolio M, and the beta of each security return regressed against the return on M, where M in Figure 3 is also the market portfolio in Figure 1.

In **Figure 4**, the points labeled 1 vs. P, 2 vs. P, and 3 vs. P show expected return on the vertical axis against $\beta_{i,P}$ plotted on the horizontal axis. The points labeled 1 vs. M, 2 vs. M, and 3 vs. M show the same expected returns plotted against $\beta_{i,M}$. The three observations for each case are connected by lines. We see that the three points that represent expected returns and betas-versus-P lie on a single straight line whereas the three points representing expected returns and betas-versus-M do not lie on a straight line. The implication is that there is a linear relationship between expected returns and betas-versus-P but no such relationship between expected returns and betas-versus-M. In other words, for some choice of a and b, Equation 8 holds if the betas in Equation 8 are from regressions against P but no such a and b choice exists when the betas are from regressions against M. More generally, if Market Portfolio M is any point on $\ell\ell'$, then a linear relationship exists between expected return and beta. In contrast, if M is any point off $\ell\ell'$, there is no such relationship (see Roll 1977; Markowitz 1987; Markowitz and Todd).

Limited Borrowing. In this section, I introduce a risk-free asset into the discussion. The Sharpe–Lintner CAPM assumes A1–A4 including unlimited borrowing at the risk-free rate. These assumptions imply that the market portfolio is a mean–variance efficient portfolio and that expected returns are linearly related to betas against the market portfolio. In this section, I illustrate that this conclusion no longer follows if borrowing is either not permitted or permitted but limited.

To illustrate this idea, the example in Table 1 is modified so that Security 3 now has 0 variance and a (risk-free) return of $r_0 = 3$ percent, as shown in **Table 4**. We continue to assume the budget constraint (Equation 1) and

$$X_1 \geq 0 \text{ and } X_2 \geq 0. \tag{11a}$$

$X_3 > 0$ represents lending at the risk-free rate; $X_3 < 0$ represents borrowing at the same rate. Prohibited borrowing would be represented by the constraint

$$X_3 \geq 0. \tag{11b}$$

Table 3. Three Risky Securities in Market Portfolio *M* of Figure 3

Security	Percent in M	$\text{cov}_{i,M} = M_i V_i$	$\beta_{i,M}$
1	0.30%	0.0097	0.36
2	0.19	0.0027	0.10
3	0.51	0.0459	1.71

Note: $\text{var}(M) = 0.0268$; $\beta_{i,M} = \text{cov}_{i,M}/\text{var}(M)$.

Figure 4. Relationship between Expected Returns and Betas versus an Efficient and an Inefficient Market Portfolio

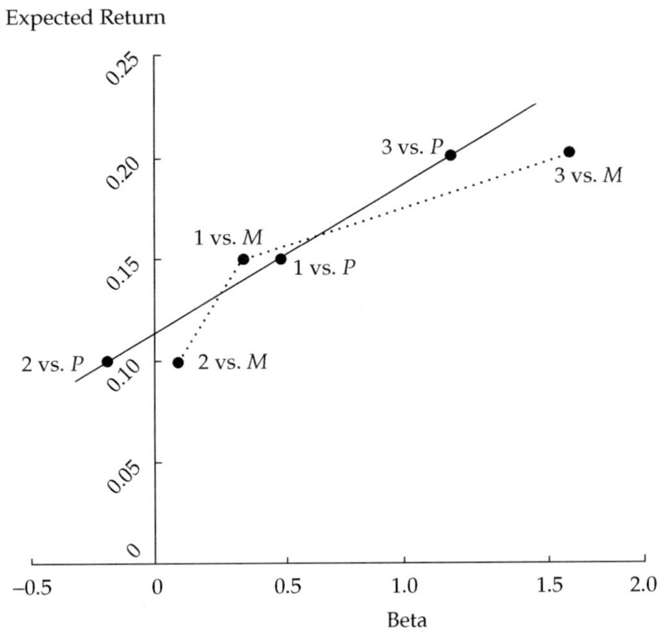

Borrowing limited to, for example, the equity in the account would be represented by

$$X_3 \geq -1.0. \quad (11c)$$

Unlimited borrowing would be represented by the constraints of Budget Equation 1 and Nonnegativity Requirement 11a, with no constraint on X_3.

In **Figure 5**, as in Figure 1, the horizontal axis represents X_1, the fraction of the portfolio invested in Security 1; the vertical axis represents X_2, the fraction invested in Security 2. As before, X_3 is given implicitly by Equation 3. If borrowing is forbidden, then the set of feasible portfolios is, as before, on and in the triangle with vertices (0,0), (1,0), and (0,1). If no more than 100 percent borrowing is permitted, the set of feasible portfolios is the points on and in the triangle whose vertices are (0,0), (2,0), and (0,2). If unlimited borrowing is permitted, the set of feasible portfolios is the entire positive quadrant.

Table 4. Expected Returns and Standard Deviations of Three Securities Including Cash

Security	Expected Return	Standard Deviation
1	0.15%	0.18%
2	0.10	0.12
3	0.03	0.00

Figure 5. Market Portfolio when Borrowing Permitted but Limited

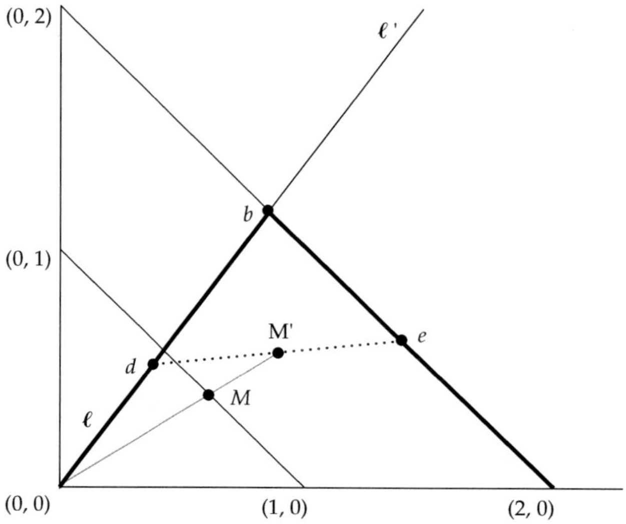

In our example assuming uncorrelated returns, when borrowing is unconstrained, the set of efficient portfolios is the set of portfolios that satisfies

$$X_1 = \frac{h(E_1 - r_0)}{V_1} \tag{12a}$$

and

$$X_2 = \frac{h(E_2 - r_0)}{V_2} \tag{12b}$$

for any zero or positive choice of h. This line is the ray that starts at the origin (0,0)—the all-cash portfolio—and proceeds into the positive quadrant along line $\ell\ell'$ in Figure 5 passing through the point (0.43, 0.57) for the example in Table 4. When borrowing is not limited, the efficient set proceeds along $\ell\ell'$ without bounds. If investors cannot borrow more than 100 percent of equity, then the efficient set cannot go beyond the line connecting (2,0) and (0,2); that is, it cannot go beyond point b = (0.86, 1.14). From that point, under Nonnegativity Requirement 11c, the efficient set moves along the line connecting (0,2) and (2,0) until it reaches the point (2,0), representing the portfolio that is 200 percent invested in the highest-yielding security, namely, Security 1 in the present example.

Suppose some investors choose portfolio d = (0.39, 0.51) on one segment in Figure 5 and all others choose portfolio e = (1.40, 0.60) on the other segment. Then, "the market"—including cash or borrowing—is a point between them, such as M'. Portfolio M is M' "normalized" so that the "market portfolio" adds up to 100 percent. Neither M nor M' is an efficient portfolio. Nor is there a linear relationship between expected returns and betas regressed against either M or M'. Such a relationship exists only if M is on $\ell\ell'$. The fact that the market is inefficient implies that there is no representative investor. No rational investor holds either M or M'.

Generalizations

Mean–variance efficient sets are computed in practice for models ranging in size from toy problems with two, three, or four assets to small problems with a dozen or so asset classes to large problems containing thousands of securities. To calculate an efficient frontier, the "critical line algorithm" (CLA) accepts as inputs any vector of expected return estimates, any matrix of covariance estimates (even a singular covariance matrix), and any linear equality or inequality constraints on the choice of portfolio (such as upper bounds on individual security holdings, sums of security holdings, or weighted sums of security holdings). From these inputs, the CLA produces a piecewise linear set of efficient portfolios. This set of portfolios "looks like" the ones in Figures 1–5, except that now the sets are difficult to draw because a portfolio in an analysis with 1,000 securities requires approximately a 1,000-dimensional space to be plotted. (When portfolio choice is subject to a budget constraint, a 999-dimensional space is sufficient.) Although we cannot plot points on a 999-dimensional blackboard, the basic mathematical properties of points, lines, and efficient sets in 999-dimensional space are the same as those in 2-dimensional space. The diagrams in Figures 1–5, which illustrate these properties, can help our intuition as to the nature of the properties in higher-dimensional spaces.

One property of points and lines that is the same in 999-dimensional space as it is in 2-dimensional space is that two points determine a line. In particular, all portfolios that lie on a straight line in an any-dimensional space may be obtained by investing amounts X_a and X_c in Portfolios P_a and P_c on the line. P_a and P_c may be any two fixed, *different* portfolios on the line. As in the three-security case, X_a and X_c are subject to constraining Equation 7 and either may be negative. If X_a is negative, then $X_c > 1.0$ and Point (Portfolio) P obtained by allocating X_a to P_a and X_c to P_c lies outside the interval connecting P_a and P_c, beyond P_c. The other cases—with $X_c < 0$ or with $X_a \geq 0$ and $X_c \geq 0$—are as described in the discussion of the two-fund separation theorem for the three-security case.

Suppose that there are n securities (for $n = 3$ or 30 or 3,000), that not all expected returns are the same, and that the n securities have a nonsingular covariance matrix. If the only constraint on the choice of portfolio is

$$\sum_{i=1}^{n} X_i = 1, \tag{13}$$

then the portfolios that minimize portfolio variance V_P for various values of portfolio expected return E_P lie on a single straight line $\ell\ell'$ in $(n - 1)$-dimensional portfolio space. Expected return increases as one moves in one direction on this line, decreases in the other direction. The set of efficient portfolios in this case is the ray that starts at the V_P-minimizing portfolio and moves on $\ell\ell'$ in the direction of increasing E_P. Repeated use of the two-fund separation theorem shows that if all investors hold portfolios somewhere on this ray, the market portfolio will also be on this ray and, therefore, will also be efficient. Thus, the efficiency of the market portfolio when $n = 3$ and Equation 1 is the only constraint generalizes to any n with Equation 13 as the only constraint.

Next, consider an investor subject to a no-shorting constraint,

$$X_i \geq 0, i = 1, \ldots, n, \tag{14}$$

as well as a budget constraint (Equation 13). For simplicity, assume that one security has the greatest expected return (albeit, perhaps, just slightly more than the second-greatest expected return). When Budget Equation 13 *and* Nonnegativity Requirement 14 are the constraints, and the only constraints, on portfolio choice, the critical line algorithm begins with the portfolio with highest expected return, namely, the portfolio that is 100 percent invested in the security with highest expected return. The CLA traces out the set of efficient portfolios from top to bottom (i.e., from this portfolio with maximum expected return down to the portfolio with minimum variance). The computation proceeds in a series of iterations. Each iteration computes one piece (one linear segment) of the piecewise linear efficient set. Each successive segment has either one more or one less security than the preceding segment. If the analysis includes a risk-free asset (or, equivalently, risk-free lending), the last segment to be computed (the one with the lowest portfolio mean and variance) is the one and only segment that contains the risk-free asset (Tobin 1958).

This characterization of efficient sets remains true if limited borrowing is allowed, as illustrated in Figure 5. It also remains true when short selling is permitted but is subject to a Reg T or similar constraint (see Jacobs, Levy, and Markowitz, forthcoming). In this case, if no other constraints are included (such as upper bounds on holdings), then short sales subject to Reg T can be modeled by an analysis with $2n + 3$ variables. The first n variables represent long positions; the second n variables represent short positions; and the final three variables represent, respectively, lending, borrowing, and slack in the Reg T constraint. These variables are subject to the following constraints:

$$\sum_{i=1}^{n} X_i + X_{2n+1} - X_{2n+2} = 1, \tag{15a}$$

$$\sum_{i=1}^{2n} X_i + X_{2n+3} = 2, \tag{15b}$$

and

$$X_i \geq 0, \text{ with } i = 1, \ldots, 2n + 3. \tag{15c}$$

The portfolio with maximum expected return typically contains two variables at positive levels (perhaps a short or long position plus borrowing). As in the case without short positions, the CLA traces out the efficient frontier in a series of iterations—each iteration producing one piece of the piecewise linear efficient set, each piece having one more or (occasionally) one less nonzero variable than did the preceding piece.

A great variety of mean–variance efficient sets are computed in practice. For example, some are computed for asset classes; some of these results are then implemented by index funds. Other efficient set analyses are performed at the individual-security level. Among the latter, analyses differ as to which securities constitute "the universe" of securities from which the portfolio optimizer is to select for its portfolios. Some permit short positions; some do not.

For comparability with the classic CAPM, let us assume here that all investors perform their mean–variance analyses in terms of individual securities rather than asset classes, all use the same universe of "all marketable securities," and either all include short sales (subject to a Reg T–like constraint) or all exclude short sales.

Even so, there properly should be a variety of portfolio analyses generating a variety of frontiers. Because different institutions have different liability structures, they properly have different efficient sets of marketable securities. For example, an insurance company or pension fund, with liabilities determined outside the portfolio analysis, should choose portfolios that are efficient in terms of the mean and variance of assets minus liabilities. When different investors properly have different efficient sets, the question of whether the market portfolio is a mean–variance efficient portfolio raises the question: efficient for whom?

For comparability with the CAPM, let us assume that all investors may properly ignore their particular liability structure in computing the efficient frontier; each uses the same mean, variance, and covariance estimates for the same universe of marketable securities; and each is subject to the same constraints. In other words, we assume that they all generate and select portfolios from the same mean–variance efficient frontier.

In tracing out this frontier, the CLA starts at the high end with an undiversified portfolio. It proceeds in a sequence of iterations that generate "lower" segments of the piecewise linear efficient frontier (i.e., segments with lower portfolio mean and lower portfolio variance). Each successive segment adds or deletes one security (or possibly a short position) on the list of active securities. Thus, if the universe consists of, say, 10,000 securities, then if all securities are to be demanded by someone, this universal efficient frontier must contain at least 10,000 segments. If investors have sufficiently diverse risk tolerances, they will choose portfolios on different segments. Some will prefer portfolios on one or another of the typically less diversified high-risk/high-return segments. Others will select portfolios on one or another of the typically more diversified lower-risk segments. The market is an average, weighted by investor wealth, of portfolios selected from these diverse segments. Although it is mathematically possible for this average to accidentally fall on the efficient frontier, such an outcome is extremely unlikely.

Thus, in this world that is like the CAPM but has realistic constraints, the market portfolio is typically not an efficient portfolio. Therefore, there is no representative investor and expected return is not a linear function of regressions of security returns against the market.

So What?

This section presents some implications of the preceding analysis.

So What #1. A frequent explanation of why observed expected returns do not appear to be linearly related to betas is that the measures of market return used in the tests do not measure the true, universal market portfolio that appears in the CAPM. The conclusion is that to test the CAPM, we need to measure returns on a cap-weighted world portfolio. The preceding discussion implies, however, that before spending vast resources on ever finer approximations to returns on this cap-weighted universal portfolio, we should note that CAPM Conclusion 2 (that expected returns are linearly related to betas) is not likely to be true if real-world constraints are substituted for Assumption 4 or Assumption 4′.

So What #2. Traditionally, some investments were thought of as businessmen's risks while others were thought appropriate for widows and orphans. The CAPM, assuming A1–A4, concludes that one and only one portfolio is efficient for all investors. The only difference should be the amount of cash or borrowing with which the portfolio is combined. In contrast, when borrowing is limited and short sales are prohibited or subject to real-world constraints, the composition of the portfolio of risky securities changes radically from one end to the other of the efficient frontier. At the high end, it contains few securities, usually with a predominance of those with high expected return. At the low end, it tends to be more diversified, with a more-than-proportional presence of the less volatile securities. In other words, the high end of the frontier will indeed tend to be dominated by businessman-risk securities, whereas the low end, although perhaps spiced up and diversified with some more-volatile securities, will typically have more than its proportionate share of widow-and-orphan securities.

So What #3. The linear relationship between expected returns and betas (against the market portfolio return) that is implied by the CAPM is the basis for a standard "risk-adjustment" calculation. This calculation is used, for example, to determine which of two projects that a company might pursue would best enhance its stock market value or which of two securities, groups of securities, or investment strategies has performed best. Because the existence of a linear relationship between expected returns and betas is questionable, the reliability of its use in risk adjustment must be questioned.

It might seem at first that the use of the CAPM risk-adjustment formula is indispensable for decisions like those I just described because there is no alternative. This is not the case. In particular, concerning the desirability of an asset class with a particular return pattern, a frequent practice now is to run an efficient frontier with and without the asset class. (This practice is subject to the essential caveat that future returns are not necessarily like those of the past, but the CAPM adjustment is subject to this same caveat.) The comparison of frontiers with and without the asset class avoids Assumptions 4 and 4′ and Conclusion 2.

Concerning the choice between two projects, I previously considered their effect on a company's stock price under the assumption that the stock appears in some but not all segments of investors' efficient frontiers (Markowitz 1990). The resulting computation is similar to that of the CAPM but involves only investors who own the company's stock. In other words, the calculation takes into account the company's clientele. For estimating the effects of investment policy in a dynamic world with mean–variance investors holding different beliefs and real-world constraints, Jacobs et al. (2004) proposed detailed, asynchronous simulation. Potentially, the simulated market could also include investors other than those with mean–variance objectives.[3] In sum, the position that "there is no alternative" to the CAPM for risk-adjustment calculations was never completely true and is certainly not true now.

So What #4. The implications of the CAPM are taught to MBA students and CFA charterholders. The lack of realism in A4 and A4′ is rarely pointed out, and the consequences of replacing these assumptions with more realistic assumptions are rarely (if ever) discussed. Worse, often the distinction between the CAPM and mean–variance analysis is confused. Not only do some say or suggest that if investors use mean–variance analysis, C1 and C2 will follow; some say or suggest that if an investor uses mean–variance analysis, C2 should be assumed to hold among inputs.

Despite its drawbacks as illustrated here, the CAPM should be taught. It is like studying the motion of objects on Earth under the assumption that the Earth has no air. The calculations and results are much simpler if this assumption is made. But at some point, the obvious fact that, on Earth, cannonballs and feathers do not fall at the same rate should be noted and explained to some extent. Similarly, at some point, the finance student should be shown the effect of replacing A4 or A4′ with more realistic constraints and the "so what" should be explained.

About 30 years ago, Fama (1976), in Chapter 8, explained the main points of the present article: that A4 or A4′ are not realistic and that if more realistic assumptions are substituted, C1 and C2 no longer follow. The two principal differences between Fama's presentation then and the current presentation are (1) my use of certain ("portfolio space") diagrams to illustrate the source and possible extent of the market portfolio inefficiency and (2) our respective conclusions concerning "so what." Fama's conclusion at the time was that what one could say about models with more realistic versions of A4 or A4′ was that they "fall substantially short of interesting and testable propositions about the nature of capital market equilibrium. For such propositions, we have to rely on" the CAPM (p. 305). My own conclusion is that it is time to move on.

Conclusion

The CAPM is a thing of beauty. Thanks to one or another counterfactual assumption, it achieves clean and simple conclusions. Sharpe did not claim that investors can, in fact, borrow all they want at the risk-free rate. Rather, he argued:

> In order to derive conditions for equilibrium in the capital market we invoke two assumptions. First, we assume a common pure rate of interest, with all investors able to borrow [without limit] or lend funds on equal terms. Second, we assume homogeneity of investor expectations. Needless to say, these are highly restrictive and undoubtedly unrealistic assumptions. However, since the proper test of a theory is not the realism of its assumptions but the acceptability of its implications, and since these assumptions imply equilibrium conditions which form a major part of classical financial doctrine, it is far from clear that this formulation should be rejected—especially in view of the dearth of alternative models leading to similar results. (pp. 433–434)

Now, 40 years later, in the face of the empirical problems with the implications of the model, we should be cognizant of the consequences of varying its convenient but unrealistic assumptions. In particular, we should be cognizant of what more realistic assumptions concerning investment constraints imply about how we should invest, value assets, and adjust for risk.

Appendix A. Finding a Probability Distribution for a Given Efficient Set

To construct a probability distribution of coconut production whose means, variances, and covariances imply a specific three-security efficient set, you may proceed as follows. The simplest distribution to construct with the requisite efficient set is a finite population with S equally likely sample points, $s = 1, \ldots, S$, with r_i^s as the return on security i if sample point s occurs. The procedure is as follows:

First, use the procedure described in Chapter 11 of Markowitz (1987) or Markowitz and Todd to produce an expected return vector, $\boldsymbol{\mu}$, and a covariance matrix, $\mathbf{C}$, that gives rise to the specified efficient set. (There are always many $\boldsymbol{\mu}$'s and $\mathbf{C}$'s that will serve. Start with any.) This step is not necessary if a $\boldsymbol{\mu}$ and a $\mathbf{C}$ are already given, as in the example in the text.

Second, by using a program that finds the eigenvalues and eigenroots of $\mathbf{C}$, you can find a matrix $\mathbf{B}$ such that $\mathbf{C} = \mathbf{B}'\mathbf{B}$.[4]

Third, let $\mathbf{R}^a$ be a matrix containing a finite sample space for three random variables with 0 mean and covariance matrix $\mathbf{I}$. For example,

$$\mathbf{R}^a = \frac{\sqrt{2}}{4}\begin{pmatrix} 1 & 1 & 1 & 1 & -1 & -1 & -1 & -1 \\ 1 & 1 & -1 & -1 & 1 & 1 & -1 & -1 \\ 1 & -1 & 1 & -1 & 1 & -1 & 1 & -1 \end{pmatrix}$$

$$= r^a_{i,j},$$

where $r^a_{i,j}$ is the value of the ith random variable in state (sample point) j.

Then, $\mathbf{R}^b = \mathbf{BR}^a$ is the matrix of a sample space of three random variables with 0 mean and covariance matrix $\mathbf{C}$. And $\mathbf{R}^c = (r^b_{i,j} + \mu_i)$ has covariance $\mathbf{C}$ and expected return μ. If $\mathbf{R}^c$ has any negative entries and if k is the magnitude of the largest in magnitude negative $r^c_{i,j}$, then $\mathbf{R}^d = (r^c_{i,j} + k)$ is the matrix of a sample space of hypothetical coconut production with nonnegative output and with the specified efficient set.

Notes

1. Some conclusions remain unchanged if we assume heterogeneous rather than homogeneous beliefs; other conclusions apply to average predictions rather than unique predictions.
2. A3 asserts that the market is strong-form efficient in the Fama (1970) taxonomy. Thus, what I will show is that, even if the market is strong-form efficient, the market portfolio is not necessarily a mean–variance efficient portfolio.
3. Simulation analysis as presented by Jacobs et al. (2004) would hardly have been feasible in 1964 when Sharpe presented the CAPM. Computer and software development since that time makes such simulation quite manageable.
4. For example, see Franklin (2000). The formula is a corollary of Section 4.7, Theorem 3. Also, see Section 7.3, Equation 21 for an alternative factorization of **C**.

References

Fama, Eugene F. 1970. "Efficient Capital Markets: A Review of Theory and Empirical Work." *Journal of Finance*, vol. 25, no. 2 (May):383–417.

———. 1976. *Foundations of Finance: Portfolio Decisions and Securities Prices.* New York: Basic Books.

Franklin, Joel N. 2000. *Matrix Theory*. Mineola, NY: Dover Publications.

Jacobs, Bruce I., Kenneth N. Levy, and Harry M. Markowitz. 2004. "Financial Market Simulation." *Journal of Portfolio Management* (30th Anniversary):142–152.

———. Forthcoming. "Portfolio Optimization with Factors, Scenarios, and Realistic Short Positions." *Operations Research*.

Lintner, John. 1965. "The Valuation of Risk Assets and the Selection of Risky Investments in Stock Portfolios and Capital Budgets." *Review of Economics and Statistics*, vol. 47, no. 1 (February):13–37.

Markowitz, Harry M. 1987. *Mean–Variance Analysis in Portfolio Choice and Capital Markets.* Oxford, U.K.: Basil Blackwell.

———. 1990. "Risk Adjustment." *Journal of Accounting, Auditing and Finance*, vol. 5 (Winter/Spring):213–225.

Markowitz, Harry M., and Peter Todd. 2000. *Mean–Variance Analysis in Portfolio Choice and Capital Markets* (revised reissue with chapter by Peter Todd). New Hope, PA: Frank J. Fabozzi Associates.

Roll, Richard. 1977. "A Critique of the Asset Pricing Theory's Tests, Part I: On Past and Potential Testability of the Theory." *Journal of Financial Economics*, vol. 4, no. 2 (March):129–176.

Sharpe, William F. 1964. "Capital Asset Prices: A Theory of Market Equilibrium under Conditions of Risk." *Journal of Finance*, vol. 14, no. 3 (September):425–441.

Tobin, J. 1958. "Liquidity Preference as Behavior towards Risk." *Review of Economic Studies*, vol. 25, no. 2 (February):65–86.

The Investment Value of an Idea

Jack Treynor

The first step in appraising investment value is translating what we know today about an asset into implications for its future. And the way an idea evolves is fundamentally different from the way either a plant or a brand franchise evolves. The cash flow of each of the three "asset classes" has its own time pattern.

For example, every capital good—lift truck, engine lathe, backhoe, power loom—embodies a solution to a particular problem. From the date of its manufacture until it arrives at the scrap yard, a capital good embodies the solution—the same idea (or set of ideas). As soon as a better solution becomes available, manufacturers will stop making the old capital good. But the examples already in service will continue for many years, even after the solution they embody becomes the marginal solution—even after they cease to be scarce and, hence, to contribute to their user's investment value.

But what about the value of the *idea* embodied in the capital good? Does it belong to the user or the manufacturer? Consider what happens when the buyer drives a new car—a capital good—away from the dealer. If its secondhand value exceeds what he paid for it, then at least the part of the value of the innovations embodied in the car belongs to the new owner. But if, as folklore suggests, the price goes down, then the new owner has paid at least full value for those innovations. Does the same thing happen to new tankships? New airliners? If so, then the *ideas* from which a new model derives its value belong to the seller (i.e., the manufacturer).

Why Ideas Are Risky

The value of the idea to the manufacturer ends with the arrival of an idea that solves the same problem better, faster, or cheaper. More often than not, it will be spawned by a different technology, developed by a different company.[1] But the better idea does not actually "arrive" when the metaphorical bulb lights up in the inventor's head. The challenger does not displace the current champion until the challenger's development is complete.

The value of an idea lasts only until a better idea—completely developed—arrives. No one knows when that will occur, but we can calculate the probability that the challenger will arrive in a given year.

Jack Treynor is president and CEO of Treynor Capital Management, Inc., Palos Verdes Estates, California.

Consider fusion. Like fission, it produces no carbon dioxide and, hence, no global warming. But unlike fission, it is allegedly safe (no Three Mile Islands or Chernobyls) and clean (no radioactive waste to store under Yucca Mountain). Twenty years ago, scientists estimated that fusion was ten years away from completing its development. Today, scientists are still estimating that fusion is ten years away from completing its development. Until then, manufacture of fossil-fuel generating plants will continue. And the implications for global warming are dire. As they raise the standards of living for their vast populations, China and India are rapidly increasing energy consumption.

Ideas with potential investment value go through four stages:

1. *Research*. Does the idea have enough economic potential to warrant the investment to make it practical? If so, it enters Stage 2.
2. *Development*. Although George Stephenson's steam locomotive was patented in 1815, the Stockton and Darlington Railway in England did not begin operations until 1830. Although Rudolf Diesel's version of the internal combustion engine was invented in 1893, it did not begin to replace the steam locomotive until the late 1920s.
3. *Application*.
4. *Death*, which occurs suddenly when a better idea is fully developed. When manufacturers stopped making (and railroads stopped buying) steam locomotives, the value of Stephenson's idea ended.[2]

A sword of Damocles hangs over every valuable idea. The probability that the sword will fall in any given future year is, of course, an investment judgment. (Do ideas change faster in the fields of biotechnology and software than they do in certain gray-belt industries?) This article spells out ways in which the consensus judgment regarding the mortality rate enters into the market price of the idea—and into its systematic risk.

When Will the New Replace the Old?

Fusion, monoclonal antibodies, and fuel cells are ideas with huge economic promise. When will they be fully developed? Nobody knows. They represent a risk to current, fully developed technologies, but the risk they pose is actuarial.

We can express this ignorance with a number—a probability that development will be completed in a given year. Because the completion of the rival's development is the death knell for the established technology, the two events have the same probability. For the old technology, it is a mortality rate.

Consider the present value of the current technology's rent in Year 10: If the challenger's development is completed in Year 9, then that rent contributes nothing to the present value. But, of course, we do not now know when the challenger will arrive. So, we reduce the Year 9 value of Year 10's rent by the factor

$$1 - \gamma,$$

where γ is the mortality rate (the probability that the challenger completes commercial development in any given year). The Year 9 value will not contribute to the Year 8 value, however, if the challenger's development is completed in Year 8, and so on. Therefore, the *expected* value of the reigning champion one year hence is its *market* value—call it ν—discounted by the probability that the challenger *does not* complete development:

$$(1 - \gamma)\nu.$$

Table 1 demonstrates a useful approximation for small values of γ.

Let ρ be the market discount rate for such ideas. If the expected value of the champion one year hence can be approximated by

$$(1-\gamma)\nu \approx e^{-\gamma}\nu,$$

then its market value now is

$$e^{-\rho}(1-\gamma)\nu \approx e^{-(\rho+\gamma)}\nu.$$

If the economic rent enjoyed by the champion is f a year, its value now is

$$\begin{aligned}\nu &= f\int_0^\infty e^{-(\rho+\gamma)t}dt \\ &= \left.\frac{-fe^{-(\rho+\gamma)t}}{\rho+\gamma}\right|_0^\infty \\ &= \frac{-f}{\rho+\gamma}(0-1) \\ &= \frac{f}{\rho+\gamma},\end{aligned}$$

so the practical effect of adding the mortality rate to the market discount rate is to increase the rate at which future scarcity rents are discounted back to the present.

Consider the case in which the market discount rate is 10 percent and the mortality rate for the current champion is 10 percent. **Table 2** shows the present value of a dollar of future economic reward, discounted at 20 percent over the intervening years. As the reader can see, it hardly matters whether we impose an arbitrary cutoff at Year 32—or, for that matter, at Year 16. The chance that the current champion will survive every future challenge is slim indeed. But we allow for that consideration when we "discount" for both appropriate capital-market discount rate ρ and mortality rate γ.

Growth Companies

In their important 1961 paper, Merton Miller and Franco Modigliani argued that mere growth does not create any incremental value for investors unless the added assets are worth more than they cost. But Miller and Modigliani were probably thinking about conventional investment assets.

Table 1. Accuracy of Approximation for Small Values of γ

γ	$e^{-\gamma}$	$1-\gamma$
0.10	0.9048	0.90
0.15	0.8607	0.85
0.20	0.8187	0.80
0.25	0.7788	0.75
0.30	0.7408	0.70

Table 2. Value of $1.00 of Economic Reward (market discount rate = 10 percent, mortality rate = 10 percent, discount of 20 percent)

No. of Years Hence	Discount Factor
1	$0.8187
2	0.6703
4	0.4493
8	0.4493
16	0.0408
32	0.0017

Unless a challenger successfully completes its development in the interim, the expected value of the idea next year will be roughly the same as the value this year. So the investor's expected reward is simply this year's economic rent on the idea and the investor's rate of return is

$$\frac{f}{v} = \frac{\rho + \gamma}{f} f$$
$$= \rho + \gamma.$$

But this return is bigger than the return on conventional assets with the same market discount rate.

The explanation is simple: This return is the rate of return on the idea until it is successfully challenged. In hindsight, a company that derives its value from ideas that have survived previous challenges will appear to have a very exciting track record. Until its ideas are overtaken by better ideas, such a company will outperform normal companies. Are ideas the only legitimate source of the growth in "growth" companies?

Systematic Risk

Valuable ideas apparently contain an extra element of *specific* risk. But what about their *systematic* risk? Adding the mortality rate to the market discount rate increases the sensitivity of the discounted value to short-term prospects for the economy. To simplify the math, assume the following:

1. There are no rents from the idea in hard times.
2. Development of potential competitors continues.

So the idea's present value depends on how long hard times are expected to last. Under these circumstances, Panel A of **Table 3** shows the discount factors for a range of values for γ. Panel B provides the corresponding values of a benefit stream of $1.00 a year when it is subjected to discounts for both (1) an undelayed benefit stream subject to the indicated ρ and γ and (2) delaying the benefit stream the indicated number of years.

As the reader can see, the investment value of an idea can be very sensitive to the immediate prospects for prosperity. The short term is more important in valuing ideas than it is in valuing plant.

More generally, let t be the number of bad years the consensus expects. Then, for the present value of an economic rent of $1.00 a year, we have

$$v = \frac{e^{-(\rho + r)t}}{\rho + \gamma}$$

Table 3. Idea's Present Value in Hard Times of Various Duration
($\rho = 0.10$)

γ	1 Year	2 Years	4 Years	8 Years
A. Discount factors				
0.10	0.82	0.67	0.45	0.20
0.15	0.78	0.61	0.37	0.14
0.20	0.74	0.55	0.30	0.09
0.25	0.70	0.50	0.25	0.06
0.30	0.67	0.45	0.20	0.04
B. Discount factors: Benefit stream of $1.00 a year				
$0.10	$4.10	$3.35	$2.25	$1.00
0.15	3.12	2.44	1.48	0.56
0.20	2.47	1.83	1.00	0.30
0.25	2.00	1.43	0.71	0.17
0.30	1.68	1.13	0.50	0.10

and

$$\frac{dv}{dt} = -(\rho + \gamma)\,v,$$

and for the effect of a change in consensus t on the idea's rate of return,

$$\left(\frac{1}{v}\right)\left(\frac{dv}{dt}\right) = -(\rho + \gamma).$$

But expectations regarding a change in the market's estimate of t affect most asset values to some degree. And when unforeseen events change these expectations, the result is *systematic risk*.[3] So γ, which measures the idea's *specific* risk, also has a big impact on its systematic risk. Because a portfolio of ostensibly unrelated ideas will have a large element of systematic risk that cannot be diversified, lenders will want to be able to reach other assets.

To summarize:

- The risk of sudden death can be incorporated into estimates of investment value by simply adding the appropriate mortality rate to the market discount rate.
- Ideas for which the Damoclean sword has not yet fallen will reward investors with rates of return higher than the market rate. Shares of their corporate owners will behave like growth stocks.
- An idea will exhibit more systematic risk than conventional investment assets with the same value. Because it cannot be diversified away, this risk places special burdens on the owner's capacity for risk bearing.

Wealth Borrowers and Wealth Lenders

Obviously, one household's liability is another household's asset. Only slightly less obvious is that one household's ownership of government debt is some other hapless household's future tax liability. When the balance sheets of all the households in society are summed, the lendings and borrowings cancel, leaving only the real assets. It follows that the total wealth available to bear the risk in these assets is identically equal to their total value.

The function of wealth is to bear society's investment risks. The other contributors to a business enterprise—workers, suppliers, bankers, and so on—will not contribute until they are satisfied that the business's equity is big enough to insulate them from risks they are not paid to bear. If an asset has sufficiently small value in relation to its risk, society will require the bearer of its risk to have other sources of wealth—assets whose value is larger in relation to their risk.

The equity in a levered corporation is an indication of the value available to protect lenders from the risk in its assets. The high degree of leverage in real estate suggests that the value in buildings is large in relation to their risk. It frees up the remainder of the value to bear other risks. But most real estate is mortgaged, and most publicly owned corporations are levered. The implication is that some other asset must exist whose risk is larger in relation to its value. If corporate and real estate assets are lenders of risk-bearing wealth (i.e., wealth *lenders*), where are the wealth *borrowers*?

Entrepreneurial Risk

A study released in January 1967 titled "Technological Innovation: Its Environment and Management," often referred to by the short name "The Connor Report" (named for John Thomas Connor, who was U.S. Secretary of Commerce from January 1965 to January 1976), sought to identify the new ideas in the first half of the 20th century that had created the most jobs (Connor 1967). It found that "the most important inventions come from independent inventors"—that is, from somebody's garage or basement. "The Connor Report" listed 31 such inventions, including Xerography, the Polaroid camera, power steering, the automatic transmission, Kodachrome, the vacuum tube, air conditioning, rockets, streptomycin, penicillin, and the helicopter.

John Heaton and Deborah Lucas (2000) estimated the value of new ideas currently in development at approximately $10 trillion. This number may seem big in comparison with the value of stocks, but there are, of course, a lot of garages and basements—many attached to houses with mortgages. What is special about what Heaton and Lucas called "entrepreneurial risk" is the high ratio of risk to value. Ideas have a higher ratio of risk to value than conventional assets—plant and brand franchises—with the same market discount rate.

Households have assets with a lot of value in relation to their risk—value that is potentially available to lenders—as long as they do not incorporate. But without the limitation on liability conferred by incorporation, proprietors are cautious about their spending, preferring to develop an idea in the basement or the garage.

Realizing the economic potential of an idea may require manufacturing facilities, raw materials, work-in-progress and finished goods inventories, accounts receivable—in other words, a lot of relatively conventional, low risk-to-reward assets. When a venture has accumulated enough of the low risk-to-reward assets to reduce its overall risk-to-reward ratio sufficiently, it is at last ready for incorporation—which obviously has to precede its IPO.

Notes

1. Can the owner of the currently valuable technology invent its successor? Baldwin-Lima-Hamilton Corporation made great steam locomotives. How did they fare with diesels? Curtis-Wright Corporation's turbo-compound radials powered the fastest piston-engine airliner. How did Curtis-Wright fare with jet engines? How did IBM fare with operating system software? Bell Labs with printed circuits? Professor Lynn Stout of the UCLA Law School has pointed out a serious *agency problem* that works against the owner of today's solution providing tomorrow's solution: The human capital of the corporation's staff is invested in the old technology. To speed the arrival of the new technology may not be in their interest, even if it is in their employer's interest.
2. Steam continued in active service until 1960 in certain Class I railroads.
3. When the systematic risk increases, ρ increases—and we are off to the races.

References

Connor, John T. 1967. "Technological Innovation: Its Environment and Management." Washington, DC: U.S. Government Printing Office.

Heaton, John C., and Deborah Lucas. 2000. "Portfolio Choice and Asset Prices: The Importance of Entrepreneurial Risk." *Journal of Finance*, vol. 55, no. 3 (June):1163–98.

Miller, Merton H., and Franco Modigliani. 1961. "Dividend Policy, Growth, and the Valuation of Shares." *Journal of Business*, vol. 34, no. 4 (October):411–433.

Investing Success in Two Easy Lessons

Charles D. Ellis, CFA

Successful investing sounds easy—avoid harm and work for your long-term objectives—but learning the lesson may take too many years for the power of compounding to benefit us.

Successful investing should be easy. Obviously, it is not. But in my more than 40 years, mostly in the privileged position of trusted advisor to the leaders of major investment and securities firms, two investment lessons stand out for me as particularly valuable and easy to use. Anyone who "gets it" on these two easy lessons will do well. Like career "bookends," one lesson came early and one came late in over four decades of continuous learning about investing.

In Munich, Germany, while visiting my son Chad and his wife Trish last summer, we agreed to cheer for their friend who was running in a marathon. Their friend had run several marathons, so she had a realistic plan and knew that at about 11 o'clock, she would pass a particular church. So, we were stationed there, and right on schedule, she came by. We cheered lustily; she waved—and was quickly gone.

We went off to lunch at a *Wursthaus* and then took the tram out to Munich's Olympic Park. As we walked from the tram station to the stadium and the marathon's finish line, we passed a trio of cheerful Kenyans who had already completed the race—probably coming in 1st, 2nd, and 3rd—and were going home. Our friend wouldn't finish the race for nearly an hour.

The organizers of the Munich Marathon had arranged an attractive way to finish: Runners came into the stadium through a tunnel that was filled with vapor and then burst out into the sunlight as they entered the Olympic stadium, with only one short lap around the stadium left to go. The runners—nicely encouraged—loved it.

Sitting in the stadium with a few hundred other fans, we enjoyed watching runners—individually and in small groups—come through the portal entrance and into the stadium for the final lap to the finish line. The runners were all different in age, dress, and running style, but in one particular way, they were all the same: Runner after runner—on entering the stadium, seeing the crowd, and hearing the scattered but

Charles D. Ellis, CFA, is chairman of Investors Education, New York City.

friendly applause—reached high overhead with both arms in the traditional triumphal "Y" and held it for at least half a minute as, grinning in victory, they ran out the final lap.

At first, it seemed strange. Didn't they know the Kenyans had won long ago? As time went by—and we were there nearly two hours because our friend had caught a cramp and had to slow down—it might have seemed stranger and stranger to see later runners act like champions, heroes, and winners. Then it hit me: They *were* winners. They were *all* winners—because each runner had achieved her or his own realistic objective.

Some finished in *less* than three hours; some in *only* three hours; some in "only" three and a half hours. Others beat their prior best times. Some won simply by completing the whole marathon—some for their first time and others for their last time.

The powerful message: Each runner had achieved his or her own realistic goal, so each was a true winner and fully entitled to make the Big Y and run the victory lap.

If, as investors, we each thought and acted the same way—understanding our capacities and our limits—we could plan the race that would be right for us and, with the self-discipline of a long-distance runner, run our *own* race to achieve our *own* realistic objectives. In investing, the good news is clear: *Everyone can win.* Everyone can be a winner.

The secret to winning the Winner's Game in investing is simple: Plan your play and play your plan to win *your* game. And if you do not think and work that winning way in investing, you will, by default, be playing the Loser's Game of trying to "beat the market"—a game that almost every investor will eventually lose.

My other favorite investing insight came more than 40 years ago. A freshly minted MBA, I was in a training program on Wall Street (at Wertheim & Company). As part of our training, we met once a month for the hour before lunchtime with the heads of various departments—syndicate, block trading, research, municipal bonds, and so on—for an introductory explanation of each unit's work.

One day, we were happily surprised to learn that the senior partner had agreed to take a Thursday slot to discuss the larger picture. Joseph K. Klingenstein—known to his friends as "Joe" and to us as "JK" (except when he was or might be present, in which case he was *always* "Mr. Klingenstein")—wore pince-nez glasses and was patrician, dignified, and erect.

As Mr. Klingenstein spoke about the history of his firm and of Wall Street and its traditions, we listened quietly—but not, I fear, conscientiously. At 10 minutes before noon, Mr. Klingenstein had finished his talk and asked, "Do you young gentlemen have any questions?"

Silence.

The silence was broken by the brightest and certainly the most outspoken of our little group. "Yeah, Mr. Klingenstein, I've got a question for you. You're rich, Mr. Klingenstein. We all want to be rich too, Mr. Klingenstein. So, what can you tell us from all your experience, Mr. Klingenstein, about how to get rich like you, Mr. Klingenstein?"

Of course, you could have heard the proverbial pin drop—or a butterfly land on a marshmallow. We were mortified. Such a way to speak to such a very great man!

At first, Joseph K. Klingenstein appeared to be angry, perhaps *very* angry. But then, to our great and collective relief, it became clear that he was silent because he was thinking—thinking carefully about his many investment experiences. Finally, looking directly at his questioner, he said simply and clearly, "Don't lose."

After JK rose and left the room, we all went off to lunch, where we agreed, "If you ask a stupid question, you get a stupid answer."

As the years have passed, Mr. Klingenstein's advice has come back to me again and again. Now, I know that in two simple words, JK gave us the secret of investing successfully. While all the chatter and excitement is taking place about big stocks, big gains, and "three-baggers," long-term investment success really depends on *not losing*—not taking major losses.

We all know that a 50 percent loss requires a *double* the next time up just to get even, but still we strive for the Big Score, even though we also know full well that accidents happen most often to too-fast drivers; that Icarus got too close to the sun; that Enron Corporation, WorldCom, and many dot-coms had *very* high "new era" multiples before their obliteration.

Large losses are forever—in investing, in teenage driving, and in fidelity. If you avoid large losses with a strong defense, the winnings will have every opportunity to take care of themselves. And large losses are almost always caused by trying to get too much by taking too much risk.

If, as investors, we could learn to concentrate on wisely defining our own long-term objectives and learn to focus on not losing as the most important part of each specific decision, we could all be winners over the long term. And if it is too late for any of us because our best years are behind us, it is not too late to tell our children or grandchildren.

Alpha Hunters and Beta Grazers

Martin L. Leibowitz

There is a great philosophical divide between passive, efficiency-based "beta grazers" and active "alpha hunters." The explosive growth of hedge funds, of both the traditional and the long-only format, has contributed to this widening chasm between intensely proactive investors and those funds that are indexed or semi-indexed.

This Reflections article presents my personal observations on the general subject of active investing and on the nature, persistence, and discernibility of various market inefficiencies that could give rise to such investment opportunities. Ironically, these behavioral biases can act as frictions as well as opportunities, and this ambiguity may help explain why a few notable investors appear to be almost continuously successful while other active investors fall well short of their alpha targets.

At the outset, we should note that there is a middle ground where relatively passive, non-zero-sum forms of alpha return can be found. As described in a series of articles (Leibowitz 2004; Leibowitz and Bova 2005a, 2005c), these "allocation alphas" arise because the volatility risk of typical institutional portfolios is overwhelmingly dominated by their home-market equity exposure. By tilting their strategic allocations toward a more balanced allocation, institutions can often garner enhanced expected returns with only modest increases in marginal volatility. The level of expected benefit obviously depends on the institution's specific return–risk assumptions.

Unlike truly active alphas, *allocation* alphas are broadly accessible through a semipassive process of moving toward an effective strategic allocation. As such, they are akin to the civilized sort of protein-seeking found in shopping at the local supermarket, with the selections determined by personal taste and dietary constraints. These readily available allocation alphas serve a critical and valuable role in moving a fund toward optimal strategic allocation. Allocation alphas are quite distinct, however, from the truly active alphas derived from

Active alphas are derived from exploiting acute and chronic inefficiencies. They are hard to capture, but the great investors have been able to do so over many, many years.

Martin L. Leibowitz is a managing director at Morgan Stanley, New York City.

tracking down—and bagging—the fleeting and elusive opportunities that arise from market inefficiencies. Both forms of alpha offer the potential for enhanced return, and they can sometimes be combined to create exceptional opportunities. They are quite different concepts, however, and are pursued in different ways. Having made this distinction, I focus the remainder of this article on the truly active-skill-based investments that are intended to add alpha above and beyond the returns passively available in any asset class or strategic portfolio.

Truly Active Alphas

Much of the literature on truly active investing has focused on so-called anomalies—sources of incremental return that appear to have some degree of persistence. In addition, a number of elegant formalizations have been developed for incorporating active return–risk prospects into the investment decision process (Sharpe 1991; Grinold and Kahn 2000; Waring and Siegel 2003; Asness 2004). This discussion should be broadened, however, to include consideration of all frictions and behavioral biases—persistent as well as occasional—that might serve as fundamental sources of inefficiency. Such inefficiencies are not always exploitable: They may take the form of overshoots at certain times and undershoots at other times, their exploitation may be blocked by counterforces or technical restrictions of various sorts, or they may resolve themselves very slowly—or never.

We need to understand, however, that these sources of inefficiency are multifold, broad based, and continually renewing themselves. Most importantly, we need to understand that they really do exist—even if they are not always available, discernible, or directionally consistent. Such pockets of inefficiency at times become reasonably discernible and actionable—to certain active investors. Thus, their very existence becomes one facet of an argument (albeit an admittedly still incomplete argument) for the possibility of successful active investing.

Another argument (also incomplete) is the historical fact that a handful of investors has produced extraordinary performance over a span of many years—often together with equally extraordinary cross-sectional success in their choices of disparate investments. The approaches of these great investors—Warren Buffett, Bill Miller, Leon Levy, Dave Swensen, Jack Meyer—differ in numerous aspects, but as pointed out by Peter Bernstein (2005), the investors share the common feature of not being in the mainstream (i.e., they are all contrarians in one way or another). The great ones share a number of positive characteristics—focus, patience, a clear-cut philosophy, a willingness to go beyond the diversification mantra and accept high concentration risks, an innovation-prone attitude, the organizational sponsorship and personal fortitude to endure significant periods of underperformance, and a disciplined process for pursuing their goals. And in various ways and at various points in time, they have all been willing to stake significant chips on their convictions.

With respect to this latter point, one might well recall Charles Ellis's (1998) wonderful characterization of most investors as playing what in tennis parlance is called "the loser's game." In the loser's game, weekend players, with their readily returnable forehands and backhands, square off against each other and the one who misses the last return loses. The message is to play a consistent game and to avoid miss-hits. It is generally good advice for B players—and beta grazers!

The great ones, however—in tennis and in investing—go one big step beyond. They play a disciplined game until the moment they see what looks like a grand opportunity. At that moment, they move into *carpe diem* mode, gather up their prowess, and take a calculated risk to proactively and aggressively force a win.[1]

Even the great Fischer Black was fascinated by the potential for exploitable inefficiency, although he certainly knew that such opportunities would not be easy, widespread, or available to all. He once famously answered a question about how his view of the investing world had evolved after moving from the Massachusetts Institute of Technology to Goldman Sachs with "the view is much clearer from the banks of the Charles than from the banks of the Hudson." Earlier in his career, he had delivered a wonderful talk at the University of Chicago under the title "Yes, Virginia, There Is Hope," which was later published in the *Financial Analysts Journal* (Black 1973). In that talk, he reported on his study of the Value Line Ranking System, which would have produced superior performance over a long span of years if followed religiously (and with transactional-cost efficiency!).

Chronic and Acute Inefficiencies

Some of my pet sources of inefficiencies are behavioral and organizational distortions that I have observed over the years. I certainly do not mean to imply that they are exploitable anomalies, but they do represent the raw nuclear material out of which discernible opportunities could arise.

In perfectly efficient markets, all information would be immediately embedded in prices. The market would go through a sequence of quantum leaps from one equilibrium value to another. Investors would have no need to trade except for liquidity purposes. It would be hard to make a living working in such an idealized world. Fortunately, for those of us in the financial arena, the reality is that the markets are always in transition from one state of inefficiency to . . . maybe equilibrium but, more likely, a new state of inefficiency.

Inefficiencies come in many forms and subforms, but they can be roughly classified as either chronic or acute. *Acute inefficiencies* are the discernible opportunities that can be exploited by accessible arbitrages. With acute inefficiencies, the surrounding uncertainties can be hedged or minimized. Their resolution occurs quickly, well within the relevant time frame of arbitraging participants. *Chronic inefficiencies* tend to be less discernible, more ambiguous, more resistant to rapid resolution from available market forces, and generally longer term in nature. This distinction relates to Jack Treynor's (1976) wonderfully suggestive concept of "fast ideas versus slow ideas."

Obviously, one would prefer to hurl fast ideas at acute inefficiencies, but by their very nature, fast ideas have a short half-life. And that half-life may be condensing with the explosive growth in hedge funds. But even in this era of the hedge fund, only a small minority of market participants spend their days in a high-performance hunt for acute inefficiencies. The vast majority of investors, and certainly the bulk of the assets, swim with the broad currents, while looking for less-fleeting incremental opportunities.

Within this mainstream, one has expanses of apparent efficiency coexisting with pockets of chronic inefficiencies. Chronic inefficiencies arise from structural and behavioral sources, such as trading frictions, organizational barriers, imbalances in capital flows, valuation ambiguities, lack of catalysts for resolution, convoy or herding behavior, artificial peer comparisons, rebalancing inconsistencies, compulsive confirmation seeking, filtering of conflicting data, misreading of market signals, inertia, formulaic action plans, and overly rigid "policy portfolios." These types of chronic inefficiencies can be quite persistent. Few arbitrageurs have mandates that allow them to pursue long-term opportunities, and their absence contributes to the longevity of such inefficiencies. As the well-known saying goes: The market can remain irrational far longer than you can hang onto your position—or your career.

Process vs. Outcome. A much-discussed behavioral bias is the tendency to overemphasize recent historical results. As every mutual fund prospectus states, "Past performance should not be taken as a guide to future performance." That warning, although true, is not much help when few other hard facts are available. A more ominous rephrasing would be, "Past performance is not even a good guide to the *quality of the decisions* that went into that past performance." Yet, the ultimate issue is the soundness of the decision process itself: Was all knowable information incorporated? Was the reasoning thorough and sound? Were alternative scenarios considered and contrary views sought? Was a well-planned implementation and monitoring program established—and then followed? Was there a routine postmortem analysis of lessons learned? And are organizational discipline and staff continuity sufficient to achieve consistency in the decision process itself?

Unfortunately, the sort of retrospective analysis that includes these questions occurs more often when the outcomes are bad than when they are good. Participants would be well advised to conduct such postmortems even when the outcomes are happy ones, however, and to ask what *really* led to success. Was the positive result achieved for the reasons thought, or was it simply good fortune in this particular instance?

Even when presented with a regime that has every evidence of success—but only a probabilistic success—few investors are able to bring themselves or their organizations to consistently follow its path. The pressures of benchmarks, peer comparisons, standard accounting, liability and expenditure demands, limited organizational risk tolerance, managerial self-doubt—all can lead to lurching departures from prescribed disciplines, even ones with a high—but probabilistic—success prospect. After all, even a strategy whose success is mathematically provable will generate long runs of underperformance. Indeed, a topic in probability theory deals specifically with the risk of ruin—and the ultimate odds of ruin always favor the infinitely resourced casino.

Convoy Behavior. Traditional modes of investing in the financial markets involve absolute or relative valuations of various market segments or securities—a process in which ambiguities, complexities, and externalities abound. Inefficiencies and opportunities do exist in this area, but they are far from clearly discernible and can only be seen "through a glass darkly."

Many chronic inefficiencies have their roots in the behavioral biases of mainstream participants. For example, consider the herding behavior of institutional funds. Participants in the financial markets find themselves on a sea of ambiguity. They may try to climb up the mast to see what lies ahead, to look for islands of opportunity, but they are always battered by the waves, the weather, and the uncertainties of navigating in uncharted waters. Is there any surprise that one sees so many sailing in convoys?

It is no coincidence that most institutional portfolios are tightly clustered, with total volatilities falling in the 10–11 percent range—regardless of the fund's mission, liability structure, sponsor strength, or funding status (Leibowitz and Bova 2004). When such ambiguity abounds, people naturally assume that their peer groups might just have the right idea. This behavior is not totally irrational where theory is more art than science and where the expertise-to-luck ratio is often tilted in favor of luck. Moreover, a sufficient critical mass of investors with a common belief, even an erroneous one, can forge a pricing consensus that becomes a de facto reality that must be taken seriously.

Another issue is the valuation horizon of the average investor. The true efficient marketeer might argue that the market is continuously efficient over time. It is interesting to speculate, however, whether most investors have some specific span of time—perhaps from six months to three years—on which they focus their investment and valuation decisions. If so, then investors with longer horizons may reap a somewhat larger risk premium than average investors do. In terms of Treynor's fast–slow dichotomy, the advantage might go to investors who are either faster or slower than this hypothetical norm.

Another behavioral bias is the tendency to seek the opinions of other "experts" who can confirm one's own views, which results in what might be called a "compounding consensus." Actually, instead of seeking confirmation, one should actively solicit *contrary* views, hear them out, consider them objectively, and then try to recognize that the financial markets themselves always reflect some balance of conflicting views. In theory, one should always start with the hypothesis that the market is well priced. Then, before acting on any potential opportunity, one should (1) try to ascertain why the market is priced where it is, (2) become convinced that the basis for this current price does not fully reflect the true opportunities, (3) believe that there is some process whereby one's views of the true state of affairs will eventually come to be widely discernible (and in a more compelling fashion than has obviously happened to date), and (4) conclude that this "discernment" will transpire within a relevant time span.

Bayesian Rigidity. The compulsion to seek confirmation also relates to how the unfolding of events is interpreted. The "rigid Bayesians" will relentlessly try to retain their old views in the face of new information. To help counter this all-too-human inclination, one could write down the explicit reasoning behind a projected outcome and then establish the milestones that would have to occur if events took the anticipated path. Such a write-up would be akin to the contingency plans military establishments routinely create for a wide spectrum of geopolitical scenarios.

A French marquis once said:

> He who makes detailed plans about every potential course of action, and then decides—in advance and in great detail—how to respond to the various contingencies that might arise, and then further proceeds to address the subsequent situations that could follow each possible outcome, etc., etc.—this man will make very few mistakes [actually, I'm not sure that this part is true], but he will also do very little [I *am* sure that this part is true].

Yet, although the market's fast pace may limit how much contingency planning makes sense, the investment management profession surely could devote more effort in this direction.

Price-Target Revisionism. Another area of curious behavior has to do with price targets. When a long position is taken and the market moves favorably, the price rise tends to be taken as a confirmation of the wisdom of the purchase decision. To the extent that a price target was established at the outset, the investor may then be tempted to find some rationale for revising the target upward. This revisionism has some rather obvious dangers. A more rational approach would be to assume that as the price moves toward the original target, the prospect for further incremental return decreases while the risk increases. So, as a first cut, one should think in terms of selling off a portion of the position as it moves up. Thus, investors would be well advised to have a plan to reduce the positions as the original target is approached—the burden of proof (or at least the burden of argument) being placed on the investor who wishes to maintain the original position and/or revise the price target upward.

When the market moves against one's position, one might reasonably conclude that the market is giving a clear signal that one is wrong. A more common belief is that the market is wrong and that greater return is to be expected from the lower price. To counter the natural tendency to avoid a frontal look at deteriorating positions, a help, again, might be to have a series of adverse-event milestones that could act as trip wires to signal serious reconsideration. A substantive adverse move should be the basis for asking what the market is trying to reveal and for vigorously seeking those contrary views.

The Ebullience Cycle. Another common behavior is the "unopened envelope" syndrome. Back in the old days when physical envelopes were the primary delivery vehicle for individuals' portfolio statements, a persistently dreary market would lead to these envelopes being redelivered—unopened—into the "circular file." Such a state of denial when the market moves against one is totally human, especially when deciding what to do about it, if anything, is not easy. The unopened envelope reinforces individuals' propensity for inaction in the face of losing positions.

The opposite phenomenon is, of course, that when the markets are moving up, the incoming envelope is eagerly awaited and ripped open with great vigor. High spirits are rampant, and risks are more comfortable. In this ebullient atmosphere, both individual and institutional investors are inclined to hold on firmly to their winning positions, which are shining examples of their brilliance. They may even invest more aggressively, leading to the phenomenon that Jack Bogle (2005) cited of markets providing one return, the mutual funds providing something less, and the investors getting even less (a number that is rarely measured, except by the individuals in pain). This problem of making ever-greater investments as the market rises is a classic cycle that is not likely to abate.

Rebalancing Behavior. Market movements typically elicit different responses from four types of actors: holders, rebalancers, valuators, and shifters (Leibowitz and Hammond 2004).

- *Holders.* As noted, in a deteriorating market, individuals tend to leave their envelopes unopened and positions unchanged. This "holding pattern" effectively reduces their equity allocations.
- *Rebalancers.* Institutions behave very differently from holders. When the market pushes an institutional fund away from its policy portfolio allocation, it usually quickly rebalances back to the original percentage weights. In essence, institutions act as "formulaic rebalancers."
- *Valuators.* Valuators take positions based on the belief that the market is either cheap (or rich) or that it will continue (or reverse) its recent direction. Valuators can obviously play in two directions. As the market moves down, they may, based on the belief that the market has become cheap and will reverse itself, act as contrarians. As momentum players, they may view the market's decline—on either a technical or a fundamental basis—as a harbinger of further downward pressure.
- *Shifters.* This category really represents a transient reaction rather than an ongoing style. Investors in any of the first three categories may find themselves becoming shifters at some point in time. Shifting occurs when a fundamental change in asset allocation is required because of circumstances intrinsic to a fund's or an individual's situation rather than because of their assessment of the market's valuation.[2] That is, shifting is a fundamental move from one strategic stance to another. For example, individuals may increase their short-term fixed-income allocations when suddenly faced with an imminent liquidity need—loss of a job, an upcoming move, a looming major purchase, medical contingencies, and so on.

Institutions are more resistant to shifting behavior. Most institutional funds have a policy portfolio that serves as an anchor for their overall strategy. The policy portfolio is intended to be the best possible passive portfolio that encapsulates all relevant information about the nature of the fund, its purpose, and how it interacts with prospective returns and risks in the financial markets. Policy portfolios have great organizational value in forming a baseline for structuring and controlling the investment management process. Following normal market movements, institutions try to rebalance back to their policy portfolios. Significant shifts tend to take place only after a major reallocation study or under extreme organizational duress. A downside to policy portfolios is that they tend to be defined somewhat arbitrarily, to be specified in greater detail than is justified, to be sustained over a longer time than is appropriate, and to form a high barrier for any tactical departure. Bill Jahnke (1999), Rob Arnott (2004), and Bernstein (2004) have written eloquently about the behavioral distortions that can arise from an overly rigid commitment to policy portfolios.

Market Impact

These different responses may either exacerbate or moderate market movements. Obviously, the holders will have little effect on the market; they are out of the game, so to speak. The rebalancers will tend to have a smoothing effect: As the market goes down, they buy more; as the market goes up, they sell. Within the valuator category, the contrarians and "reversionists" will act as moderators whereas those pursuing momentum strategies will have an exacerbating effect. Because shifting tends to become more urgent (and probably more widespread) in adverse conditions, shifters will generally exacerbate market moves.

This four-part categorization also indicates something about how new flows are invested. Holders and rebalancers will usually invest their new funds congruently with their existing allocations. (However, individuals do seem to exhibit somewhat more proactive flexibility in investing their new funds than with their existing allocations. This behavior is rather curious.) Valuators, of course, will make fresh decisions about where to deploy new funds, but this type represents a relatively small part of overall new fund flows. The bulk of flows is concentrated in holders and rebalancers—those with relatively rigid channels who tend to direct new investments largely toward their current allocations.[3]

Rebalancing and Market Efficiency

The rebalancing behaviors themselves may become sources of market inefficiency. Consider which of the behaviors really make sense. Suppose a fund starts with a portfolio that mirrors the market as a whole. One could argue that, in a strictly efficient market, price movements would move the fund's portfolio in concert with the evolving equilibrium, and in this case, holding behavior might make eminent sense. Most funds do not, however, have a portfolio that reflects the market as a whole (certainly not on purpose). Moreover, at least in the case of individuals, holding behavior is more likely to be the result of inertia, not sophisticated reasoning.

Some formulaic rebalancers believe they are adhering to an appropriate response in an efficient market. There is some inconsistency, however, in reestablishing the same allocation after an "efficient market" has made a major alteration in global asset weights. After all, a downward move reduces the asset's weight in the market portfolio, which argues for rebalancing back to an allocation somewhat lower than the original policy portfolio weight.

One sometimes hears the rationale for formulaic rebalancing presented in terms of buying cheaper after a decline and selling expensive assets after a rise. But if one really believes that the market has become discernibly cheaper as a result of a decline, shouldn't the right move be to establish an even larger position rather than to rebalance back to the original position? After all, if the policy allocation were done afresh, then (given the newly cheaper valuation) the revised allocation should be even more aggressive than before. Thus, one can reasonably argue that rebalancing should, in general, lead not to a resurrection of the original allocation but, rather, to a higher or lower percentage weighting!

Ideally, rational rebalancing should not be rigidly tethered to a fixed policy portfolio but should respond more fluidly to market signals—to the extent they are interpreted either as an efficient restructuring of the global portfolio or as a *discernible* change in valuation. The problem, of course, is that large investment organizations are not designed to facilitate such judgmental flexibility. And as one astute chief investment officer put it, "Better to have a rigid rebalancing by prior agreement than a portfolio that deteriorates into a holding pattern because the organization lacks the confidence or the will to reestablish the policy portfolio weightings—or to even move back in that direction."

The behavior of valuators is integrally tied into the issue of *discernibility*. To the extent that discernible valuation opportunities truly exist, why not try to take advantage of them? Of course, with valuators, the big question is whether their business models *compel* them to make tactical and timing decisions even when no market opportunities meet this test of "reasonable discernibility."

Risk as Risk to the Policy Portfolio

A fund's strong reluctance to being forced to shift away from its policy portfolio may play an underappreciated role in setting the fund's risk tolerance and in shaping its policy portfolio in the first place. When an institution shifts to a lower-risk allocation, it departs from the policy portfolio that was previously considered to represent an optimal allocation. Institutional funds are understandably reluctant to move away from pre-established policy portfolios. Indeed, their rebalancing behavior is specifically geared toward sustaining this portfolio structure. Most institutional managers view it as most unfortunate if the fund is forced by an extreme market movement—or by the fund's investment committee—to abandon the presumably optimal approach and shift into a lower-risk strategy.

Potential trigger points for such mandated shifts lurk in the background of every investor's mind, however, acting as fence posts that define the outer limits of tolerable risk. These fence posts may also play a feedback role in setting the policy portfolio's overall risk level in the first place. For example, suppose adverse movements of 15–20 percent are considered to be the tolerable outer limit of the risk envelope. Then, a fund might reasonably wish to control the prospect of any such triggering event by reducing its probability to a minimal level (say, 10 percent). This shortfall constraint implies a portfolio volatility (risk) level in the 10–11 percent range, which happens to be exactly where most institutional funds are clustered.

Two further observations on this issue of risk. One is that the standard measure of risk, volatility, is an estimate of the range of returns *at a given horizon*. As pointed out by Mark Kritzman (2000) and by Kritzman and Don Rich (2002), this end-of-horizon distribution is not the same as the distribution of outcomes that could occur at some intermediary time. That distribution is much wider. And logically, this "riskier" intermediary distribution should determine when trigger points might be activated.[4]

The Illusion of Growth Eternal

Participants in the financial markets are intrinsically oriented toward an optimistic view of a world with a continuously compounding growth of value. Reality reminds us, however, that wealth can also be destroyed—both by "whimpers" and by "bangs." Sidney Homer and I (2004) once posed the following question: If a Roman soldier put just one drachma in a savings account and let it compound at 4 percent throughout the ages, how much money would his descendants have today? The answer turned out to be so many drachmas that, at virtually any exchange rate, it would amount to far more than the total existing wealth in the world. This outcome led to a follow-up question: What happened to it all? The sobering answer is that wealth is destroyed by war, inflation, devaluation, pandemic, political collapse, repudiation, obsolescence, virulent competition, bankruptcy, financial debacle, revolutionary technology, nonproductive investment, and so on. The natural inclination to deny the phantom of such discontinuities may be necessary for moving things forward, but it may also be a chronic source of inefficiency.

Conclusion

Participants in the financial markets often find themselves sailing on a sea of ambiguity through broad patches of fog, bouts of heavy weather, and occasional balmy periods that may prove only to be the center of passing storms. One can elect the passive approach—fly the beta flag and allow one's portfolio to float on the "index currents." Or one can choose to be an active alpha-seeking investor and try to chip away at the many chronic inefficiencies and behavioral biases that we know exist, even though we can't clearly discern how they are priced and whether they will profitably regress toward equilibrium within a reasonable time. With chronic inefficiencies, by their very definition, discernibility will always be somewhat clouded. (Otherwise, they would become acute—and would be long gone.) So, with these opportunities, one is always acting on imperfect knowledge and playing the odds. But without actively scanning the horizon and being poised to move on reasonably discernible opportunities, investors will surely have no chance of reaping the incremental return inherent in the grand continuous march toward efficiency.

The great investors are like the great sailors: They have the courage to set forth, they know where they want to go, they have a strong gyroscope to keep them on course, they have appropriate respect for the dangers of the sea and its potential for radical shifts in weather and currents, and they are not afraid to be alone for long stretches.

Notes

1. Although I argue for the possibility of successful active investing, I do not wish to suggest that everyone can be a winner. Indeed, they cannot. And the narrowness of the list of great investors attests to that dour fact. The great mass of investors should treat the market as being highly efficient and should start with the null hypothesis that all assets are fairly priced.
2. In some cases, market movements do ultimately lead to a portfolio shift. For example, a rule of thumb says that many individuals will let their allocations drift until a 15–20 percent decline from some high-water mark forces them to seriously reconsider their risk tolerances. I am drawing a distinction, however, between shifts based on a market-driven change in risk tolerance and those reallocations that are directly valuation motivated.

3. The large majority of existing dollar assets are also controlled by holders and formulaic rebalancers, which leads to the interesting question of whether the key risk premiums between asset classes are being priced by a relatively minor segment of the investing universe.
4. An even more severe criterion would be based on the range of declines from a high-water mark (Leibowitz and Bova 2005b).

References

Arnott, Robert D. 2004. "Managing Assets in a World of Higher Volatility and Lower Returns." In *Points of Inflection: New Directions for Portfolio Management* (Charlottesville, VA: CFA Institute):39–52.

Asness, Clifford. 2004. "An Alternative Future." *Journal of Portfolio Management* (Special Anniversary Issue):94–103.

Bernstein, Peter L. 2004. "Overview: A Fifth Point of Inflection." In *Points of Inflection: New Directions for Portfolio Management* (Charlottesville, VA: CFA Institute):1–5.

———. 2005. "Alpha: The Real Thing, or Chimerical?" *Economics and Portfolio Strategy* (15 March).

Black, Fischer. 1973. "Yes, Virginia, There Is Hope: Tests of the Value Line Ranking System." *Financial Analysts Journal*, vol. 29, no. 5 (September/October):10–14.

Bogle, Jack. 2005. "The Mutual Fund Industry 60 Years Later: For Better or Worse?" *Financial Analysts Journal*, vol. 61, no. 1 (January/February):15–24.

Ellis, Charles. 1998. *Winning the Loser's Game*. New York: McGraw-Hill.

Grinold, Richard C., and Ronald N. Kahn. 2000. *Active Portfolio Management*. 2nd ed. New York: McGraw-Hill.

Homer, Sidney, and Martin L. Leibowitz. 2004. *Inside the Yield Book*. Princeton, NJ: Bloomberg Press.

Jahnke, William. 1999. "Why Setting an Asset Allocation Policy Is a Bad Idea." *Journal of Financial Planning* (February). Available online at www.fpanet.org/journal/articles/1999_Issues/jfp0299-art5.cfm.

Kritzman, Mark P. 2000. *Puzzles of Finance*. New York: John Wiley & Sons.

Kritzman, Mark P., and Don Rich. 2002. "The Mismeasurement of Risk." *Financial Analysts Journal*, vol. 58, no. 3 (May/June):91–99.

Leibowitz, Martin L. 2004. "The β-Plus Measure in Asset Allocation." *Journal of Portfolio Management*, vol. 30, no. 3 (Spring):26–36

Leibowitz, Martin L., and Anthony Bova. 2004. "Structural Betas: The Key Risk Factor in Asset Allocation." Morgan Stanley Research Notes (21 June).

———. 2005a. "The Efficient Frontier Using 'Alpha Cores'." Morgan Stanley Research Notes (7 January).

———. 2005b. "Convergence of Risk." Morgan Stanley Research Note (April).

———. 2005c. "Allocation Betas." *Financial Analysts Journal*, vol. 61, no. 4 (July/August):70–82.

Leibowitz, Martin L., and P. Brett Hammond. 2004. "The Changing Mosaic of Investment Patterns." *Journal of Portfolio Management*, vol. 30, no. 3 (Spring):10–25.

Sharpe, William F. 1991. "From the Board: The Arithmetic of Active Management." *Financial Analysts Journal*, vol. 47, no. 1 (January/February):7–9.

Treynor, Jack L. 1976. "Long-Term Investing." *Financial Analysts Journal*, vol. 32, no. 3 (May/June):56–59.

Waring, M. Barton, and Laurence B. Siegel. 2003. "The Dimensions of Active Management." *Journal of Portfolio Management*, vol. 29, no. 3 (Spring):35–52.

The Relentless Rules of Humble Arithmetic

John C. Bogle

During the glorious financial excesses of the recent era, we in the investment community basked in the sunlight of prosperity that is almost unimaginable. But in this environment, our community developed a vested interest in ignoring the obvious realities of financial market returns. It's been said—I think by my detractors—that all I have going for me is "an uncanny ability to recognize the obvious." But as we look ahead to a far less forgiving investment environment, we all must face these truths.

This problem is not new. Two and a half millennia ago, Demosthenes warned, "What each man wishes, he also believes to be true." More recently, and certainly more pungently, Upton Sinclair marveled, "It's amazing how difficult it is for a man to understand something if he's paid a small fortune not to understand it."

But we all must understand the realities of our investment system, for they are central to the operation of the system of financial intermediation that underlies the collective wealth of our citizenry and the accumulation of assets in our retirement systems. While the Bush administration defines our system as the "ownership society," I call it the "investment society." But whatever words we use, the future of capitalism depends importantly on our understanding the realities of our system.

The investment community is ignoring the reality that the costs of financial intermediation are devastating the net return actually delivered to investors.

The Cost Matters Hypothesis

The overarching reality is simple: *Gross returns in the financial markets minus the costs of financial intermediation equal the net returns actually delivered to investors.* Although truly staggering amounts of investment literature have been devoted to the widely understood EMH (the efficient market hypothesis),

John C. Bogle is president of The Vanguard Group's Bogle Financial Markets Research Center, Valley Forge, Pennsylvania.

Editor's Note: This article was developed from Mr. Bogle's presentation to the *FAJ* 60th Anniversary conference titled *Reflections and Insights: Provocative Thinking on Investment Management* (February 2005). The opinions expressed in this article do not necessarily represent the views of Vanguard's present management.

precious little has been devoted to what I call the CMH (the cost matters hypothesis). To explain the dire odds that investors face in their quest to beat the market, however, we don't need the EMH; we need only the CMH. No matter how efficient or inefficient markets may be, the returns earned by investors as a group must fall short of the market returns by precisely the amount of the aggregate costs they incur. It is the central fact of investing.

Efficient Market Hypothesis	Cost Matters Hypothesis
• Strong evidence	• Overwhelming evidence
• Sound explanation	• Obvious explanation
• Mostly true	• Tautologically true

Nonetheless, the pages of our financial journals are filled with statistical studies of rates of market returns that are neither achievable nor achieved. How can we talk about "creating positive alpha" without realizing that after intermediation costs are deducted, the system as a whole has negative alpha? Of what use is speculation about the amount of the equity risk premium when 100 percent of the return on the 10-year U.S. Treasury note (or T-bill, if that's what you prefer) is there for the taking while as much as 50 percent or more of the real return on stocks can be consumed by the costs of our financial system? How can we ignore the fact that, unlike those children in Garrison Keillor's fictional Lake Wobegon, we investors are, as a group, average before costs but below average after our costs are deducted?

The idea that investors as a group must be average goes back more than a century, expressed by Louis Bachelier in his PhD thesis at the Sorbonne in 1900: "Past, present, and even discounted future events are [all] reflected in market price." That's essentially what the EMH says. Nearly half a century later, when Nobel Laureate Paul Samuelson discovered Bachelier's long-forgotten thesis, he confessed that he oscillated between regarding it as trivially obvious and regarding it as remarkably sweeping. Of course, Bachelier was right. However, when he went on to conclude that "the mathematical expectation of the speculator is zero," Bachelier was *wrong*. He didn't go far enough. For the fact is that the mathematical expectation of the speculator and the long-term investor alike is not zero. It is zero minus the cost of playing the game, a shortfall to the stock market's return that is precisely equal to the sum total of all those advisory fees, marketing expenditures, sales loads, brokerage commissions, legal and transaction costs, custody fees, and security-processing expenses. And that is the essential message of the CMH.

Relentless Rules That Are Eternal

With that background, let me now turn to the quotation that inspired the title of this essay. In *Other People's Money* (1914), Louis D. Brandeis, who later became one of the most influential jurists on the U.S. Supreme Court, railed against the oligarchs who a century ago controlled both investment America and corporate America. He described their self-serving financial management and interlocking interests as "trampling with impunity on laws human and divine, obsessed with the delusion that two plus two make five." He predicted (accurately, as it turned out) that the widespread speculation of that era would collapse—"a victim of the relentless rules of humble arithmetic." He then added this unattributed warning (perhaps from Sophocles): "Remember, O Stranger, arithmetic is the first of the sciences, and the mother of safety."

As it is said, the more things change, the more they remain the same. The history of the era that Brandeis described may not be repeating itself exactly today, but (paraphrasing Mark Twain) it rhymes. America's investment system—our government retirement programs, private retirement programs, and indeed all of the securities owned by stockowners as a group—is plagued by the relentless rules of humble arithmetic. Because the returns investors receive come only *after* the deduction of the costs of our system of financial intermediation—as a gambler's winnings come only from what remains after the croupier's rake descends—those relentless rules devastate the long-term returns of investors. Applying Brandeis's formulation to these contemporary issues, we seem obsessed with the delusion that a 7 percent market return, minus 2.5 percentage points for costs, still equals a 7 percent investor return.

No one knows the precise amount of the intermediation costs of our financial system.[1] However, we do have data for some of the major cost centers. During 2004, revenues of investment bankers and brokers came to an estimated $220 billion; direct mutual fund costs came to about $70 billion; pension management fees, $15 billion; annuity commissions, some $15 billion; hedge fund fees, about $25 billion; fees paid to personal financial advisors, maybe another $5 billion. These financial intermediation costs alone—even without including the investment services provided by banks and insurance companies—came to approximately $350 billion, directly deducted from the returns that the financial markets generated for investors.

Moreover, the price of intermediation has soared. In 1985, the annual revenues of these cost centers were in the $50 billion range. In the bubble and postbubble era (since 1996) alone, the aggregate costs of financial intermediation may well have exceeded $2.5 trillion, all dutifully paid by our stockowners and stock traders. Of course, some of these costs create value (for example, liquidity). But, by definition, those costs cannot create *above*-market returns. To the contrary, they are the direct cause of *below*-market returns, a dead weight on the amount earned by investors as a group. In investing, all investors together get precisely what they *don't* pay for. So, it is up to all of us in the financial community to develop a more efficient way to provide investment services to our clients.

The Mutual Fund Industry

The largest of all U.S. financial intermediaries is the mutual fund industry. In my article (Bogle 2005) about the fund industry, in which I've now spent 56 years, I examined the changes that have taken place during this long period and asked whether these changes are for better or for worse. I regret to report that the answer to the question is "for worse."

Consider this summary:[2]

- We have created a mind-boggling number of new and often speculative funds that demand unnecessarily complex choices by investors.
- We've moved from investment committees focused on the wisdom of long-term investing to portfolio manager "stars" engaged in the folly of short-term speculation.
- We've enjoyed an enormous growth in our ownership position in corporate America along with a paradoxical and discouraging diminution of our willingness to exercise that ownership position responsibly, if at all.
- We've imposed soaring costs on our investors that belie the enormous economies of scale in money management.

- Our reputation for integrity, sadly, has been tarred by the brush of a broad-ranging series of scandals.
- Among the larger management companies that dominate the field, we've moved away from private ownership in favor of public ownership, and then to ownership by financial conglomerates.
- We've changed from a profession with aspects of a business to a business with aspects of a profession

The evidence clearly supports the conclusion that the mutual fund industry has moved from stewardship to salesmanship. To this dispiriting analysis of the past, I would add a warning about the future: Unless we return to our traditional role as trustees of other people's money, the mutual fund industry will falter and finally fail—a victim of, yes, the relentless rules of humble arithmetic. I love this industry too much to remain silent and let that happen without putting up a fight.

The Record. The record of the past two decades indicates that the humble arithmetic I have described—Gross Return minus Cost equals Net Return—has proven dangerous to the wealth of the families who have entrusted their hard-earned wealth to mutual funds. In fact, it has destroyed their wealth in almost precisely the measure that the CMH suggests. Investors have learned, and learned the hard way, that in mutual funds, it's not that "you get what you pay for" but that "you get what you *don't* pay for."

Table 1 shows that over the past 20 years, a simple low-cost, no-load stock market index fund that replicated the Standard & Poor's 500 Index delivered an annual return of 12.8 percent—just a hair short of the 13.0 percent return of the market itself. During the same period, the average equity mutual fund delivered a return of 10.0 percent, a shortfall to the index fund of 2.8 percentage points a year and less than 80 percent of the market's annual return. Compounded over that period, each $1 invested in the index fund grew by $10.12—the beneficiary of the magic of compounding returns—whereas each $1 in the average fund grew by just $5.73, a shriveled-up 57 percent of the index fund's cumulative return—the victim of the tyranny of compounding costs.

These data are before taxes. When after-tax data are used, the annual gap between the equity fund and the index fund soars far higher, rising from 2.8 percentage points to 4.1 percentage points a year. The average fund deferred almost no gains during this period; the index fund deferred

Table 1. Average Equity Fund vs. S&P 500 Index Fund, 1983–2003

	S&P 500 Index Fund		Average Equity Fund		
Measure	Rate	Profit on $1.00	Rate	Profit on $1.00	Fund Percent of Index Profit
Gross return	13.0%	$10.52	13.0%	$10.52	100%
Fund lag	–0.2		–3.0		
Pretax return	12.8%	10.12	10.0%[a]	5.73	57%
Taxes	–0.9		–2.2		
After-tax return	11.9%	8.47	7.8%	3.49	41%
Inflation	–3.0		–3.0		
Real return	8.9%	$ 4.50	4.8%	$ 1.55	34%

[a]Lipper reported return reduced by 0.3 pp for estimated survivor bias and 0.3 pp for sales charges.

nearly all. (Deferred taxes may be the ultimate example of how you get what you don't pay for.) Cumulatively, the average equity fund produced, not 57 percent of the market's after-tax return, but only 41 percent.

In fairness, however, the wealth accumulated in the index fund and the average equity fund should be measured not only in nominal dollars but also in real dollars. As Table 1 shows, the real annual return for the index fund drops to 8.9 percent and for the equity fund, to 4.8 percent, obviously the same gap of 4.1 percentage points. But when we reduce both returns by the identical 3.0 percentage points a year for inflation, it will hardly surprise those who know their humble arithmetic that the compounding of those lower annual returns further widens the cumulative gap. Over the past 20 years, the cumulative profit on each $1 initially invested in the equity fund after costs, taxes, and inflation comes to just $1.55 in real terms—only 34 percent of the index fund real profit of $4.50.

A casual look at the stock market over the past two decades, then, reflects a 13 percent annual return that produced a profit of $10.52 on each dollar initially invested. But the underlying reality reflects an outcome almost light years away. After investment costs and taxes are deducted each year in nominal dollars, and after the erosion of inflation, the annual return for the average equity fund tumbles to 4.8 percent, with an accumulated real profit of just $1.55, only one-seventh the amount of the apparent profit on the market portfolio.

Fund Returns vs. Investor Returns. To make matters worse, the stark reality is that the return of the average equity *fund* greatly overstates the return earned by the average equity fund *investor.* When we consider what fund investors actually earn, as shown in **Table 2**, the shortfall to the market return worsens dramatically.

As this industry came to focus more and more on marketing and less and less on management, we deluged investors with a plethora of enticing new funds, at ever-rising costs. Our marketing experts responded with alacrity to the waxing and waning of market fads and fashions, most obviously with the "new economy" funds of the late market bubble. Aided and abetted by the fund industry, investors not only poured hundreds of billions of dollars into equity funds as the stock market soared to its high but also characteristically selected the wrong funds. In addition to the wealth-depleting penalty of fund costs, then, fund investors paid one substantial penalty for the counterproductive *timing* of their investments and another large penalty for the unfortunate *selection* of the mutual funds they chose to own.

Table 2. Average Equity Fund Investor vs. S&P 500 Index Fund, 1983–2003

	S&P 500 Index Fund		Equity Fund Investor		
Measure	Rate	Profit on $1.00	Rate	Profit on $1.00	Investor Percent of Index Profit
Gross return	13.0%	$10.52	13.0%	$10.52	100%
Fund lag	–0.2		–3.0		
Net fund return	12.8%	$10.12	10.0%	$ 5.73	57%
Timing/selection	0.0		–3.7		
Net return	12.8%	$10.12	6.3%	$ 2.39	24%

Intuition suggests that these costs were large, and the data we have, although not precise, confirm that hypothesis. The asset-weighted returns of mutual funds—which are easy to estimate by examining each fund's quarterly cash flows—lag the standard time-weighted returns by fully 3.7 percentage points a year. Adding that shortfall to the 2.8 percentage point annual lag of time-weighted returns of the average equity fund relative to the S&P 500 Index fund over the past two decades, we see that the asset-weighted returns of the average equity fund stockholder fell behind the index fund by a total of 6.5 percentage points a year. Average annual pretax nominal returns for the period: index fund, 12.8 percent; equity fund investor, 6.3 percent—less than one-half of the stock market's annual return.

Applying the tyranny of compounding not only to the actual costs of fund operations but also to the even larger costs of, well, fund ownership, we find that each $1 invested at the outset by the average fund investor, before taxes and inflation, grew by only $2.39 over the full period, compared with the growth of $10.12 that came from simply owning the low-cost index fund. That is, investors received only 24 percent of the wealth that might easily have been accumulated simply by holding a low-cost, unmanaged stock market portfolio.

Much of this extra lag came from the specialized (usually speculative) funds that the industry created and promoted. For example, as **Table 3** shows, during the bull and bear markets we experienced in 1998–2003, the asset-weighted returns of the industry's six largest broadly diversified funds lagged their time-weighted annual returns by an average of less than a single percentage point. The asset-weighted returns of the six largest specialized funds, in contrast, lagged their time-weighted returns by an average of more than 11 percentage points.

Table 3. Performance of 2000's Six Largest Diversified and Sector Funds

	Time Weighted			Asset-Weighted Return	Asset Weighted minus Time Weighted
Fund	1998–2000	2001–2003	1998–2003	1998–2003	
Diversified funds					
Fidelity Magellan	14.4%	–5.6%	3.9%	3.7%	–0.2%
Vanguard 500 Index	12.3	–4.2	3.7	2.4	–1.3
Investment Company of America	14.2	1.0	7.4	6.7	–0.7
Janus Fund	20.2	–11.0	3.4	0.9	–2.5
Fidelity Contrafund	15.2	0.4	7.5	7.9	0.4
Washington Mutual	9.6	2.8	6.2	5.5	–0.7
Average annual return	14.3	–2.7	5.4	4.5	–0.9
Cumulative return	49.0%	–7.9%	37.0%	30.0%	–7.0%
Sector funds					
TRP Science & Technology	23.5%	–19.1%	–0.1%	–8.8%	–8.7%
Seligman Communication and Information	13.5	–2.4	5.3	2.0	–3.3
AB Global Technology	28.0	–15.7	3.9	–9.5	–13.4
Vanguard Health Care	34.2	1.4	16.7	13.7	–3.0
Fidelity Select Electronics	37.0	–10.2	10.9	0.0	–10.9
Munder NetNet	35.7	–21.6	3.1	–25.7	–28.8
Average annual return	28.6	–11.3	6.6	–4.7	–11.4
Cumulative return	113.0%	–30.0%	47.0%	–25.0%	–22.0%

Compounded during the six-year period that included the bubble and its aftermath, the gap in returns was astonishing. The specialized funds produced a positive time-weighted annual return of 6.6 percent but lost a cumulative 25 percent of client wealth. Despite a slightly lower time-weighted annual return of 5.4 percent in the broadly diversified large funds, client wealth was enhanced by 30 percent during the period—an additional 55 percentage points in wealth accumulation.

The "Marketingization" of the Fund Industry. The stark arithmetic that illustrates the huge sacrifices of wealth incurred by fund investors has been driven by two costly and counterproductive trends. One is the marketingization of the mutual fund industry, in which most major firms have come to create and market whatever funds will sell.

One reasonable proxy—obviously an imperfect one—for differentiating a marketing firm from a management firm is the number of funds it offers. The data, which come from a Fidelity Investments study of the 54 largest firms managing about 85 percent of the industry's long-term assets, clearly support the proposition that fund firms that have avoided being dominated by a marketing ethic have provided distinctly superior performance.

On the one hand, as shown in **Table 4**, the 9 firms that each operate fewer than 15 mutual funds clearly dominate the upper reaches of the rankings, holding six of the seven top spots. The firms focused on few funds outpaced almost 80 percent of all their common rivals (i.e., their large-cap growth fund versus other large-cap growth funds, their balanced fund versus other balanced funds, etc.) during the 10-year period studied (1994–2003). On the other hand, the 45 firms with more than 15 funds (averaging 52 funds each) focused on offering a broad line of fund "products" to the public, outpaced only about 48 percent of their peers and hold 36 of the 37 lowest ranks. Marketing focus, apparently, comes at the expense of management success.

"Conglomeratization" of the Fund Industry. The other trend that has ill served investor interest is the conglomeratization of the fund industry, in which giant international financial institutions, eager to get a piece of the action for themselves—a share of the huge profits made in money management—have gone on a buying binge. (The trend toward conglomerated public ownership, while little noted, has been dramatic. Until 1958, all fund management firms were privately held.)

Again, a powerful pattern prevails, with funds operated by privately held management companies holding an impressive edge in investors' returns over funds owned and operated by financial conglomerates. **Table 5** compares the relative returns of the funds managed by the 13 private companies that remain today and the funds managed by the 41 public companies—those that are held either directly by public investors (7 firms) or indirectly by publicly owned financial conglomerates (34 firms).

The funds managed by the 13 firms under private ownership (averaging 34 funds and totaling \$1.3 trillion in assets) outpaced 71 percent of their peers and held eight of the top nine spots.[3] The 34 fund managers under the aegis of conglomerates (averaging 47 funds and totaling \$1.6 trillion in assets) outperformed only 45 percent. The other 7 publicly held firms (averaging 55 funds each and with \$0.6 trillion in assets) outperformed 60 percent. In all, public firms held 32 of the 34 bottom spots on the list.

Table 4. Number of Funds vs. Relative Returns, 1994–2003
(firms offering 15 or fewer funds are shaded)

Firm	Equal-Weighted Outperformance	No. of Funds	Firm	Equal-Weighted Outperformance	No. of Funds	Firm	Equal-Weighted Outperformance	No. of Funds
Dodge & Cox	98%	4	Waddell & Reed	61%	45	Eaton Vance	49%	73
First Eagle	97	5	USAA	61	31	Morgan Stanley Adv.	49	50
Calamos	91	8	Oppenheimer	60	48	Goldman Sachs	49	34
So. Eastern/Longleaf	90	3	MFS	59	61	The Hartford	48	33
American Funds	79	26	Prudential	59	49	Putnam	47	54
Royce	79	14	New York Life	58	22	John Hancock	47	35
Harris Associates	77	7	US Bancorp	57	37	Dreyfus	45	126
Vanguard	76	75	Columbia Mgmt.	56	72	Delaware	44	56
PIMCO	76	51	AllianceBernstein	55	57	Strong	44	42
Franklin Templeton	71	100	Banc One	54	36	Thrivent Financial	44	25
T. Rowe Price	71	72	Neuberger Berman	54	14	Trusco Cap	43	24
Janus	70	21	Lord Abbett	53	27	Merrill Lynch	40	58
ING	69	60	Scudder	52	65	Aim	39	62
Nuveen	65	36	Van Kampen	52	43	Nations Funds	38	42
American Century	64	54	Federated	52	37	American Express	37	60
WM Advisors	64	15	Evergreen	51	57	BlackRock	36	32
Davis	62	7	Citigroup	50	57	Pioneer	33	24
Fidelity	62	207	Wells Fargo	50	39	JP Morgan	32	38

Note: Performance rankings ignore the impact of sales charges and include only A-class shares.

Source: Fidelity Investments.

Table 5. Relative Returns and Organizational Structure
(private firms are shaded; publicly held, nonconglomerate firms are in boldface)

Firm	Equal-Weighted % Outperformance	Firm	Equal-Weighted % Outperformance	Firm	Equal-Weighted % Outperformance
Dodge & Cox	98	**Waddell & Reed**	**61**	Goldman Sachs	49
First Eagle	97	USAA	61	Morgan Stanley Adv.	49
Calamos	91	Oppenheimer	60	**Eaton Vance**	**49**
So. Eastern/Longleaf	90	Prudential	59	The Hartford	48
Royce	79	MFS	59	John Hancock	47
American Funds	79	New York Life	58	Putnam	47
Harris Associates	77	US Bancorp	57	Dreyfus	45
PIMCO	76	Columbia Mgmt.	56	Strong	44
Vanguard	76	AllianceBernstein	55	Delaware	44
T. Rowe Price	**71**	Banc One	54	Thrivent Financial	44
Franklin Templeton	**71**	Neuberger Berman	54	Trusco Cap	43
Janus	**70**	Lord Abbett	53	Merrill Lynch	40
ING	69	Van Kampen	52	Aim	39
Nuveen	**65**	Scudder	52	Nations Funds	38
American Century	64	**Federated**	**52**	American Express	37
WM Advisors	64	Evergreen	51	BlackRock	36
Davis	62	Wells Fargo	50	Pioneer	33
Fidelity	62	Citigroup	50	JP Morgan	32

Note: Performance rankings ignore the impact of sales charges and include only A-class shares.
Source: Fidelity Investments.

From these compelling data, it seems reasonable to assume that publicly held firms run by far-removed managers who may well have never looked a fund independent director in the eye are in the fund business primarily to gather assets, build revenues, and enhance their brand names. Such a firm is, with some logic, likely to be far more concerned about the return on *its* capital than the return on the capital entrusted to it by its mutual fund owners. (We saw something of that syndrome in the recent scandals, in which the largest offenders were owned by conglomerates.)

Of course, the conglomerate's managers have a clear fiduciary duty to the conglomerate's owners as well as to the owners of its funds. But the record suggests that when fund fee schedules are considered and new fund "products" created, the conglomerate resolves these dilemmas in favor of its own public owners, ignoring the invocation in the Investment Company Act of 1940 that funds must be organized, operated, and managed in the interests of their shareholders.

Looking Ahead. Despite the problems I have described, fund investors (at least those investors who didn't jump on the bull market bandwagon late in the game) seem satisfied with earning the decidedly modest positive returns achieved by their funds during the bull market of the past two decades. They seem willing to ignore the generally hidden costs of fund investing, oblivious to the tax inefficiency, happy to think in terms of their returns in nominal rather than real dollars, and comfortable in assuming that the responsibility for the mistakes made in fund timing and fund selection are theirs alone.

But suppose we are entering an era of lower returns. What are the implications of these findings for long-term wealth accumulation? Let's measure what might be the typical experience in terms of the investment horizon of a young investor of today. Assume the investor has just joined the workforce and is looking forward to 45 years of employment until retirement and then to enjoying the next 20 years in retirement that the actuaries promise—a total time horizon of 65 years.

If the stock market is kind enough to favor investors with a total return of 8 percent a year over that period and if annual mutual fund costs are held to 2.5 percentage points, the return of the fund investor will average 5.5 percent. By the end of the long period, a cost-free investment at 8 percent will carry an initial $1,000 investment to a final value of $148,800, a profit of $147,800. However, as **Figure 1** shows, the 5.5 percent net return will increase the investor's cumulative wealth by only $31,500, bringing the final value of the investor's investment to $32,500. In effect, the amount paid over to the financial system, also compounded, will come to $116,300.

In other words, the investor who put up 100 percent of the capital and assumed 100 percent of the risk would receive only 21 percent of the return. The financial intermediaries, who put up 0 percent of the capital and assumed 0 percent of the risk, would enjoy a truly remarkable 79 percent of the return. Indeed, the cumulative return of our young capitalist saving for retirement would fall behind the cumulative return taken by the financial croupiers after the 29th year, less than halfway through the 65-year period. Devastating as is this diversion of the spoils of investing, apparently few investors today have either the awareness of the relentless rules of humble arithmetic that almost guarantee such a shortfall in their retirement savings or the wisdom to understand the tyranny of compounding costs over the long term.

The Wealth of the Nation

If our system of retirement savings were not the backbone of the wealth of the nation and our economic strength, perhaps this wealth-depleting arithmetic would not matter. But retirement savings *are* the backbone, and the arithmetic *does* matter. Our corporate pension plans hold $1.8 trillion in stocks and bonds; our state and local pension plans, another $2.0 trillion. Private noninsured pension reserves total $4.2 trillion; insured pension reserves, $1.9 trillion; government pension reserves, $3.1 trillion; life insurance reserves, $1.0 trillion—for a total of $10.2 trillion, or nearly one-half of total family assets (other than cash and savings deposits).

Figure 1. The Cumulative Lag Caused by 2.5 Percent Costs in an 8 Percent Market

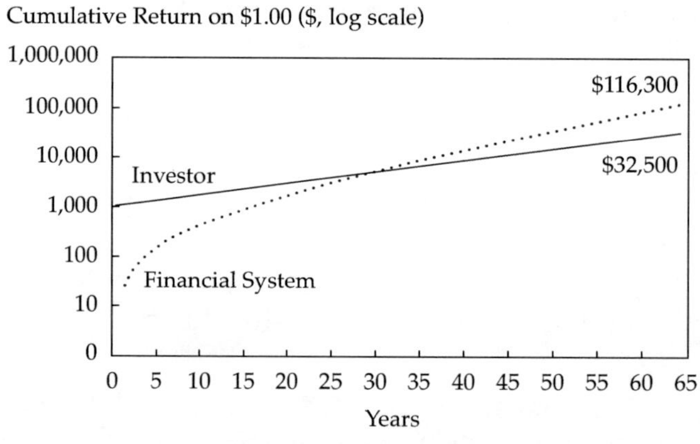

Since 1970, U.S. national policy has been to increase private savings for retirement by providing tax-sheltered accounts, such as IRAs and defined-contribution pension, thrift, and savings programs [usually 401(k) plans]. The present administration seems determined to extend the reach of these tax-advantaged vehicles, together with the amount that each family may invest in them each year. So, how do the relentless rules of arithmetic affect our investment society or, if you prefer, our ownership society?

Certainly, the earlier data on relative returns show that the retirement savings of U.S. families are too important to the wealth of the nation to be entrusted to the mutual fund industry. Moreover, the system of tax incentives provided to investors clearly hasn't resulted in adequate wealth accumulation. Only about 22 percent of our workers are using 401(k) savings plans, only about 10 percent have IRAs, and about 9 percent have both. Even after three decades of experience with these tax-advantaged plans, the average 401(k) balance is now a modest $33,600, and the average IRA $26,900—hardly the kind of capital with the potential to provide a comfortable retirement.

In addition, the massive shift that has taken place from defined-benefit plans to defined-contribution plans does not seem to be working well from an investment standpoint. Not only have DB plans produced higher returns than DC plans during the period 1990–2002 (144 percent versus 125 percent), they have done so with far less volatility; in the recent down-market years, DB plans fell only about half as much (–12 percent versus –22 percent). Part of the cumulative shortfall over the 12-year period, of course, can be traced to the higher costs imposed on investors in DC plans, dominated by mutual fund holdings.

The Humble Arithmetic of Pension Plans

Clearly, the nation's foray into DC plans is not doing the job it should in producing a solid base for retirement savings. But our DB plans have done far worse, not because of the returns they have earned, but because of the excessive returns they have projected. The financial statements of U.S. corporations are rife with aggressive assumptions about future returns that have fostered substantial underfunding of their pension plans. Even as interest rates tumbled and earnings yields steadily declined during the past two decades, projections of future returns soared.

In 2000, for example, General Motors Corporation was projecting a 10 percent annual return on its pension plan, compared with the 6 percent assumption it was using in 1975. Why? It based the projection largely on "long-term historical returns." The higher the stock market rose and the more interest rates tumbled, the higher the pension plan's expected returns rose, and not only in the GM model. Amazingly, General Motors was essentially saying, "The more stocks have gone up in the past, the more they'll rise in the future."

Corporate America's projections of pension fund returns are both a national scandal and an accident waiting to happen. Consider from the standpoint of the relentless rules of humble arithmetic what might today be reasonable in projecting future returns of pension plans. **Table 6** provides the data for a conventional pension portfolio of 60 percent U.S. equities and 40 percent U.S. bonds. The projected return of 7.5 percent for the stock portfolio is based on realistic expectations—today's 2 percent dividend yield and historical earnings growth of about 5.5 percent—and assumes no change in the current P/E multiple of 21 times reported earnings.

Table 6. Realistic Return Assumptions: Corporate Pension Plan

	1	2	3	4 (2 – 3)
Asset Class	Allocation	Projected Return	Expenses	Net Return
Equities	60%	7.5%	1.5%	6.0%
Bonds	40	4.5	0.5	4.0
Weighted total	100%	6.3%	1.1%	5.2%

The present yield on a conservative portfolio of U.S. Treasury and corporate bonds suggests a projected bond return of about 4.5 percent, bringing the gross portfolio return to 6.3 percent. Deducting estimated annual plan expenses (fees, turnover costs, etc.) of 1.1 percent from the gross return, the arithmetic takes us to a net return of 5.2 percent, less than two-thirds of the 8.5 percent total projected by the average large U.S. corporation. A company making that kind of projection for its pension plan is either looking for trouble or trying to engineer upward the earnings it reports to its shareholders.

General Motors currently uses that 8.5 percent assumption, which seems outlandish on the face of it. When I pursued this issue with GM, I was told that the traditional policy portfolio of 60 percent stocks and 40 percent bonds is history; GM has added alternative investments, such as venture capital, and "absolute return" investments, such as hedge funds. It's easy enough to understand that change, so let's make some reasonable assumptions about what this new policy portfolio might hold:[4]

- 30 percent in U.S. equities,
- 40 percent in U.S. bonds,
- 10 percent in venture capital, and
- 20 percent in hedge funds.

Table 7 shows one example of the returns that would be required from each of these four asset classes to reach that 8.5 percent target. The market returns for equities and bonds are unchanged, so the equity managers would have to beat the stock market by 3.0 percentage points a year and the bond managers would have to beat the bond market by 0.25 percentage point. Then, let's generously assume that the venture capital market will return 12 percent, with smart managers who earn almost 18 percent, and that hedge funds will earn an average 10 percent return, with smart managers who earn 17 percent. Then, let's deduct investment costs, as we must. Voila! The pension fund reaches its goal of 8.5 percent a year!

But now consider the possibility that these returns actually will be achieved. Equity managers who can beat the market by 3 percentage points a year are conspicuous by their absence. (And the quest for such outperformance presumes the assumption of considerable risk.) Consider too that the assumed venture capital returns are far above even the historical norms that were inflated by the speculative boom in IPOs during the market madness of the late 1990s. And consider not only the high (10 percent) assumed average hedge fund return but the obviously staggering odds against finding a group of so-called absolute-return managers who can consistently exceed that return by 6–7 percentage points a year over a decade. Surely most investment professionals would consider these Herculean assumptions absurd.

Table 7. Getting to an 8.5 Percent Return: A Template for Corporate Annual Reports

	1	2	3	4	5 (2 + 3 – 4)
Asset Class	Allocation	Projected Return	Value Added[a]	Expenses	Net Return
Equities	30%	7.5%	3.0%	1.5%	9.0%
Bonds	40	4.5	0.25	0.5	4.2
Venture capital	10	12.0	5.50	3.0	14.5
Hedge funds	20	10.0	6.50	3.0	13.5
Weighted total	100%	7.2%	2.8%	1.5%	8.5%

[a]Required to produce expected rate of return.

Of course, no one can really know what lies ahead. Assumptions are, after all, only assumptions. But that is not my point. My point is that each corporation's annual report should present to shareholders a simple table like Table 7 so that its shareowners can make a fair determination of the reasonableness of the arithmetic on which the pension plan is relying to calculate its pension fund return assumptions. Such a report should be placed high on the list of financial statement disclosure priorities, and I would hope that serious analysts will take this issue directly to corporate managers and challenge the reasonableness of any assumptions deemed excessive. Corporate boards rarely touch this issue, but shareholders ought to force it to the fore.

The seemingly outlandish returns being assumed by corporations for their pension plans have been a major factor in the growing negative gap between the assets and the liabilities of corporate pension plans. The future of DB plans is fraught with challenges that can only be described as awesome. A recent report by Morgan Stanley's respected accounting expert Trevor Harris (with Richard Berner, 2005) put it well:

> Years of mispriced pension costs, underfunding, and overly optimistic assumptions about mortality and retirement have created economic mismatches between promises made and the resources required to keep them. Corporate defined-benefit plans as a whole are as much as $400 billion underfunded. State and local plans, moreover, may be underfunded by three times that amount. Those gaps will drain many plan sponsors' operating performance and threaten the defined-benefit system itself, especially if markets fail to deliver high returns, or if interest rates remain low.

Excessive return assumptions, insufficient contributions, and the almost universal failure to consider the profound long-term erosion of market returns engendered by investment costs have combined to create this serious savings shortfall that pervades our nation's private pension system, our government pension systems, our individual retirement plans, and our defined contribution plans. Much of the responsibility for that failure can be laid to the unwillingness of the financial community to recognize the relentless rules of humble arithmetic.[5]

Comparative Advantage or Community Advantage?

If we are to create greater wealth accumulation for investors, we in the investment profession must focus on these broad issues. Yet we continue to focus nearly all of our attention on the search for the Holy Grail of achieving superior performance for our own clients, seemingly ignoring the fact that all market participants as a group earn average returns. Put another way, in terms of the returns we earn for our clients, we in the investment community are, and must be, average.

Here, I want to make a point about the difference between "comparative advantage" and "community advantage." Much—sometimes I think almost all—of what I read in the learned journals of finance has to do with comparative advantage, such as picking winning stocks or capitalizing on a market inefficiency that improves performance relative to the total market or gaining an edge in return over professional rivals. Yet we ply our trade in what is essentially a closed market system, and we can't change whatever returns the markets are generous enough to bestow on us. So, each dollar of advantage one investor gains in the market comes only at the direct disadvantage of other market participants as a group.

Of course, each of us believes that we ourselves are not average, that we can gain a sustained edge over the market. But we can't all be right. A recent article in the *New Yorker* (Gawande 2004) noted the great fear: "What if I turn out to be average? Yet, if the bell curve is a fact, then so is the reality that most [investors] are going to be average." The article continued:

> There's no shame in being one of them, right? Except, of course, there is. Somehow, what troubles people isn't so much being average as settling for it. Averageness is, for most of us, our fate.

Alas, in the world of money management, the picture is even darker. For we are average only before investment costs are deducted. After costs, we are losers to the market—that relentless rule of humble arithmetic that we want to deny but cannot. Put another way, costs shift the entire bell curve of variations in our individual performance to the left.

But it is a rule of life that none of us want to be average, and competition to be the best is, up to a point at least, healthy. Our efforts to win, however fruitless in the aggregate, provide the transaction volumes that are required for liquidity and market efficiency. Yet, paradoxically, the closer we move to market efficiency, the closer we come to a world in which the EMH becomes a tautology.

Of course, management fees and transaction costs also fatten the wallets of fund managers and Wall Street's financial intermediaries. If the successful strategy of a given fund manager remains undiscovered and sustained, that firm will attract more dollars under management, diverting fees into its pockets from the pockets of its rivals. Such success may even allow the firm to charge higher fees, thereby increasing (albeit only modestly, at least at first) its advisory fee revenues. Yet, again paradoxically, when that happens, by definition, the net returns earned by all investors as a group are commensurately reduced.

Realizing that the upshot of all our feverish investment activity is to advantage Peter at the expense of Paul is doubtless vaguely painful to investment professionals. The dream that we can all achieve success defies Immanuel Kant's categorical imperative that we must "act so that the consequences of our actions can be generalized without self-contradiction." Yet our best and brightest souls continue to compete—arguably, ever more vigorously—in this game of comparative advantage that is inevitably a zero-sum game before costs and a loser's game after costs.

Warren Buffett's crusty but wise partner, Charlie Munger, shares my concern that in the field of money management, as far as the interests of clients are concerned, there can be no net value added, only value subtracted. Here's what he had to say about the commitment of so many exceptional people to the field of investment management:

> Most money-making activity contains profoundly antisocial effects . . . As high-cost modalities become ever more popular . . . the activity exacerbates the current harmful trend in which ever more of the nation's ethical young brain-power is attracted into lucrative money-management and its attendant modern frictions, as distinguished from work providing much more value to others.[6]

Adam Smith's invisible hand may give a minority of money managers a competitive edge, but it cannot improve the lot of investors as a group.

Yet we do have it within our power to do exactly that—to create a community advantage that provides value to all investors. And that can be achieved only by slashing the costs of financial intermediation and reducing the overcapacity present in our investment business today in the form of, for example, the grossly excessive number of mutual funds and the staggering levels of stock-trading activity.

If capitalism is to flourish, enriching the returns of all investors as a group must be a vital goal for our investment society. Yet the triumph of managers' capitalism over owners' capitalism in corporate America has been paralleled by an even greater triumph of managers' capitalism over owners' capitalism in investment America—the field of money management. So long as money-making activity simply shifts returns from the pedestrian to the brilliant or from the unlucky to the lucky or from those who naively trust the system to those who work at its margins, then of course, it has "profoundly antisocial effects." If we vigorously work to reduce system costs, thereby increasing investor returns while holding risk constant, wouldn't we be making capitalism work better for all stockowners? And wouldn't that create, well, profoundly *social* effects that are the diametrical opposite of the antisocial effects that so concern Munger?

Our Intermediation Society. Two powerful forces stand in the way of realizing the idealistic goal of "beginning the world anew" in investment America. One of those forces is money. The field of financial intermediation has become so awesomely profitable to its participants that the vast sums of money we earn has become a narcotic. We have become addicted to enormous profits. The second force may be even more powerful: the reliance of investors on financial intermediaries to protect their interests. We may *think* we live in an ownership society—albeit one that has miles to go before it achieves its promises—but each passing day brings fewer actual direct owners of our wealth-generating corporations.

The fact is that we now live in an intermediation society, in which the last-line owners—essentially, our mutual fund shareholders and the beneficiaries of our public and private pension plans—have to rely on their trustees to act as their faithful fiduciaries. Yet largely because of the dollar-for-dollar trade-off in the money management business (in which the more managers take, the less investors make), there is far too little evidence of such stewardship today. But if our 100-million-plus last-line stockowners and beneficiaries rise up, however, and demand that their stewards provide them with, well, stewardship, then all will be well in investment America—or at least far better for our clients than it is today.

We need to change not only the costs and the structure of our system of financial intermediation but also the philosophy of its trustees. Way back in 1928, New York's Chief Justice Benjamin N. Cardozo put it well:

> Many forms of conduct permissible in a workaday world for those acting at arm's length are forbidden to those bound by fiduciary ties. A trustee is held to something stricter than the morals of the marketplace . . . . As to this there has developed a tradition that is unbending and inveterate . . . . Not honesty alone, but the punctilio of an honor the most sensitive, is then the standard of behavior . . . . Only thus has the level of conduct for fiduciaries been kept at a level higher than that trodden by the crowd.[7]

Yet somehow, in today's world of caveat emptor, of the marketplace as the ultimate arbiter of what's right, and of "get while the getting's good," too large a portion of our financial community seems to have lost sight of that standard.

The Next Frontier. In early 2005, as I approached the completion of my new book on today's counterproductive form of capitalism (forthcoming 2005), I was reading the January/February 2005 issue of the *Financial Analysts Journal*, which included my history of how the mutual fund industry has changed over the past 60 years. I was drawn to Keith Ambachtsheer's insightful essay "Beyond Portfolio Theory: The Next Frontier."

His perceptive thesis questioned the conventional wisdom that the next frontier in investing is about "engineering systems to create better financial outcomes for investors." He suggested that we ought to be thinking more about information theory—knowledge about the costs of investing, for example—and agency theory—the conflicting economic interests that manager/agents confront when they make decisions on behalf of their investor/principals. He wrote of seeking "better outcomes" for investors by virtue of a material reduction in intermediation costs and a "value for money" philosophy in which the driving force is service to clients and beneficiaries. I can only express my deep appreciation for his willingness, without any prior consultation with me, to stand up and be counted on these issues that are at the core of the reflections I present here.

I have been fortunate to play a role in articulating these issues for a full half century, culminating in the creation of The Vanguard Group as a truly *mutual* mutual fund complex all those many (30-plus) years ago. "The Vanguard Experiment," as we called it in its early years, was an effort to set the standard for a new kind of financial intermediation designed to give investors their fair share of whatever returns our markets are kind enough to deliver. Had I not "walked the walk" of truly mutual investing ever since, I would hardly be in a position to "talk the talk" of this essay.

Walking the Walk

It has been a singular and wonderful walk, one that has enabled us to keep investor costs low and investor performance commensurately high. As a result, Vanguard has arguably achieved not only an artistic success but also a remarkable commercial success. Our share of mutual fund assets has now risen for 23 consecutive years—going from 1.8 percent in 1981 to 11.0 percent in mid-2005, as shown in **Figure 2**. It is a revelation to compare that trend with the market share of Massachusetts Financial Services (MFS), our longtime rival of the 1950s and 1960s.

Figure 2. Market Share of Vanguard and MFS, 1961–2004

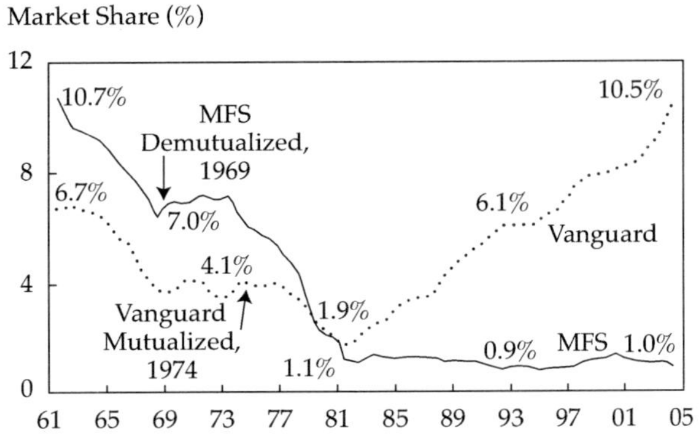

Note: As of January. The percentage changes after conversion were +156 percent for Vanguard and –86 percent for MFS.

Ironically, MFS converted from its own original mutual structure to a typical public (and later conglomerate) ownership in 1969, just before we did exactly the reverse five years later. Although their conversion was hardly the sole cause of the sharp tumble in market share MFS experienced (also shown in Figure 2) from 9 percent to 1 percent, it surely could not have helped. To the limited extent exemplified in these two contrasting patterns, investors are speaking, and their voice is loud and clear: They want their interests placed front and center.

I hope you will forgive the vested nature of this conclusion. It merely brings me full circle to the early words in this essay about the importance of "recognizing the obvious." Surely Vanguard's turning creed into deed is a validation of the words of famed entrepreneurial economist Joseph A. Schumpeter, who asserted that "successful innovation is not an act of intellect, but of will." The fund industry has yet to emulate the innovation that is Vanguard, but I guarantee you that our pioneering outpost will not stand alone at the frontier forever. "The relentless rules of humble arithmetic" that I've pounded home in this message and the attendant CMH and related fiduciary concepts will, sooner or later, resonate with the investing public. That public will accept nothing less than that we in the financial community live up to the responsibilities we are duty bound to honor. Forewarned is forearmed.

Notes

1. It's high time for someone (perhaps for CFA Institute) to conduct a careful study of the system and find out.
2. I recognize that there are fund organizations that are exceptions to these generalizations. The number, however, is surprisingly small.
3. Group averages have been adjusted for sales charges and B-class shares.
4. Possible variations on the new policy portfolio and its potential returns are myriad.
5. The rules of arithmetic apply also to Social Security and the issues surrounding privatization, but these are topics for another day.
6. Munger was speaking at a meeting of the Foundation Financial Officers Group in Santa Monica, California, 14 October 1998.
7. From the decision in *Meinhard v. Salmon* (1928).

References

Ambachtsheer, Keith. 2005. "Beyond Portfolio Theory: The Next Frontier." *Financial Analysts Journal*, vol. 61, no. 1 (January/February):29–33.

Berner, Richard, and Trevor Harris. 2005. "Financial Market Implications of Pension Reform." Morgan Stanley Research, Global Economic Forum (18 January): www.morganstanley.com/GEFdata/digests/20050118-tue.html.

Bogle, John C. 2005. "The Mutual Fund Industry 60 Years Later: For Better or Worse?" *Financial Analysts Journal*, vol. 61, no. 1 (January/February):15–24.

———. Forthcoming 2005. *The Battle for the Soul of Capitalism*. New Haven, CT: Yale University Press.

Brandeis, Louis D. 1914. *Other People's Money*. New York: F.A. Stokes.

Gawande, Atul. 2004. "The Bell Curve." *New Yorker* (6 December):82–91. Available online at www.newyorker.com/fact/content/?041206fa_fact.

Biases and Lessons

Henry Kaufman

During the 60 years of the *Financial Analysts Journal*'s existence, the financial markets have undergone dramatic changes. They have grown in size much more than the economy itself, and many new credit instruments now play important roles in portfolio management and trading activities. Today, the volume of new issues and secondary-market trading is awesome in comparison with only a few decades ago.

Together with the unprecedented growth and innovations, however, have come financial mishaps, scandals, and credit market upheavals. We have experienced credit and speculative bubbles, large gyrations in interest rates, and the rise and fall of financial buccaneers who have more than equaled in their misbehavior their predecessors in U.S. financial history. All of this disorder should have taught important lessons to anyone involved in the financial markets—investors, institutions, and official authorities. I suspect that we have not yet learned them well, however, and that many financial misconceptions and biases persist.

Today's financial community is suffering from a failure to learn the lessons of the past and from biases that cannot be overcome by all our quantitative techniques.

Marketability vs. Liquidity

Despite all the missteps that have occurred, many market participants still lose sight of the distinction between the *marketability* and the *liquidity* of an obligation. Of course, when financial assets are securitized, as many have been, they do become more marketable than when they were lodged on the balance sheet of some institution. Often, however, securitized financial assets can give the false impression of seamless marketability. The fact is, marketability varies considerably over the financial cycle. The narrow credit spreads that seem to give emerging market debt and corporate junk bonds such allure when the financial system is awash with credit are only temporary symptoms of

Henry Kaufman is president of Henry Kaufman & Company, Inc., New York City.

Editor's Note: This article draws from Chapter 16 of Kaufman's *On Money and Markets: A Wall Street Memoir* (New York: McGraw-Hill, 2000).

marketability, not true liquidity. To be sure, these issues can be sold and are, therefore, definitionally marketable when credit market conditions tighten—but only with considerable price concessions and in relatively modest volume.

Marking to Market

With the rapid growth of securitization, the practice of marking to market has gained increasing importance. Accounting guidelines and regulatory guidelines have encouraged this movement, but the pitfalls of marking to market need to be recognized. It is an imperfect process. It tends to overstate values and offer investors false comfort. When market conditions deteriorate and liquidity declines, can one really claim that the last quoted price (even in organized markets or quoted by dealers in the OTC market) is the real market price? Much depends on the size of the security holding, the credit quality of the obligation, and the activity of other market participants. Indeed, large institutions can never liquidate a sizable portion of their assets quickly. In that sense, they are captives of a country's well-being.

Quantitative Models

Another aspect of our dynamic financial markets that we need to continually be aware of is that the modeling of risks has great limitations. Dependence on risk modeling is increasing in the management of investment portfolios and in trading practices. Underlying it is the belief that financial risks are knowable, can be calculated with mathematical precision by massaging historical data, and can be diversified. The shortcomings of this approach are occasionally exposed by large losses and even financial failures. For example, Long-Term Capital Management was a prominent user of mathematical model–based tactics.

The increasing reliance on quantitative modeling is understandable. After all, the quantitative and econometric techniques developed in the last generation have given investors and portfolio managers a new sense of confidence in their ability to forecast financial trends and behavior. By compiling and analyzing historical data and by building models that take into account current variables, econometricians try to predict the movement of interest rates, stock prices, inflation, unemployment, and so on.

What we all know now, however, is that, although historical trading patterns are a useful starting point for assessing risk, they are *only* a starting point. Most instances of sudden deterioration in the credit standing of a corporate or government borrower are not predictable. They reflect submerged weaknesses in underlying economic or financial structures that are not captured by the available data. Models, which are basically backward looking, are essentially useless when an underlying structure changes—a key example of which is loss of liquidity. In the case of managing elaborate positions of options and other complex financial derivatives, models that provide good formulas for conducting dynamic hedging in normal circumstances are of no assistance when transactions cannot be made without huge price concessions.

Another aspect of relying on quantitative modeling that we should be cautious about is that rational analytical techniques cannot predict extremes in financial behavior. During times of financial euphoria or investor panic, these techniques become virtually worthless. The reason is fairly simple: The vast majority of models rest on assumptions about normal and rational financial behavior. But during market manias, logical and analytical minds do not prevail. The historical record is clear: Few analysts have been able to predict when a panicky bear or raging bull would appear, and fewer still have known how far it would go. Such markets are driven more by hubris, elation, fear, pessimism, and the like—emotions that the current models do not, and perhaps cannot, compute—than they are by reason.

Biases in Forecasting

Related to these underlying biases is the rise and prominence of "the consensus forecast." In large measure, this development reflects an all-too-human propensity to minimize risk and avoid isolation. There is comfort, after all, in running with the crowd. Doing so makes it impossible for one to be singled out for being wrong and allows one to avoid the envy or resentment often directed at those who are right more often than not. As a practical matter, however, the consensus forecast cannot be accurate. If a large number of market participants could anticipate big shifts in economic and financial behavior, they would act accordingly, heading off the dramatic changes in the first place.

Our forecasting is biased by the weight of history. Many projections—whether of an individual corporation's earnings or of standard macroeconomic indicators—are based on an assumption that past cyclical patterns will repeat in the future. This bias has been reinforced by statistical averaging, which has become easier and easier to do, thanks to advances in computational power in recent years. This widespread impulse—to believe that the future is grounded in the past—is understandable but should be viewed with great caution and skepticism. To be sure, repetitive patterns occur in the broad pattern of economic and financial change. But the critical ingredient in making good projections is often a matter of identifying what *differs* from the past.

Some biases in the forecasting process are chronic. One of the most profound is the clear bias against negative predictions, either about the financial markets or about the economy. From the President's Council of Economic Advisers—which rarely if ever sees recession on the horizon—to individual corporations and financial institutions—which assiduously avoid talk of near-term difficulties—good news and neutral news both drive out bad news.

There are many reasons for this bias. On the most general level, people are inclined to optimism as a way of coping with the often harsh realities of life. According to one anthropologist, optimism has been a key biological mechanism for the survival of our species.[1] The realities of the workplace also tend to mute pessimistic prognostications. And, of course, negative forecasts make for bad politics. Even though the negative forecasts often are the accurate forecasts, they can cut short the careers of political leaders, interfere with the aspirations of business managers, and imperil the performance records of financial managers.

Throughout my professional career, I have encountered the fallout that comes to those who make negative predictions. In the 1970s, I repeatedly warned of pernicious high inflation rates and the attendant sharp rise in interest rates. In the 1970s and 1980s, I was one of only a handful of analysts to make unwelcome predictions about the damaging effects of the debt explosion and of the poor supervision of financial institutions. Such admonitions earned me the sobriquet "Dr. Doom." Even so, I never wavered from the conviction that accuracy is better than false hope in financial forecasting.

The Growth Bias

Even if one could deliver an absolutely correct—albeit dire—forecast of impending crisis, who has the will or capacity to take advantage of it? Among the ranks of large business organizations—the central wealth-creating institutions in our economy—few are able to make good use of bad news. Top managers rarely have the power to reverse an expansionary course. Large corporations are pressured by internal constituencies and external stakeholders to push for continued growth. Their people, their machinery, their procedures—all are geared to build market share and to expand.

When contraction or crisis forces corporate restructuring, seldom is the process managed with vision. It is normally undertaken under duress, when the very survival of the organization is threatened. The behavioral bias toward growth blinds many managers to the frequent need to manage the downward slope of the business cycle with the same attention they give to the upward climb.

Ironically, when downsizing does come, the resulting write-offs—certainly a reflection of earlier management errors—often are heralded by the market. The lack of intellectual honesty in such situations extends to the accounting treatment of the losses, because tax laws allow the write-offs to be taken as one-time charges against earnings, thereby insulating them from the company's operating earnings. A more authentic approach would force the company to go back and restate the overly cheerful operating earnings of the past by distributing the losses from the unprofitable activity over its entire lifetime within the company.

Financial Trusteeship

The most important lesson that we have not yet learned well is that people in finance are entrusted with an extraordinary responsibility—namely, other people's money. This basic fiduciary responsibility too often has been forgotten in the high-voltage, high-velocity financial environment that has emerged in recent decades. With financial assets extraordinarily mobile, with growing corporate access to debt financing that is perceived to be just as secure as the liquid assets actually owned by the company, and with the absorbing excitement of the trading floor (which for some becomes a sort of game, an end in itself), the notion of financial trusteeship is frequently lost in the shuffle.

The shabby events of the recent past demonstrate that those of us in the profession of finance neither can nor should escape public scrutiny. After all, the huge liabilities of our leading financial institutions are derived from the assets of millions of individual households, businesses, and government. Only a small percentage of the total footings of financial institutions represent their own risk capital. For this reason, we in finance are hardly isolated, insulated, or independent from the external world. (If we were, finance might quickly become the world's most popular profession!) It is our job to make critical judgments about how to channel money and credit into a broad range of economic activities. To carry out this singular and crucial task properly requires objectivity and a strong appreciation of the public trust in our hands.

When this responsibility is not carried out, where is the source of laxity? First of all, senior managers of financial institutions must bear part of the responsibility. They must hammer home the central truth about professional behavior: Breaking the rules is not merely a breach of ethics and of law; it is poor business. To be engaged in questionable financial dealings may well cost a financial institution millions of dollars and imperils client relationships. The lure of huge near-term profits and the financial benefits that will accrue to the firm has compromised the behavior and contributed to the downfall of quite a few senior people in our profession.

To some extent, this failure in behavior is also a result of the shortcomings in our professional schools. They have become so quantitative in their teachings—with the rise of model building, quantitative risk analysis, and econometrics in required course work—that economic and financial history, ethics, and the values and responsibility inherent in prudent financial behavior (the lessons of financial history) have been downplayed. Thus, business schools have catered to the immediate needs and demands of the financial markets and have forsaken their broader responsibilities. Some change for the better, however, seems to be in the offing. As a result of the recent financial excesses, universities are starting to rectify some of the curricular deficiencies.

A large part of the burden for limiting financial excesses, nevertheless, rests on the shoulders of the official authorities, especially the Board of Governors of the Federal Reserve System. The reason is that excessive credit creation breeds excessive credit practices in the private sector. The Fed has not coped well in dealing with this recurring problem. The basic objective of monetary policy is to balance sustainable economic growth with price stability. But most people associate price stability with the stability of the prices of goods and services. Prices, however, have two other key dimensions: the prices of *real* assets, such as housing and commercial property, and the value of financial assets. To what extent should the Fed take into account inflation in asset prices when formulating monetary policy? There is a political dimension to this difficult question, because the simple fact is that inflation in asset prices is quite popular, whereas inflation in the prices of goods and services typically hurts the average individual or family in very tangible ways. Still, excessive inflation in financial asset prices sets in motion a series of forces that, over time, can undermine the foundation of a stable economy. For one thing, such inflation stifles incentives to save. It can breed excesses in business investment, can contribute to undue economic and financial concentration, and can encourage questionable flows of funds into risky markets at the hands of inexperienced investors.

The Fed's historical record when it comes to dealing with changes in financial asset values has been asymmetrical. The record shows that when asset values have fallen suddenly, the Fed has eased monetary policy to provide greater liquidity to the financial markets and to counteract the decline in domestic spending that might result from the loss of financial wealth. When asset prices have advanced strongly, however, escalating financial wealth and loose financing and investment practices, the Fed generally has not responded by tightening monetary policy in a timely fashion. This asymmetry has given rise in the market to an expectation that faulty investments will be bailed out by the central bank. And political support for this policy approach is growing.

Final Word

Eventually, many of these neglected lessons and biases will be learned and overcome. If history is any guide, however, the learning may well not occur until after another round of financial adversity.

Note

1. Lionel Tiger, *Optimism: The Biology of Hope* (New York: Simon & Schuster, 1979).

Consistent Alpha Generation through Structure

William H. Gross, CFA

Successful money management over long periods of time rests on a three- to five-year "secular outlook" and the "structural" composition (the genetic makeup) of the portfolio.

My first (and, up until now, only) published article in the *Financial Analysts Journal* (Gross 1979) was one of the proudest achievements of my career, although looking back on it, I realize that the ideas in the article were surpassed many times over by Myron Scholes, Fischer Black, Robert Merton, and a myriad of others associated with option theory (see, for example, Black and Scholes 1973; Scholes 1972; Merton 1973).

My 1979 article came at option pricing from the standpoint of the market. It was a trader's perspective that attempted to apply real-time price levels for "cushion" bonds (callable corporate bonds) in a context of value based on day-to-day experience. Crude as it was, it was nevertheless a forerunner of my efforts to apply theory, psychology, and common sense to the construction of bond portfolios that would outperform indices and competitors over long periods of time with minimal volatility.

After more than 30 years of managing institutional and individual bond monies, I have gradually come to the understanding that successful money management over long periods of time rests on two, somewhat disparate, foundations. The first is "a secular outlook"—that is, a three-year to five-year forecast that forces one to think long term and to avoid the destructive bile arising from the emotional whipsaws of fear and greed. Such emotions can convince any investor or management firm to do exactly the wrong thing during "irrational" periods in the market.

The second foundation is what might be called the "structural" composition of portfolio management, and whether the reader agrees or disagrees with the secular thesis, I would argue that those who fail to recognize the structural elements of the investment equation will leave far more chips on the table for other, more astute investors to scoop up than they could ever imagine. A portfolio's structure is akin to its genetic makeup: It is how it is constructed without regard to short-term strategic decisions. Structure incorporates principles that are

William H. Gross, CFA, is chief investment officer at PIMCO, Newport Beach, California.

longer than secular, principles that are nearly paramount and should be able to deliver alpha during years when the manager's magic touch—to use a basketball metaphor—seems to have disappeared or when there's simply a time-out on the court, with secular investment opportunities few and far between. Duration, curve, credit, volatility, and other less obvious tilts to a portfolio's steady-state status are what I mean when I speak of a portfolio's inherent structure, although some tilts are more volatile than others and, therefore, produce less risk-adjusted alpha.

Some examples of successful investment structures will give the reader a clearer idea of the concept. Banks have a formidable investment structure: Borrow short near the risk-free rate; lend longer and riskier. If a bank does not overdo the structural model (and they can and have), profits are almost guaranteed on a long-term basis as long as capitalism as we know it survives. Insurance companies, with their "free" reserves and predictable liabilities, have another financial structure almost guaranteed to generate a positive return on capital. Closer to portfolio managers is the structure of Warren Buffett's Berkshire Hathaway, which depends on "float" (about which he frequently writes and talks). This structure, combined with his bottom-up, secular stock picks, has produced one of the world's great fortunes and investment success stories.

In addition to their profit-generating elements, these structures share the common element of longevity, near permanence. They span time periods beyond the secular segments of three to five years, which define typical forecasting periods, and secular stretches of inflation/disinflation that have endured for several decades. An investment's structural magic, then, comes from its "Methuselahian" ability to persist.

The successful structure I am most familiar with is PIMCO's well-known approach labeled the BondsPLUS structure, which has morphed into specific products such as StocksPLUS. These structural models have been more than additive to our clients' bottom lines for many years now. Both the bond and the stock products involve the use of financial futures or future-related investments and the successful placement of the residual cash into higher-yielding, slightly longer-dated investments. As in banking structures, this structural model involves borrowing short via futures priced at nearly the risk-free rate and lending slightly longer. The quality of the debt securities we use, however, tends to be much higher—Aa+ on average—than that which the securities banks use.

By using futures, mortgage rolls, and swaps, we are not actually borrowing money; rather, we are investing in bondlike assets that reflect a borrowing rate slightly less than risk-free/LIBOR-based financing rates. Because these instruments (the "reserves," or "float," as Buffett would call them) absorb little actual cash, the cash is then free to be invested in 6-month to 12-month, higher-yielding securities with yield pickups of 50 bps or more and of quality near Aaa. This 50 bp spread provides a structural advantage to the bond and S&P 500 Index portfolios in almost all yield-curve scenarios except that of an extended negative yield curve (à la 1979–1981). If we use a 40 percent combination of U.S. Treasury futures, mortgage forwards, and swaps in the portfolios, we can enhance performance by (0.40 × 50) or 20 bps a year without even breathing hard.

Our second primary structure involves the selling of unlevered volatility. I use the term "unlevered" from the outset because it was the selling of *levered* volatility that was a major structure, and structural failure, at Long-Term Capital Management. Although structures based on the sale of volatility made sense for LTCM (as they do for PIMCO), LTCM's massive leverage and vulnerability to financing sources added to these strategies made for a potent and deadly mix.

Hedge funds have a particularly short time in which to avoid failure because they are vulnerable to financing sources (this vulnerability was clear when the sources pulled the plug on LTCM). PIMCO is not a hedge fund, so it is not vulnerable in the same way. We are mindful, however, of the "average life" of investment firms. This time frame implies that we have perhaps three to four years before an average client will pull his or her funding if performance is below par. That average life, then, becomes the time frame within which we can "safely" use structural models. It is a time frame far shorter than the one used by banks, insurance companies, or Berkshire Hathaway.

A recent speech by Peter Fisher (2002), former under secretary of the Treasury and potential successor to Alan Greenspan as chairman of the Federal Reserve Board, addressed "the transparency, depth and resilience of the interest rate volatility market"—that is, the part of market structure I have been describing. He suggested what I have been outlining for the past few pages: "Market structure matters," he said; by "market structure," he meant "the overall structure, dynamics and flow of the interest rate volatility market." And the price involved in the buying/selling of volatility is an inherent part of that structure. (We outlined this aspect to clients in early 1988 in an "Investment Outlook" subtitled "Selling the Noise.")

In addition to the "noise" content of volatility, which allows for overpricing, other inherent features of volatility-based option prices lead to structural overvaluation and thus to profitable structural sales. Fisher noted:

> Two major players hold positions that require the rest of the market systematically to be short volatility. One is the federal government, and the other is the American homeowner, through the mortgage market.

Turned upside down, with a PIMCO slant tacked on, Fisher's statement says that because the U.S. government and U.S. homeowners are systematic buyers of volatility (with little recognition of the price they are paying), others can profit structurally by taking the other side of the bet.

How does one get in line to do this? First, it can be done by owning a disproportionately large percentage of mortgages relative to an index. Owning a mortgage is nearly the same thing as owning an agency note (e.g., a Freddie Mac, Federal Home Loan Mortgage Corporation, note) and selling the attached prepayment option to the individual homeowner. It results in a higher yield while carrying the risk of prepayment (or, conversely, duration extension) at exactly the wrong times in the interest rate cycle. Although Fisher argued in his speech that the mortgage volatility market is not necessarily "complete" with regard to price discovery, I believe that historical returns and sociological factors involved in the pricing of the mortgage "option" overwhelmingly favor the holder of the mortgage-backed security and, therefore, the explicit seller of prepayment options. Long-term performance numbers for mortgages versus straight agency notes, for instance, favor mortgages over almost any five-year (or longer) period since the origination of the Ginnie Mae (Government National Mortgage Association) pass-through in the mid-1970s.

The mispricing/overpricing of the prepayment option is the fundamental explanation. The U.S. homeowner, it appears, knows little about the worth of his prepayment option but is more than willing to pay for it via higher interest rates. The opportunity to prepay seems to be an inherent component of a U.S. homeowner's cultural ethic. No amount of massive buying by us or by the agencies themselves in the past decade or so seems to have "arbitraged" away the overpricing of this option. Over the years, our overweighting of mortgages has added perhaps 10 bps annually to performance.

Volatility can be sold in other forms also. For example, explicit sales of put and call options on Treasury futures and swaps can add incremental return to clients' portfolios. Typically, 10 percent of the notional value of portfolios that allow the practice are optioned at any time during the year via out-of-the-money "strangles" (option strategies in which the investor holds a position in both a call and put with different strike prices but with the same maturity and underlying asset). The logic in this case, in contrast to the fleecing of the 30-year mortgagee, is based not only on selling the noise that exaggerates volatility but also on the principle of reversion to the mean and the "lottery ticket" mentality long established in psychology, sociology, and history textbooks. (This is not to say that markets always revert to the mean or that buyers of lottery tickets never hit the big one, but the odds favor option sellers as opposed to option buyers.) Option pricing in this market structure follows the random walk theology of academicians rather than the real-world, real-time experience of astute portfolio managers. These option sales add 5–10 bps of performance annually for our clients.

In addition, volatility can be sold via overweighting the front end of the yield curve relative to an index. Historical information ratios are maximized in duration space by purchasing 12-month to 18-month securities and rolling them back up the curve every quarter. (The dynamics of this strategy, although real and historically potent, are perhaps better left for another paper, to be written by my successor celebrating the 120th anniversary of the *FAJ*!)

Before I leave the topic of structural investing, I want to use a poker analogy to sum up what I've written. Buffett is fond of saying that if you sit down at a poker table and you can't look around and find the fish, "you be the fish." The same thing applies in investing—although in this day and age, it would be unwise to assume that any investor, especially any institutional one, is a fish. From a structural standpoint, however, there may be market participants that, because of their inherent character or the role they play, provide profits to structural investors taking the other side of the bet. Those fish are probably most easily identified as (1) the American homeowner and (2) the investor in short-term cash and money markets who requires liquidity nearly overnight and perpetual overnight peace of mind. Our BondsPLUS and volatility sales programs depend on such fish, and they form the schools of structural plankton on which mighty whales feed.

The essence of my structural investment thesis is that applying the appropriate structure to an investment portfolio over long periods of time can add value and alpha before any strategizing—short-term or secular—takes place. How wonderful to start off the New Year knowing that your portfolio is odds-on to generate alpha without the necessity to outsmart the market via short-term strategies!

Recent trends involving hedge funds, the use of leverage, and the fascination with the "carry trade" (borrowing short and investing long) assuredly threaten short-term performance of some structural models. But for the investor with enough staying power, the alpha-generating properties of these strategies over long periods of time should survive what could be a lengthy winter to emerge ultimately into the inevitable spring.

Individuals as well as institutional money managers, by the way, can apply this structural philosophy. Want to emulate a bank, an insurance company, or a PIMCO plan in your own investment portfolio? You have simple ways to do it these days via the futures and options markets. The trick is to first recognize who you are and what your investment time frame is. Structural investing will not necessarily succeed over short periods of time (as LTCM found out).

And it will not generate positive alpha in every year. The probability of success depends on matching the structure with the liquidity of an institution's liabilities and, in the case of an individual, to your own investment time frame, emergency requirements for funds, and discipline and resolve to follow a consistent plan. With high levels of confidence that you know yourself in each of these areas, however, you can use a structural investing approach to greatly increase your odds of generating alpha relative to the bogey in almost any portfolio. I advise readers contemplating using such a strategy to do it but not overdo it. And pick your structures in concert with your long-term secular view of the economy.

References

Black, Fischer, and Myron Scholes. 1973. "The Pricing of Options and Corporate Liabilities." *Journal of Political Economy*, vol. 81, no. 3 (May/June):637–659.

Fisher, Peter R. 2002. Remarks of Under Secretary of the Treasury Peter R. Fisher to the Bond Buyer's Financial Innovations and Derivatives Conference, New York (7 June): www.treas.gov/press/releases/po3158.htm.

Gross, William H. 1979. "Coupon Valuation and Interest Rate Cycles." *Financial Analysts Journal*, vol. 35, no. 4 (July/August):68–71.

Merton, Robert C. 1973. "The Theory of Rational Option Pricing." *Bell Journal of Economics and Management Science*, vol. 4, no. 1 (Spring):141–183.

Scholes, Myron S. 1972. "The Market for Securities: Substitution versus Price Pressure and the Effects of Information on Share Prices." *Journal of Business*, vol. 45, no. 2 (April):179–211.

Implementation Efficiency

Richard Grinold

Investment management relies on an ability to understand and manage three forces: return, risk, and cost. The understanding, if not the management, of risk and return is well advanced in the finance field—stemming from Markowitz's notion of mean–variance efficiency and Sharpe's economic explanation of expected return. In that risk–return landscape, any presumed potential for adding investment value can be summarized by the information ratio—that is, the expected exceptional return (alpha) divided by the amount of risk assumed in pursuit of that exceptional return.

Alas, potential is one thing and delivery is another. The ability to move the cup of investment potential to the lip of the bottom line is restricted by institutional and economic realities and, in some cases, by a lack of attention to the task. The institutional limitations are constraints that are either self-imposed or imposed by a principal. The economic realities are costs. These costs take many forms, but the largest costs and the costs most dependent on the investment manager's actions stem from trading. The world of return, risk, and cost is not well understood and is a significant challenge in advancing the theory of portfolio management.

This article describes a strategic framework for thinking about and analyzing costs or, more broadly, implementation losses. I use the notions of covariance and correlation that are central in the study of risk and return and have been effectively exploited by Clarke, De Silva, and Thorley (2002, 2005) in their study of implementation efficiency.

The information ratio is key to measuring active investment potential. However, analysts should not concentrate on the information ratio to the exclusion of investment objectives. As the objective, I use the active management version of mean–variance utility that consists of portfolio alpha minus two penalties—one for active risk and one for implementation costs. This objective is variously called "risk-adjusted alpha"

The implementation losses resulting from transaction costs and investment constraints can be measured by an analysis of risk, covariance, and correlation.

Richard Grinold is director of research at Barclays Global Investors, San Francisco.

or "certainty-equivalent alpha." I concentrate on the effect of constraints and costs on the objective value. The objective and the information ratio are linked because the strategy that maximizes risk-adjusted alpha in a constraint- and cost-free environment also has a maximum information ratio. When there are costs and constraints, that link breaks down, but happily, my work can characterize the impact of costs and constraints on both the objective and the information ratio.

The two barriers to implementation efficiency are opportunity costs and implementation costs. Opportunity costs are the loss in benefits an investor would anticipate if the investor were not limited by constraints or deterred from acting by the presence of trading costs. Implementation losses are associated with the transactions the investor attempts. These losses include the direct cost of trading, anticipated market impact, and the estimated losses associated with trades attempted but not completed. This article presents a model for the loss of value added with and without the consideration of implementation costs. The exposition tends toward the technical, but most of the theoretical development is relegated to Appendix A.

General Results: Before Costs

This section introduces the notation and terminology used in the framework's development and presents the general results before implementation costs.[1]

Notation and Terminology. We consider a universe of N assets and indicate *active* positions as holdings vectors

$$\mathbf{h}_X = \left(h_1^X, h_2^X, \ldots, h_N^X\right)$$

and

$$\mathbf{h}_Y = \left(h_1^Y, h_2^Y, \ldots, h_N^Y\right)$$

for, respectively, positions X and Y. Risk is measured with an N-by-N covariance matrix (which is assumed to be nonsingular):

$$\mathbf{V} = \left(V_{n,m}\right).$$

The risk of position X is

$$\omega_X = \sqrt{\mathbf{h}'_X \mathbf{V} \mathbf{h}_X},$$

and the respective covariance and correlation of positions X and Y are given by

$$\begin{aligned}\omega_{X,Y} &= \mathbf{h}'_X \mathbf{V} \mathbf{h}_Y \\ &= \omega_X \rho_{X,Y} \omega_Y.\end{aligned}$$

We have a forecast of exceptional asset return that is

$$\boldsymbol{\alpha} = \left(\alpha_1, \alpha_2, \ldots, \alpha_N\right).$$

With this forecast, we can calculate the alpha of any position P as

$$\alpha_P = \alpha' \mathbf{h}_P.$$

The information ratio of the position is

$$IR_P = \frac{\alpha_P}{\omega_P}.$$

Our investment criterion is risk-adjusted or certainty-equivalent alpha. For position P, it is

$$U_P = \alpha_P - \left(\frac{\lambda}{2}\omega_P^2\right).$$

For example, with $\lambda = 40$ and risk levels ω_P of 1 percent, 2 percent, 3 percent, and 4 percent, the respective risk penalties would be 0.20 percent, 0.80 percent, 1.80 percent, and 3.20 percent.

Important Attributes. Any strategy P has three attributes that help explain the level of implementation efficiency. These attributes relate any position P with the ideal position, Q; thus, we can compare where we are with where we would like to be. The attributes are as follows:

- *Transfer coefficient*. In general, the correlation between any two positions, say X and Y, is $\rho_{X,Y}$. When one of these is ideal position Q, we use the shortcut notation $\tau_P \equiv \rho_{P,Q}$.
- *Risk commitment*, which is the ratio of the volatilities of positions P and Q—that is,

  $$\chi_P = \frac{\omega_P}{\omega_Q}.$$

- *Backlog position*. Let

  $$\mathbf{h}_{Q-P} = \mathbf{h}_Q - \mathbf{h}_P$$

  be the difference between ideal implementation Q and actual implementation P. Think of $\mathbf{h}_{Q-P}$ as the trade one would have to make to transform P into Q. The item of interest to us is the variance of the backlog position, backlog risk:[2] ω_{Q-P}.

The Basic Equation. We start with a simple and useful relationship. It connects two quantities—the alphas, $\boldsymbol{\alpha}$, and the active-position positions, $\mathbf{h}_Q$, in an equation using the covariance matrix, $\mathbf{V}$, and the coefficient of risk aversion, λ. I call this the *basic equation* and refer to it repeatedly:

$$\boldsymbol{\alpha} = \lambda \mathbf{V} \mathbf{h}_Q. \tag{1}$$

The basic equation says that the alpha of each asset is proportional to its covariance with the return on active position Q. The usual interpretation of Equation 1 is that position Q captures the information in the alphas in a mean–variance-efficient manner. I consider an alternative interpretation of the basic equation after I state the results.

Results. For any position P,

$$IR_P \equiv \frac{\alpha_P}{\omega_P} = \tau_P IR_Q, \tag{2}$$

where τ_P is the transfer coefficient. Our ability to implement effectively is proportional to our degree of alignment with Q.

The loss in objective value when we move from the ideal Q to some actual P is also easily captured:

$$U_Q - U_P = \frac{\lambda}{2}\omega_{Q-P}^2, \tag{3}$$

where ω_{Q-P} is the risk of the backlog position.

From Equation 2, we immediately see that $IR_P < IR_Q$ unless P is perfectly correlated with Q (i.e., $\tau_P = 1$). From Equation 3, we note that $U_P < U_Q$ for any $P \neq Q$.

Recall that χ_P is the ratio of the volatilities of P and Q, so Equation 3 can be rearranged as

$$\frac{U_P}{U_Q} = 2\tau_P\chi_P - \chi_P^2 \leq \tau_P^2. \tag{4}$$

Thus, in terms of our objective, before costs, a transfer coefficient of $\tau_P = 0.7$ limits us to *at most* 49 percent of the potential value added.

Example. **Figure 1** shows how the transfer coefficient of an optimal portfolio that is constrained to be long depends on volatility ω_P. In this case, the average risk of the individual assets is shown increasing from 15 percent to 35 percent. Position sizes tend to be inversely related to volatility; thus with high-volatility assets, one bumps into the long-only restriction less often than with low-volatility assets.

Reverse Engineering. Basic Equation 1 can be used in another interesting way. Rather than start with the forecasts (alphas) and use Equation 1 to solve for active position $\mathbf{h}_Q$, we could start with $\mathbf{h}_Q$ and then use the basic equation to calculate the alphas. This method is called "reverse engineering" or "grapes from wine."[3] An illustration follows:

Suppose we start with a forecast alpha as per basic Equation 1 and find a position, S, that is the best we can do when we consider mandated constraints but ignore trading costs and any additional constraints. Then, we proceed as if we had started with forecasts $\hat{\alpha} = \lambda \mathbf{V}\mathbf{h}_S$ and analyze implementation efficiency relative to that modified standard.

Figure 1. Transfer Coefficient for Various Asset Volatility Levels and Levels of Active Risk

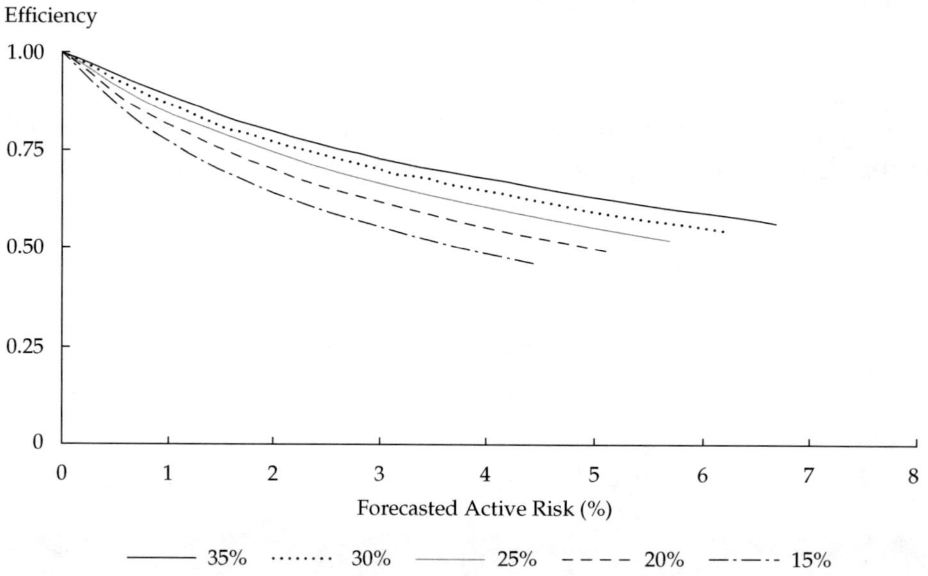

Source: Grinold and Kahn (2000b).

When we add the additional complication of trading costs and other constraints, our optimization yields the positions P. This simple equation shows how one can relate the implementation P to the intermediate standard, S:

$$IR_P = \left(\frac{\tau_P}{\tau_S}\right) IR_S = \tau_P IR_Q. \tag{5}$$

***Ex Ante* and *Ex Post*.** Our results have been expressed in terms of forecasted information ratios and predictions of risk-adjusted returns. We can examine these criteria on an *ex post* (realized) basis. Doing so adds considerable noise to the process, however, and raises a host of issues, such as: "Our policy limiting large active positions in growth stocks reduces efficiency on an *ex ante* basis but actually helps on an *ex post* basis. Does this mean our constraint improves implementation efficiency?" Such questions come in infinite varieties. If one tries to limit an investment process in K ways, some of these limitations will turn out to help on an *ex post* basis. Does this particular outcome prove anything? It might, but our first presumption should be that the result is a backhand form of data mining. A more judicious course would be to establish a prior hypothesis—something like: "Our most extreme forecasts for growth stocks are likely to be based on a false premise"—and then take steps to either substantiate that hypothesis, dig a great deal deeper into the extreme forecasts, or rein in the alphas in a more formal manner (i.e., identify the problem, verify that it exists, and attack the problem at its source).

Allocation of Opportunity Loss to Constraints and Costs

If constraints and trading costs exist, we need informed judgment to split the opportunity cost between them.[4] We might, as suggested previously, do an incremental analysis. In the cost and constraint case, the analysis could involve optimizing four times:

1. with no constraints or costs: optimal value $U_1 = U_Q$,
2. with constraints and no costs: optimal value U_2,
3. with costs and no constraints: optimal value U_3, and
4. with both costs and constraints: optimal value $U_4 = U_P$.

We know that $U_1 \geq U_2 \geq U_4$ and $U_1 \geq U_3 \geq U_4$. We could attribute either $U_1 - U_2$ or $U_3 - U_4$ to the constraints, or we could waffle and say that $[(U_1 - U_2) + (U_2 - U_4)]$ divided by 2 is attributable to the constraints and $[(U_1 - U_3) + (U_3 - U_4)]$ divided by 2 is attributable to the trading costs. There is no right answer and considerable wiggle room. The difficulty compounds as we add additional sources of constraints or costs.

In this section, I present an elegant way to waffle and show how it applies in the case of constraints and trading costs.[5] It works in great generality, and an investor has to solve the problem only once. If we face several constraints and multiple sources of cost (e.g., spread and market impact), we can use the concept I describe here to allocate the opportunity loss among the several sources.

In any optimization, we obtain an equation for each asset; thus, we have N equations, called the "first-order conditions." The first-order conditions are a generalized version of "setting the derivative equal to zero." The resulting set on N equations can be written as a variation of basic Equation 1:

$$\alpha = \lambda \mathbf{V} \mathbf{h}_P + \mathbf{c} + \mathbf{t}, \tag{6}$$

where **c** is a term related to constraints and **t** reflects the marginal trading costs.[6]

Here are three ways to interpret Equation 6:

1. If we start with alpha equal to $\alpha - (\mathbf{c} + \mathbf{t})$ and ignore both constraints and trading costs, we will find P as our optimal position.
2. If we start with alpha equal to $\boldsymbol{\alpha} - \mathbf{c}$ and ignore constraints, we will find P as our optimal position.
3. If we start with alpha equal to $\boldsymbol{\alpha} - \mathbf{t}$ and ignore trading costs, we will find P as our optimal position.

So, a portion of our alpha has been consumed by the constraints and costs. How do we apportion the loss between the two? Here is one way.

First, we link the lost alpha with positions. We define positions $\mathbf{h}_C, \mathbf{h}_T$ through the linear equations

$$\mathbf{c} = \lambda \mathbf{V} \mathbf{h}_C \tag{7a}$$

and

$$\mathbf{t} = \lambda \mathbf{V} \mathbf{h}_T. \tag{7b}$$

These positions have alphas and risks. Indeed, the variances, ω_C^2, ω_T^2, and covariance, $\omega_{C,T}$, play a role in what follows. Note that Equations 1, 6, and 7 together with our definition of the backlog imply that

$$\begin{aligned} \mathbf{h}_{Q-P} &= \mathbf{h}_Q - \mathbf{h}_P \\ &= \mathbf{h}_c + \mathbf{h}_T. \end{aligned} \tag{8}$$

The loss in objective value, before costs, is

$$\begin{aligned} U_Q - U_P &= \frac{\lambda}{2} \omega_{Q-P}^2 \\ &= \frac{\lambda}{2}\left(\omega_C^2 + 2\right)\left(\omega_{C,T} + \omega_T^2\right). \end{aligned} \tag{9}$$

Equation 9 can be conveniently split, Solomon fashion, to become

$$U_Q - U_P = \frac{\lambda}{2}\left(\omega_C^2 + \omega_{C,T}\right) + \frac{\lambda}{2}\left(\omega_{C,T} + \omega_T^2\right). \tag{10}$$

We then attribute opportunity loss $\lambda/2(\omega_C^2 + \omega_{C,T})$ to the constraints and attribute opportunity loss $\lambda/2(\omega_{C,T} + \omega_C^2)$ to the trading costs.[7]

In addition, of course, we should deduct the implementation costs of trading to obtain an after-cost objective value or information ratio. The generalized after-cost calculation is complicated; the next section provides an analytic solution in a special case.

Specific Model: After-Cost Results

In special circumstances, we can find analytic after-cost results for both the information ratio and the objective. In the previous section, I compared ideal implementation Q with any other implementation P. In this section, I consider a specific implementation P that is optimal with transaction costs explicitly considered. Thus, the results for P are an upper bound on any strategy choice. Also, in contrast to the previous sections, I need to make several assumptions. Thus, we have an illustrative result. It shines a beam of light into an otherwise dark space; it does not turn the lights on.

Trading costs influence implementation efficiency in two ways. First, we have to pay for the trades we make. More insidious is what I call "the intimidation factor"; that is, trading costs deter us from trading and we let opportunities slip by. Indeed, when costs are extremely high, we do not even attempt any trades. We thus pay no costs, but we lose all opportunities. We must account for the trades we forgo as well as the trades we attempt.

The trades we make give rise to implementation costs. Some sources of implementation costs are observable—such as bid–ask spreads, commissions, and taxes. Other implementation costs are not observable but are inferred; we temporarily push up the prices of the assets we buy and depress the prices of the assets we sell. This buying too high and selling too low eventually manifests itself in lower investment performance, which is called "market impact." Because not all of the trades we attempt will actually be completed, we must account for this disappointment as well. Finally, a true, dynamic optimization method senses potential future costs. Thus, increasing an active position today represents a commitment to eventually unwind the trade. When that prospective cost is considered, we will take smaller active positions.

To develop the after-cost results, we need some additional notation. Let c_P be the annual costs (more on this later) for maintaining position P. Because our goal is to explore the nature of the after-cost information ratio and the risk-adjusted return after costs, we need these measures, which are, respectively, $(\alpha_P - c_P)/\omega_P$ and $U_P - c_P$.

The model depends on a number of assumptions. To focus on costs, we assume that there are no constraints.

We need four components to fill out the structure:

- an information process,
- a trading-cost model,
- specification of the optimal policy, and
- an intertemporal link.

The Information Process. We rebalance the positions at periods of length Δt; in the examples that follow, we take a week, $\Delta t = 1/52$. A typical period is the interval of time $(t - \Delta t, t)$. Suppose that at time $t - \Delta t$, the ideal position is $\mathbf{h}_Y$ and the alphas are $\boldsymbol{\alpha}(t - \Delta t)$. These variables are linked by the basic equation as follows:

$$\boldsymbol{\alpha}(t - \Delta t) = \lambda \mathbf{V} \mathbf{h}_Y. \tag{11}$$

At time t, the alphas change and position $\mathbf{h}_Q$ becomes our new ideal; again, as per Equation 1,

$$\boldsymbol{\alpha}(t) = \lambda \mathbf{V} \mathbf{h}_Q. \tag{12}$$

You can see from the notation that we are assuming no change in either the risk aversion, λ, or the covariance matrix, $\mathbf{V}$.

The time $t - \Delta t$ alphas fade toward zero as old information loses relevancy. Let HL stand for the half-life (in years) of our information. The half-life is used to define gamma, which denotes the retention rate of the alphas (with $1 - \gamma$ the loss each period), as $\gamma = (0.5)^{\Delta t/HL}$. The parameter γ plays a key role in what follows. To get a feel for these numbers, suppose we are examining weekly periods and a half-life of three or nine months. For a three-month half-life, γ would be 0.948, and for a nine-month half-life, γ would be 0.982. The expected alphas at time t are $\gamma\boldsymbol{\alpha}(t - \Delta t)$.

Old information ebbs away as new information flows in. We denote the new information $\Delta\boldsymbol{\alpha}$. It is random with mean zero and is unrelated to the current alphas [i.e., knowing $\boldsymbol{\alpha}(t - \Delta t)$ is no help in predicting $\Delta\boldsymbol{\alpha}$]. Putting these pieces together, we can describe the simple, mean-reverting dynamics of the alpha process:

$$\boldsymbol{\alpha}(t) = \gamma\boldsymbol{\alpha}(t - \Delta t) + \Delta\boldsymbol{\alpha}. \tag{13}$$

The risk aversion and covariance matrix do not vary, so the ideal positions, Equations 11 and 12, inherit the simple dynamics (Equation 13) of the alphas. We define $\Delta\mathbf{h}$ as the change in positions caused by the arrival of new information. It is linked to the new information through the equation $\Delta\boldsymbol{\alpha} = \lambda\mathbf{V}\Delta\mathbf{h}$, then Equation 13 determines how our ideal position moves through time from Y to Q:

$$\mathbf{h}_Q = \gamma\mathbf{h}_Y + \Delta\mathbf{h}, \tag{14}$$

where the expected values of $\Delta\mathbf{h}$ and $\mathbf{h}'_Y\,\mathbf{V}\Delta\mathbf{h}$ are zero.[8]

Trading Costs. The ideal position moves from Y to Q while the actual active position moves from what I will term Z during the period $(t - \Delta t, t)$ to P for the period $(t, t + \Delta t)$. We assume that the trading costs for getting from Z to P are proportional to the tracking variance (tracking error squared) between positions Z and P. Thus,

$$c_P\Delta t = \frac{\hat{\eta}}{2}\omega_{P-Z}^2, \tag{15}$$

where $\hat{\eta}$ is a parameter used to adjust the level of trading costs.

This assumption can, at best, be described as an approximation. The economic motivation is that the other side, also known as the market, will have to take on the risk of this trade to fill our order. We assume that the price for taking on that risk is going to be proportional to the hedging cost, and we assume, in addition, that the hedging cost will be proportional to the variance of the trade basket. Among the shortcomings of this assumption is the fact that many of the observable implementation costs of trading increase in a linear way with the amount of trading. Indeed, Keim and Madhavan (1996) presented evidence that the inferred market-impact cost increases with the three-halves power, not the square we have assumed. The trading-cost assumption is the weakest link in the argument, and I shall take care not to strain it unduly in interpreting the results.[9]

Equation 15 measures the transaction costs for any single rebalance. Because we will rebalance $1/\Delta t$ times a year, c_P is the annual cost (run rate). If we define η as $\eta \equiv \hat{\eta}\Delta t$, then the annual costs are

$$\frac{\eta}{2}\omega_{P-Z}^2.$$

For example, with weekly rebalancing and a 0.17 percentage point (17 bps) tracking error between the positions Z and P, if $\hat{\eta} = 100$, the annual cost is

$$52 \times \frac{100}{2} \times (0.0017 \times 0.0017) = 0.77 \text{ percentage points a year.}$$

The cost paid per week is 1/52 of this amount.

Optimal Position. Optimal strategy P wants to be in two places at the same time.[10] Being close to Q allows us to capture investment opportunity, but being close to our prior position, Z, allows us to control trading costs. In a single-period model, the optimal policy is simply a mixture of the two. In a dynamic model, the optimal policy is slightly more complicated.

In a dynamic model, the decisions taken today will have cost implications for the future; therefore, we set our sights somewhat lower than ideal portfolio Q. Two (easily calculated) parameters, ψ and δ, both of which are between 0 and 1, determine the optimal policy. The parameter ψ is the amount we scale back the alphas. The parameter δ maintains the balance between the transaction costs and the opportunity loss of being far from the resulting less-than-ideal position. Rather than trying to be spot on position $\mathbf{h}_Q$, we settle for less and try to stay close to $\psi\mathbf{h}_Q$. Given a current position $\mathbf{h}_Z$ and the ideal position $\mathbf{h}_Q$, we choose position $\mathbf{h}_P$ according to the following equation:

$$\mathbf{h}_P = (1-\delta)(\Psi\mathbf{h}_Q) + \delta\mathbf{h}_Z, \text{ with } 0 < \delta < 1 \text{ and } 0 < \Psi < 1. \tag{16}$$

Calculation of the Parameters. The alpha and risk-penalty terms of the objective are in terms of annual run rates—that is, percentages per year. The transaction costs, however, are point costs. Indeed, one of the hurdles a dynamic management process faces is trying to convert the transaction costs also into annual run rates. In the relatively simple model presented here, we do so explicitly.

We start on this path by defining an effective risk aversion via

$$\hat{\lambda} = \frac{\lambda\Delta t}{2}\left[1+\sqrt{1+4\left(\frac{\hat{\eta}}{\lambda\Delta t}\right)}\right]. \tag{17}$$

Then, the policy parameters are

$$\delta \equiv \frac{\hat{\eta}}{\hat{\lambda}+\hat{\eta}} \tag{18a}$$

and

$$\psi \equiv \frac{1-\delta}{1-\gamma\delta}. \tag{18b}$$

The parameter $\hat{\lambda}$ places the risk aversion and trading costs on a similar basis. In that spirit, δ measures the relative size of the trading costs.

The good news for users of single-period optimization is that if we scale the three terms—alpha, risk, and transaction costs—of a *single-period* optimization correctly, we obtain the same solution as the dynamic optimal policy. This single-period optimization will do the trick:

$$\max_{\mathbf{h}}\left[\psi\alpha'\mathbf{h} - \frac{\lambda}{2}\mathbf{h}'\mathbf{V}\mathbf{h} - \left(\frac{\hat{\eta}}{2}\right)\left(\frac{\lambda}{\hat{\lambda}}\right)(\mathbf{h}-\mathbf{h}_Z)'\,\mathbf{V}(\mathbf{h}-\mathbf{h}_Z)\right]. \tag{19}$$

Two adjustments are necessary: (1) scale back the alphas, and (2) use an amortization factor, $\lambda/\hat{\lambda}$, to put the transaction costs on a run-rate basis.

Intertemporal Link. Our model up to this point has involved four positions and two dates. The transitions are

Date: $t-\Delta t \to t$.
Ideal: $Y \to Q$.
Actual: $Z \to P$.

We assume that the system is in equilibrium. To be explicit:

- The active risks of Y and Q are the same, $\omega_Y = \omega_Q$.
- The active risks of Z and P are the same, $\omega_Z = \omega_P$.
- The relationship between (Y,Z) and (Q,P) is stable; thus, the transfer coefficient is the same in all periods, $\tau_Z = \rho_{Z,Y} = \rho_{P,Q} = \tau_P$.

An immediate consequence of this equilibrium assumption is that the correlation between the prior ideal position, Y, and the current ideal position, Q, is equal to γ.

This structure allows us to ascertain important properties of the resulting strategy. We saw in the previous section that the transfer coefficient, τ_P, is a key measure of implementation efficiency. Our model allows us to see how the basic drivers of the investment process, γ as a measure of the shelf life of our information and δ as a measure of the relative size of the trading costs, determine the correlation of the two positions. The relationship is

$$\tau_P = \sqrt{\frac{1-\delta^2}{1-\gamma^2\delta^2}} < 1. \tag{20}$$

The transfer coefficient increases as the half-life of the signals (and therefore γ) increases, and it decreases as costs (and therefore δ) increase. We would suspect that faster-moving information and higher costs would reduce the transfer coefficient; Equation 20 shows us how and to what extent.

I illustrate these results in a series of examples. In all of them, the period is one week (so, $\Delta t = 1/52$), risk aversion is $\lambda = 20$, the information ratio is $IR_Q = 1.5$; thus, we have the potential for value added of $U_Q = 5.625$ percent a year.

Figure 2 illustrates the sensitivity of the transfer coefficient, the first important attribute, to changes in costs and the half-life of the information. In Figure 2 and those that follow, half-lives of 1, 2, 3, and 4 quarters are considered. The cost is scaled from a base-case number. Thus, 1.80 on the horizontal axis represents an 80 percent increase in costs and 0.52 represents a case where the costs are roughly half the costs in the base case.

The second important attribute is risk commitment, given as $\chi_P = \omega_P/\omega_Q$; it is the relative volatility of the actual and ideal strategies. The risk commitment plays a central role in evaluating the after-cost certainty-equivalent return and after-cost information ratio. Costs always induce lower volatility than the volatility of the ideal (costless) strategy, Q; thus, $\chi_P < 1$. The lower volatility can be considered the exposure to the strategy that we are willing to accept. We can determine this important attribute in terms of (γ,δ):

$$\chi_P = \psi\sqrt{\left[\frac{1-\delta}{1+\delta}\right]\left[\frac{(1+\gamma)\delta}{(1-\gamma)\delta}\right]} < \tau_P. \tag{21}$$

The parameters τ_P and χ_P are sufficient to describe implications of the costs for the investment process. Note also that they are easily measured in actual applications as, respectively, the correlation between our ideal Q and actual P and the relative volatility of P and Q.

The attributes of the optimal policy are given here (recall that U_Q is the annual certainty-equivalent return from following the ideal strategy):

$$\frac{\alpha_P}{U_Q} = 2\tau_P\chi_P, \tag{22a}$$

Figure 2. The Transfer Coefficient as a Function of Cost and Information Half-Life

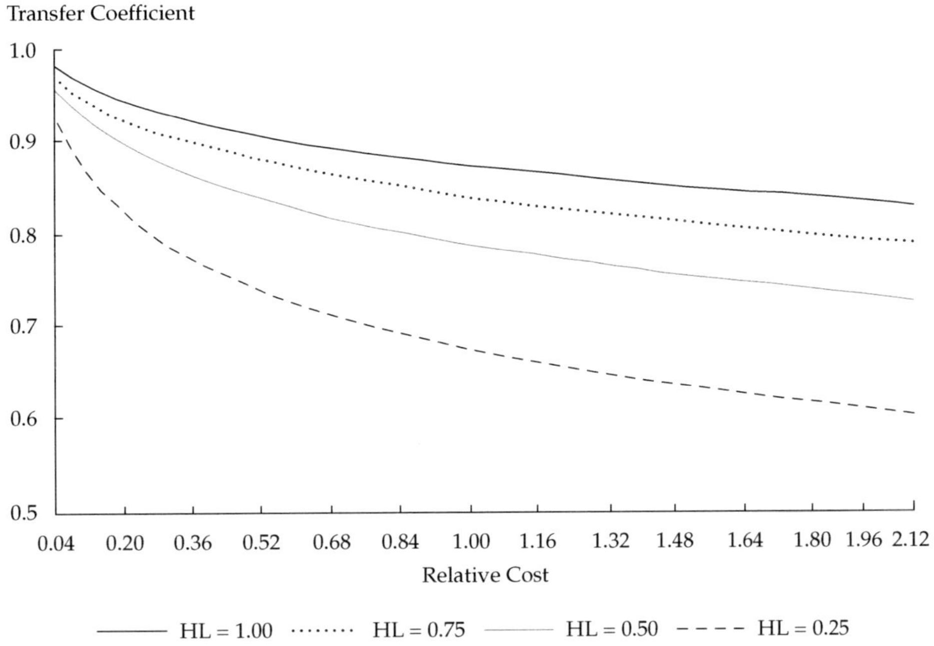

$$\frac{c_P}{U_Q} = \tau_P \chi_P - \chi_P^2, \tag{22b}$$

$$\left(\frac{\lambda}{2}\right)\left(\frac{\omega_P^2}{U_Q}\right) = \chi_P^2, \tag{22c}$$

and

$$\frac{(U_P - c_P)}{U_Q} = \tau_P \chi_P. \tag{22d}$$

It is interesting to look at the cost in more detail. When unit costs are low, costs at the strategy level, c_P, are also low. When unit costs increase to a high level, c_P will decrease as we gradually withdraw from the strategy. The result can be highly nonlinear, as can be seen in **Figure 3**.

In detailed simulations of portfolio management processes, I have usually observed that transaction costs incurred are relatively insensitive to the cost levels. There seems to be a unit elasticity of cost; costs being up 10 percent implies turnover going down about 3.5 percent, and the total spent on trades remains about the same. We can see that characteristic in the long, relatively flat parts of the curves for the relatively longer-lived signals in Figure 3.

The same is not true for indirect costs, the opportunity loss. **Figure 4** shows the sizable and increasing opportunity loss as costs increase. At the limit, 100 percent of the opportunity is lost.

The bottom line—according to our objective—is Equation 22d, which shows the fraction of value added. The graph lines in **Figure 5** have a shape and ordering similar to those of the transfer coefficient shown in Figure 2. The magnitudes, however, are different. In the case of extremely high costs and a short half-life, the investor can extract only about 12 percent of the potential benefits. This effect is clear in the algebra because $\tau_P \chi_P < \tau^2{}_P < \tau_P$.

Figure 3. Annual Cost Incurred as a Function of Unit Cost and Information Half-Life

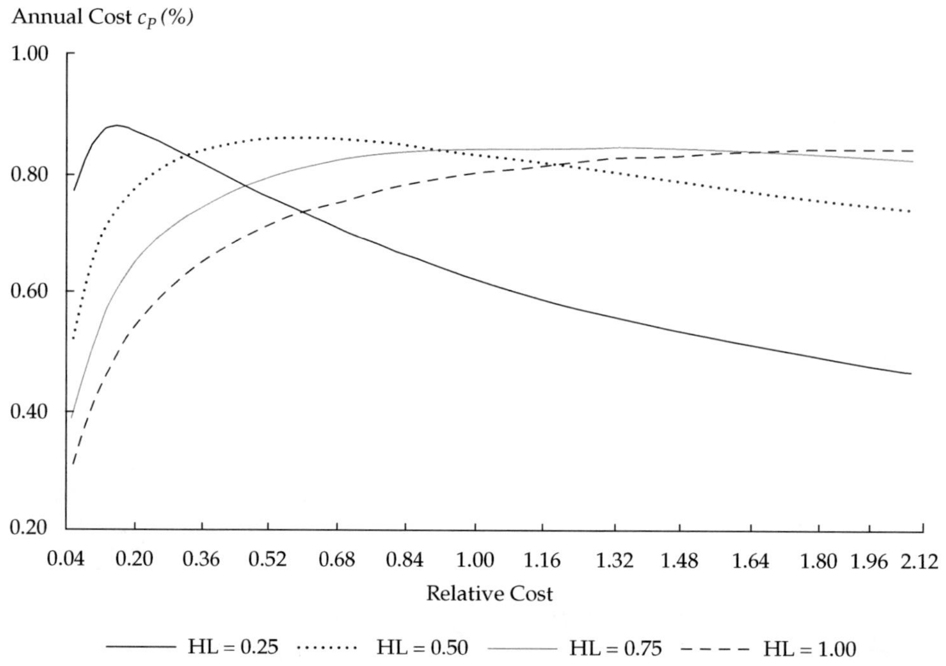

Figure 4. Opportunity Loss as a Function of Unit Cost and Information Half-Life

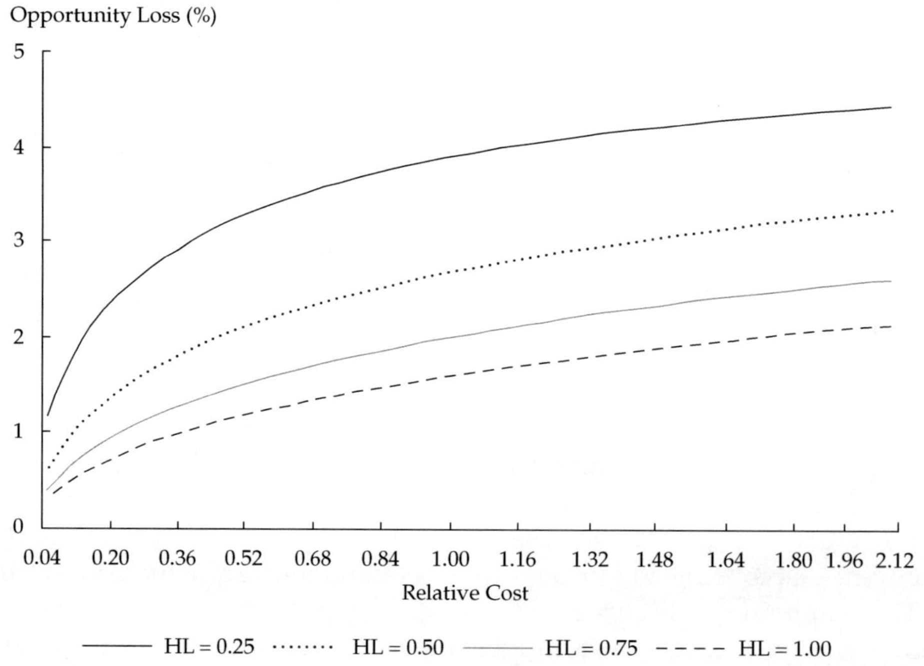

Figure 5. Fraction of Potential Value Added That Is Captured

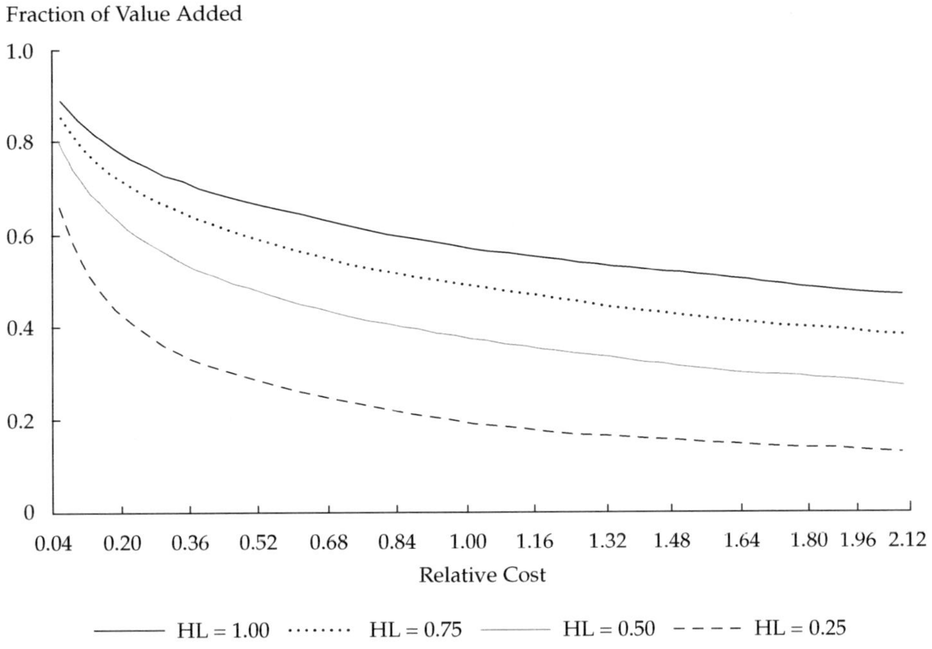

The final result is in terms of implementation efficiency as measured by the before- and after-cost information ratios:

$$\frac{\alpha_P}{\omega_P} = \tau_P IR_Q \tag{23a}$$

and

$$\frac{\alpha_P - c_P}{\omega_P} = \left(\frac{\tau_P + \chi_P}{2}\right) IR_Q. \tag{23b}$$

The before-cost result must agree with the general results. The after-cost results must, of course, be worse. Equation 23b makes the difference explicit, and **Figure 6** makes clear that the effect can be large.

Figure 6 shows the fraction of IR_Q that strategy P will yield on both a before- and after-cost basis. The arrows indicate the link between the before-cost and after-cost results for the long (one year) and short (one quarter) half-lives.

Figure 7 illustrates these results in terms of an active, after-cost frontier that demonstrates the alpha minus cost that can be attained in various combinations of active risk and costs.

Conclusion

The study of implementation efficiency relies on a comparison of ideal and actual implementation. The yardstick for comparison is the active investment version of mean–variance utility—alpha minus a penalty for active risk. In analyzing the general results (comparing any implementation with the ideal), I found that the loss in objective value depends on the risk of the basket trade needed to move from actual position P to ideal position Q—we call this backlog risk. In addition, the analysis confirmed and generalized the notion of the transfer coefficient as a measure of the fraction of the before-cost information ratio that is being captured. Indeed, I showed that the fraction of utility that is captured is bounded above by the square of the transfer coefficient.

Figure 6. Relative Information Ratios before and after Costs

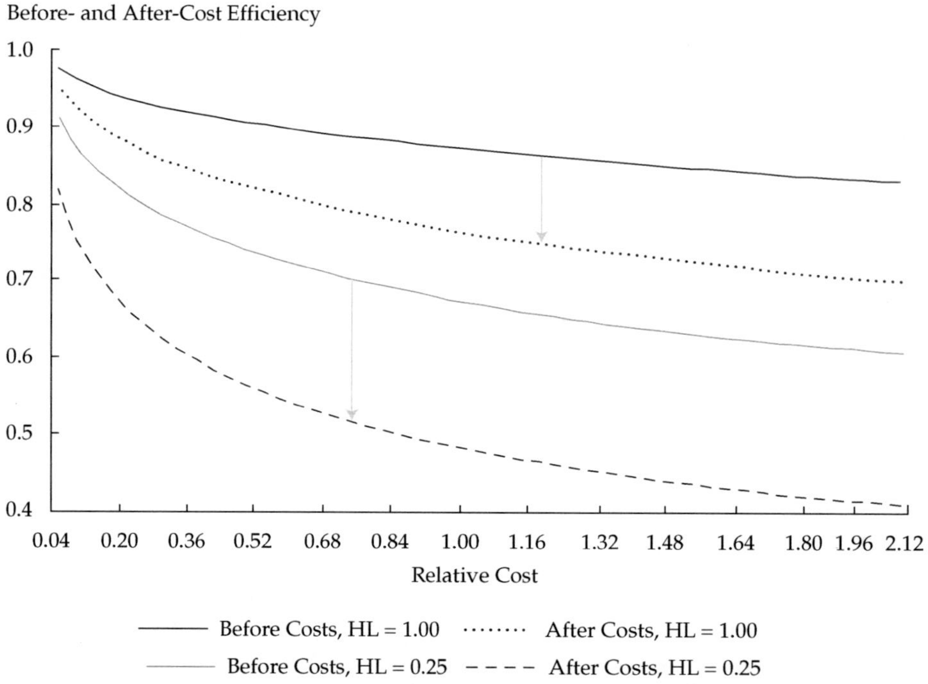

Figure 7. The Active, After-Cost Frontier

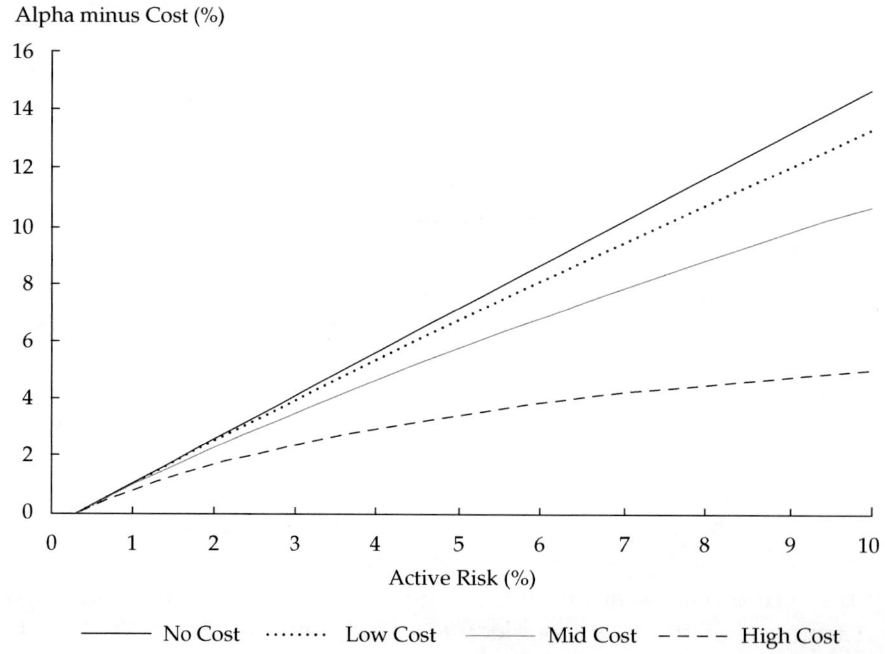

Next, I demonstrated how we could attribute opportunity loss to multiple sources and thus suggested how implementation might be improved.

After-cost results are more difficult to obtain. We examined a specific case with transaction costs and no constraints. The transaction costs were assumed to be proportional to the variance of the trade under consideration. Under these (and other, less heroic) assumptions, we obtained simple expressions for implementation efficiency after costs. The model has an intriguing aspect in that it seems to mimic behavior seen in more complicated backtests and simulations: As trading costs rise because of an increase in assets under management, costs paid tend to stay roughly constant as the portfolio manager responds by reducing active risk, reducing turnover, and slowing down the trading process. The true impact of trading costs lies in opportunity loss, not in costs actually paid.

Appendix A

In what follows, we are considering only portfolios with residual (active) risk that is positive; $\mathbf{h}_Q \neq \mathbf{0}$ and $\mathbf{h}_P \neq \mathbf{0}$ are the active positions. The covariance matrix is $\mathbf{V}$, and we use the notation

$$\omega_{P,P} \equiv \omega_P^2 = \mathbf{h}'\mathbf{V}\mathbf{h}_P$$

and

$$\omega_{P,Q} \equiv \mathbf{h}'_P\mathbf{V}\mathbf{h}_Q = \omega_P\rho_{P,Q}\omega_Q.$$

Other definitions are as follows:

The risk-adjusted (certainty-equivalent) alpha is given by

$$U_P \equiv \alpha_P - \frac{\lambda\omega_{P,P}}{2}, \tag{A1}$$

the tracking variance of P and Q is

$$\omega_{Q-P}^2 = \omega_Q^2 - 2\omega_{P,Q} + \omega_P^2, \tag{A2}$$

and the information ratio of P is

$$IR_P \equiv \frac{\alpha_P}{\omega_P}. \tag{A3}$$

Proposition 1. If

$$\alpha = \lambda\mathbf{V}\mathbf{h}_Q, \tag{A4a}$$

then

$$IR_Q = \lambda\omega_Q \tag{A4b}$$

and

$$U_Q = \frac{\alpha_Q}{2} = \frac{\lambda\omega_{Q,Q}}{2} = \frac{IR_Q^2}{2\lambda}. \tag{A4c}$$

■ *Proof*. If we premultiply the basic equation (Equation A4a) by $\mathbf{h}_Q$, we get

$$\alpha_Q = \lambda\omega_{Q,Q} = \lambda\omega_Q\omega_Q, \tag{A5a}$$

which, when divided by ω_Q, implies

$$IR_Q = \frac{\alpha_Q}{\omega_Q} = \lambda\omega_Q. \tag{A5b}$$

Equation A4c of the first proposition can be handled the same way by using the definitions in Equations A1 and A5:

$$\frac{\lambda\omega_{QQ}}{2} = \frac{(\lambda\omega_Q)(\lambda\omega_Q)}{2\lambda} = \frac{IR_Q^2}{2\lambda}. \tag{A6}$$

Proposition 2. Let $\chi_P \equiv \omega_P/\omega_Q$. If $\alpha = \lambda \mathbf{V}\mathbf{h}_Q$, then for any portfolio P,

$$\alpha_P = \lambda\omega_{P,Q}, \tag{A7a}$$

$$IR_P = \rho_{P,Q} IR_Q, \tag{A7b}$$

$$U_Q - U_P = \frac{\lambda\omega_{Q-P}^2}{2}, \tag{A7c}$$

and

$$\frac{U_P}{U_Q} = 2\chi_P\tau_P - \chi_P^2 \le \tau_P^2. \tag{A7d}$$

Proof. For Equation A7a, premultiply Equation A4a of Proposition 1 by $\mathbf{h}_P$ to yield

$$\alpha_P = \lambda\omega_{PQ} = \lambda\omega_Q\rho_{P,Q}\omega_P = IR_Q\rho_{P,Q}\omega_P. \tag{A8}$$

Recall that $\rho_{P,Q} = \tau_P$, the transfer coefficient of P.

If we divide both sides of Equation A8 by ω_P, we have Equation A7b.

For Equation A7c, note that

$$\frac{\lambda}{2}\omega_{Q-P}^2 = \frac{\lambda}{2}\omega_{Q,Q} - \lambda\omega_{P,Q} + \frac{\lambda}{2}\omega_{P,P}. \tag{A9}$$

From Equation A4b, we have $U_Q = (\lambda/2)\omega_{Q,Q}$. From Equation A8, we have $\alpha_P = \lambda\omega_{Q,P}$. Finally, we have the definition of objective value: $U_P = \alpha_P - (\lambda/2)\omega_{P,P}$. When these three facts are combined with Equation A9, we obtain

$$\begin{aligned}\frac{\lambda}{2}\omega_{Q-P}^2 &= U_Q - \left(\alpha_P - \frac{\lambda}{2}\omega_{P,P}\right) \\ &= U_Q - U_P,\end{aligned} \tag{A10}$$

as desired.

For Equation A7d, note that

$$\frac{\lambda}{2}\omega_{Q-P}^2 = \frac{\lambda}{2}\omega_{Q,Q}\left(1 + \chi_P^2 - 2\chi_P\tau_P\right); \tag{A11}$$

thus,

$$U_Q - U_P = U_Q\left\{1 + \chi_P^2 - 2\chi_P\tau_P\right\}, \tag{A12}$$

which, together with Equation A4c from Proposition 1 and some rearranging, gives us the first half of Equation A7d.

From simple optimization, we see that

$$\max_y \left\{2y\tau_p - y^2\right\} = \tau_P^2, \tag{A13}$$

so

$$2\chi_P\tau_p - \chi_P^2 \le \tau_P^2, \tag{A14}$$

which is the second part of Equation A7d.

Notes

1. Derivations are in Appendix A. Equation 2 is from Grinold and Kahn (2000a and the previous edition). Equation 2 was used as a measure of implementation efficiency in Grinold and Kahn (2000b) and called "shrinkage." Clarke et al. coined the term "transfer coefficient" and showed its central role as a measure of implementation efficiency.
2. If we know ω_Q^2, then any two of these attributes are sufficient to find the third because $\omega_{Q-P}^2 = \omega_Q^2(1 + \chi_P^2 - 2\chi_P\tau_P)$.
3. The capital asset pricing model follows the same logic, with the "market portfolio" playing the role of $\mathbf{h}_Q$ and the expected return on all assets playing the role of α.
4. This section follows and expands on the ideas found in Grinold and Easton (1998).
5. In private communication in 2003, Steven Thorley presented an elegant solution that views position P as a mix between Q and some other position, say R, that is uncorrelated with Q. In our notation, R would be defined through the equation $P = (\chi_P\tau_P)Q + R$; R is all risk and no alpha.
6. For an asset that is not being traded, the marginal trading cost is ambiguous. You can resolve the ambiguity by choosing the value that satisfies Equation 6.
7. For multiple sources (of constraints or costs), say K sources, the generalized form of Equation 6 is $\alpha = \lambda\mathbf{V}\mathbf{h}_P + \sum_{k=1,K}\mathbf{c}_k$. If we define position $\mathbf{h}_k$ by $\mathbf{c}_k = \lambda\mathbf{V}\mathbf{h}_k$ and the covariance between sources j and k as $\omega_{k,j} = \mathbf{h}'_k\mathbf{V}\mathbf{h}_j$, the cost attributed to k is $\lambda/2\sum_{j=1,K}\omega_{k,j}$.
8. This last, $\mathbf{h}'_Y\mathbf{V}\Delta\mathbf{h} = 0$, follows from our assumption that $\boldsymbol{\alpha}(t-\Delta t)$ cannot be used to forecast $\Delta\boldsymbol{\alpha}$.
9. The trading-cost assumption is not robust along the time dimension. Suppose a position turns over 52 percent a year. If costs are linear, it matters little whether this cost is 1 percent a week for 52 weeks, 13 percent a quarter for four quarters, or 26 percent each six months. With a quadratic cost structure, the cost effectively disappears as we chop it into smaller and smaller pieces. If we change the interval between rebalances, the cost parameter should also be recalibrated.
10. The results presented in this subsection are from Grinold (forthcoming).

References

Clarke, Roger, Harinda de Silva, and Steven Thorley. 2002. "Portfolio Constraints and the Fundamental Law of Active Management." *Financial Analysts Journal*, vol. 58, no. 5 (September/October):48–66.

———. 2005. "Performance Attribution and the Fundamental Law." *Financial Analysts Journal*, vol. 61, no. 5 (September/October): 70–83.

Grinold, R. Forthcoming. "A Dynamic Model of Portfolio Management." *Journal of Investment Management*.

Grinold, R., and K. Easton. 1998. "Attribution of Performance and Holdings." In *Worldwide Asset and Liability Modeling*. Edited by J. Mulvey and W.T. Ziemba. New York: Cambridge University Press.

Grinold, R., and R. Kahn. 2000a. *Active Portfolio Management: Quantitative Theory and Applications*. 2nd ed. New York: McGraw-Hill.

———. 2000b. "The Efficiency Gains of Long–Short Investing." *Financial Analysts Journal*, vol. 56, no. 6 (November/December):40–53.

Keim, Donald B., and Ananth Madhavan. 1996. "The Upstairs Market for Large-Block Transactions: Analysis and Measurement of Price Effects." *Review of Financial Studies*, vol. 9, no. 1 (Spring):1–36.

History Lessons for 21st Century Investment Managers

Paul McCulley

The U.S. national system can be described as a democratic capitalist society. Most Americans assume that such a system is a good thing: We embrace both democracy and capitalism. But democracy and capitalism are inherently in conflict, and this conflict is a source of major structural changes in our economy and secular trends in asset performance.

Managers would be wise to use the history of the shifting ascendancy between capitalism and democracy as a guide in interpreting the secular changes now occurring in the U.S. economy.

Marriage of Democracy and Capitalism

Democracy is founded on a simple socialist principle—one person, one vote—which assures that each person (theoretically, at least) has equal influence in the system. Capitalism, in contrast, is founded on the principle of "one dollar, one vote," which is known as a "cumulative voting system." The more dollars a person or voting entity has, the more votes that person or entity has and, therefore, the more influence in the system. This difference leads to an inherent conflict between these two coexisting systems—one that offers equal influence to each person and one that offers variable influence depending on wealth.

Like all marriages, the one between democracy and capitalism is far from perfect, but it seems to work better than most, and the key variable that makes it work is the rule of law, because within the rule of law is the ingredient that capitalism most requires—the sanctity of property rights. Democracy's gift to capitalism is property rights. Capitalism cannot function without property rights. And property rights cannot be guaranteed by a society that does not have a sense of equity and justice. Justice, however, cannot be guaranteed under the capitalist principle of cumulative voting, because a voting system based on wealth implies that the wealthy can buy better justice,

---

Paul McCulley is a managing director and portfolio manager at Pacific Investment Management Company, Newport Beach, California.

Editor's Note: This article was developed from a presentation published in *Points of Inflection: New Directions for Portfolio Management* (Charlottesville, VA: CFA Institute, 2004).

at which point justice loses its value along with property rights and the rule of law. Democracy—founded on the principle of "one person, one vote"—creates a framework in which all are afforded equal justice and no one is supposed to get the best justice that money can buy.

The system is like a delicately balanced seesaw: Democracy and capitalism sit at either end, teetering continuously up and down, and the rule of law and property rights act as the fulcrum in the middle.

Like the U.S. national system as a whole, the U.S. economy, including its markets, is by nature mixed. It consists of a public sector—call it "we-the-people," or government—and a private sector—call it "we-the-markets," or capitalism. Secular changes (or points of inflection) occur when the weights in our economy shift. These shifting weights are manifested as either a bull market in we-the-people power or a bull market in we-the-markets power. One such secular change occurred in the 1979–81 period. Another such secular change is occurring right now, and it will have a tremendous effect on how investment professionals manage investments in the years ahead.

The 1979–81 secular change put an end to the bull market in government that had dominated the economy during the 1960s and 1970s. It ushered in the beginning of a bull market in capitalism, which dominated the economy in the 1980s and 1990s. Thus, from 1979 to 1981, the invisible hand of the markets won out over the visible fist of the government. This bull market was the defining characteristic of the 1980s and 1990s, and it was hugely important because of a single conclusive variable—inflation. In the long sweep of history, bull markets in government have been shown to be inherently inflationary and bull markets in capitalism, inherently disinflationary. Thus, when an economy swings from one type of bull market to the other, the economy has reached a secular inflection point in inflation.

Over the long run, the most important economic variable to get right is inflation. By understanding the status of inflation, investment managers can more effectively determine the relative valuation of tangible assets, financial assets, and the various components within each of those categories. If investment managers can accurately assess which power is going to be in ascendancy (we-the-people or we-the-markets), they are likely to forecast inflation accurately. Many other strategic choices will naturally follow from that forecast.

Bull to Bear

The 1960s and 1970s constituted an inflationary period—a bull market in government and a bear market in capitalism. It ended because the bull market in government eventually created a lethal brew called "stagflation," which is the proximate reason that we-the-people, through the electoral process, decided to shift our weight toward a more market-based economy.

President Carter's Cardigan Moment. Some people believe that the bull market in government died on the day in August 1979 that Paul Volcker became chairman of the U.S. Federal Reserve. That is not a bad day to choose. I prefer to think that the change actually occurred on the evening in 1978 when President Jimmy Carter appeared on national television wearing a cardigan sweater and told us that we, the American people, were suffering from a malaise. Many people remember the malaise speech, but perhaps not as many people remember why he was wearing a cardigan sweater. The cardigan was part of his energy program. At the time of the malaise speech, the United States did not have a capitalist energy sector. It had a government-controlled energy sector. It also had a serious energy shortage. And part of President Carter's solution for the shortage, which he recommended that evening to the American people, was to turn the thermostat down to 65 degrees and put on a sweater.

The American people responded with hearty disagreement. It was the beginning of a turn in the U.S. psyche, an inflection point: The visible fist of government was about to be slapped aside by the invisible hand of the markets.

Good Things. The 1960s and 1970s were a terrible time for financial assets. Stagflation is not a prescription for making lots of money on Wall Street. But the 1960s and 1970s offered many wonderful examples of the self-correcting nature of our democratic capitalism. Our society did some good things in the 1960s and 1970s, things that we can feel proud of as U.S. citizens, things that capitalism could never have accomplished. I mention these things because I want to discredit the notion that a bull market in government is axiomatically a bad thing.

First, we-the-people declared that capitalism may not discriminate on the basis of race. We-the-people reaffirmed that we did, indeed, believe in the proposition that all men and women are created equal, and we-the-people, therefore, established within our rule of law a prohibition against discrimination on the basis of race. Capitalism would never have done that. We-the-people did it.

Second, we-the-people declared, "Thou shalt not discriminate on the basis of gender." Capitalism would never have come to that conclusion by itself. We-the-people did.

And third, we-the-people told capitalists, "Thou shalt not pollute and destroy our public property (i.e., our environment). You must internalize in your profits the externalities of your behavior." We-the-people declared that some things are owned by all of us. These things constitute our collective property, which, like private property, is protected by the concept of property rights.

I am proud of these developments, and I think that most Americans are proud that we took such measures in the 1960s and 1970s.

Three Power Shifts. The problem with the 1960s and 1970s was that after we-the-people made a number of decisions that capitalism would not have made on its own, the bull market in government drove capitalism into a bear market, which eventually led to President Carter appearing on national television in a cardigan sweater. It was time to shift the weights in our mixed economy from the public sector back toward the private sector. It was also time for some serious asset reallocation. Three power shifts occurred that helped create the market-based economy of the 1980s and 1990s—a shift in monetary policy, a shift in fiscal policy, and a shift in regulatory policy.

- *Monetary policy*. President Carter appointed Volcker chairman of the Federal Reserve in August 1979. On the same day, he effectively wrote his own pink slip and gave Volcker a mandate to shift monetary policy from the political process to the markets.

To make this shift, Volcker had to do something that the Federal Reserve is supposed to be reluctant to do—throw our economy into recession. Recessions offend democratic sensibilities. Recessions do not inflict pain on an equitable basis. Recessions hurt the weakest among us, so the political process is naturally predisposed against tight monetary policy. But in 1978, the United States actually borrowed money to fund its current account deficit in nondollar currencies. It was a sad day, and these borrowed amounts became known as Carter Bonds. Because of such developments, the American people were willing to tolerate a recession to combat the nefarious inflationary problem they were facing.

- *Fiscal policy*. The second power shift that laid the foundation for the market-based economy actually occurred in the 1990s under President Bill Clinton. We-the-people, for reasons that are still unclear to me, decided that we wanted to de-lever ourselves, to shift from budget deficits to budget surpluses and pay off our collective national debt, which is a very difficult thing for a democratic economy to do because a government that de-levers is a government that is reducing its own power. Typically, nobody likes to give up power. But giving up power is exactly what we-the-people did in the 1990s.

There was, of course, an economic rationale to this de-levering: Budget deficits crowd out private-sector investment, and private-sector investment (under the umbrella of capitalism) is inherently more productive than government-sector investment. Therefore, reducing the budget deficit reduces the crowding out of private-sector investment.

Once the deficit was eliminated and the government started running surpluses, the government not only stopped crowding out private-sector investment; it actually began crowding such investments in.

- *Regulatory policy*. The third power shift occurred in regulation, which is, in essence, a process by which we-the-people infringe on private-sector property. I use the word "infringe" as a descriptor, not in a pejorative sense, because regulation is not inherently bad. For example, assume you own your car; you have a title for it, and it is your car. Your ownership is protected under property rights. But we-the-people do impose some regulations. We say, "Thou shalt not drive your car while you are drunk." That is a regulation, and most people would agree that it is a good regulation.

We-the-people also say, "Thou shalt not drive your car faster than 65 miles per hour on the interstate." Many people feel less certain that this is a good regulation, as demonstrated by the fact that 7 mph over the speed limit seems to be the default standard.

My point is that regulation is not inherently bad. It can, however, go too far, as it had by the end of the 1970s.

Rise of We-the-Markets

The result of the overregulation in the 1970s was a period of deregulation that began, actually, in the Carter Administration with deregulation of the airlines. That move was followed by deregulation of the financial system, deregulation of the utilities, and finally, in 1996, deregulation of telephone service. Deregulation thus restored private-sector property rights.

Those three things together—tight money, fiscal discipline, and deregulation—resulted in the bull market in capitalism that, in turn, produced the variable that determined everything else—falling inflation.

Beer, Ballparks, and Disinflation. Capitalism is inherently disinflationary because capitalism is inherently about competition, which is a process of creative destruction. That is, under the framework of capitalism, no profit margin endures for long. Downward pressure on prices is naturally promoted.

As an example, consider one portion of the economy that was not deregulated during the 1980s and 1990s—the beer concessions at major-league ballparks. No matter what ballpark a fan might visit, a beer costs $6.00. Why is this so? It is a regulated market. It is a market with a barrier to entry. It is a monopoly. It is not a capitalist market. What would happen if beer concessions were deregulated? Entrepreneurs would enter the market, and the sequence of events would go something like this:

> The first entrepreneur goes out and buys a pickup truck and a couple kegs of beer—which are called "investments" in GDP accounts—and begins offering beer at $5.50 per serving, not $6.00. This is called "disinflation," and assuming there is some price elasticity of demand, the consumption of beer rises. Thus, the economy experiences more investment, disinflation, and an increase in consumption. But other potential vendors think that a price of $5.50 per serving still provides an excess profit margin. So, another entrant appears and lowers the price of beer still more. Now, people become exuberant about the profit potential for selling beer at the ballpark. So, another entrepreneur enters the market, and the price of a serving of beer drops to $4.00. At this point, venture capital discovers this wonderful profit-making opportunity and entrants four, five, and six appear. Beer is now going for $2.25 per serving, and the first entrepreneur has gone public with an IPO. Exuberance is working. Inflation is going down, down, down. The story finally ends with 17 guys selling beer at the ballpark for 25 cents a serving and a stadium full of drunks.

This is exactly what happened to the telecom industry and the price of a long-distance phone call at the end of the 1990s. What was the cost of a long-distance call by the end of the 1990s? Not even a quarter.

Thus, shifting to a more capitalist model, tightening money, crowding in private-sector investment, and deregulating industries led to falling inflation, which was the dominant theme of the 1980s and 1990s.

Five Strategies for Success in 1980. If an investment manager had understood the implications at the turn of the tide in 1980, he or she would have needed to do five things to be successful.

1. *Sell tangible assets into financial assets.* Falling inflation is inherently bearish for tangible assets in relation to financial assets. Disinflation is directly negative for pricing the product of tangible assets. Disinflation is directly positive for the valuation of stocks and bonds.
2. *Overweight stocks in relation to bonds.* The reason for selling financial assets into a portfolio overweighted in stocks is that disinflation and a bull market in capitalism have their most profound effect on the longest duration asset, which is equity.
3. *Overweight growth in relation to value.* A bull market in capitalism will take P/E multiples up because of falling inflation and the shifting of shares of GDP toward corporate profits. Investment managers will want a call option on the upside.
4. *Overweight government bonds in relation to corporate bonds.* This action may seem counterintuitive. Investment managers may think, "If we have a bull market in capitalism, shouldn't we be holding corporates?" But a bull market in capitalism, including the crowding in of private-sector investment, means a crowding in of private-sector default risk, so a bull market in capitalism is not bullish for corporate bonds.
5. *Overweight the U.S. dollar.* This move follows from the proposition that if the United States is going to have a party in celebration of capitalism, the rest of the world will want to attend the party, and the cover charge for the party will be denominated in dollars.

If an investment manager did these five things in 1980, the resulting portfolio looked pretty good in 1990: light on tangible assets, long on financial assets, overweight in stocks, overweight in growth stocks, overweight in government bonds, and long on the dollar.

Capitalism's Cardigan Moment

The party celebrating capitalism was a great one, but all parties must come to an end, and so did this one. Whenever one sector of our mixed economy has been in power for too long, it suffers from hubris. Government suffered from hubris at the end of the 1970s; capitalism suffered from hubris at the end of the 1990s.

The best example of hubris in capitalism in that decade is the market's convincing itself that the more capitalist an economy is, the gentler its business cycle will be. Therefore, by accepting the notion that capitalism will take the boom and bust out of our economy, the equity market reduced the equity risk premium to the point that it went negative. The reality, unfortunately, is that although capitalism can reduce inflation, it actually introduces more risk of boom and bust, as John Maynard Keynes explained in Chapter 12, "The State of Long-Term Expectation" (or "Animal Spirits," as the chapter is commonly called), of *The General Theory of Employment, Interest, and Money* (see Keynes 1965).

Capitalism offers the opportunity to get rich, but it also requires the occasional duty of going broke. Socialism is inherently calmer than capitalism.[1] Therefore, if an economy moves toward a more capitalist system, its participants should expect a more agitated business cycle, not a calmer one.

The problem with socialism, of course, is that it has revolutions every 50 years or so. Between revolutions, it offers a fairly calm sort of existence, whereas capitalism presents us with a state of continuous revolution. The process is called "creative destruction," and it leads to periods of irrational exuberance and irrational doom. Capitalists involved in the equity market were confronted by capitalism's inherent instability when three bubbles burst at the end of the 1990s—the equity valuation bubble, the business investment bubble, and the corporate leverage bubble. Tobin's q predicted that an equity bubble would lead to a business investment bubble. Franco Modigliani and Merton Miller predicted that those two bubbles would lead to a corporate debt bubble. All three occurred as predicted

And all three burst just as the economy reached the end of a welcomed disinflation. Thus, we saw a unique inflection point: The bubbles burst at a 2 percent inflation rate, which means that the economy had a fundamental need to reflate. Otherwise, the economy would have been in danger of a Minsky-style debt deflation, which occurs when the entire corporate sector decides to rehabilitate its balance sheet (see Minsky 1986). For individual companies, such a decision represents rational behavior. Collectively, however, it embodies the paradox of thrift: Not all companies can rehabilitate their balance sheets at the same time. Nevertheless, that is exactly what the corporate sector tried to do, and it introduced the distinct risk of a deflationary spiral, at which point a new bull market in government was born.

Three Power Shifts in Reverse. That we are, in fact, living in a bull market in government can be demonstrated by examining the reverse of the three power shifts that I discussed earlier—shifts in monetary policy, fiscal policy, and regulation.

- *Monetary policy*. Monetary policy is under the guidance of Federal Reserve Board Chairman Alan Greenspan. Since the bursting of the three bubbles in the late 1990s, monetary policy in the United States has been geared, quite appropriately, toward saving capitalism from its deflationary self by reflating. The power of the monetary printing press, which we-the-people own, has been turned to generating higher inflation. How quickly the Fed returns monetary policy to a neutral stance, whereby it neither stimulates nor slows the economy, will depend on how successful this reflation is.

- *Fiscal policy*. Fortunately for the United States, we-the-people have forgotten that nonsense about de-levering ourselves, and we have shifted from a budget surplus to a huge budget deficit. The United States is re-levering itself, which is precisely what is needed when the private sector is trying to de-lever itself. So, the Federal Reserve is printing $20 bills and the federal government is borrowing $20 bills.
- *Regulation*. The United States is re-regulating along a number of fronts, but the one that seems most significant is embodied in the Sarbanes–Oxley Act of 2002, which regulates corporate governance. Sarbanes–Oxley is the anti-drunk-driving bill for CEOs. It states, in effect, "Thou shalt not drive the car of U.S. capitalism while drunk with hubris and greed. If you do, your pinstripes will no longer be vertically aligned; they will be horizontally aligned."

Capitalism's hubris exposed the United States to deflation risk, and it offended our democratic sensibilities. We are now in a corrective process.

Five Strategies in an Era of Inflation. Assuming that I am right and that the United States is at an inflection point where capitalism is in retreat and the power of we-the-people is in ascendancy, it is fair to conclude, on a secular horizon, that inflation will rise. I have no idea what the U.S. Consumer Price Index will be next week, next month, or next year. But if we have indeed reached the antithesis of 1981, then inflation is going to go up, and that development holds many implications for investment portfolios. Investment managers will need to reverse the five strategies needed for success in 1980, thus realigning their portfolios toward a mix of public- and private-sector investments that better matches the macroeconomic environment.

1. *Overweight tangible assets and TIPS in relation to nominal financial assets*. If we are indeed entering a we-the-people bull market and a period of secularly rising inflation, a successful portfolio will need more tangible assets. It will also need Treasury Inflation-Indexed Securities (originally "Treasury Inflation-Protected Securities," commonly called "TIPS"), which did not even exist in the 1980s. TIPS are T-bonds whose principal value is adjusted to reflect actual inflation, a feature that makes them compare favorably with nominal bonds, whose yields reflect only the market's estimate of inflation. Although TIPS performed well in the past several years as real yields fell, they still offer relatively cheap insurance against inflation. TIPS valuations are supported by the fact that real rates have been lower during reflationary, government-oriented periods than during disinflationary, private sector–dominated times.
2. *Balance stocks and bonds*. Unfortunately, both stocks and bonds are going to offer lousy returns in the years ahead because rising inflation is both a damper on P/E multiples and a corrosive for total returns on bonds. Stocks and bonds had their glorious two-decade run, but now they face a headwind. If I were forced to choose, I would overweight bonds in relation to stocks, partly because I consider stocks to be a call option on capitalism. And if capitalism checks into the Betty Ford Center for balance sheet rehabilitation, the call option is not worth much.
3. *Overweight value in relation to growth*. The coming environment is not one in which growth stocks will perform well. They were strong performers in the late 1990s, but that rally was about the nation reembracing the U.S. enterprise as a going concern. Now, we must think in terms of normalized relative valuations and performance, which means a bias toward value.

4. *Overweight private-sector obligations.* A bull market in government is actually a bull market in credit quality. Current valuations are rich in the corporate bond market, but secularly speaking, investors should shift from government debt to private debt.
5. *Overweight nondollar assets in relation to the dollar.* In the United States, rising inflation and a more government-controlled economy will weigh heavily on the dollar's value over the secular horizon. What is more, the sheer size of the U.S. current account deficit—an inevitable consequence of "successful" reflation—implies a surplus of dollars globally relative to private global demand.

Conclusion

Based on the lessons of history, success in portfolio management depends on adjusting appropriately to the prospective weights in our mixed economy, not to the weights as they used to exist. Investment managers cannot afford to extrapolate from returns of the prior regime to project returns into the future. The returns of the 1980s and 1990s arose from a bull market in capitalism and falling inflation, and those conditions do not appear on the secular horizon. If investment managers take seriously their fiduciary mandate to anticipate the future and not simply extrapolate from the past, they cannot use the returns of the 1980s and 1990s as the foundation for a prudent, forward-looking efficient frontier.

I am extremely grateful to Scott Martin, a vice president at Pacific Investment Management Company (PIMCO), who assisted in the preparation of this article. The opinions expressed in the article are the author's and not necessarily those of PIMCO.

Note

1. One of the redeeming characteristics of socialism, in fact, is its calmness. Just think in terms of the postal service or a department of motor vehicles. They offer no one the opportunity to get rich, but neither do they require anyone to go broke.

References

Keynes, John Maynard. 1965 (first published in 1936). *The General Theory of Employment, Interest, and Money*. Fort Washington, PA: Harvest Books.

Minsky, Hyman. 1986. *Stabilizing an Unstable Economy*. New Haven, CT: Yale University Press.

Rubble Logic: What Did We Learn from the Great Stock Market Bubble?

Clifford S. Asness

It's not what we don't know that hurts us; it's what we know for sure that just ain't so.

Mark Twain

Good advice and accurate pricing are too important to be left to the kind of "logic" we saw in the Great Bubble, so a postmortem is crucial for analysts and managers.

The *Financial Analysts Journal*'s 60th anniversary happens to coincide with the five-year anniversary of the peak of the Great Stock Market Bubble of 1999–2000. The proximity in time, with just a bit of distance, makes this year an appropriate time to consider what we may have learned from this momentous event.

"Rubble Logic" is what should be left over now that we have passed through "Bubble Logic," the title of an unpublished book draft (Asness 2000a) that was my contribution to a small but stalwart group of practitioners and academics arguing back in 1999–2000 that the stock market, and technology stocks in particular, were priced at unsustainably high levels.[1] Several members of this group have shared that work in the *FAJ*, which makes this review especially appropriate as part of the 60th anniversary commemoration. "Bubble Logic" was my disparaging term for the tortured stories and sometimes outright lies necessary to justify prices in 1999–2000. Now that the bubble has burst, the most important question is: What have we learned from this devastating experience?

Before continuing, I must disclose certain inadequacies in this article's title and subtitle. First, the term "rubble" is misleading. Stock prices today, although not at bubble levels, are still quite high—something certainly not conveyed by the term "rubble." Second, although I repeatedly discuss lessons we have "learned," many of these lessons are things we knew before the bubble but collectively forgot during those heady

---

Clifford S. Asness is founding and managing principal at AQR Capital Management, LLC, New York City.

Editor's Note: The views and opinions expressed in this article are those of the author and do not necessarily reflect the views of AQR Capital Management, LLC, its affiliates, or its employees.

times. Third, whether we have even now fully internalized the lessons is questionable. Finally, I treat these lessons as if everyone agreed on what we have learned, but obviously, they are simply my opinions. A more accurate title would be "Things I Believe We Already Knew about Investing but Forgot during the Bubble and May Still Be Forgetting Now, So It Is Probably a Good Idea to Go Over Them Again." Unfortunately, although more accurate, it is very long, fails to rhyme with my original work, and completely lacks pith.

Long-term average stock returns are a poor forecaster of the future

> *I don't know much about history, and I wouldn't give a nickel for all the history in the world. History is more or less bunk.*
>
> Henry Ford

On the face of it, using historical stock returns as a reasonable forecast for the future seems unimpeachable. It is certainly common, and the method is simple and clear. Basic statistical analysis is conducted on stock returns over some long-term period, and the future returns are expected to act similarly.

But although seemingly reasonable, this method can produce some strange results. For instance, suppose investors carried out this exercise in July 1982. They would have found an average annualized compound real (above U.S. Consumer Price Index inflation) return on the S&P 500 Index since the end of World War II (i.e., January 1946) that would lead to a forecast of 4.9 percent returns a year. Over the next 17 1/2 years (through the end of 1999), however, the average annual real return on stocks turned out to be 15.3 percent. Updating the calculation from 1946 through the end of 1999—a longer period, so it might make the investor more sure of the method—would result in an annual average return of 8.4 percent over inflation. That's a nice return to expect in the future! But over the next few years—from the end of 1999 through the end of 2004—the average annualized real return on the S&P 500 turned out to be –5.0 percent. (Whoa, nobody said anything about negative!) Finally, looking at the whole period at the end of 2004 (1946–2004) provides an average annual return on stocks of 7.2 percent over inflation. QED.

This example is contrived, because it uses particular extreme end points and then looks at returns over only the next few years, but although intentionally extreme, it makes the important point that forecasts derived from past averages, even if long-term averages, are often actually backwards. That is, after periods of strong returns, trailing average returns are higher than normal, and because these periods almost always come with increases in valuation, expected returns are actually lower for the future. When it comes to forecasting the future, especially when valuations (and thus historical returns) are at extremes, the answers we get from looking at simple historical average returns are bunk.

Higher prices today mean lower expected returns tomorrow

> *A fanatic is one who can't change his mind and won't change the subject.*
>
> Sir Winston Churchill

In the case of P/Es, I am the fanatic. I have been showing the same evolving valuation information in **Figure 1** and **Table 1** for at least six years. Figure 1 shows the P/E multiple of the S&P 500 for 1881–2004 based on Robert Shiller's (2000) method of using the 10-year average of real earnings

Figure 1. S&P 500 P/E, 1881–2004
(price divided by 10-year real earnings)

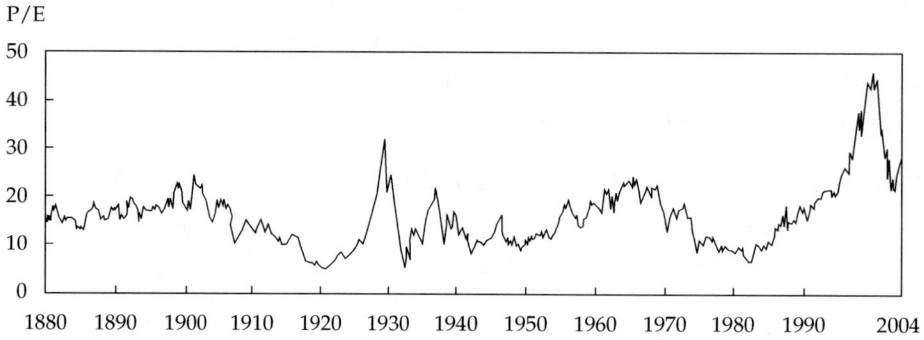

Note: Annual dates are as of December.

for the "E" in P/E.[2] Table 1 presents the data for each rolling decade for 1927–2004 and puts it into one of six buckets based on the starting value of the P/E multiple. So, we can examine the future 10-year performance of the S&P 500 (in real terms) when starting out in each bucket.

First, note in Table 1 that median future returns (average returns produce similar results) fall sharply with rising starting P/Es. Next, consider the hallowed property of equity returns—that stocks never lose if held for the long term. Well, if a decade is your idea of the long term, then this adage is true only when prices start out in the lower three valuation buckets. When prices start out more expensive, there are decades when stocks not only lose to inflation but lose big.[3]

In short, starting equity valuation is a powerful long-term forecaster of future stock returns, but admittedly, valuation is perilously close to irrelevant when forecasting the short term. Investors are always admonished to ignore the short term, however, when it comes to potential losses on equities but told, at the same time, that valuation does not matter because stocks often advance in the short term even when expensive. To the contrary, although the story in Table 1 is far from perfect if examined in more depth (stocks certainly do well in some decades despite starting out expensive), Table 1 shows that a long-term investor should seriously consider entry price.[4]

Table 1. S&P 500 Returns Starting from Different P/Es, 1927–2004

		Return	
Low	High	Median (annual)	Worst (total)
5.2	10.1	10.9%	46.1%
10.1	11.9	10.7	32.0
11.9	14.6	10.0	4.0
14.6	17.2	7.6	–20.9
17.2	19.9	5.3	–32.0
19.9	31.7	–0.1	–35.5
31.7	46.1	Here be dragons!	

Finally, please note the last row of the table. "Here Be Dragons" is a phrase once used on old maps for parts of the world that had not been visited yet. Results for P/Es in this range do not make it into the table because we have not yet observed a 10-year period starting from these rarified levels. We did visit this new world briefly in 1999–2000, but we did not stay long. So far since then, the table is being filled in with, as you would expect, negative real returns.

Today's high stock prices have two possible meanings

More than any other time in history, mankind faces a crossroads. One path leads to despair and utter hopelessness. The other, to total extinction. Let us pray we have the wisdom to choose correctly.

Woody Allen

The current S&P 500 P/E (around 27) puts the market in the high end of the highest bucket in Table 1 for which we have observed a full decade. An immediate logical conclusion might be to expect a zero real return on stocks over the next decade. This expectation may be less obvious than it sounds. Historically, stocks have done poorly when starting out very expensive for two reasons (this explanation works in reverse for cheap prices). The first is that when stocks are expensive, they are "lower yielding," whether measured in dividends or earnings, which implies that (barring any further valuation changes or large changes in growth rates) returns will be lower. The second is that valuations can change, and historically, when they have started out high, they have subsequently fallen—that is, reverted to the mean. Thus, those buying stocks when they were expensive suffered a double whammy. Both reasons were clearly at work for those buying near the peak in 1999–2000. The future from here is hard to predict because we do not know whether mean reversion in P/Es has to happen. If it does not, stocks will still be expected to return less in the future than they have historically (because of the lower-yield effect) but will not return zero as in Table 1. Estimates based on using a Gordon-type dividend discount model (which effectively assumes steady-state valuation) lead to forecasts of about 4 percent real returns (6–7 percent nominal returns if inflation stays in the 2–3 percent range). These figures are low in light of history but not a 10-year disaster.

P/Es might, in fact, stay at these lofty levels. I am keenly aware of the dangers of forecasting anything like a "permanently high plateau" for valuations, which has always been wrong before, but the intellectual argument that P/Es have on average, in fact, been too low throughout history is not without teeth. Academics have long had a name for the idea that equities have been too cheap—the "equity premium puzzle." Essentially, according to most economic models, stocks have been too good a deal.

Equity exposure is far cheaper to get these days than in the past, which means that, even if gross returns are lower, net returns may be comparable, so investors are justified in paying permanently higher P/Es and receiving permanently lower gross (but not net) returns. If, after 100 years, investors have finally figured out the equity premium puzzle or are responding to this changing cost structure, prices may not have to fall sharply over the next few years. It also means that the lower-return environment is here to stay. A truly long-term investor or an investor with more future cash flows than present cash (and a borrowing constraint) does not necessarily favor permanently higher prices and lower returns simply to avoid a crash.

Although high prices have usually led to sharp price declines in the past (and then better returns going forward), intellectual honesty demands that we recognize the other possibility—no long-term mean reversion in prices but permanently lower expected returns.[5]

There are caveats. Those who might accept the idea that investors are truly cognizant of, and comfortable with, a lower equity risk premium in the future must also accept some sobering facts. First, the following logic does not hold: "Sure the risk premium is lower, but I have learned that equities always win if you hold them for at least 20 years, so lower but guaranteed positive returns are still good." Equities have, in fact, never lost to inflation over any 20-year historical period. But that fact is more a statement about their past average returns than about their risk. If the equity risk premium is much smaller in the future, the probability of equities losing over a 20-year period is much larger than if the premium were higher. Second, investors need to use the lower equity premium when making plans. So, pension funds with their assumed market returns and individuals with their "when can I retire" spreadsheets have to assume equities will rise at about a nominal 6–7 percent a year (and a whole portfolio, including bonds, with costs, taxes, and inflation, will rise considerably less). It is inconsistent to believe that stock prices do not have to fall now (because people have learned to accept a lower equity risk premium) and still to use a 10+ percent a year return assumption.

The question of whether high prices mean permanently low returns or near-term very bad returns followed by more historically normal results is one of the most crucial puzzles currently facing capital markets. Little can change the high probability that high prices lead to lower expected returns in the future, but the timing is very much up in the air.

Long-term investors should not be 100 percent in stocks

Take calculated risks. That is quite different from being rash.

George S. Patton

A bit of conventional wisdom that was particularly rampant during the bubble days is that long-term investors should be 100 percent in equities. It is wrong. Recall from that first long-ago finance class the diagram in **Figure 2**. It illustrates the concept that under certain assumptions, all investors should own the same portfolio of risky assets and should lever that portfolio if they want more expected return for risk or add cash (delever it) if they want less risk (expected return). Forget the baggage of the capital asset pricing model that often comes with the diagram; the principle is more general. Subject to some real-world constraints (transaction costs, bankruptcy risk, etc.), investment decisions should clearly be made in two steps. First, find the best portfolio of risky assets (highest return per risk); then, lever or delever based on personal preferences for risk.

Suppose an investor tried this approach with U.S. stocks and government bonds and ran the experiment through the recent bull market (1982–2004). **Figure 3** shows the growth of $1 in four portfolios. In order of final finish, 100 percent equities is not the top finisher. The best portfolio is called "Levered 60/40," and it is based on the realized prior 20-year volatility of the 60/40 stocks/bonds portfolio levered to a volatility equal to 100 percent stocks. Because the 60/40 portfolio unlevered is less volatile than 100 percent stocks, the Levered 60/40 portfolio involves borrowing and buying more of the 60/40 portfolio until it is as historically volatile as stocks. This portfolio wins by a healthy margin. Moreover, the worst periods—something to consider when examining any levered strategy, which by definition entails bankruptcy risk—are generally more benign for Levered 60/40 than for 100 percent equities.

Figure 2. Return vs. Risk Efficient Frontier

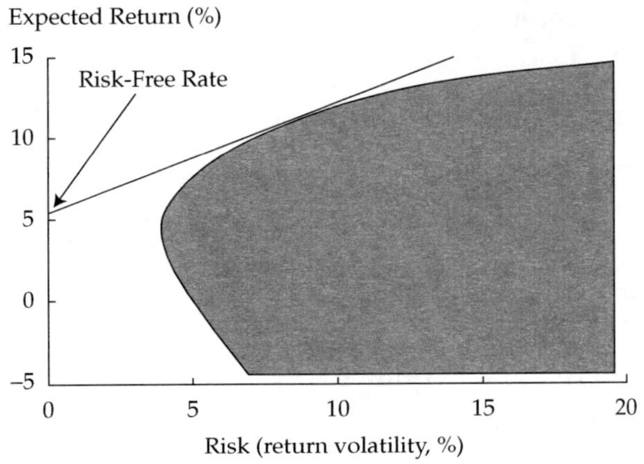

On the one hand, this experiment is not entirely fair because I used a T-bill and no transaction costs to lever, which is clearly aggressive.[6] On the other hand, I considered only government bonds as the alternative to equities. Broadening the asset mix (to, e.g., corporate bonds, international assets, commodities) would strengthen the empirical results. Much of the bang from this analysis comes from the fact that, although bond returns have historically lagged stock returns, the reason is primarily that bonds are less volatile assets, not that they have far lower Sharpe ratios.

Constraints permitting, and with reasonable costs and a reasonable mix of assets, I doubt that even the most aggressive long-term investor would want to own a portfolio of 100 percent stocks; it forgoes the benefit of diversification, which increases risk-adjusted return.

Figure 3. Performance of Four Portfolios: Growth of $1, 1982–2004

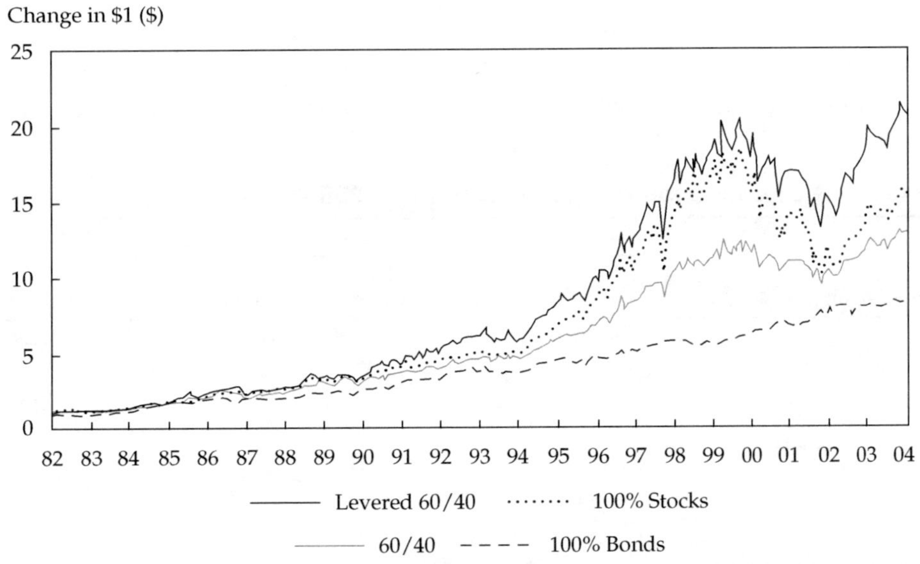

International diversification is not a waste of time

You should always go to other people's funerals; otherwise, they won't come to yours.

Yogi Berra[7]

A legion of academic and practitioner papers has questioned the diversification benefit of adding international equities to a U.S. equity portfolio. These authors usually make an argument like the following: The whole idea of diversifying is for downside protection, but the worst days, weeks, and months for international equities occur at similar times and magnitudes as they do for U.S. equities. So, why bother?[8,9]

Investors looking for international equities to protect them during a U.S. crash are indeed looking in the wrong place. But the diversification benefits of international equity investing should be judged over the same time frame as U.S. equity investing. Many fans of equity investing will tolerate nearly any amount of pain in the short term while preaching that we must keep our eyes on the long-term prize. But when they examine international diversification, they focus on how it works over days, weeks, or months. Not fair.

Table 2 is from an analysis of international diversification over longer horizons from multiple countries' perspectives (Asness, Krail, and Liew, forthcoming). The table shows returns for worst 1-year, 5-year, and 10-year periods. For each country, we examined, from the home country's perspective, the home country's worst case and the worst case for a simple global portfolio that equally weighted the countries. From every country's perspective for each time horizon, worst-case returns for a simple global portfolio are better than for the home country. Furthermore, in most cases, they are materially better. The quintessential recent example is Japan. In the United States, many learned papers in the past 15 years have attacked the idea of diversifying internationally; in Japan, the papers are probably arguing the exact opposite. Unless one country is going to permanently outperform the other, both sets of papers cannot be right.

Table 2 is only a five-country example, the portfolios were not capitalization weighted, and the example does not deal with transaction costs and taxes, but the data are highly indicative. Theory and common sense both suggest that, with no systematic differences in expected returns,

Table 2. Returns to International Investing, 1950–2004

	Worst 1 Year		Worst 5 Years		Worst 10 Years	
Home Country	Home Country	Global Portfolio	Home Country	Global Portfolio	Home Country	Global Portfolio
Japan	–45.0%	–43.0%	–50.3%	–44.9%	–53.8%	–42.9%
Germany	–54.4	–42.6	–53.3	–46.2	–44.6	–35.5
United Kingdom	–60.8	–45.9	–65.7	–33.1	–61.3	–21.9
France	–53.0	–43.4	–52.9	–41.5	–57.9	–21.2
United States	–47.5	–45.4	–46.4	–37.7	–39.9	–11.3
Average	–52.1%	–44.1%	–53.7%	–40.7%	–51.5%	–26.5%
Average difference between Global and Home portfolios	8.0		13.0		25.0	

Notes: Returns are continuously compounded and inflation adjusted. Reported returns are not annualized. Differences are in percentage points.

a more diversified portfolio is safer than a less diversified portfolio. Unless you have a strongly held view that your country will deliver superior returns over the ensuing long term (and, please, if you believe it, do so for a better reason than "it has done better for a while"), the case for international diversification is rock solid.

Dividends are good and for some surprising reasons

How little you know about the age you live in if you think that honey is sweeter than cash in hand.

Ovid

In the heyday of the bubble, companies were particularly reticent to pay dividends. In fact, paying dividends was in some ways a black mark. It said to the market that you had no confidence in your growth opportunities. Many authors (e.g., Arnott and Bernstein 2002) have pointed out the historical importance of dividends to the total long-term return on stocks. They cannot, however, prove that dividends are actually necessary. If companies pay less in dividends but reinvest the money prudently, investors are no worse off (and, considering the effect of taxes, perhaps better off) because lower dividend payments show up as higher earnings growth. This outcome fits common sense well and, although not a precise version, is much in the spirit of the Modigliani–Miller dividend irrelevance theorem. Long-term dividend irrelevance should be the "base case" theory. The "bubble case" theory would be the notion that (1) companies are so flush with growth opportunities that paying dividends would be crazy and (2) those not paying dividends will grow *more* than fast enough to make investors whole for the forgone dividends.

One way to examine the accuracy of these two theories is shown in **Figure 4**. The x-axis represents the starting dividend payout ratio (dividends paid divided by the previous year's earnings) every rolling month for the S&P 500 for all post–World War II decades. The y-axis shows the subsequent 10-year earnings growth. According to the base case (dividend irrelevance), the line of best fit should be downward sloping; that is, as the company pays out fewer dividends, it should grow more. The line for the bubble case should be similar, although we would expect a more extreme downward slope as the forgone dividends did more than their share as reinvestment.

Well, the line is not downward sloping, certainly not sharply downward sloping; rather, it is clearly upward sloping. When companies collectively pay out more in dividends, their collective earnings tend to grow strongly faster over the next decade than when they pay out less.[10]

We do not know why this startling result exists. A working hypothesis involves how corporate managers behave and what they believe when paying or not paying large dividends. When companies pay out large dividends (relative to earnings), it may mean they are confident that the future will be bright (companies loathe cutting dividends, so they would not pay them if the future looked grim). Also, when companies pay large dividends, they are forced to be frugal in choosing investment projects (or ask the capital markets for more money when needed), so perhaps they then choose investments more wisely. Conversely, when companies pay out small dividends, they either may know they are running on fumes (as when earnings were inflated in 1999) or are engaged in "empire building" (that is, managers like to run big companies and may imprudently overinvest in bad projects when they have abundant reserves of company cash).

Thus, historically, dividends are not simply an important part of total stock returns; they are an important aspect of corporate governance. Not a bad combination.

Figure 4. Payout Ratios and Earnings Growth, 1946–2001

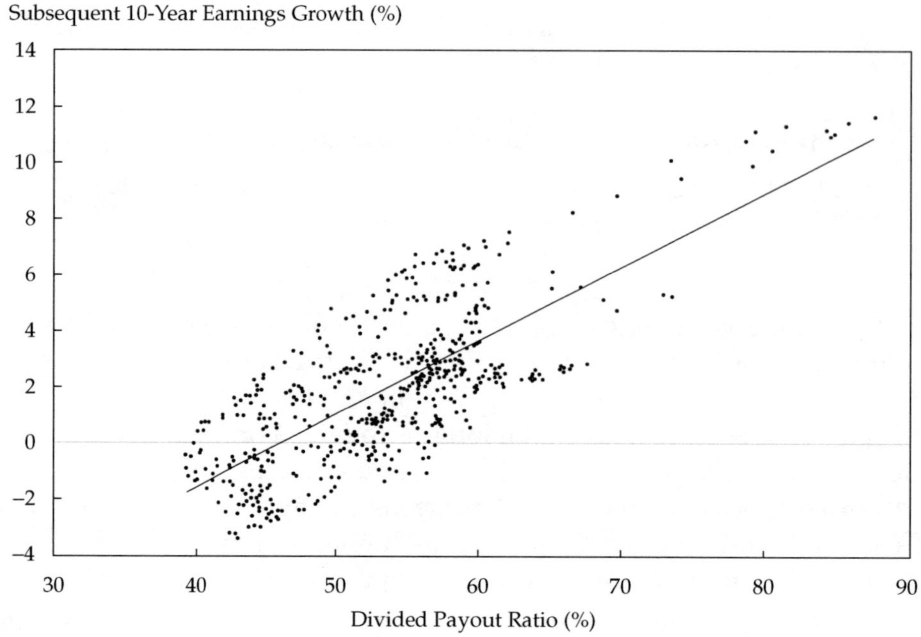

Source: Modeled on Exhibit 2 from Arnott and Asness (2003), which built on work of Bernstein (1997a, 1997b).

Earnings do not grow at 10 percent a year

History is the version of past events people have decided to agree upon.

Napoleon Bonaparte

During the bubble, the aggregate five-year earnings growth forecast from Wall Street analysts hit 15 percent a year for the S&P 500 and 30 percent a year for the NASDAQ 100 Index. Those figures exemplify the forecasting of growth above any possible reality. And it occurs often, albeit usually in milder form. Companies routinely claim they expect double-digit future growth, and commentators on cable business news will repeatedly state that 10 percent growth for the aggregate market is pretty much the norm.

Unfortunately, the past 75 years, a period marked by great performance of the U.S. economy and stock market, demonstrate that 10 percent is way too high. Realized EPS growth for S&P 500 stocks has been less than 2 percent above inflation for this period (see, e.g., Arnott and Bernstein; Ibbotson and Chen 2003). At the individual stock level, Chan, Karceski, and Lakonishok (2003) showed that despite analysts' willingness to aggressively forecast the growth of individual companies, they are incredibly bad at forecasting the relative long-term (with long-term really being anywhere past a year out) growth of companies.

Some analysts accept the past data but predict a much brighter future. They have many reasons. One argument is that companies pay fewer dividends than they used to and thus will grow faster. As noted, this argument is historically backward. Another is that productivity growth is and will remain strong. If true, the outcome will be great for all our standards of living, but historically, productivity growth has benefited consumers, and perhaps labor, more than the owners of capital. The Internet boom is a perfect example: Prices went down dramatically for consumers, but profits were tiny.

Finally, we need to translate real EPS growth into nominal growth, which is what most people use in practice. If we take a forecast of 2 percent long-term real EPS growth and add it to an assumed steady 2–3 percent inflation from now on, we find that history favors a 4–5 percent long-term nominal EPS growth for the future. I bet Wall Street does not agree.

The Fed Model must be fought

A nickel isn't worth a dime today.

Yogi Berra

The so-called Fed Model is a popular, simple, one-step model for valuing the stock market.[11] The Fed Model values the stock market by comparing the inverse of the P/E of the S&P 500, called the earnings yield or E/P, with the yield on the 10-year U.S. T-bond, Y. If E/P > Y, the stock market is deemed cheap; if E/P < Y, stocks are expensive; E/P = Y is considered the fair-value point.

The arguments in favor of the Fed Model generally follow one of two lines of reasoning. One is its apparent common sense: When stocks are paying more than bonds, stocks are cheap, and vice versa. The second is that, empirically, it "works." **Figure 5** shows that the stock market's E/P and the bond market's Y have clearly moved together over time.

Neither of these lines of reasoning is valid. First, the Fed Model is not simply common sense. The fatal flaw in the Fed Model is the comparison of a real (invariant-to-inflation) quantity with a nominal quantity. This comparison is often called the "money illusion" and is certainly not common sense.[12]

Second, Figure 5 shows only that investors have used the Fed Model to price stocks for the past 40 years; it does not show that they were correct to do so. I believe they used the Fed Model in error and to their own detriment.[13]

Figure 5. Earnings/Price vs. Yield, 1965–2001

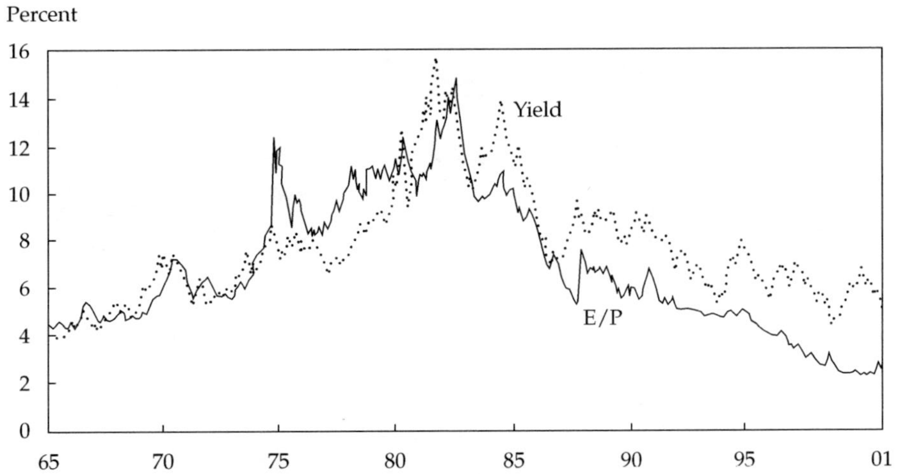

Source: Modeled on Exhibit 1 in Asness (2003).

So, the Fed Model is based on flawed logic. What happens when investors consistently use a model that is wrong? Well, consider **Figure 6.**

Figure 6, which draws on Asness (2003), shows each month from 1965 onward in one of five buckets based on the level of interest rates that month. So, Bucket 1 represents the months where Y ended in the bottom 1/5 of all months (very low interest rates), and Bucket 5, the top 1/5 (very high interest rates). The dark bars represent the average real return of the stock market for the prior 10 years before the month in question. The result is the stuff of Fed Modeler dreams. When interest rates were low, the stock market, on average, performed phenomenally (more than 10 percent above inflation). This relationship is monotonically declining, ending in a paltry average real return of 2 percent when interest rates were at their highest. There is only one small problem: The dark bars are 10-year periods ending in either low or high interest rates. The white bars represent average real returns over the *next* 10 years. They are completely backward from a Fed Model perspective. Future real returns rise as interest rates increase. The average real return on the S&P 500 when starting from the lowest interest rates is actually negative. Looking forward, the best time to buy stocks is actually when interest rates are high. It is, if you will, an Anti-Fed Model.

The reason is really simple. Investors have indeed historically (since 1965 or so) used the Fed Model to price stocks, but again, they have been wrong to do so. The dark bars work so nicely because when interest rates are low (high), investors are currently paying an inflated (depressed) P/E for stocks based on their Fed Model, so it is a good (bad) time to *have* owned stocks for the last 10 years. By the same token, these inflated prices mean it is a bad (good) time to own them for

Figure 6. Annualized Real Returns to Stock Portfolios Based on 10-Year Bond Yields, 1965–2001

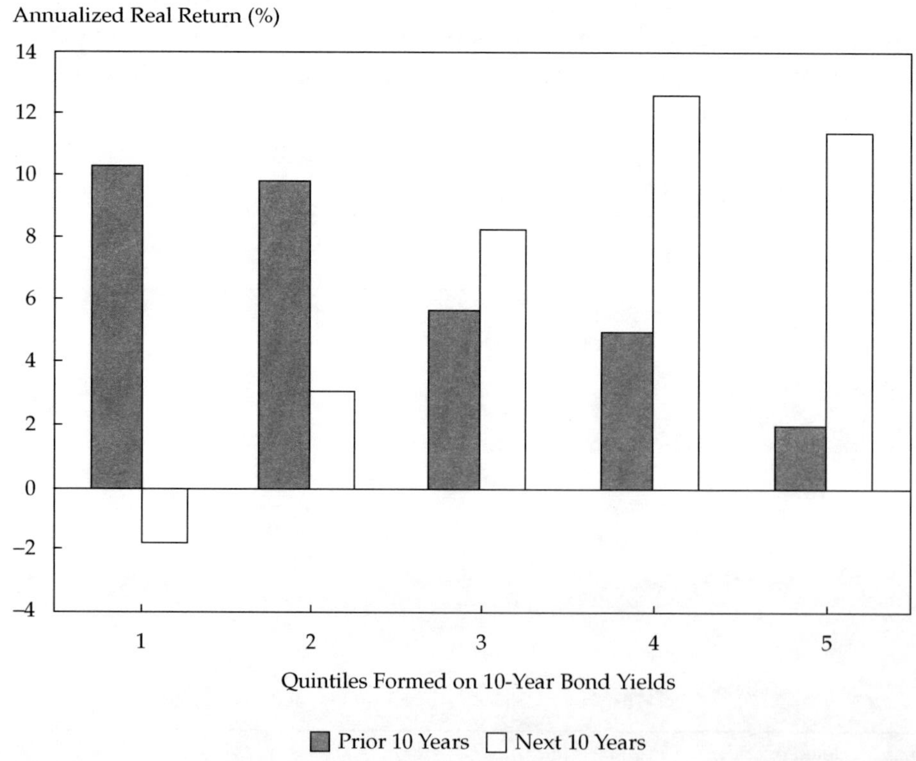

the *next* 10 years. It is not the interest rates that are actually relevant; rather, it is the P/E on the stock market that comes along with high or low rates. The Fed Model is useful only for explaining the error that investors rather consistently seem to make when pricing stocks, not for justifying that error.[14] It is very strange to see investors consistently making an error and then recommending that error to future investors on precedent—which is precisely what strategists advocating the Fed Model are doing.[15]

Value wins in the long term

> *Let us be thankful for the fools. But for them the rest of us could not succeed.*[16]
>
> Mark Twain

Before the bubble, value investing, the idea of buying out-of-favor stocks at low prices and shunning glamorous stocks at high prices, was favored by many academics and perfectly respectable on Wall Street (Graham and Dodd 1934). Then, the logic of the bubble said value investing "does not work anymore." This logic appeared to be right for a while. **Figure 7** illustrates the poor performance of one well-known version of a value strategy during the bubble period. HML stands for "high book-to-market stock minus low book-to-market stock." The solid line is the growth of a dollar invested in cash, and the dotted line is the growth of a dollar invested in cash plus the HML excess return during the bubble. This investment is called the "HML Hedge Fund" because it is the gross return on a hedge fund that went long the H stocks and short the L stocks (so, during the bubble, it was long a lot of "old economy" stocks and short a lot of "new economy," technology, stocks).

Figure 7. Bubble Performance of a Value Strategy, August 1998–2000

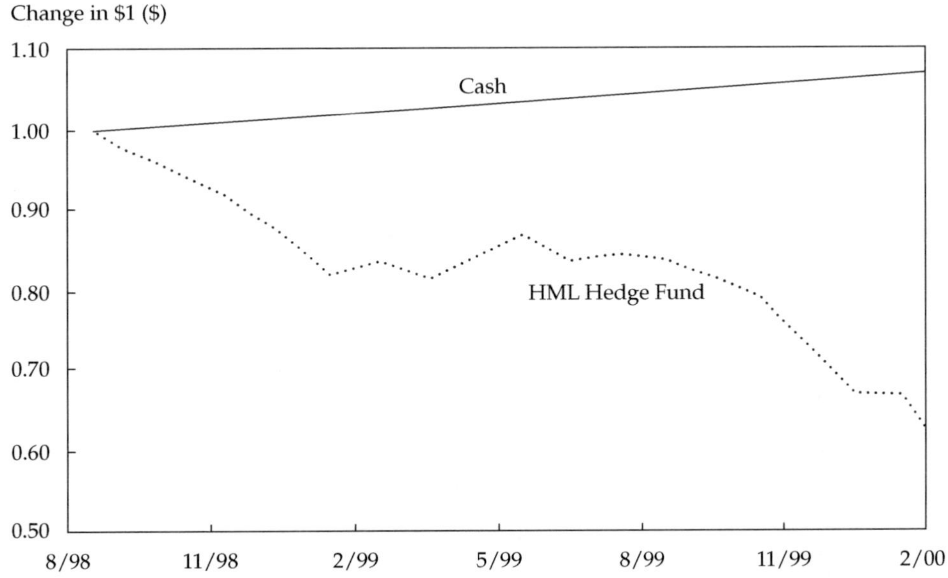

Note: Returns are gross of transaction costs and fees.

Source: Returns are from Kenneth French's website, available at mba.tuck.dartmouth.edu/pages/faculty/ken.french/.

The total gross return on this normally well-behaved value strategy was a devastating –41 percent (nearly 50 percent below the cash return) and with few up months to give the manager and clients hope—not a situation even the most stoic long-term investor found easy to tolerate.

Value proponents at the time could respond with a graph like that shown in **Figure 8**, in which the period begins in 1926. Their argument was that value had a long history of producing positive returns and the then-recent poor returns were just a blip.

Of course, during the bubble, such protestations were dismissed as theoretical, visionless, and (most damning) "driving by looking through the rear-view mirror" because, obviously, the giant dip at the end of the period was not an aberration but the new economy taking over forever.

Figure 9, which extends Figure 8 through the present, speaks for itself. After a brief departure (brief from a historical, not a personal, perspective; living through it took eons), value is back on trend. The view in the now-*schadenfreude*-tinted rear-view mirror once again looks quite scenic.

"Arbitrage" has real limits; everyone votes on stock prices

It has been said that democracy is the worst form of government except all the others that have been tried.

Sir Winston Churchill

How many have thought something like the following? "It does not matter if a few, or even many, fools exist; market prices will still be accurate if there are rational arbitrageurs out there"? I did, and it is not true. Shleifer and Vishny (1997), who used the term "the limits of arbitrage," showed that even a sure thing is not a sure thing if one faces any form of bankruptcy risk (e.g., the risk in 2000 that a value manager would go out of business before the investor could be proven right). More recently, Fama and French (2004) showed us formally that unless the stupid and misinformed exactly cancel each other out (i.e., for every stupid person overpricing something there is one

Figure 8. To-Date Performance of a Value Strategy, 1926–2000 (log scale)

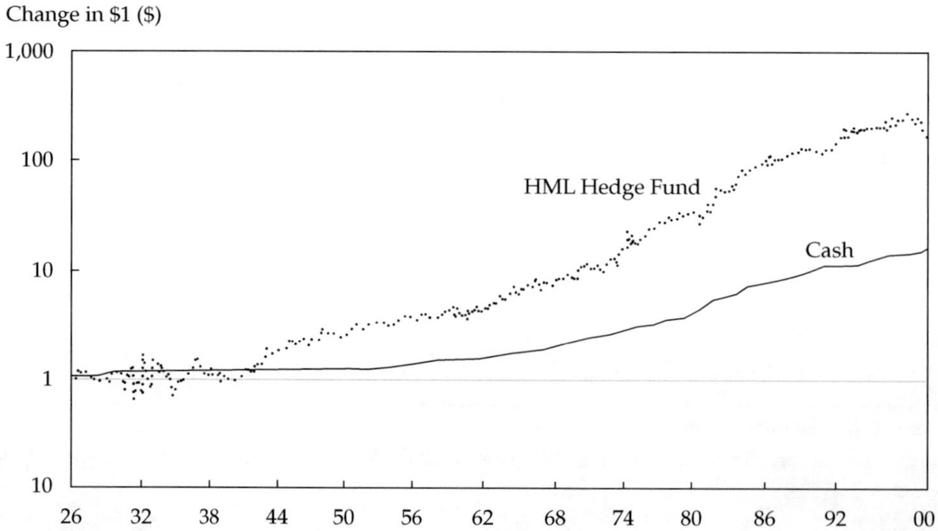

Figure 9. Long-Term Performance of a Value Strategy, 1926–2004 (log scale)

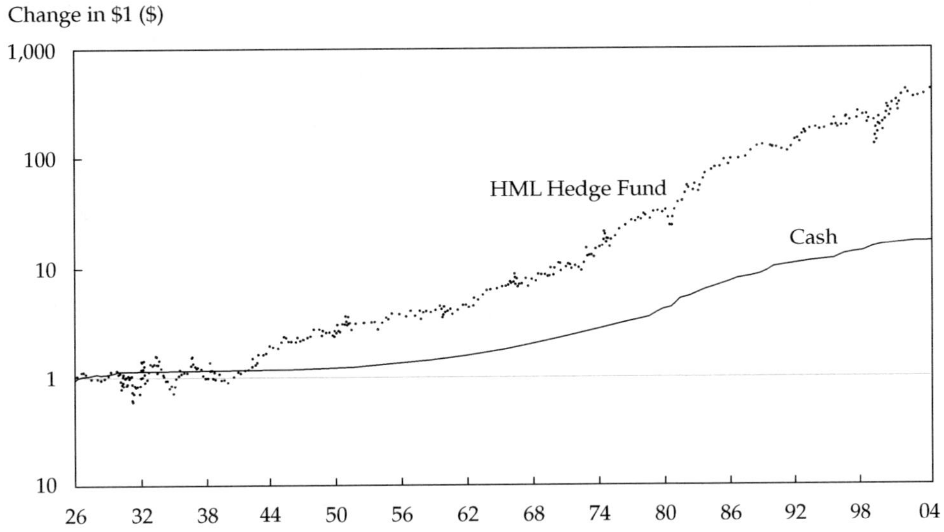

underpricing it), their net views will be reflected in prices. The Fama–French idea is similar in spirit to the work of Shleifer and Vishny. It recognizes that the "rational arbitrageur" does not find sure things but simply good bets when someone else is being stupid. And every good bet still has risk. Thus, rational arbitrageurs will *reduce* mispricing—but not enough to drive prices back to fully rational levels, because doing so would be too little gain for too much risk.

In the Bubble Logic of 1999–2000, many investors thought the market could not be wrong, so (as a tautology) prices must be rational and perhaps "the market" was seeing something all of us could not see. If the foolish all get a vote, however, and have an impact on final prices, then at times, more fools are more foolish than normal—and the result could be a bubble.

Wall Street and the media are not looking out for you

I don't want any yes-men around me. I want everybody to tell me the truth even if it costs them their jobs.

Samuel Goldwyn

From the perspective of post-bubble 2005 after the many scandals, the observation that Wall Street is not looking out for you should be less than Earth shattering. Still, the idea of benevolent rock-star analysts and strategists dispensing sage and useful advice to investors was an important part of the bubble.

Wall Street exists largely to sell stocks and bonds and to broker stock and bond transactions in both directions, not to make intellectually honest arguments. Similarly, the media exist to sell media. Speaking the truth may or may not be in both of their long-term interests, but investors must recognize that it is not always done. Most importantly, both groups do far better in a bull than in a bear market, and both behaved poorly during the bubble.

Of course, some strategists spoke their bearish minds, and some analysts said "sell" before it became fashionable, and some clear-headed members of the media bored their editors by not going for the hype. But these laudatory examples were simply the occasional exceptions that proved the overwhelming rule.[17]

The very idea of Wall Street making impartial recommendations about its own products is a strange one. Imagine a General Motors "transportation strategist" telling consumers, "We kind of like cars in here, maybe some light trucks in a portfolio context . . . ." Similarly, a large part of Wall Street's business is selling *new and used* stocks and bonds, which strangely they do make recommendations about.

Moreover, stock returns are basically unforecastable in the short run, and in the long run, only valuation works, which is just bad TV. Imagine a Wall Street guru saying, "Stocks will return an expected 6–7 percent over the long haul, but frankly, we, and everyone else, have no idea what will happen in the next few weeks or months or even years." Now, think of it repeated every day. Not only is it not bullish; what is worse, it is boring! The long-term story is boring precisely because, as a long-term story, it appropriately changes quite slowly. So, both the bullish bias and the bias toward avoiding the boring are working against the consumer here, and it is unlikely that Wall Street's peculiar practice of recommending its own products, with ever-evolving rationales, will soon change.[18]

You cannot trust Wall Street to compare apples to apples

"I'd say he's done more than that." When asked if first baseman Don Mattingly had exceeded expectations for the current season.

Yogi Berra

The bubble saw the rise of the concept of *pro forma* analysis. Since then, *pro forma* has been ridiculed by legions of open-eyed commentators, but sadly, it does not die. In concept, there is nothing wrong with looking at a company's earnings excluding something that is, in the analyst's opinion, truly nonrecurring. Companies themselves decide what to do in their *pro forma* statements, however, and sell-side analysts (although perhaps not the lapdogs of 1999) usually follow the companies' choices. And firms that gather and report earnings use what the majority of these analysts decide they should use. It is a scary system.

For a common form of *pro forma* abuse (see Asness and Casscells, forthcoming), consider the following typical statement among sell-side strategists: "We calculate the current P/E of the S&P 500 to be about 16 [or some other close-by number]. This is right in the range of historical average P/Es, so the market's valuation is on sure footing." The tricky part is that when an analyst calls a P/E of 16 about average, the analyst is usually calculating the current P/E for the S&P 500 from "forecasted" "operating" earnings. Both words are dangerous. "Forecasted" generally means "higher than today and probably higher than what will really occur tomorrow," and "operating" is a form of *pro forma* calculation that throws out bad things. Operating P/Es are almost always lower than trailing GAAP P/Es, and the historical evidence about long-term average P/Es comes mainly from trailing GAAP numbers. In fact, our history of forecasted operating P/Es (from 1976 on) shows that, on average, they are about 25 percent less than trailing P/Es—thus averaging about 12. Moreover, the period from 1976 to today is still, net, a period of expensive stock prices, so the true long-term average of forecasted *pro forma* P/Es is probably even lower than 12. Thus, analysts should not compare today's forecasted operating P/Es of around 16 with the historical average of GAAP trailing P/Es and declare current prices average; they should compare the forecasted P/Es with the much lower historical average of similar forecasted operating P/Es and should note that stocks are still quite expensive.

Finally, I will note one good use of *pro forma*. I am *pro forma* 6′ 2″ tall and have all my hair. Sadly, my wife is a stickler for GAAP.

Options issuance is an expense

A lie told often enough becomes the truth.

Vladimir Ilyich Lenin

For years, by winning a calculated campaign of lobbying in favor of misinformation, companies have avoided expensing their stock option grants by relegating these expenses to footnotes. I have reviewed already the many arguments for expensing options and refuted the many illogical arguments to the contrary (Asness 2004). Those who argue (generally for self-serving purposes) that corporate managers should be allowed to give themselves companies without even recording the cost should be ashamed of themselves.

Option expensing seems to be on the way to becoming mandatory. I will believe it when it is a fact, because many vested, venal, and vengeful interests are against it.[19] Of course, when option expensing becomes mandatory, we will probably soon afterward have a new entry into the *pro forma* sweepstakes as many companies choose to report *pro forma* earnings that delete the very real expense of options.[20]

Timing the market is not all bad

The generation of random numbers is too important to be left to chance.

Robert R. Coveyou
Oak Ridge National Laboratory

During the heyday of the bubble, Wall Street had a particularly schizophrenic relationship with the strategy based on short-term forecasting called "market timing." On the one hand, a substantial amount of the bubble was built on short-horizon investing in general. An obvious example is the rise of the day trader. A more subtle example is Wall Street strategists at the time touting their "year-end price target" for the S&P 500. They might not have called this practice "timing," but if acting on a short-term forecast is not timing, what is it?[21] Of course, when investors even considered *selling* their stocks, they would be treated to a lengthy discourse on Wall Street conventional wisdom (this time mostly from the buy side) that market timing is an investing sin.

My comments in this section will also be schizophrenic. I strongly agree with the general recommendation not to regularly engage in short-term market timing, but I take serious issue with the idea that you should never engage in *long-term* timing because such a policy aids and abets bubbles. And I take serious issue with Wall Street's favorite antitiming argument.

First, let me say that 99 times out of 100, "avoid market timing" is a good piece of advice. The transaction costs, tax effects, and general unpredictability of the market—all make timing a dicey proposition.

However, what Wall Street is often really saying is, "Ignore the price of what I am selling you." Wall Street is in the business of selling you stocks and does not want you leaving the market. Now, if a salesperson of any other purchase told you to ignore the price because "it will all work out over the very long run," you would run clutching your wallet. In particular, to bolster its antitiming case, Wall Street often uses the evidence of how much return you can miss by being out of the market for just a little while. But amazingly, the same people completely leave out the almost symmetrical upside if you are right. Of course, a short-term bet has a downside, but it also has an upside! So, although perhaps usually good advice, "do not try to time the market" cannot mean ignore price entirely, and it cannot be based on looking only at the negative possible outcomes. If being price sensitive means timing the market but timing the market is a cardinal sin, then prices have no anchor to reality. Thus, although I agree that short-term market timing is almost always a bad idea, changing your exposure to the stock market based on current prices with a long horizon in mind, and perhaps acting only at extremes, seems like a form of market timing that would be beneficial to those willing to follow such a strategy and to healthy markets in general.

The general public is full of bored, innumerate gamblers[22]

After years of disappointment with get-rich-quick schemes, I know
I'm gonna get rich with this scheme . . . and quick!

Homer Simpson

Many people are natural gamblers; they like to be entertained and are not good at math. For example, many people like lotteries (Statman 2002)—which are entertaining games that have negative expected returns and offer the small chance of a huge payoff. Many people like the casino's video poker game. It has fun flashing lights, and as with lotteries, the player loses on average (and certainly if the game is played long enough) but over short intervals, can win for a while. In both these cases, presumably even the most innumerate player knows that the enterprise is a negative-expected-value game (although they might not put it that way).

Now, consider on-line trading, particularly during the bubble. It is obviously a ton of fun, and it was clearly sold as a positive-expected-return game with huge positive skewness (remember those truck drivers in the commercials with their own private islands). What if Las Vegas could follow this strategy—could convince their video poker players that they would actually win on average and win more the longer they played? You would have to pry the players out of their seats with the Jaws of Life!

The nature of these bored, mathematically challenged investors relates to the lessons of the rubble because, as discussed earlier, they all get a vote on stock prices. Many people still see the stock market as entertainment, a chance to get rich quick, or both, and many are still doing the math wrong.

Do-it-yourself trading is a bad idea

If at first you don't succeed, failure may be your style.

Quentin Crisp

Countless exhortations can be heard (they were particularly prevalent during the bubble but are still very much in vogue) to individuals to "take control" of their own financial future by making their own trades and investments (usually online). A typical exhortation is, "Yes, you can!" when it comes to managing your own active investment portfolio. I am here to tell you, "No, you can't!"

Forget the prior section's misanthropy, which, if accurate, calls attention to an obvious hurdle (the average person's innumeracy and gambling problem). There is simply massive evidence that professional full-time active managers with degrees in this field have great difficulty beating low-cost index funds. Yes, perhaps the professionals have some biases, constraints, and distractions, and perhaps a smart person dedicated full-time to active management of his or her own money might clobber the indices. As down-home, golly gee nice as it sounds, it is not likely.

Consider these common exhortations: "With as little as one hour a week of homework, you can pick great stocks!" Or "You should just buy what you know"—implying that your common sense is better than the efforts of highly motivated professionals. You cannot pick great stocks this way, and your common sense is not better. You can trade your own stocks to entertain yourself—and to hope for the big payoff. And just like such entertainment and hope at Las Vegas, it has a cost.

Have we collectively "learned" these lessons?

> *Thank you for sending me a copy of your book. I'll waste no time reading it.*
>
> Moses Hadas

Despite many negative signs, I see some positive portents that we have learned many of the lessons of the bubble. The idea that long-term returns from here will be low has certainly gained traction. The stock market return forecasts of Wall Street strategists are still higher than what is likely to occur, but they have come way down from their former steady median forecasts of 15 percent a year. Most importantly, prices are now only high versus history, not insane.

However, all is not rosy. The debate on Social Security offers an interesting window into whether we have learned to avoid thinking in Bubble Logic. A crucial issue in this debate involves investing Social Security funds in the stock market, either through private accounts or directly by the government. Casual study of the widespread arguments in favor of such a policy reveals the following Bubble Logic:

- quoting long-term historical stock returns to determine the expected stock return for today's Social Security investor (i.e., ignoring current valuation);
- noting that investors have never lost in stocks if held for long periods, such as 20 years (i.e., ignoring that at a lower risk premium, stocks will lose with much higher probability in the future, even over the long term);
- most egregiously, acting as if we all, collectively, even had the option of investing *more* retirement money in stocks. We do not. In the short term, we cannot collectively move $1 net into stocks because we can only buy them from someone else, presumably someone saving for her or his retirement, so we cannot all invest more in stocks. All we can do is force prices higher and the long-term risk premium even lower.[23]

If at any point I had felt that the need for this retrospective article had faded with the receding of the bubble, the Social Security debate, with its mix of old and new Bubble Logic, has rejuvenated me.

Some constructive advice

Investing is simple, but not easy.

Warren Buffett

Despite all the criticism I have leveled at our collective understanding, we basically know how to invest. A good analogy is to dieting and diet books. We all know how to lose weight and get in better shape: Eat less and exercise more. But as Warren Buffett would say, that is simple—but not easy. Investing is no different.

Some simple, but not easy, advice for good investing and financial planning in general includes

- diversify widely,
- keep costs low,
- rebalance in a disciplined fashion,
- spend less,
- save more,
- make less heroic assumptions about future returns,
- when something sounds like a free lunch, assume it is not free unless very convincing arguments are made—and then check again,
- stop watching the stock markets as if they were on ESPN, and
- work less on investing, not more (after finishing this article, of course).

Perhaps the most important advice, in true Hippocratic fashion, is: Do No Harm! You do not need a magic bullet. Little can change the fact that current expected returns on a broad set of asset classes are low versus history, and explicitly or implicitly "levering up" low expected returns to make them high is not usually a great idea. Stick to the basics with discipline, and ignore Bubble Logic.

Conclusion

Speak the truth, but leave immediately after.

Slovenian Proverb

The stock market is quite wonderful. It is a long-term wealth creator and democratizer. It is a bringer of economic efficiency, and aside from bubble times, it prices things far more accurately than any other system yet devised. Furthermore, stock prices, although not "rubble" or even down to long-term averages, are indeed far more reasonable today than when they were a true bubble back in 1999–2000. Clearly, whether the lessons of Bubble Logic have been learned sufficiently or not, they are far closer to being learned today than a few years ago. Expected returns to investors following "simple but not easy" investing are positive, and although returns are low historically, they are still reasonable. My message, if not optimistic, is not nearly as deeply pessimistic as it was five years ago.

As cynical as I have been about "strategists" and "analysts" and salespeople of many stripes, this criticism is also, almost by definition, a statement of the importance of these people doing their jobs well in a free capitalist society. We have certainly seen what happens when they do it poorly. The societal importance of careers in finance is often downplayed in comparison with the many other paths that more obviously and directly aid people. Perhaps that view is justified by how Wall Street has performed to date, but if the investment manager and the analyst do their jobs well, they provide good advice and accurate pricing—which are exceptionally important and something to be proud of because capitalism depends on them and freedom and abundance depend on capitalism. Good advice and accurate pricing are certainly too important to be left to Bubble Logic.[24]

Those who were kind enough to give me comments on this work are too numerous to mention by name; I thank them all. Also, I would like to thank my wife, Laurel; my partners, David Kabiller, Bob Krail, and John Liew; and Brad Asness—not simply for their comments but for listening to me rant and rave through much of the bubble and its aftermath, which was the catalyst for this article and its unpublished predecessor. Finally, of course, I would like to thank Al Gore, without whom there would be no Internet and, possibly, no Great Stock Market Bubble of 1999–2000 about which to write.

Notes

1. In fact, given that the original "Bubble Logic" was never formally published, I am going to feel free to plagiarize my own work and use some parts of the original here. This plagiarism concerns me a bit as, frankly, I fear I may be litigious.
2. Some argue that using past 10-year average earnings may be inferior to using more current measures, such as trailing 1-year earnings or Wall Street forecasts of future earnings. Each method has obvious advantages and disadvantages. (I focus on Wall Street forecasts later.) The 1-year measure is more timely, but it may include many transient components that could render P/Es calculated from the earnings less meaningful. The earnings crash of 2001–2002 is an example. The 10-year measure is more dated but smooths the transients. In simple tests of the ability of each measure to forecast future (10 and 20 years forward) total earnings, the 10-year method of Shiller was a clear victor (these tests are available from the author).
3. Table 1 is impressive, but it suffers from some statistical weaknesses. We do not have many independent 10-year periods to observe, and the results have been strengthened by an in-sample bias, in that starting price is used to sort in-sample returns.
4. Some people criticize arguments like that implied by Table 1 by pointing to historical cases of stocks delivering attractive returns, even for a decade, when starting out at high prices. Even the best cases, however, generally decline as starting price rises. When prices are high, average future real returns are low; worst cases are much worse, and best cases are weaker, although not nonexistent. I am not claiming that valuation is a near-perfect forecaster. Rather, in 10-year regressions, it seems to forecast 30–40 percent of the variance of future stock returns. It will not always work over the next decade (nothing does), but to dismiss valuation as irrelevant when it gets a decade wrong is quite silly.
5. Actually, intellectual honesty demands that we review a third possibility—that higher valuation levels signal permanently higher levels of expected earnings and dividend growth and thus no lower expected returns in the short or long term. This future is supported by almost zero evidence in the data but cannot be ruled out as a possibility.
6. I am also being a little tricky in my choice of time period because 1982–2004 was not only a bull market for stocks but also a massive bull market for bonds. I have shown elsewhere (Asness 1996) that this section's findings are general.
7. Disclaimer: I have not exhaustively checked whether my Yogi Berra quotations are truly his or merely attributed to him. I'll let Yogi explain with his purported comment "I really didn't say everything I said."
8. A much sillier argument, which was especially popular in the bubble, goes: U.S. equities have outperformed international equities for the past 5–10 years or so, so why bother? This argument propounds momentum investing pure and simple. U.S. equity has done better than international portfolios largely as a result of decades of upward revaluation. Forecasting more of the same kind of outperformance as when valuation changes were driving the outperformance is not only wrong; it is probably backwards.
9. Another version of this argument notes that correlations between countries go up during bear markets. This observation is accurate, but the more relevant problem is that all markets seem to go down at the same time.

10. Arnott and Asness (2003) conducted a bevy of robustness checks, in all of which, this result survived unscathed.
11. The Federal Reserve Board itself actually shows no tendency to favor the Fed Model; it is mentioned in obscure minutes of meetings and testimony along with many other models and hypotheses. Chairman Alan Greenspan has made several comments on the illusion underlying the Fed Model. Nevertheless, the name "Fed Model" wrongly implies a certain stamp of approval on this flawed metric.
12. The money illusion was perhaps first noted in this context by Modigliani and Cohn (1979).
13. As shown in Asness (2000b, 2003), the simple relationship between E/P and Y breaks down if extended back in time prior to 1965 but can be resuscitated if relative perceptions of stock and bond market risks are accounted for in the model. For a full discussion of flaws in the Fed Model, see Asness (2003).
14. In its role of explaining investor behavior, the Fed Model may be useful for the intrepid tactical asset allocator, but that short-term horizon is very different from the long-term horizon discussed here.
15. Many investors and analysts make the same error by using the venerable dividend discount model to value stocks. In a typical DDM, the analyst or strategist forecasts the future cash flows to a stock or the stock market, then discounts these cash flows back at some rate (often a U.S. Treasury rate plus a risk premium). When interest rates fall, the DDM's user often lowers the discount rate but *not* the forecast of future cash flows; thus, the user finds that the stock or stock market should rise in value. This approach is the same error made by the Fed Model, and those who use DDMs this way are subject to the same long-term consequences of grossly overpaying (underpaying) for stocks when interest rates are low (high). Similar logic is being applied to real estate investments, where the idea that low inflation/interest rates support a bullish real estate market is currently ubiquitous. This idea has to be wrong. Although real estate may appear more affordable when interest rates are low (because monthly payments are low), so, presumably, is average nominal income growth (the analogy to slower nominal corporate earnings growth in the Fed Model). More generally, how can a "real" asset (in both the literal sense and the sense of an asset that is an inflation hedge) change in fundamental value when only nominal, not real, interest rates change? Perhaps the next paper should be on the real estate bubble and the logic that powers it; the parallels are apt (and the five-year follow-up using the term "rubble" might be more literal).
16. I apologize to all my efficient market friends for the blatant behavioral bias implied in this quotation.
17. During the bubble, a queue formed of courageously bearish strategists and analysts who decided to "retire," often with the stated purpose of "spending more time with my family." They were replaced with happier, more bullish prognosticators—many of whom also discovered, in the bear market, that their families needed their attention.
18. I am not making a plea for regulation; everyone should have the right to his or her opinion. As a believer in caveat emptor, I would simply like to see the emptors start caveating more.
19. In fact, as this article is being prepared, the U.S. SEC is proposing, at industry request, to put off by another six months the requirement to expense. The reasons they give amount to "the dog ate my Black–Scholes spreadsheet" and make for some very sad reading.
20. One of the more amusing current financial stories is about companies changing their option policy now that options soon must be expensed. The reason many are giving is that they can no longer afford options. Let me be very clear: *Options were always and will always be expenses*. They are no more or less affordable now than before. What these companies mean is that they will not be able to lie about the expenses by hiding them in the footnotes.
21. There is nothing necessarily wrong with being short term. Short-term strategies, short-term momentum strategies in particular, might have validity (see, for instance, Jegadeesh and Titman 1993; Asness 1999). However, these strategies are probably not applicable to the average investor.
22. AQR Capital Management, LLC, would like to reemphasize that the views and opinions expressed herein are those of the author and do not necessarily reflect the views of AQR, its affiliates, or its employees. Should Cliff run for office one day, he intends to deny that this section exists.
23. In the long term, we can move more money into stocks because more stocks can be created. This process can have some positive effects (one person's expected return is another's cost of capital), but taken to excess, it encourages the creation of dicey ventures—as we certainly saw during the bubble.
24. Finally, by way of apology for all the quotations, here is one about me: "He wrapped himself in quotations—as a beggar would enfold himself in the purple of Emperors"—Rudyard Kipling.

References

Arnott, Robert D., and Clifford S. Asness. 2003. "Surprise! Higher Dividends = Higher Earnings Growth." *Financial Analysts Journal*, vol. 59, no. 1 (January/February):70–87.

Arnott, Robert D., and Peter L. Bernstein. 2002. "What Risk Premium Is 'Normal'?" *Financial Analysts Journal*, vol. 58, no. 2 (March/April):64–85.

Asness, Clifford. 1996. "Why Not 100% Equities." *Journal of Portfolio Management* (Winter):29–34.

———. 1999. "The Power of Past Stock Returns." Working paper, AQR Capital Management.

———. 2000a. "Bubble Logic or How to Learn to Stop Worrying and Love the Bull." Unpublished manuscript, AQR Capital Management (June).

———. 2000b. "Stocks vs. Bonds: Explaining the Equity Risk Premium." *Financial Analysts Journal*, vol. 56, no. 2 (March/April):96–113.

———. 2003. "Fight the Fed Model." *Journal of Portfolio Management*, vol. 30, no. 1 (Fall):11–24.

———. 2004. "Stock Options and the Lying Liars Who Don't Want to Expense Them." *Financial Analysts Journal*, vol. 60, no. 4 (July/August):9–14.

Asness, Clifford, and Anne Casscells. Forthcoming. "Comparing Apples to Apples, the Stock Market Is Expensive." Working paper, AQR Capital Management.

Asness, Clifford, Robert Krail, and John Liew. Forthcoming. "International Diversification: Have We Missed the Forest through the Trees?" Working paper, AQR Capital Management.

Bernstein, Peter L. 1997a. "Stock/Bond Risk Perceptions and Expected Returns." In *Economics & Portfolio Strategy*, Peter L. Bernstein, Inc. (1 February).

———. 1997b. "Payouts and Payoffs and an Interesting Erratum." In *Economics & Portfolio Strategy*, Peter L. Bernstein, Inc. (15 March).

Carhart, Mark M. 1997. "On Persistence in Mutual Fund Performance." *Journal of Finance*, vol. 52, no. 1 (March):57–82.

Chan, L., J. Karceski, and J. Lakonishok. 2003. "The Level and Persistence of Growth Rates." *Journal of Finance*, vol. 58, no. 2 (April):634–684.

Fama, Eugene E., and Kenneth R. French. 2004. "Disagreement, Tastes, and Asset Prices." Working Paper No. 2004–03, Tuck Business School.

Graham, Benjamin, and David Dodd. *Security Analysis*. New York: McGraw-Hill (also see later editions).

Ibbotson, Roger G., and Peng Chen. 2003. "Long-Run Stock Returns: Participating in the Real Economy." *Financial Analysts Journal*, vol. 59, no. 1 (January/February):88–98.

Jegadeesh, Narasimhan, and Sheridan Titman. 1993. "Returns to Buying Winners and Selling Losers: Implications for Stock Market Efficiency." *Journal of Finance*, vol. 48, no. 1 (March):65–91.

Modigliani, F., and R. Cohn. 1979. "Inflation, Rational Valuation and the Market." *Financial Analysts Journal*, vol. 35, no. 2 (March/April):24–44.

Shiller, Robert J. 2000. *Irrational Exuberance*. Princeton, NJ: Princeton University Press.

Shleifer, Andre, and Robert W. Vishny. 1997. "The Limits of Arbitrage." *Journal of Finance*, vol. 52, no. 1 (March):35–55.

Statman, Meir. 2002. "Lottery Players/Stock Traders." *Financial Analysts Journal*, vol. 58, no. 1 (January/February):14–21.

Perspectives on the Equity Risk Premium

Jeremy J. Siegel

The equity risk premium, or the difference between the expected returns on stocks and on risk-free assets, has commanded the attention of both professional economists and investment practitioners for many decades. In the past 20 years, more than 320 articles, enough to fill some 40 economics and finance journals, have been published with the words "equity premium" in the title.

The equity risk premium determines asset allocations, projections of wealth, and the cost of capital, but we do not have a simple model that explains the premium.

The intense interest in the magnitude of the premium is not surprising. The difference between the return on stocks and the return on bonds is critical not only for asset allocation but also for wealth projections for individual investors, foundations, and endowments. One of the most asked questions by investors is: How much more can I expect to earn from shifting from bonds to stocks?

Academic interest in the equity premium surged after Mehra and Prescott published a seminal article in 1985 titled "The Equity Premium: A Puzzle." By examining the behavior of the stock market and aggregate consumption, they showed that the equity risk premium, under the usual assumptions about investor behavior toward risk, should be much lower than had been calculated from the historical data. Indeed, Mehra and Prescott stated that the equity premium in the U.S. markets should be, at most, 0.35 percent instead of the approximately 6 percent premium computed from data going back to 1872.

The Mehra–Prescott research raised the following question: Have investors been demanding—and receiving—"too high" a return for holding stocks based on the fundamental uncertainty in the economy, or are the models that economists use to describe investor behavior fundamentally flawed? If the returns have been too high, then analysts can justify increased asset allocation to equities and reduced allocation to bonds; if the models are flawed, economists need to develop new models to describe investor behavior.

Jeremy J. Siegel is the Russell E. Palmer Professor of Finance at the Wharton School, University of Pennsylvania, Philadelphia.

My discussion of the equity risk premium will be divided into three parts: (1) a summary of the data used to calculate the equity premium and discussion of potential biases in the historical data, (2) analysis of the economic models, and (3) discussion of the implications of the findings for investors and for forecasts of the future equity premium.[1]

Historical Returns on Stocks and Bonds

In this section, I present historical asset returns since 1802, define the equity premium, and discuss biases in the historical data that affect future estimates of the equity premium.

Equity Returns. The historical returns on stocks, bonds, and bills and the equity risk premium for the U.S. markets from 1802 through 31 December 2004 are in **Table 1**.[2] Both the arithmetic mean of the annual data, which is the "expected return" used in the capital asset pricing model (CAPM), and the compound (or geometric) return, which is the return most often used by individual and professional investors, are given in Table 1.[3] The last columns display the equity risk premium in relation to both long-term U.S. government bonds and T-bills. Returns and premiums are broken down into two subperiods in Panel A, into three major subperiods in Panel B, and into the major bull and bear markets since World War II in Panel C.

The stability of the real (inflation-adjusted) return on stocks over all long periods is impressive.[4] The compound annual real return on equity has averaged 6.82 percent over the past 203 years and, as Panels B and C show, settled between 6.5 percent and 7.0 percent for each of the three major subperiods and for the post–World War II data. This return is about twice the growth of the economy and includes the risk premium above risk-free assets that investors have demanded to hold stocks.

Table 1. Historical Real Stock and Bond Returns and the Equity Premium

	Real Return						Stock Return minus Return on:			
	Stocks		Bonds		Bills		Bonds		Bills	
Period	Comp.	Arith.	Comp.	Arith.	Comp.	Arith.	Comp.	Arith.	Comp.	Arith.
A. Long periods to present										
1802–2004	6.82%	8.38%	3.51%	3.88%	2.84%	3.02%	3.31%	4.50%	3.98%	5.36%
1871–2004	6.71	8.43	2.85	3.24	1.68	1.79	3.86	5.18	5.03	6.64
B. Major subperiods										
1802–1870	7.02%	8.28%	4.78%	5.11%	5.12%	5.40%	2.24%	3.17%	1.90%	2.87%
1871–1925	6.62	7.92	3.73	3.93	3.16	3.27	2.89	3.99	3.46	4.65
1926–2004	6.78	8.78	2.25	2.77	0.69	0.75	4.53	6.01	6.09	8.02
C. Post–World War II full sample, bull markets, and bear markets										
1946–2004	6.83%	8.38%	1.44%	2.04%	0.56%	0.62%	5.39%	6.35%	6.27%	7.77%
1946–1965	10.02	11.39	–1.19	–0.95	–0.84	–0.75	11.21	12.34	10.86	12.14
1966–1981	–0.36	1.38	–4.17	–3.86	–0.15	–0.13	3.81	5.24	–0.21	1.51
1982–1999	13.62	14.30	8.40	9.28	2.91	2.92	5.22	5.03	10.71	11.38
1982–2004	9.47	10.64	8.01	8.74	2.31	2.33	1.46	1.90	7.16	8.32

Note: "Comp." stands for "compound"; "Arith." stands for "arithmetic."

When the period for which stock returns are analyzed shrinks to one or two decades, the real return on stocks can deviate substantially from the long-run average. Since World War II, returns in major market cycles have fluctuated from a 10.02 percent annual real equity return in the bull market of 1946–1965 to a –0.36 percent annual real equity return in the bear market of 1966–1981; in the great bull market of 1982–1999, the return doubled the 203-year average.

Fixed-Income Returns. The middle columns in Table 1 show that real bond returns, in contrast to stocks, have experienced a declining trend in the past two centuries. From 1802 through 2004, the average annual compound real return on long-term bonds was about half the equity return, but in the 19th century, real bond returns were nearly 5 percent. Since the end of World War II, the bond return has averaged less than 1.50 percent. The 3.31 percent average real return over the last two centuries is approximately equal to the real growth of the economy, but in the post–World War II period, real returns on bonds have fallen far below economic growth.[5]

The real return on short-dated T-bills has fallen even more sharply than the return on bonds over the past two centuries. For the entire period, real T-bill returns averaged 2.84 percent, 67 bps below the return on long-term bonds. Average short-term rates were 34 bps above long-term rates for 1802–1870, but they were 57 bps below long rates from 1871 through 1925 and have been 156 bps below long rates since 1926.

The increase in the spread between long rates and short rates was caused partly by the increased liquidity of the T-bill market, which lowered short rates, and partly by the increase in the inflation premium investors have required on long-term bonds over much of the post–World War II period.

The Equity Premium. The decline in the real return on bonds, combined with the relative stability of the real return on equity, has increased the equity premium over time, as the last columns in Table 1 show. Over the 1802–2004 period, the equity risk premium as measured from compound annual returns and in relation to bonds rose (see Panel B) from 2.24 percent to 2.89 percent to 4.53 percent. Measured in relation to T-bills, the equity risk premium has increased even more.

The Risk-Free Rate: Long or Short? Should the equity risk premium be measured against the rate of short-term or long-term government bonds? In the simple representations of the CAPM, the risk-free rate is calculated against the rate on short-term risk-free assets, such as T-bills. When an intertemporal CAPM is used, however, a short rate may not be appropriate.[6] Investors should hedge against changes in investment opportunities, as represented by changes in the real risk-free rate. And in an intertemporal context, a risk-free asset can be considered an annuity that provides a constant real return over a long period of time.[7] The return on this annuity is best approximated by the returns on long-term inflation-indexed government bonds. In the United States, inflation-indexed government bonds were not introduced until 1997, so real returns on bonds before that date must be calculated *ex post* by subtracting inflation from nominal bond yields.

Calculation of the Equity Premium. The equity risk premium can be defined by the reference asset class, time period chosen, or method of calculating mean returns so as to take on a wide range of values. Its maximum value is calculated by using the *arithmetic* mean return of historical stock returns and subtracting the mean return on the highest-quality short-dated securities, such as T-bills. Measured in this way, the equity premium in the United States since 1802 has been 5.36 percent and since 1926, has been 8.02 percent. When *geometric* mean returns are used, the equity premium shrinks to 3.98 percent since 1802 and 6.09 percent since 1926. If we calculate the equity premium against long-dated (instead of short-term) bonds, the compound premium falls farther—to 3.31 percent over the past 202 years and 4.53 percent since 1926.

So, over the period from 1926 to the present, the premium can differ by 3.5 percentage points depending on whether long- or short-dated securities are used or arithmetic or geometric returns are calculated. Notwithstanding, the premium calculated by any of these methods far exceeds the magnitude derived in the Mehra–Prescott model.

Biases in Historical Equity Returns. In calculations of the equity risk premium, certain biases must be recognized: the international survivorship bias; failure to take transaction costs and diversification benefits into account; investor ignorance of risks, returns, and mean reversion; taxes and individuals' pension assets; and biases in the historical record of bond returns.

- *International survivorship bias*. Some economists claim that the historical real return on U.S. equities quite probably overstates the true expected return on stocks (Brown, Goetzmann, and Ross 1995). They maintain that the United States simply turned out to be the most successful capitalist country in history, a development that was by no means certain when investors were buying stock in the 19th and early 20th centuries.

Because the economic outcome in the United States was better than expected, U.S. returns may overstate the *expected* return on stocks. The cause is a phenomenon called "survivorship bias." This bias will exist whenever stock returns are recorded in successful equity markets, such as those in the United States, but omitted where stocks have faltered or disappeared outright, such as they did in Russia.

To address survivorship bias and to compile definitive series of long-term international stock returns, three U.K. economists—Dimson and Marsh from the London School of Business and Staunton from the U.K. statistical center—examined stock and bond returns over the past century in 16 countries. Their research, published in *Triumph of the Optimists: 101 Years of Global Investment Returns,* found that the superior returns on stocks over bonds is not characteristic of the U.S. market alone but exists in virtually all countries (see Dimson, Marsh, and Staunton 2002, 2004). **Figure 1** shows the average annual real stock, bond, and bill returns of the 16 countries they analyzed from 1900 through 2003.

Real equity returns ranged from a low of 1.9 percent in Belgium to a high of 7.5 percent in Sweden and Australia. Stock returns in the United States, although quite good, were not exceptional. U.S. stock returns were exceeded by the returns in Sweden, Australia, and South Africa.

If an equal investment had been placed in each of these markets in 1900, the average annual real return on stocks from 1900 through 2003 would have been 6.0 percent a year, not far below the U.S. return of 6.5 percent.[8] Furthermore, in the countries where real equity returns were low, such as Belgium, Italy, and Germany, real bond returns were also low, so the equity premium in Italy and Germany as measured against bonds was actually higher than the premium in the United States. In fact, the compound annual return of an equal amount invested in stocks in each country surpassed an identical amount in bonds in each country by 4 percent a year, only slightly less than the 4.6 percent equity risk premium found for the United States over the same time period.

Figure 1. Real Returns on International Assets, 1900–2003

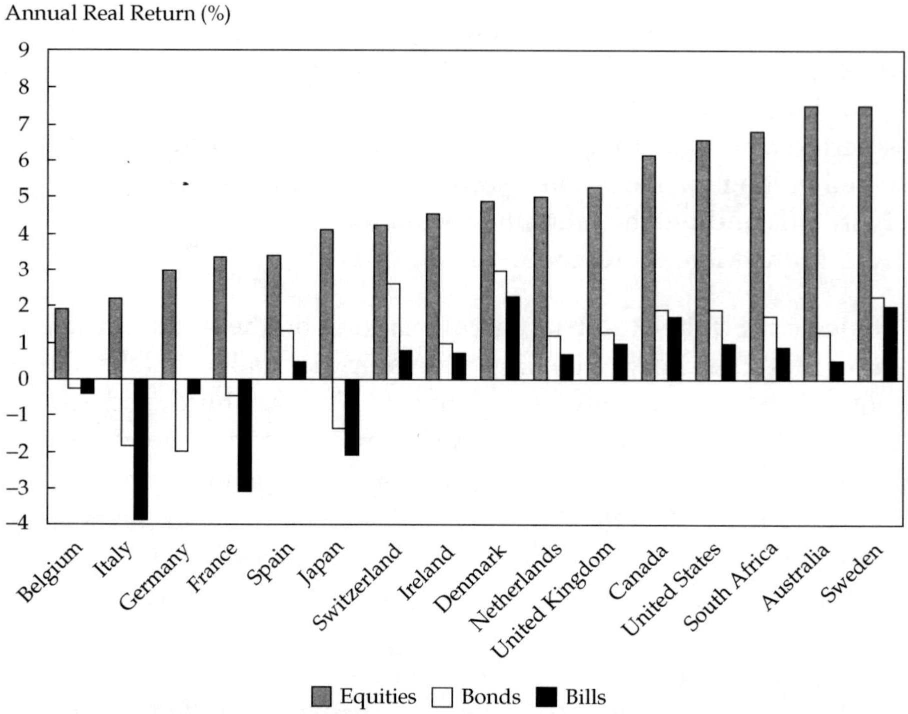

When all the information was analyzed, the authors concluded:

> While the U.S. and the U.K. have indeed performed well . . . there is no indication that they are hugely out of line with other countries. . . . Concerns about success and survivorship bias, while legitimate, may therefore have been somewhat overstated [and] investors may have not been materially misled by a focus on the U.S. (Dimson, Marsh, and Staunton 2002, p. 175)

The high historical equity premium is a worldwide, not just a U.S., phenomenon.[9]

- *Transaction costs and diversification.* The returns used to calculate the equity premium are derived from published stock indices, but investors may not have realized these returns in their portfolios. Transaction costs in the equity markets were far higher over most of the period than they are today.

Low-cost indexed mutual and exchange-traded funds were not available to investors of the 19th century or most of the 20th century. Before 1975, brokerage commissions on buying and selling individual stocks were fixed by the NYSE at high levels. Moreover, it is not unreasonable to assume that until recently, transaction costs involved with replicating a market portfolio with reinvested dividends subtracted 1–2 percentage points a year from stockholder returns.[10] So, the *realized* equity returns were probably much lower than those calculated from published data.

- *Investor ignorance of risks, returns, and mean reversion.* Because data on long-term stock returns were not available until the second half of the 20th century, investors in the past were probably ignorant of the true risks and returns from holding stocks and may have underestimated the return and/or overestimated the risk of equities. When Fisher and Lorie (1964) first documented long-term returns in the 1960s, many economists were surprised that even when the Great Depression was included, stocks yielded such a high rate of return.

Another advantage of stocks that until recently was not recognized is the evidence of *mean reversion* of long-term equity returns.[11] In the early development of capital asset pricing theory, financial returns were modeled as random walks whose risk increased as the square root of the time period. But examination of long-term data strongly suggests a predictable component of stock returns that makes the returns less variable over long periods than they would be if mean reversion did not exist. Mean reversion increases the desirability of stocks as assets for long-term investors.

Ignorance of the historical risks and returns of various asset classes may have led to a general underpricing of equities as an asset class. This result, in turn, may have raised realized returns higher than would be justified if stocks were priced by investors with full knowledge of the distribution of stock returns.[12]

- *Pension assets and taxes*. The evolution of U.S. federal tax policy also may have influenced stock returns. The tremendous increase in tax-sheltered plans over the past several decades has greatly increased the demand for equities. For example, in 1974, ERISA established minimum standards for pension plans in private industry and allowed equities to play a greatly expanded role in asset accumulation.

McGrattan and Prescott (2003) argued that the increase in tax-sheltered savings has led to a significant drop in the average tax rate on equities. This drop may have boosted stock returns and, to the extent that stocks substituted for bonds, lowered the real return on fixed-income assets.

- *Biases in historical bond returns*. Real government bond returns may have been biased downward in the period since 1926, especially since World War II. Bondholders clearly did not anticipate the double-digit inflation of the 1970s and 1980s.

Table 1 shows the extraordinarily poor bond returns in the 35 years following World War II. Of course, when inflation was brought down in the 1980s and 1990s, interest rates returned to the levels of the immediate postwar period. But the resulting bull market in bonds did not offset the losses of the inflationary 1960s and 1970s because, although the inflation rate returned to its earlier level, the *price level* did not. So, over the entire inflation cycle, bondholders suffered a permanent loss of return. This phenomenon is one reason real bond returns since World War II have averaged only 1.4 percent, less than half their historical level.[13]

Models of the Equity Premium

The biases just discussed have probably raised the historical return on equities and, therefore, the historical value of the equity risk premium. Nevertheless, accounting for these biases is unlikely to reduce the premium to the level that Mehra and Prescott maintain is consistent with reasonable levels of risk aversion. So, we are compelled to analyze whether the assumptions of the models used to describe investor behavior are, in fact, reasonable representations of investor and financial market behavior.

The equity premium puzzle is centered on the "reasonable" level of risk aversion for investors. Recall that risk premiums exist because individuals are assumed to have declining marginal utility of consumption. How fast this utility declines measures the investor's degree of risk aversion. In early risk models, the investor's utility function, U, was assumed to be a function of wealth, W, such that

$$U(W)=\left[\frac{1}{(1-A)}\right]W^{(1-A)}. \tag{1}$$

The parameter A is the coefficient of relative risk aversion, or the percentage change (elasticity) of the marginal utility of wealth caused by a 1 percent change in the level of wealth. In other words, A is directly related to the pain felt by investors when their wealth falls.

With this utility function, and under the assumption that returns are lognormally distributed, the arithmetic equity premium, EP, can be approximated by

$$EP \approx A(\sigma^2), \tag{2}$$

where σ is the standard deviation of returns on an investor's portfolio. If we use 0.18 as the standard deviation of annual stock market returns and an (arithmetic) equity risk premium of 8 percent as measured from annual data since 1926, we obtain a level of risk aversion, A, of 2 or 3.[14]

These levels of risk aversion produced by the early models seemed reasonable. With a risk aversion of 2, an individual would be willing to pay 4 percent of his wealth to insure against an equal probability of a 20 percent rise or 20 percent fall in wealth. If A equals 3, this insurance payment would be 5.6 percent of wealth.

But Equation 1 is not correctly specified. Economists knew that wealth is a proxy for consumption, which is the correct variable to put into the utility function. Putting consumption into the utility function led to the development of the "consumption CAPM" (CCAPM) popularized by Breeden (1979).

There is an important empirical difference between the consumption-based CAPM and the wealth-based CAPM. Per capita consumption, as measured by national income account statistics, fluctuates far less than the value of wealth. The standard deviation of the growth of consumption is only about 4 percent, so the variance of changes in the stock market is almost 20 times greater than the variance of the changes in consumption.

If we plug the variance of consumption of 0.16 percent and an equity premium of 8 percent into Equation 2, we find a risk aversion of 50. If investors were really this risk averse, they would pay an insurance premium of 17 percent to avoid an equal probability of a 20 percent rise or fall in their wealth. For investors to act this risk averse is implausible. In other words, if individuals actually have a risk aversion coefficient of 2 or 3, the equity risk premium implied in the CCAPM is much smaller, on the order of 0.3–0.4 percent. The intuition here is that historical changes in consumption are not large enough to significantly alter utility, so investors are willing to take nearly a "fair bet" with stocks.[15]

Another way of looking at this issue is that the standard CAPM assumes that changes in wealth cause equal changes in consumption, but in reality, movements in the stock market are not associated with dramatic changes in consumption. Any risk that is not strongly correlated with consumption should not require a large risk premium, and empirically, the returns on equities fall into that category.[16]

The equity premium puzzle was not the only anomaly implied by the consumption CAPM. Weil (1989) showed that not only did the CCAPM imply that the historical equity premium was too large, but it also implied that the historical real rate of return on bonds, given economic growth and reasonable risk-aversion parameters, was far too small. This anomaly was called the "risk-free rate puzzle." These two puzzles were related to the "excess volatility puzzle," which had been explored earlier by Shiller (1981), who showed that stock prices have been too volatile to be explained by changes in subsequent dividends.

These puzzles are caused by the fact that the stock market has fluctuated far more than the underlying economic variables, such as aggregate consumption or GDP.

Finding the Model That Fits the Data

Before attempting to change the basic model summarized by Equation 1 with consumption substituting for wealth, I should note that some economists believe that the high levels of risk aversion implied by the model are not necessarily unreasonable. Kandel and Stambaugh (1991) pointed out that, although high levels of risk aversion may lead to unreasonable behavior with respect to large changes in consumption, the behavior may not be implausible for small changes in wealth. For example, to avoid a 50/50 chance of your consumption rising or falling by 1 percent if your coefficient of risk aversion is 10, you would pay 5 percent of the gamble. Even if risk-aversion coefficient A is as high as 29, which best fits the data in the Kandel–Stambaugh model, an investor would pay only 14.3 percent of the gamble to avoid the risk of a 1 percent rise or fall in wealth. Neither of these actions appears unreasonable.

Fama, agreeing that a large risk-aversion coefficient is not necessarily a puzzle, stated:

> a large equity premium says that consumers are extremely averse to small negative consumption shocks. This is in line with the perception that consumers live in morbid fear of recessions (and economists devote enormous energy to studying them) even though, at least in the post war period, recessions are associated with small changes in per capita consumption. (1991, p. 1596)

In evaluating these arguments, however, remember that in the domain of retirement savings, the stakes are large relative to wealth or yearly consumption. A typical faculty member at age 55 saving, say, 10 percent of her salary a year might well have half or more of her wealth (including future earnings) in her retirement account. Similarly, university endowments are a substantial portion of the wealth of private universities. And even with mean reversion of equity returns, the 10-year to 20-year standard deviation of equity returns is substantial. So, we seem to be back in the high-stakes category, where high values of risk aversion lead to absurd behavior.

Changes in the Utility Function. In an attempt to solve the puzzle, most economists have been driven to modify the consumption-based utility function represented by Equation 1 to justify a higher equity premium without requiring an implausibly high level of risk aversion. A popular generalization of Equation 1, pioneered by Epstein and Zin (1989), breaks the rigid link between risk aversion (investor reaction to changes in consumption over a *given period of time*) and the reaction to changes in consumption over time, called the *intertemporal rate of substitution*, which affects the real rate of interest. This class of utility functions has been fruitful in explaining low real rates but does not go far in explaining the equity premium.

Another line of research makes utility a function not only of current consumption but also of some "benchmark" level of consumption. If the benchmark is taken to be prior levels of consumption, then individuals are taken to be sensitive not only to their level of consumption today but also to how it has changed from yesterday. Thus, individuals are assumed to take time to adjust to new levels of consumption, a behavior that can be described as "habit formation."

Constantinides (1990) showed that habit formation makes an investor more risk averse to a short-run change in consumption, leading to higher "short-run" risk aversion than "long-run" risk aversion. Evidently, once one has tasted the good life, it is difficult to adjust one's consumption downward. A similar approach was taken by Campbell and Cochrane (1999), who claimed that utility is a function of consumption over and above some habit that is slow to change. Therefore, in a recession, risk aversion increases markedly even though in absolute terms, recessions exhibit relatively small declines in consumption. The equity premium, as well as all other risk premiums, does indeed increase in recessionary periods.

Abel (1990) examined asset pricing when an individual's utility is derived not only from the individual's own consumption but also *relative* to the consumption of others around them—what he termed "catching up with the Joneses." This utility function is less risk averse if everyone's income moves up and down together, but when individuals compare their living standards with others', the comparison makes individuals act very risk averse. This utility function helps solve the real rate puzzle but is not much help in explaining the equity premium.[17]

An alternative approach, elaborated by Benartzi and Thaler (1995), is built on the "cumulative prospect theory" proposed by Tversky and Kahneman (1992). Prospect theory shares the claim that utility is based on benchmarks, so today's level of consumption is important, but prospect theory, which is a pioneering model in behavioral finance, asserts that asset *returns*, rather than consumption or wealth, are arguments of the utility function. In these models, investors dislike losses much more intensely than they like gains. When the utility function is based on *changes* in wealth rather than *levels* of wealth, investors are referred to as "loss averse" rather than "risk averse."[18]

When investors have these loss-averse preferences, their attitudes toward risky assets depend crucially on the time horizon over which returns are evaluated. For example, loss-averse investors who compute the values of their portfolios every day would find investing in stocks unattractive because stock prices fall almost as often as they rise. Investors who check returns less frequently have a higher probability of seeing positive returns. The concept of loss-averse preferences explains why individuals are so risk averse in the short run, what Benartzi and Thaler called "myopic loss aversion."

Uncertain Labor Income. The previous models assumed that the only important source of uncertainty is the return on equity. A more realistic way to model uncertainty would be to recognize that labor income is also uncertain. This fact can markedly change investors' behavior toward the risks in financial markets.

Uncertain labor income may explain why risk aversion increases in a recession; it is well known that unemployment and the number of layoffs affect workers' decisions. During recessions, stocks frequently sell at large discounts relative to their long-term values, a factor that increases long-run equity returns.

The inability to borrow large sums against labor income also means that many workers, especially young workers, are not able to hold as much equity as they would like, even though their "human capital," measured as the value of their future labor income, is high. Constantinides, Donaldson, and Mehra (2002) reported that this phenomenon can have important consequences for asset pricing. Older workers do hold equity, but this age cohort displays greater risk aversion than younger workers because older workers have much more limited ability to offset portfolio losses by changing their work effort. As a result, the economy in general displays the greater risk aversion of the older generation, for whom future consumption is more geared to the level of financial assets than to income. Indeed, Mankiw and Zeldes (1991) found that large stockholders' consumption reflects a larger sensitivity to market fluctuations than does the consumption of smaller stockholders.

Modeling the Risks to Consumption and Equities. Another path to justifying the equity risk premium, rather than changing the form of the utility function, is to reexamine the statistical properties of consumption and stock returns. The standard approach is to assume that both the growth of consumption and the return on stocks are stochastic processes marked by lognormal distributions with constant expected returns. Although this specification is analytically tractable and reasonably replicates the behavior of the historical data, it may not be correct.

Weitzman (2004) argues in a working paper that we do not know the exact distributions of output in the economy, so treating the historically estimated means and standard deviations as known parameters is incorrect. Uncertainty about the true means and variances of the distribution signifies that the probability distributions of consumption and stock returns have fatter tails than assumed in the lognormal distribution.

We know that stock returns do, in fact, have far fatter tails than implied by lognormality. If lognormality prevailed, the probability of the 19 percent decline in the S&P 500 Index that occurred on 19 October 1987 would be less than 1 in 10^{71}, so even if we had had billions of exchanges operating daily for the last 12 billion years (the estimated age of the universe), there would be virtually no chance of observing this event. Yet, the decline did occur, and it may have dramatically increased investors' perceptions of equity risk.

Weitzman shows that, in the absence of risk-free assets, these fatter-tailed distributions alter the analytics of the equity premium dramatically. Instead of yielding an extremely low equity premium, these distributions yield an arbitrarily high equity premium for any level of risk aversion. Furthermore, this model has the ability to explain a low risk-free rate *and* the "excess volatility" of the stock market.

This research is not unrelated to the earlier studies of Rietz (1988), who speculated shortly after Mehra and Prescott's research that investors fear a lurking "disaster state" of extreme negative consumption that has not yet been realized. Such fear would lead to a higher equity premium.[19] Recently, Barro (2005) found strong support for this theory in the data for international markets.

In a similar vein, Bansal and Yaron (2004) rewrote the stochastic properties of the consumption and dividend growth models. Instead of modeling consumption growth as uncorrelated through time, they assumed it has a small long-run predictable component that is affected by past growth. So, a shock to consumption influences its expected growth as well as the expected growth of dividends many years into the future, which can have a dramatic impact on the valuation of equities.[20] When this consumption process is combined with time-varying variance, the Bansal–Yaron model, like Weitzman's approach, has the capability of explaining all the asset pricing puzzles.[21]

Practical Applications

The practitioner might ask: How does the equity premium puzzle matter to investors? This question should be analyzed in the following way.

If the equity premium should be only a fraction of 1 percent, as the basic economic model suggests, then either stocks should be priced much higher or bonds should be priced much lower than they have been on a historical basis.[22] If stock prices rose and bond prices fell, the result would lower the forward-looking returns on equities and raise returns on fixed-income assets, thereby lowering the equity premium. Clearly, if investors believe this narrower premium will prevail at some time in the future, they should be fully invested in stocks now.

But this scenario is highly unlikely to occur. Although the future equity premium is likely to be somewhat lower than in the past, few believe investors will hold stocks if their expected return is only a fraction of a percent above the return of risk-free assets.

Yet, we should not dismiss the equity premium puzzle. The search for the right model has yielded insights that can give practitioners guidance in structuring their clients' portfolios. One promising area is the work on habit formation, which implies that there may be a significant difference in an investor's short-term and long-term attitudes toward risk. This research suggests that an advisor may find it worthwhile to explore the investor's reaction to lowering consumption in a short time frame versus lowering it in a longer time frame, when other adjustments can be made to ease the impact of a reduced standard of living.

A related issue is the importance of examining labor income as a component of portfolio choice. Individuals whose labor income is uncertain and whose borrowing capabilities are low should hold a lower allocation of equities. Those with highly marketable skills should hold a higher fraction in equities. Those who are near retirement and have no flexibility to change their labor income will be more risk averse than investors with marketable labor skills.

A high equity premium can arise from assuming that investors demand a minimum level of consumption that must be attained in any investment plan, no matter what the time period to adjust. The effect is equivalent to assuming that risk aversion becomes extremely high at low levels of consumption. This approach has given rise to the growth of "liability investing," in which investors, especially those approaching retirement, fund what they deem absolute minimum expenditures with risk-free assets, such as Treasury Inflation-Indexed Securities (informally called TIPS), with the remainder being subject to the usual risk and return trade-offs (see Waring 2004).

Investors who suffer from myopic loss aversion, the condition in which the downs in the market deliver much more pain than the ups deliver pleasure, should be advised to set their best allocations and then assess the value of their portfolios infrequently. Blind trusts controlled by outside advisors might be the best strategy for the investors who are particularly sensitive to losses.

Financial planners must also evaluate their clients' fears of remote but catastrophic events and evaluate the likelihood of such events. In some economic states, such as a terrorist strike or a nuclear attack, equities could suffer extreme losses. Practitioners should note that these events will also affect the value of government bonds, so what are considered risk-free assets may even no longer exist.[23] War and other conflicts that destroy wealth also cannot be ruled out. Furthermore, over a very long horizon, there is the possibility that capitalism as a form of economic organization may cease to exist and that the wealth of the propertied classes will be expropriated. For investors with fears of these remote, yet not inconceivable, events, a financial advisor must determine whether the equity premium is sufficient to overcome the outcomes.

Future of the Equity Risk Premium

Despite the fact that the models that economists taught in their classes predicted a small equity premium, most academic economists, even at the peak of the bull market in 2000, maintained a personal estimate of the equity premium (which, presumably, they taught to students) close to the historical mean realized premium since 1926—that is, about 6 percent (compound) or 8 percent (arithmetic) over T-bills.

For his 2000 paper, Welch surveyed a large number of academic economists, who estimated the arithmetic premium of stocks over short-term bonds at 7 percent, about 100 bps below the 1926–2004 average.[24] If we subtract 2 percentage points to convert to the geometric average and then subtract a further 150 bps to convert from short-run to long-run bonds, we obtain a geometric equity premium of stocks over bonds of about 3.5 percent.

Professional money managers apparently have a lower estimate of the equity risk premium than do academics. At a CFA Institute conference I spoke to in early 2004, Peter Bernstein—noted author, money manager, and an organizer of the conference—asked the large crowd of professional investors whether they would be inclined to hold in their portfolios a preponderance of equity over fixed income if they knew that the equity premium was 3 percent. A majority raised their hands. When he asked the same question with a 2 percent premium, most of the audience did not.[25]

I noted in the opening of this article that persuasive reasons support a lower forward-looking real return on equity than the return found in the historical data. The sharp drop in the cost of acquiring and maintaining a diversified portfolio of common stocks, not only in the United States but now worldwide, should increase the price of equities and lower their future return. If we assume these annual costs have been brought down by 100 bps, then the future real return on equities should be 5.5–6.0 percent, about 1 percentage point lower than the historical range of 6.5–7.0 percent. Although these returns are below the historical average calculated from indices, investors today will receive the same realized return from stocks as they obtained earlier when trading costs were higher.

For bonds, the question is whether real future returns should be higher than the 2.25 percent average recorded since 1926. Until recently, I believed that the answer was unambiguously yes. The historical real return on bonds was biased downward by the inflation of the 1970s. Indeed, when TIPS were issued in 1997, their real yield was 3.5 percent, and it climbed to more than 4 percent in 2000. If we assume future real bond returns will be 3.5 percent and real stock returns will be between 5.5 percent and 6 percent, the equity premium will be between 2 percent and 3 percent, a level that would leave most money managers satisfied with their equity allocations.

But in the last few years, the real return on protected government bonds has dropped sharply. TIPS yields, which had been as high as 3 percent in the summer of 2002, fell to 1.5 percent in 2005. The causes of the drop are not well understood but may be related to such factors as fear of a decline in growth because of the decline in the number of workers, the increased risk aversion of an aging population, the excess of saving over investment, manifesting itself through the demand for U.S. government bonds from developing Asian countries, or the increased demand for fixed-income assets by pension funds seeking to offset their pension liabilities. Another possibility is that bondholders believe central banks will keep inflation low, so they view government bonds as true hedges against disaster scenarios ranging from armed conflict to terrorist attacks—and even natural disasters.

If the equity premium is 2–3 percent and real bond yields remain at 1.5 percent, the projected real return on stocks is only about 4 percent. Some noted analysts believe that real stock returns will indeed be this low because this return comports with a 2 percent dividend yield plus the 2 percent long-term real growth of per share dividends found in long-run stock data (Bernstein and Arnott 2003).

I believe, however, that this forecast of real stock returns is too low. First, future dividend growth should be higher than the historical average because the dividend payout ratio has fallen dramatically, which enables companies to use retained earnings to finance growth.[26] Second, future real stock returns can be predicted by taking the earnings yield, which is the inverse of the well-known P/E. This approach works extremely well with long-run data because the average historical P/E of 15 has corresponded to a 6.7 percent real return on stocks. The P/E taken from data in August 2005 points to a 5.5–6.0 percent real stock return. As mentioned earlier, the higher level of stock prices relative to earnings is justified by the steep decline in the costs of holding a fully diversified equity portfolio.

Finally, I believe that the pessimism about future economic growth is unwarranted. In my opinion, the negative impact of the aging of the developed world's population will be more than offset by accelerating growth in the developing world, which will lead to rapid worldwide growth over the next several decades.[27] Forward-looking equity returns of an internationally diversified portfolio should therefore be in the range of 5.5–6.0 percent. If the real return on bonds remains in the 1.5–2.0 percent range, because of increased risk aversion or other factors unrelated to economic growth, then the equity risk premium has probably risen to a level that comports with the post-1926 data.

Conclusion

The equity premium is a critical number in financial economics. It determines asset allocations, projections of retirement and endowment wealth, and the cost of capital to companies. Economists are still searching for a simple model that can justify the premium in the face of the much lower volatility of aggregate economic data. Although there are good reasons why the future equity risk premium should be lower than it has been historically, projected compound equity returns of 2–3 percent over bonds will still give ample reward for investors willing to tolerate the short-term risks of stocks.

Notes

1. Many excellent academic reviews of the equity premium puzzle are available. Cochrane (2005) of the University of Chicago has provided a complete updated review.
2. The stock series is from a combination of sources. Data for 1802–1871 are from Schwert (1990); data for 1871–1925 are from Cowles (1938); data for 1926–2004 are from the CRSP capitalization-weighted indexes of all NYSE, Amex, and NASDAQ stocks. More extensive descriptions of the data can be found in Siegel (2002).
3. As an approximation, the geometric return is equal to the arithmetic return minus one-half the variance of the return. For a fuller description, see the subsection "Calculation of the Equity Premium."
4. Smithers and Wright (2000) called this stable long-term return "Siegel's Constant."
5. Theoretically, real interest rates do not necessarily equal growth. The real rate is also a function of the time rate of discount and the level of risk aversion.
6. See Merton (1973) for a description of the intertemporal CAPM.
7. Campbell and Viceira (2002) indicated that the yield on the 10-year U.S. inflation-linked bond would be the closest in duration to the indexed annuity, especially for someone approaching retirement.
8. Mathematically, the average return of an equally weighted world portfolio is higher than the average equity return in each country.

9. In fact, *Triumph of the Optimists* may have actually *understated* long-term international stock returns. The U.S. stock markets and other world markets for which we have data did very well in the 30 years prior to 1900, which is when their study began. U.S. returns measured from 1871 outperformed returns taken from 1900 by 32 bps. Data from the United Kingdom show a similar pattern.
10. Before commissions were deregulated in May 1975, a typical trade—say, 100 shares at $30—paid a commission of $58.21, almost 2 percent of market value. Small odd-lot trades resulting from reinvesting dividends could cost, considering odd-lot premiums, as much as 4 percent.
11. See Poterba and Summers (1988) for early research on mean reversion and Cochrane (1999) for evidence of stock return predictability.
12. Abel (2002) explored the implications for the equity risk premium when investors had incorrect information on the distributions of returns.
13. Recently, real bond returns have fallen sharply, which is discussed later.
14. See Friend and Blume (1975) for an earlier derivation of the risk-aversion parameter.
15. Arrow (1965) showed that for small risks, investors should be risk neutral, requiring little or no premium.
16. When consumption and stock returns are not perfectly correlated, $EP = \sigma_c \sigma_W \rho_{c,W}$, where σ_c is the standard deviation of consumption, σ_W is the standard deviation of stocks, and $\rho_{c,W}$ is the correlation coefficient between the two. Because empirically ρ is about 0.2, this equation leads to approximately the same estimate of risk aversion as does the CCAPM (see Cochrane 2005).
17. Once Abel (1999) added leverage, the equity premium was better estimated.
18. In the standard model, loss aversion is equivalent to a "kink" in the utility function at the current level of consumption. The loss in utility when consumption drops below the kink is greater than the gain when consumption is above, even for tiny changes in consumption.
19. Mehra and Prescott (1988), criticizing Rietz's research, noted that a disaster state was very likely to be realized in the more than 100 years of data that Mehra and Prescott analyzed.
20. The intuition here comes from the Gordon model of stock price determination, in which small changes in the growth rate of dividends have a large impact on stock prices.
21. Note that in reconciling the volatility of stocks with underlying macroeconomic variables, the compilation of national income accounts requires a large amount of estimation and smoothing of past data, and averaged data on any index lower its volatility. As for estimation, it is well known that the "appraised" value of real estate is far more stable than the value of securities that *represent* similar assets, such as REITs.
22. Indeed, a best-selling book by James Glassman and Kevin Hassett (1999) on the stock market, *Dow 36,000*, marketed at the peak of the last bull market, maintained this thesis and predicted that stocks would have to increase fourfold to bring their real yields down to those of bonds.
23. Perhaps this fear explains why gold continues to be popular despite the fact that in portfolio models, precious metals are often dominated by stocks and inflation-protected bonds.
24. These academics predicted that other academics' estimates were higher—in the 7.5–8.0 percent range.
25. The conference was "Points of Inflection: Investment Management Tomorrow"; a webcast of the Bernstein presentation is available at www.cfawebcasts.org. Rob Arnott has been doing such surveys for a number of years and has communicated to me that most of the institutional money managers would be satisfied with an equity premium measured against bond returns of 2–3 percent (see Arnott and Bernstein 2002).
26. If retained earnings can be invested at the same rate of return as required by equity investors, a drop in the dividend yield will produce an equal rise in the future growth of dividends (see Siegel 2002). Arnott and Asness (2003), believing that company managers squander retained earnings on low-return projects, rejected my contention that real dividends will grow faster in the future.
27. See Siegel (2005) for support for these statements.

References

Abel, Andrew B. 1990. "Asset Prices under Habit Formation and Catching Up with the Joneses." *American Economic Review*, vol. 80, no. 2 (May):38–42.

———. 1999. "Risk Premia and Term Premia in General Equilibrium." *Journal of Monetary Economics*, vol. 43, no. 1 (February):3–33.

———. 2002. "An Exploration of the Effects of Pessimism and Doubt on Asset Returns." *Journal of Economic Dynamics and Control*, vol. 26, nos. 7–8 (July):1075–92.

Arnott, Robert D., and Clifford S. Asness. 2003. "Surprise! Higher Dividends = Higher Earnings Growth." *Financial Analysts Journal*, vol. 59, no. 1 (January/February):70–87.

Arnott, Robert D., and Peter L. Bernstein. 2002. "What Risk Premium Is 'Normal'?" *Financial Analysts Journal*, vol. 58, no. 2 (March/April):64–85.

Arrow, Kenneth A. 1965. *Aspects of the Theory of Risk-Bearing*. Helsinki, Finland: Yrjö Hahnsson Foundation.

Bansal, Ravi, and Amir Yaron. 2004. "Risks for the Long Run: A Potential Resolution of Asset Pricing Puzzles." *Journal of Finance*, vol. 59, no. 4 (August):1481–1509.

Barro, Robert J. 2005. "Rare Events and the Equity Premium." National Bureau of Economic Research Working Paper No. 11310 (May).

Benartzi, Shlomo, and Richard H. Thaler. 1995. "Myopic Loss Aversion and the Equity Premium Puzzle." *Quarterly Journal of Economics*, vol. 110, no. 1 (February):73–92.

Bernstein, William J., and Robert D. Arnott. 2003. "Earnings Growth: The Two Percent Dilution." *Financial Analysts Journal*, vol. 59, no. 5 (September/October):47–55.

Breeden, Doug. 1979. "An Intertemporal Asset Pricing Model with Stochastic Consumption and Investment Opportunities." *Journal of Financial Economics*, vol. 7, no. 3 (September):265–296.

Brown, S.J., W.N. Goetzmann, and S.A. Ross. 1995. "Survival." *Journal of Finance*, vol. 50, no. 3 (July):853–873.

Campbell, John Y., and J.H. Cochrane. 1999. "By Force of Habit: A Consumption-Based Explanation of Aggregate Stock Market Behavior." *Journal of Political Economy*, vol. 107, no. 2 (April):205–251.

Campbell, John Y., and Luis M. Viceira. 2002. *Strategic Asset Allocation: Portfolio Choice for Long-Term Investors.* New York: Oxford University Press.

Cochrane, John. 1999. "New Facts in Finance." *Economic Perspectives* (Federal Reserve Bank of Chicago), vol. 23, no. 3 (3rd Quarter):36–58.

———. 2005. "Financial Markets and the Real Economy." NBER Working Paper No. 11193 (March).

Constantinides, George M. 1990. "Habit Formation: A Resolution of the Equity Premium Puzzle." *Journal of Political Economy*, vol. 98, no. 3 (June):519–543.

Constantinides, George M., J.B. Donaldson, and R. Mehra. 2002. "Junior Can't Borrow: A New Perspective on the Equity Premium Puzzle." *Quarterly Journal of Economics*, vol. 117, no. 1 (February):269–296.

Cowles, A. 1938. *Common-Stock Indexes, 1871–1937*. Bloomington, IN: Principia Press.

Dimson, Elroy, Paul Marsh, and Mike Staunton. 2002. *Triumph of the Optimists: 101 Years of Global Investment Returns*. Princeton, NJ: Princeton University Press.

———. 2004. *Global Investment Returns Yearbook 2004*. ABN-AMRO (February).

Epstein, L.G., and S.E. Zin. 1989. "Substitution, Risk Aversion, and the Temporal Behavior of Consumption and Asset Returns: A Theoretical Framework." *Econometrica*, vol. 57, no. 4 (July):937–969.

———. 1991. "Substitution, Risk Aversion, and the Temporal Behavior of Consumption and Asset Returns: An Empirical Analysis." *Journal of Political Economy*, vol. 99, no. 2 (April):263–286.

Fama, Eugene. 1991. "Efficient Capital Markets: II." *Journal of Finance*, vol. 46, no. 5 (December):1575–1617.

Fisher, Lawrence, and James H. Lorie. 1964. "Rates of Return on Investment in Common Stocks." *Journal of Business*, vol. 37 (January):1–21.

Friend, Irwin, and Marshall Blume. 1975. "The Demand for Risky Assets." *American Economic Review*, vol. 65, no. 5 (December):900–922.

Glassman, James, and Kevin Hassett. 1999. *Dow 36,000: The New Strategy for Profiting from the Coming Rise in the Stock Market*. New York: Crown Business.

Kandel, Shmuel, and Robert F. Stambaugh. 1991. "Asset Returns and Intertemporal Preferences." *Journal of Monetary Economics*, vol. 27, no. 1 (February):39–71.

MaCurdy, Thomas, and John Shoven. 1992. "Accumulating Pension Wealth with Stocks and Bonds." Working paper, Stanford University (January).

Mankiw, N. Gregory, and Stephen P. Zeldes. 1991. "The Consumption of Stockholders and Non-Stockholders." *Journal of Financial Economics,* vol. 29, no. 1 (March):97–112.

McGrattan, Ellen R., and Edward C. Prescott. 2003. "Average Debt and Equity Returns: Puzzling?" Staff Report 313, Federal Reserve Bank of Minneapolis.

Mehra, Rajnish, and Edward C. Prescott. 1985. "The Equity Premium: A Puzzle." *Journal of Monetary Economics,* vol. 15, no. 2 (March):145–162.

———. 1988. "The Equity Risk Premium: A Solution?" *Journal of Monetary Economics,* vol. 22, no. 1 (July):133–136.

Merton, Robert C. 1973. "An Intertemporal Capital Asset Pricing Model." *Econometrica,* vol. 41, no. 4 (October):867–887.

Poterba, James, and Lawrence H. Summers. 1988. "Mean Reversion in Stock Returns: Evidence and Implications." *Journal of Financial Economics,* vol. 22, no. 1 (April):27–60.

Rietz, T.A. 1988. "The Equity Risk Premium: A Solution." *Journal of Monetary Economics,* vol. 22, no. 1 (July):117–131.

Schwert, William. 1990. "Indexes of United States Stock Prices from 1802 to 1987." *Journal of Business,* vol. 63, no. 3 (July):399–426.

Shiller, Robert J. 1981. "Do Stock Prices Move Too Much to Be Justified by Subsequent Changes in Dividends?" *American Economic Review,* vol. 71, no. 3 (June):421–436.

Siegel, Jeremy J. 2002. *Stocks for the Long Run.* 3rd ed. New York: McGraw-Hill.

———. 2005. *The Future for Investors.* New York: Crown Publishing.

Siegel, Jeremy J., and Richard H. Thaler. 1997. "Anomalies: The Equity Premium Puzzle." *Journal of Economic Perspectives,* vol. 11, no. 1 (Winter):191–200.

Smithers, Andrew, and Stephen Wright. 2000. *Valuing Wall Street.* New York: McGraw-Hill.

Tversky, Amos, and Daniel Kahneman. 1992. "Advances in Prospect Theory: Cumulative Representation of Uncertainty." *Journal of Risk and Uncertainty,* vol. 5, no. 4 (October):297–323.

Waring, M. Barton. 2004. "Liability-Relative Investing." *Journal of Portfolio Management,* vol. 30, no. 4 (Summer):8–19.

Weil, Philippe. 1989. "The Equity Premium Puzzle and the Risk-Free Rate Puzzle." *Journal of Monetary Economics,* vol. 24, no. 3 (November):401–421.

Weitzman, Martin L. 2004. "The Bayesian Equity Premium." Working paper, Harvard University (August).

Welch, Ivo. 2000. "Views of Financial Economists on the Equity Premium and on Professional Controversies." *Journal of Business,* vol. 73, no. 4 (October):501–538.

Dividends and the Frozen Orange Juice Syndrome

Peter L. Bernstein

A generation that grows up drinking only frozen orange juice will forget that any other form of OJ exists; a generation that grows up thinking dividends and yields don't matter are like those OJ drinkers.

A distinguished professor of finance recently paid me a visit, and in the course of conversation, we turned to the subject of dividends. My friend asked what I thought about dividends now that investors are offered the bonanza of a 15 percent top-bracket U.S. federal income tax.

The question was a thoughtful one. Why has this bonanza had so little impact on values in the stock market or on management decisions about dividend payout ratios? The question deserves more than the casual answer that I gave the professor. I begin with some facts and then follow with analysis. Have I hit on something no one else has observed?

Is Anybody Listening?

At 15 percent, this new tax rate on dividends is not merely absolutely low. The after-tax income in your pocket from dividends is now worth as much as the after-tax dollars in your pocket from capital gains. That is unprecedented. Furthermore, as Martin Leibowitz (2003) recently pointed out, with interest income still taxed at the old rates and dividend income taxed at only 15 percent, the trade-off between stocks and bonds is now more favorable than it was in the past, especially in an environment where inflation is more than 1 or 2 percent. Keep in mind that the expected return on equities equals the expected nominal bond return plus a risk premium. As inflation drives nominal bond yields higher, the tax advantage for equities—and the expected risk premium—increases at the same time. This radical change should ignite a big shift in investor preferences.

The response has been minimal. Amazing. As Sherlock Holmes taught us, if the dog does not bark, something important is going on.

Peter L. Bernstein is president of Peter Bernstein, Inc., New York City, a consulting editor of the Journal of Portfolio Management, *and author of* Against the Gods: The Remarkable Story of Risk.

There have been scattered headlines about tiny payouts initiated by Microsoft Corporation and a few other non-dividend-payers seeking a wider constituency. Otherwise, neither corporate managers nor shareowners seem to care. No statements at annual meetings or anywhere else have provided any hints that corporate managers are considering a reversion to the payout ratios of the past. Much of the bull move in stock prices since September 2002 has favored stocks that pay *no* dividends, whereas the prices of many high-yielding stocks have been hit hard in sympathy with the recent rise in interest rates. The extraordinary revision in the tax structure has been a nonevent in the markets.

At the corporate level, payout ratios for 2004 in terms of both reported and operating earnings were still down close to 30 percent, as in the glory days of the technology bubble. But did the bubble not burst? The historical anomaly is striking. From 1950 to 1989, the payout ratio on the S&P 500 Index averaged 50 percent and never fell below 38 percent, a brief low point that occurred during the huge surge in oil earnings in 1979. Now the payout ratio is scraping along at the record lows scored during the boom of the second half of the 1990s. The ratio of dividends to book value, one of our old favorites, is running about 4.5 percent, a full 100 bps below even 1999, and this is happening at a time when profit margins are historically high and borrowed money is cheap.

With the stock market up more than 30 percent since the lows it touched 15 months ago, it is obvious that the demand for dividends is approximately nil. This phenomenon makes little sense.

The Positive Case for Dividends

Dividends matter. In a famous article on the subject, Fischer Black (1976) argued that dividends are a puzzle. I find the puzzle to be the way investors react to dividends rather than the phenomenon itself. I base this assertion on two arguments, which I now set forth in detail.

The Frailty of Accounting. With the best of intentions, the earnings that accountants and managers report with such precision ("We earned $2.01 this quarter versus $1.96 last year") are nothing more than estimates, with built-in vulnerabilities. Nobody knows how to measure true earnings. Everybody knows the precise amount of a dividend declaration.

This viewpoint was valid long before the recent colorful history of hanky-panky accounting. As far back as 1972, Jack Treynor wrote:

> Reporting the change in value over an accounting period [which is what earnings purport to represent] implies an estimate of the value itself at the beginning of the period . . . a fatal circularity. (p. 42)

More recently, Jeremy Siegel (2002)—one of the most enthusiastic of the bulls on the stock market—pointed out that "the old-fashioned way" of estimating earning power always depended on dividends:

> Dividends are crucial for pricing a firm, since finance theory states emphatically that the price of a stock is not the discounted value of future earnings, but the discounted value of future dividends and cash distributions. (Opinions section)

I have made my own contribution to this line of argument (Bernstein 1979). I explained:

> The accounting data we see are a fiction. . . . Accrual accounting is an act of faith. It records as revenues money not yet received. It excludes from expenses money actually laid out if it is spent on assets expected to produce cash revenues in the future. The more the accountants accrue, the more vulnerable the company will be to a future that is different from what the accountants have assumed it will be. (p. 9)

Every financial statement is exposed to this risk.

More than 30 years ago, I proposed a U.S. SEC regulation that would forbid published earnings. All the information would be encapsulated in the dividend, a hard fact. The trend of dividends would be a clear message about how the corporation is faring. All the obfuscation and gaming of current earnings announcements would be abolished, instead of clogging up the daily headlines. Some investors and a lot of security analysts would bemoan the loss of earnings information, but of what value is information that is inherently inaccurate and, in so many cases, purposely inaccurate.

What Are Capital Gains Worth? Siegel was convinced that taxes explain the shrinking shareholder demand for dividends. "Shareholders prefer that companies use earnings to lift the price of their shares rather than pay taxes on dividends" (p. 9) was how he put it. He was in good company. Such leading theoreticians as Franco Modigliani, Merton Miller, and Fischer Black went even farther; they argued that—taxes aside—investors should be indifferent between dividends and capital gains. They had no doubt that "dividends don't matter."

I beg to differ. My position on this controversy derives from the analysis provided by Karl Marx in *Capital* (1867). Marx proposed a handy little equation to explain the workings of the capitalist system: *M-C-M′*. In words, the capitalist begins by investing Money, *M*, into Capital goods, *C*, which the capitalist expects to return more money, *M′*, than the *M* the capitalist started out with. Most of *Capital* is concerned with the sources of *M′*, but my interest here is in what this equation can tell us about the importance of dividends.

Cash is at the essence of Marx's approach. *M-C-M′* begins and ends with cash money. The capitalist may, and in Marx's world undoubtedly would, reinvest the *M′* yielded by his capital goods. But the capitalist has a choice. The critical element is the cash in the capitalist's pocket. Debts have limits. You must have cash to pay your bills.

For a rational investor, investments that never yield cash are extremely risky. What is the difference between a painting or an ounce of gold and the stock of a company that will never pay a dividend, will never repurchase shares, will never sell out for cash or a liquid security, and will never liquidate itself? The value of both depends entirely on what somebody else will pay for the asset. These investments have no "intrinsic" value. Yes, I know about Warren Buffett and Berkshire Hathaway (full disclosure: I have shares in Berkshire Hathaway), but I also know that stock even in Buffett's company is a "greater fool" game unless somewhere, sometime, there are positive odds on a cash payout in some form.

Siegel suggests that shareholders prefer companies that "use earnings to lift the price of their shares," but exactly how can companies achieve that? If we knew the answer, we would all be rich. Even buybacks cannot assure us that price appreciation is baked in the cake. The greater fool theory is what this is all about.

No one can make the market do anything. The market makes up its own collective mind. Earnings fell 12 percent between 1955 and 1961 while stock prices rose 59 percent. Earnings rose 54 percent from 1969 to 1974 while stock prices flopped 26 percent. If the relationship between earnings growth and price changes were so steady that companies could "use earnings to lift the price of their shares," we would never see any kind of volatility in P/Es.

Don't the Companies Need the Money?

The notion that growth companies cannot afford to pay dividends rests on frail assumptions. A lot of growth in earning power has taken place with high payout ratios or managers that systematically shared increases in earnings with their stockholders.

General Electric Company is an example. It has a track record of earnings growth that many others would envy, especially in view of its huge size, yet GE's payout ratio has been in the 40 percent range for many years. More remarkable is that its payout ratio in the 1990s was higher than in the 1980s. There is contrary thinking for you!

Or consider IBM Corporation, once upon a time the prototype of growth companies. During the 1950s, IBM managed to pay out more than 20 percent of earnings, even though earnings were growing at a compound annual rate of 20 percent and even though the company was intensely capital intensive because it leased rather than sold its machines. From 1956 to 1981, the IBM dividend grew 19 percent a year. That 19 percent is a handsome return all by itself, even if capital appreciation had been zero. The total accumulation of dividends over those 25 years equaled six times the original purchase price in 1956. The 1981 dividend was equal to 81 percent of the original purchase price. Does anyone know of a fast grower in today's world whose board of directors is displaying that kind of generosity—and still maintaining the growth rate?

In the years before 1990, the S&P 500 companies as a whole managed to pay out dividends and still record high earnings growth rates. The payout ratio exceeded 50 percent in every year of the 1960s, the decade when growth became the dominant theme in equity investing. Dividends were so popular in those days that a significant inverse correlation existed between payout ratios and dividend yields.

And tax differentials seem to have been no obstacle to the demand for dividends: From 1953 to the early 1980s, the top federal income tax bracket was 70 percent—versus only 25 percent on long-term capital gains. Another world! The generous tax cuts on top brackets and dividend income of the George W. Bush era have had zero impact on payout ratios or the popularity of companies with above-average dividend yields.

What about stock repurchase plans? Although there is no difference between dividends and buybacks in terms of cash flows from company checking accounts to owners' checking accounts, there is a world of difference in terms of moral obligations and assurance of a steady cash flow to shareholders. At least that was the case before the Nutty 1990s arrived on the scene. Prior to the bubble of the 1990s, stock prices always fell sharply when dividends were cut—and for good and sufficient reason. No more. In recent years, neither dividend cuts nor failed promises on buybacks have had any noticeable impact on stock prices—except on occasion to make them go up! In any case, when so many of the repurchased shares are almost simultaneously reissued to cover option grants to executives and employees, the significance of buybacks as distributions to shareholders is cloudy.

Investors have forgotten how to think about these matters. Work I did as early as 1997 demonstrated that low payout ratios lead to *lower*, not higher, rates of earnings growth. More recently, Rob Arnott and Cliff Asness (2003) prepared an elaborate analysis of this thesis that gave clear, robust, and powerful evidence that the consequences of low payouts have provoked no response from investors. The markets have yet to understand that their intuition is wholly wrong on the matter of payout ratios.

Who Needs the Money?

The folklore of the marketplace is that corporate managers know better than shareholders how to deploy the company's earnings. After all, running the company is these managers' full-time job. They must be better informed.[1]

Although this view sounds logical, it violates the theoretical foundation supporting our economic system, which is built on the credo that the market knows best. The market is often wrong, but its collective judgment over time tends to outperform the judgment of any individual participant. Why else do we emphasize rules and institutions to make the market as free and fair as possible in all areas of our economy, from finance to retailing, from banking to baking? Why else is deregulation cheered and reregulation abhorred?

Seen in that context, there is no coherent reason for company managements to retain earnings because the company "needs the money." On the contrary, shareholders are likely to be better off with the money out of management hands. Tax considerations aside, the economy would work more efficiently, with higher overall rates of return, if the law required corporate managers to distribute 100 percent of earnings, however defined. Then, the managers would have to go to the markets to finance whatever cash needs they had for expansion, debt repayment, or acquisition. A world of mandated 100 percent payouts, in which any expenditure of the stockholders' money beyond current operating expenses would have to meet the test of the capital markets, would exhibit no empire building, no cash hoarding, no unnecessary diversification.

The markets do not know everything, but they do know more than even the most vaunted managers of individual enterprises. To the extent that we inhibit market participation in capital decisions, we operate the economy at a suboptimal level.

Where Did the Demand for Dividends Go?

In light of the powerful historical evidence that companies can grow and still pay out somewhere around half their earnings as dividends, why is the demand for dividends today so small? If the theoretical case for high payout ratios is beyond dispute, why is the demand for dividends so small? In the wake of corporate and accounting scandals that one might expect to lift the demand for dividends, why is the demand for dividends so small? In view of the radical change in the taxation of dividends, why is the demand for dividends so small? As the King of Siam put it, "It is a puzzlement."

I offer an unorthodox explanation that has not received any attention elsewhere. The solution to the puzzle, I believe, lies in a phenomenon my wife, Barbara Bernstein, describes as "the frozen orange juice syndrome." A generation that has grown up drinking only frozen orange juice believes that orange juice exists only in the frozen format. Never having indulged in the real thing, they have no concept of what they are missing.

The demography of market participants provides the answer to the riddle. Low payouts and low yields are frozen orange juice that today's investors accept as normal. The following history explains how they got that way.

Chapter One. Once upon a time, there was such a thing as fresh orange juice—high payouts and high yields. For nearly 90 years, from 1871 to the end of the 1950s, except for brief pops during panic conditions, investors set dividend yields in a 4–6 percent range. Payouts were in the 50 percent area. Investors did drive dividend yields down to 3 percent in the 1929 environment, but the reaction to the Great Crash was an immediate reversion to the old range, which held until the end of the 1950s. In 1949, the S&P 500 yielded exactly 6 percent. Eight years later, even though dividends had grown by 80 percent, the dividend yield was 4.4 percent—still inside the historical range.

It is important to understand why this was so—why John Burr Williams framed his great valuation model around dividends rather than earnings. Corporate earnings data in the old days had little credibility, much less than even today in the aftermath of the accounting scandals. Most companies reported earnings to investors only annually and with almost no accompanying information. Keeping secrets from shareholders was accepted practice. For example, I own a Coca Cola Company annual report from 1953. It has a cover, a title page, a page listing officers and directors, a letter from the president of four paragraphs (one to report net profit, one to comment on high gallon sales, one to announce the time and date of the annual meeting, and one to advise that the financial statements follow). There is a balance sheet. The top line of the profit and loss statement is gross profit; the entire P&L runs to 10 lines of numbers. The report has seven brief notes and the usual auditor's report. The whole thing, including the cover, is nine pages. Try performing today's methods of security analysis on that!

Because dividends were the only information stockholders could rely on, the dividend yield dominated the P/E as a measure of value. This approach—what Siegel called "the old-fashioned way"—is what the world was like going into the boom and crash of the 1920s, and the survivors of the 1929 crash expected the old-fashioned way to return once normalcy returned.

Chapter Two. A crucial aspect of this story is that the veterans of the crash dominated Wall Street for at least three decades after the event. The terrible memories of the crash were so pervasive that few people had any interest in going to Wall Street to earn a living. And for good reason: Trading volume remained depressed for many years. From 1951, when I became an investment counselor, until 1966, annual turnover on the NYSE averaged a measly 15 percent. Volume did not surpass a billion shares a *year* until 1961.

When, in response to family pressures, I reluctantly left a commercial banking career and entered the investment counsel profession in 1951, only two other members of my Harvard class were on Wall Street. As I was, they were there because their fathers had been there. Most of our classmates were lawyers, doctors, professors, or in Washington (and proud to be there). A few were running businesses whose only relationship to the world of finance was as a user of credit. I remember well what it was like to work in an environment where everybody was older than I was, except perhaps for the secretaries. And even most of them were older; my own secretary was old enough to be my mother.

Most investors were still the wealthy individuals. Institutional investing was in its infancy. Our clients spent their incomes. Invasion of principal was a last resort, as it had been for the parents and grandparents of those people. Capital appreciation was nice, but dividends mattered, even to people in high tax brackets. The old days were alive and well back then. The orange juice was still fresh.

Chapter Three. The paradigm shift hit in the early 1960s. By that time, the veterans of the crash had died or retired. Too bad for them but lucky for me: As stock prices tripled from where they had been when I had ventured into the world of investing 10 years earlier, Wall Street began to look a lot better as place to work. In response, the business school invasion got under way, and it has persisted ever since—even the professors followed along after their students. All of a sudden, after being younger than everyone else, I found myself older than everyone else.

Sandy Weill and his friends were the young hawks in the market, and they were soon acquiring the fine old investment houses, such as Hayden Stone, Shearson Hammill, and Loeb Rhodes. The cutting edge of Weill's generation was also on the fast track at Morgan Stanley, Salomon Brothers, First Boston, and Merrill Lynch. This huge demographic cohort had no investment memory other than the record of a fantastic bull market extending all the way back to 1942. To these young investors, dividends were of no interest. Capital gains came faster and incurred less in taxes. And capital gains seemed to grow on trees anyway. I recall a client-on-the-make who came to me in the early 1960s, and the first thing he said to me was, "I can't stand more income."

The investing population was changing in the same way as the Wall Street population. Wealthy investors were diminishing in importance as owners of equities. They also fell way behind in terms of trading activity. Corporate pension funds were rapidly becoming the most important buyers of equities, and these investors reinvested their income instead of spending it—cash needs for retirements were far off in the future. Consequently, the pension funds had no particular interest in current income. The miracle of compounding was forgotten. Growth was what mattered. Dividend yields settled in at around 3 percent—now consistently less than bond yields—and returned to 3 percent even after the inflationary debacles of the 1970s.

Chapter Four. By 1990, the fast-trackers of the 1960s were growing gray hair and paunches. The new arrivals knew even less about hard times and had no memory at all of the days when dividends mattered. During the 15 years from 1975 to 1989, stock prices declined in only two years, and both of those occasions came before 1982. The super bull market of the 1990s was a tornado waiting to happen.

The bursting of the bubble in 2000–2002 changed a lot of perceptions about the credibility of earnings announcements—and of earnings projections by Wall Street's security analysts. But because nobody remembered anything much about dividends, dividends remained in the shadows in which they had been hidden for so many years. In many ways, the newcomers among the individual investors were rather like the pension funds in the 1960s. Unlike my clients of yore, these people were not *rentiers* living off their income. They were on the young side and financed their spending out of their incomes—or borrowings. They felt no need to depend on dividends for income. They socked their savings into 401(k) plans or played games like day trading, but depositing dividend checks was not a matter of any interest.

Meanwhile, none of the remarkable innovations in financial instruments of the 1990s was focusing on income. The hedge funds, the absolute return strategies, the elaborations in the use of derivatives, and portable alpha—all work as well without income as with it. The bond market, even more than in the past, has developed into a haven for traders with complex strategies and arbitrages rather than a place where people go to clip their coupons and put the bond certificates back into their safe deposit boxes. At the same time, Alan Greenspan's monetary policy has delivered the coup de grâce to income on bonds.

The Orange Juice Is Well Frozen

Except in the high-yield bond area, where current yield usually suffices to offset losses from default, income plays no role today in portfolio strategy or in the formulation of investment objectives. Even spending institutions, such as endowments and foundations, appear to put little weight on income in their deliberations (the recent tax reform has no significance for them anyway).

The real mystery is the lack of response by taxable investors to the fall in taxes on dividend income. Maybe one day soon the word will reach them that dividends have been enriched by an income tax of only 15 percent. If and when that day arrives, they will launch a whole new generation of investors who, at long last, will disdain frozen orange juice.

Note

1. A case can be made that the dividend really comes out of the price of the stock, which is marked down by the amount of the dividend on the payment date. Modigliani and Miller (1958) used this practice as proof that "dividends don't matter." I continue to profess that dividends *do* matter because they take cash away from managers.

References

Arnott, Robert D., and Clifford S. Asness. 2003. "Surprise! Higher Dividends = Higher Earnings Growth." *Financial Analysts Journal*, vol. 59, no. 1 (January/February):70–87.

Bernstein, Peter L. 1979. "Surprising the Smoothies," *Journal of Portfolio Management*, vol. 10, no. 1 (Fall):7–9.

Black, Fischer. 1976. "The Dividend Puzzle." *Journal of Portfolio Management*, vol. 2, no. 1 (Winter):5–8.

Leibowitz, Martin. 2003. "The Higher Equity Risk Premium Created by Taxation." *Financial Analysts Journal*, vol. 59, no. 5 (September/October):28–31.

Modigliani, Franco, and Merton Miller. 1958. "The Cost of Capital, Corporation Finance, and the Theory of Investment." *American Economic Review*, vol. 48, no. 3 (June):655–669.

Siegel, Jeremy. 2002. *Wall Street Journal* (13 February): Opinions section.

Treynor, Jack. 1972. "The Trouble with Earnings." *Financial Analysts Journal*, vol. 28, no. 5 (September/October):41–43.

Good News!

J. Parker Hall III, CFA

We are continuously bombarded by bad news that causes us to invest cautiously. The good news is that an investor with a diversified benchmark can have confidence in the profitability of a program of portfolio rebalancing.

During nearly 50 years in the institutional investment management business, one comes across some useful insights. One such insight relates to our reactions to market lows: How intense and bleak our feelings are during, and for a while after, a bear market. But then, looking back at the resolution of the crisis, we conclude that it was not so bad after all. We needn't have panicked. Here we are, survivors, only somewhat worse for wear from a continuous litany of scary events. And from all this turmoil, we see affirmed a second insight: A systematic rebalancing program is critical to a successful portfolio strategy. Its implementation is essential in bad times as well as good times.

First, consider the times of crisis just since World War II. The nerve-wracking events tumble out with extraordinary frequency:

1950s

- The Korean War evolves from the continuing Cold War, to be followed in the rest of the century by the Vietnam, Gulf, and Iraq wars.
- The security markets are caught up in fears of a return of the Great Depression, with equities not regaining pre-Depression highs until 1954.

1960s

- U.S. businesses go through a conglomerate craze.
- In the mid-1960s, Litton Industries proposes issuing a non-dividend-paying convertible preferred stock for the acquisition of Montgomery Ward. Under accounting rules at that time (which did not include "fully diluted" data), 100 percent of Ward's earnings would have gone to increase Litton's EPS. Talk about cheap money!

J. Parker Hall III, CFA, a frequent contributor to the Financial Analysts Journal, *was president of Lincoln Capital Management for 30 years; he resides in Winnetka, Illinois.*

- In 1968, at a speculative stock market top, three celebrity Freds—Alger, Carr, and Mates—manage mutual funds with net asset values up more than 100 percent (one Fred is up more than 100 percent two consecutive years). Adroit use is made of unregistered letter stock. These carryings-on foreshadow the late-1990s technology and telecom bubbles and related shenanigans.
- The assassinations of President John F. Kennedy, Robert F. Kennedy, and Martin Luther King, Jr., devastate us.

1970s

- In April 1970, Penn Central goes bankrupt. (The chairman of the railroad's finance committee was on the investment committee of a Lincoln Capital Management client. Despite Lincoln receiving contractual incentive compensation, the client terminated the firm after less than one year for a market timer.)
- In mid-1970, Chrysler, also without bank lines to cover maturing commercial paper, is within a day or two of bankruptcy. The Federal Reserve Board "keeps the window open late" while Manny Hanny (Manufacturers Hanover Trust), which is Chrysler's agent, scampers ahead to arrange refinancing. At the same time, the Fed offers active support to Goldman and Becker, the principal U.S. issuers of commercial paper.
- The Nifty Fifty craze tops out in early 1973. The S&P 500 Index goes down 45 percent, with many of these institutional favorites down a lot more.
- My father, one of the founders in 1947 of the FAF (Financial Analysts Federation, a forerunner of CFA Institute), says, "Parker, you haven't experienced a real bear market until it's down 90 percent." In mid-1974, I observe, "Dad, the American Stock Exchange is now down 90 percent."
- President Richard M. Nixon resigns and is pardoned by President Gerald R. Ford.
- "Predators' Balls" and Drexel Bernham produce the rise and fall of junk bonds.
- The problem of trading on inside information rises to the fore, and in January 1974, the FAF establishes new guidelines for insider trading.[1] Thirty years later, we are still trying to live up to the guidelines.

1980s

- A 30-year bear market in bonds is completed in 1981; the market goes from an interest rate trough of 1 percent in 1951 (at the time of the Treasury–Federal Reserve Accord) to an interest rate peak in 1981, with long-term U.S. Treasuries yielding 14 percent. Pain! (Lincoln actually bought some of those Treasuries at the 30 September 1981 low price.)
- The aggressive implementation of portfolio insurance and tautly stretched bond/stock valuations take the market crashing down more than 22 percent on Black Monday, 19 October 1987; futures drop down 29 percent. Tuesday starts out worse; the Fed "affirms its readiness to serve as a source of liquidity."
- Energy prices, which erupted in the 1970s, do so again in the early 1980s (and in 2003–2005). Energy stocks hit highs in October 1980, the month that Morgan Guaranty capitulates and "covers" its underweight in the energy sector of its trust clients.
- A merger and acquisition frenzy occurs.
- Latin America and Continental Illinois National Bank and Trust Company swoon.

1990s

- The decade begins with the savings and loan scandal.
- The institutional real estate market collapses.
- Long-Term Capital Management (LTCM) disintegrates (where is the hedge?); the Fed is there, again.
- Japan and Russia implode.

2000s

- We experience a Big Bear Market—a drop of 40 percent plus, the second in 70 years.
- 9/11/2001.
- Terrorism broadens.
- New York Attorney General Eliot Spitzer blows whistles.
- Malfeasance is revealed in industrial businesses, accounting, investment banking, insurance, and mutual funds. Sadly, it seems nearly everybody is involved.[2]
- Governance and ethics become the subject of renewed focus, and the Sarbanes–Oxley Act of 2002 stipulates a number of reforms.
- The dollar weakens.
- The federal deficit (and private indebtedness) balloons.
- The Pension Benefit Guaranty Corporation grows shaky.
- And the decade's only half over!

Well, there certainly has been a lot of bad news to be absorbed in a half century—nearly one nasty crisis a year. And given human nature, bad news will probably never end. *Plus ça change, plus c'est la même chose.*

Fortunately, the first insight we can gain by examining our history is that our domestic economy is extraordinarily large, diverse, and resilient. This fact plus fiscal and (especially) monetary policies have usually been effective in restoring us to stability. So, our economy should continue to successfully assimilate initially nerve-wracking events.

The second insight has to do with a beneficial portfolio idea that is reaffirmed by all this history—portfolio rebalancing. By this term, I mean a policy of systematically trimming winning segments (asset classes) and supplementing losing segments to maintain a portfolio's normal strategic proportions. Rebalancing for a diversified portfolio is a powerful—if not perfect—strategy. It is the only way I know to obtain some modest alpha without making significant active bets.

Needless to say, rebalancing won't work well if no enabling reversion to "normal" relationships occurs. Imagine the pain if one's only investment was LTCM. But as we have seen for the past 50 years, bad events don't last forever; opportunities abound for a diversified portfolio.[3] The look back at history should be reassuring and allow us to avoid being painfully panicked by all the scary events that occur with such regularity.

Of course, one must always be alert to underlying changes in a client's basic circumstances and any appropriate modification to portfolio policy. Otherwise, rebalancing offers a strategic framework that permits us to compensate for the human tendency to make disadvantageous active bets (buy winning portfolio segments, sell losing segments).

I recommend that you build this attractive strategy into your policy statement.

Conclusion

For more than five decades, the U.S. economy has demonstrated extraordinary resilience under a seemingly constant, nearly annual, barrage of scary events. This resilience reflects, among other attributes, the large, productive, and diverse nature of our economy and fruitful monetary initiatives. With respect to investment policy formation, we can be reassured by these fundamental economic strengths. In a diversified investment portfolio, the opportunity to benefit, through portfolio rebalancing, from others' misplaced fears and related (mostly futile) "timing" has obvious merit. Even as we are continuously bombarded by bad news, history shows us it can represent good news for investors.

Notes

1. I chaired this FAF committee.
2. I could repeat in 2005 what I wrote in 1971: "It isn't clear there is anything fundamentally new in the current fierce quest for higher standards of corporate accountability" ("The Professional Investor's View of Social Responsibility," *Financial Analysts Journal,* September/October:32).
3. I am involved in one relationship where the client has been invested almost completely passively for 20 years. The investment committee actually looks forward to meetings when policy guidelines have been breached, especially by a weak stock market.

Through the Years

Letter from immediate past
CFA Institute President and CEO
Thomas A. Bowman, CFA

Financial Analysts Journal: A Tradition of Public Service

"Our members look for constructive debate and for ways to move the profession forward."

The paths of the *Financial Analysts Journal* and the Chartered Financial Analyst (CFA) Program have unfolded in a complementary and intertwined pattern. In 1942, the New York Society of Security Analysts proposed the idea that its board be allowed to "confer the [Qualified Security Analyst] rating upon applicants who met designated standards," which included standards relating to (1) character, (2) education and experience, and (3) passing of an examination. This proposal was the genesis of what would come to be known as the CFA Program.

It was Benjamin Graham, at that time chair of the Standards Committee, who argued vociferously in the very first edition of *The Analysts Journal* in January 1945 (now available online at www.cfapubs.org/faj/) for a set of criteria that would define the profession of security analysis. The journal was also the brainstorm of the New York Society, so it was entirely appropriate that the first debate of the merits of a chartering program take place in the pages of *The Analysts Journal*.

In that inaugural edition, Mr. Graham noted, "Some fifty years ago, trained accountants were wrestling with a similar idea, and at that time the difficulties and drawbacks of the proposed C.P.A.

Thomas A. Bowman, CFA, was president and CEO of CFA Institute (formerly AIMR) from 1994 through 2004.

FAJ Milestones (1945–1954)

1945

First issue of *The Analysts Journal* published by the New York Society of Security Analysts, Inc., "to advance the interests of our profession [and] to encourage thoughtful discussion and debate on topics of current interest."	Benjamin Graham's farsighted article advocates the creation of a professional designation for security analysts.	George Mackintosh introduces a way to translate a company's estimated earnings into a stock price by estimating the outlook for earnings growth at the time of analysis.	H.M. Gartley discusses measuring a stock's (or portfolio's) price volatility as it rises and falls against an average.	Code of Ethics printed, beginning with: "The Security Analyst will be independent and unprejudiced. His first and final obligation is to discover the truth and to state it as he sees it."

designation no doubt appeared quite serious to many of them. Today the need for a professional rating in that field and in many others is taken for granted." Mr. Graham's vision for a professional designation was prescient. He believed that once the initial hurdles were overcome, the procedure would establish itself firmly and would come to be considered "indispensable to the public interest."

As always, there were two sides to the issue. The camp of practitioners opposed to the idea of a professional qualification was represented in the journal by Lucien O. Hooper, a former president of the New York Society. He wrote, "Unless our employers, the investing public, or some governmental regulative body force regimentation upon us, we earnestly desire to remain free from this unnecessary formalism. The life of an analyst is complicated enough without the addition of any unnecessary appurtenances."

Both men made sense, and the logic of their arguments—public interest versus demand of the industry—was the basis for many discussions during the next 60 years as publication of the *FAJ* moved from the New York Society to the National Federation of Financial Analysts Societies, then the Financial Analysts Federation and Institute of Chartered Financial Analysts, to the Association for Investment Management and Research, and finally to CFA Institute. Issues of new professional standards and continuing education continue to involve us in debate.

Despite Mr. Hooper's opposition to the idea of a qualification, he certainly shared some common ground with Mr. Graham and with the program that ultimately was adopted. He believed that before any sort of rating could be adopted, a "stated set of principles" was needed. The first statement of the Code of Ethics was printed in the July 1945 issue of *The Analysts Journal*.

Although another 18 years had to pass before the concept of a professional designation that was initially debated in *The Analysts Journal* reached fruition, there is little doubt that the logic of Benjamin Graham played a large role in its acceptance within the New York Society and among security analysts across North America. As Mr. Graham wrote, "It is hard to see why it is sound procedure to examine and register customers' brokers but not sound to apply corresponding standards to security analysts."

Perhaps more telling about this organization than the eventual triumph of Mr. Graham's point of view is that, in the end, Lucien Hooper, despite his initial opposition, went on to sit for the first CFA examination in 1963. (Ironically, Mr. Graham never did.) Mr. Hooper passed the examination and was among the first to earn his CFA charter (#165).

Our members look for constructive debate and for ways to move the profession forward—always in the pursuit of protecting the interests of the investing public. Despite our growth, despite our global expansion, these goals are as true in 2005 as they were in 1945.

1947	1948	1952	1953	1954
Pierre Bretey becomes the first editor of the *Journal*, taking over from the Editorial Board.	Lucien Hooper's "Investment Implications of American Involvement in International Politics" wins the Alexander Annual Award (a precursor to the Graham & Dodd award) for best article of 1947.	Benjamin Graham advocates that the profession collect the studies and recommendations of numerous analysts, classify them, and evaluate their accuracy and success.	Nicholas Molodovsky provides a blueprint for using the price-to-earnings ratio in the valuation process.	The *Journal* is transferred to the National Federation of Financial Analysts Societies, the forerunner of the Financial Analysts Federation and of CFA Institute. The *Journal* is considered to be the "official organ of the Federation."

Letter from a member of the first Editorial Board
Irving Kahn, CFA

Early Days at the *Financial Analysts Journal*

"We believed that getting ideas and facts out to the analysts was important."

I send the *Financial Analysts Journal* warmest congratulations on this 60th anniversary! In the beginning, when the group that became the Editorial Board started *The Analysts Journal* back in 1944–1945, we saw it as a way to communicate ideas. "Financial analysis" was such a new profession, and the postwar world was growing so rapidly. We believed that getting ideas and facts out to the analysts was important. Everybody that worked on the *Journal* in the beginning was an unpaid volunteer; we did it because we wanted to make security analysis a serious profession.

Many of us were interested in hands-on, fundamental analysis of actual companies and actual industries. The approach we pursued was to give how-to advice for day-to-day practice on analyzing company, industry, and national statistics and facts. Others, particularly the academic authors that became attracted to the *Journal*, pursued the theoretical side—theory, methodology. The challenge was then and continues today: how to bridge that gap between theory and practice.

Irving Kahn, CFA, is chairman of Kahn Brothers, New York City. His column, "Financial Analysts Digest," was published from 1964 to 1971. He was a founding member of the New York Society of Security Analysts and received his CFA charter in 1963.

FAJ Milestones (1955–1964)

1955	1957	1959	1960	1961
Edmund Mennis examines the relationship of equity indexes to the general business cycle.	Benjamin Graham presents two methods for choosing a growth factor in forecasting.	*The Analysts Journal* is renamed *Financial Analysts Journal.*	Edward Renshaw and Paul Feldstein make the case for passive investing.	First Graham and Dodd Award is announced—for the 1960 article by Fulton Boyd on investment opportunities in Latin America.

One of the ways I tried to help was to start a column in 1964 called "Financial Analysts Digest." It wasn't any great words of wisdom of my own; what I did was communicate important information by quoting other sources. For example, I would quote from the publications of the U.S. Federal Reserve Board district banks. These bank professionals were pretty smart people, and they wrote about local conditions. I wanted to describe what things were like in Kansas City or St. Louis or Dallas because companies, economies, and products were all different in those different parts of the country. Therefore, it was educational for somebody on the East Coast, like me, to read about what was going on on the West Coast.

This kind of applied education was also part of the purpose behind the train rides and other trips arranged by Pierre Bretey (first editor of the *Journal*)—trips from New York to California, Chicago to New Orleans, and so on. Bretey, who was the editor from 1947 to 1963, was a rail analyst. And in those days, a different railroad would be involved for each leg of a trip. So, at each important stop, the president of the railroad would hook on his presidential car and ride with us from, say, Cleveland to Chicago. During that time, we'd have a luncheon meeting and a dinner meeting and he'd say what was good or bad about conditions where he lived.

One of the most memorable trips is the 1966 trip we took to Japan. We flew from New York to Anchorage and Anchorage to Tokyo. The Japanese were so anxious to show how they were climbing out of the disaster of World War II that they let us see everything. We went to a small two-story building to see a poor little company that was trying to go into the radio business by copying U.S. technology. It was Sony, and today, its huge building is right across the street from me in Manhattan.

The practical and the theoretical must remain balanced in the *FAJ*. It is a challenge, and I wish the publication well as it enters the next decade.

1963		1964		
First CFA exam is given in June to 284 candidates.	The Institute of Chartered Financial Analysts is formed, and the first CFA charters are awarded to 268 people in September.	Frank Block argues for a valuation system based on price-to-book multiples.	Nicholas Molodovsky becomes editor.	Feature "Financial Analysts Digest" is introduced by Irving Kahn.

Letter from an *FAJ*
Associate Editor, 1960–1988
Edmund A. Mennis, CFA

Financial Analysts Journal: Marrying the Academic and Practitioner Worlds

> "Until these developments, practitioners in, for example, portfolio management basically collected stocks one at a time, without a method of relating them."

I am pleased but not surprised that the *Financial Analysts Journal* has thrived for 60 years. Over the many years I was associated with the *Journal* (under four editors!), I saw much success and certainly many changes.

I became involved with the *FAJ*, the Financial Analysts Federation, and the Institute of Chartered Financial Analysts (forerunners of CFA Institute) while I was working for Abe Kulp at Wellington Management Company in Philadelphia, Pennsylvania, from 1950 to

---

Ed Mennis, CFA, authored or co-authored a dozen FAJ *articles, one of which, "Corporate Earnings: Long Term Outlook and Valuation" (July/August 1971), won the Graham and Dodd Award. Another, "Security Prices and Business Cycles," was selected for inclusion in the 1995 50th Anniversary Issue (January/February). He chaired the ICFA Research and Publications Committee in 1968 when the committee was responsible for the initial development of the Body of Knowledge used for the CFA Program. As part of that effort, he co-authored* Quantitative Techniques for Financial Analysis *and spurred development of the* CFA Readings *series. For his efforts, in 1972, he was the second recipient of the Nicholas Molodovsky Award. (Molodovsky was the first recipient.) Mennis edited the* CFA Digest *from its inception in 1972 through 1986. He was chairman of the ICFA for 1970–1971 and 1971–1972. He received his CFA charter in 1965 and received the C. Stewart Sheppard Award for commitment to the profession in 1978.*

FAJ Milestones (1965–1974)

1965	1966	1968	1969
Eugene Fama lays out the case for the markets as random walks and the implications for analysts.	John Shelton explores the use of computers in security analysis.	Financial Analysts Federation awards first Molodovsky Award for contributions "of such significance as to have changed the direction of the profession" to Nicholas Molodovsky.	Jack Treynor becomes editor.

1966. My background was in financial analysis and economics, and Abe and I often discussed areas with which we thought a well-educated analyst—and later, CFA charterholder—should be familiar. I wrote several articles for the *Journal* in the 1950s, and while Pierre Bretey was editor, he asked me to be on the "Editorial Board" (we were all called "associate editors"). When Nicholas Molodovsky became editor in 1964, he asked me to stay on. The Editorial Board used to meet regularly at the Harvard Club in New York City over wonderful long dinners, where Nick would have as guests his friends from the academic and business communities, which made for exciting and stimulating discussions. And I stayed an associate editor under Jack Treynor's editorship until 1988.

Nick Molodovsky was a distinguished scholar and true gentleman. He was a Russian who had fled the Soviet Union in the 1920s, moved to Paris, and then to New York. He had an inquiring, wide-ranging mind, and he wanted to introduce practitioners to the developing ideas of leading academics in the 1960s—ideas such as the efficient market hypothesis and modern portfolio theory, which were challenging the very foundations of financial analysis. As a member of the Research and Publications Committee of the ICFA and head of its financial analysis group, Molodovsky contributed greatly to defining what we established in 1963–1965 as the CFA Body of Knowledge. Until these developments, practitioners in, for example, portfolio management basically collected stocks one at a time, without a method of relating them. Molodovsky also believed that unless analysts learned quantitative techniques and computer applications, they ran the risk of becoming illiterate in their own field.

This effort to marry the academic and practitioner worlds was continued by Jack Treynor when he became editor following Molodovsky's shocking death in 1968. Treynor wanted practitioners to be able to see and adapt the ideas of academics in day-to-day investment analysis and management. He published many articles covering quantitative techniques and methods. Of course, some people liked this direction while others didn't. The same is true today.

The *FAJ* of 2005 is on the right track in this balancing act. The articles are thought-provoking and useful, and they expand our knowledge. For example, today's practitioners must understand that the excessive returns of the late bull market could not last. They needed the bucket of cold water that Rob Arnott and Peter Bernstein threw on those false expectations many have for the future market return (*FAJ*, March/April 2002). The articles that are heavily quantitative serve as leavening in the *FAJ*—not too much, not too little. I hope the *FAJ* will remain on this road to helping investment professional serve clients, and I wish it a continued long life.

1971		1972	1974
A regular feature by John Gillis begins on "Securities Law and Regulation."	Jack Treynor analyzes why investors generally cannot beat the market.	William Sharpe discusses how to measure the risk in a portfolio based on its sensitivity to market movements and diversification.	Bruno Solnik argues that substantial risk reduction results from adding nondomestic stocks to a portfolio.

Letter from the
FAJ Editor, 1969–1981
Jack Treynor

Ideas for the People Who Make the Decisions

"I began to think that we ought to have a way to quantify the role of risk."

Being editor of the *Financial Analysts Journal* was one of the most fascinating jobs I ever held. I had written for the *Journal* when Nicholas Molodovsky was the editor. In fact, Molodovsky requested the first article I co-authored for the *Journal*. It was on estimating risk.[1] I admired the man, and I admired what he was doing with the magazine. When Molodovsky died suddenly, which was a shame, some people said, "Gee, Jack, you ought to think about doing that job." My first reaction was: Why? I had never edited anything, not even my high school yearbook. But the more I thought about it, the more appealing it became. I was working for Merrill Lynch, Pierce, Fenner & Smith at the time. I kind of created Merrill Lynch's first "quant group," and some very talented people were working in it. But because Merrill Lynch was so big, I suspected that they would want to make me a specialist of some sort. So, I thought "maybe this is an opportunity to focus on my true interest, which was the analytical problem behind investment decisions."

Jack Treynor is president and CEO of Treynor Capital Management, Inc., Palos Verdes Estates, California. He served as editor of the FAJ *from 1969 through 1981. Treynor is the author or co-author of more than 40 articles on investing published in the* FAJ*, one of which,"What Does It Take to Win the Trading Game?" (January/February), won the 1981 Graham and Dodd Award, and another, "The Only Game in Town" (March/April 1971), was reprinted in the January/February 1995 Golden Anniversary issue. Treynor received the Nicholas Molodovsky Award for "contributions to the profession of financial analysis of such significance as to change the direction of the profession . . ." in 1985.*

FAJ Milestones (1975–1984)

1975		1976	1977
Charles Ellis describes why professional money management has become a game one wins only by avoiding mistakes.	May Day ushers in the age of negotiated commission rates.	Barr Rosenberg and James Guy explain the meaning of beta systematic risk.	A regular feature, "Accounting for Financial Analysis," is established by William Norby.

I was a math major in college—partly because at the small college I attended, the department for my first love, physics, was even smaller than the math department. After serving in the U.S. Army during the Korean War, I attended Harvard Business School (where, naturally, I became interested in finance). After staying on for a year to write cases, I went to work for Arthur D. Little (ADL), where I dealt with industrial clients from Shell Oil to Honeywell and financial clients from Chase Bank to Yale University. The Yale University endowment fund was being managed virtually out of the treasurer's hip pocket. Well, some Yale alumni on Wall Street said, "That's no way to manage the Yale endowment; to beat the market, you have to manage actively!" But my interviews with money managers in Chicago, New York, Boston, San Francisco—everywhere—suggested that there was no clear agreement on the right way to manage money.

During my work experiences, I began to think that we ought to have a way to quantify the role of risk. If you change the discount rate just 1 percent on a 40-year investment, you can change the present value so much that it goes from lots more than the initial cost to lots less than the initial cost. The only answer the Harvard Business School gave me to this issue in the 1950s was that "well, you know, you use your judgment—to take risk into account, you use a bigger discount rate." (Of course, in the 1960s, Harvard moved into quantitative analysis in a big way.)

So, I took a year off from ADL to study economics and econometrics under the guidance of the late Franco Modigliani. By 1960, I had a rough draft of my CAPM paper, and in 1962 I presented it to the MIT finance faculty seminar. (Modigliani later asked me to exchange drafts of our work on capital asset pricing with Bill Sharpe.)

When Frank Block, who was then employed as chief investment officer for the Citizens and Southern Bank in Atlanta and was president of the Financial Analysts Federation (the forerunner of AIMR, which was the forerunner of CFA Institute), hired me to be the *FAJ* editor, he wanted me to bring developing methodologies to the attention of the people who make the investment decisions. To do that, we had to make some changes in our choice of papers, which meant additions to the Editorial Board. The existing board was a clever, talented bunch of guys (we had fascinating dinners at the Harvard Club once a month), but they were interested in current events; they weren't interested in methodology.

In those days, I couldn't run the *Journal* the way an academic journal is run—with double-blind refereeing and so on—because we weren't inundated with submissions. If I needed help on a piece, I'd send it to someone who could help. I went a lot by what I liked, and the result was that we started publishing a lot of quantitative material.

1978	1981	1982	1984
A regular feature, "Pension Fund Perspective," is introduced by Patrick Regan.	Mark Rubinstein and Hayne Leland explain how to use protective puts and covered calls on stocks for which there is no options market.	Charles D'Ambrosio becomes editor.	Richard Roll and Stephen Ross add unanticipated changes in four economic variables to the CAPM factors.

A number of columns were introduced during my editorship, but none of them were my idea. They reflected the expanded scope of the investment manager's responsibilities—what a manager did and had to think about. Various leaders of the FAF would say, "We need a column on XYZ." But then I had to find someone to write the column. "Securities Law and Regulation," "Accounting for Financial Analysis," and "Pension Fund Perspective" were written by people more qualified than I to write them. But I also wound up writing a number of editorials for the *FAJ* in addition to the articles I wrote.

I liked the work; I liked the chance to do my thing. I'm a problem solver, hence my interest in the principles of investing. It was a time when institutional money management—mutual funds and pension funds—was expanding rapidly. Modigliani and Merton Miller had just published their great papers on the impact of leverage and growth on investment value.[2] Harry Markowitz had published his book on portfolio theory.[3] Sharpe followed up his 1963 paper introducing the distinction between systematic and specific risk with his 1964 CAPM paper.[4] With Larry Fisher, Jim Lorie had created CRSP (the Center for Research in Security Prices) at the University of Chicago, and Rex Sinquefield and Roger Ibbotson were working with Fisher on the creation of the CRSP tapes, which made data on U.S. stock market returns available to researchers. (Mike Jensen, Dick Roll, and Gene Fama earned their doctorates at the University of Chicago.)[5]

The people stirring up this ferment of research were a natural pool for helping the *FAJ* spread the ideas of modern finance to the practitioner community. Bill Beaver, Fischer Black, Dick Brealey, Bob Ferguson, Bill Fouse, Walter Good, Marty Leibowitz, Jay Light, Tony Meyer, and Gordon Pye—all accepted my invitation to join the *FAJ* Editorial Board. And if I liked a presentation at a CRSP meeting, I would ask them to write it up for the *Journal*. I was shameless about drumming up articles!

Surprises came up all the time in the work, but I particularly recall one that threatened all the priceless work of these authors. I'm a messy person; the idea of cleaning up the desk at the end of the workday is not part of my style. So, in the morning, the same mess would be there on my desk that had been there the night before. The stuff just accumulated. The most pressing stuff was in the middle of the mess, and the less pressing stuff was out along the edges. One day, the light bulb in the lamp over my desk exploded! I quickly grabbed the cord and pulled the plug out, even though it was really too hot to handle, because I was afraid that we'd have a fire and all that work would be gone!

My account of these years at the *FAJ* would be incomplete if I didn't acknowledge the extraordinary editorial talent of Judy Kimball and the striking covers of Joe Hollis.

In closing, I want to remind readers that, although financial analysis is a young profession, it offers a special window on the world—on economics, on politics, on the psychology of leadership. The United States is struggling to demonstrate to the rich and poor of the world what capitalism can really be. We can't do this job without the unique contributions of the professional investor. The *FAJ* has a tremendous responsibility.

Notes

1. Jack L. Treynor, William W. Priest, Jr., Lawrence Fisher, and Catherine A. Higgins, "Using Portfolio Composition to Estimate Risk," *Financial Analysts Journal* (September/October 1968):93–100.
2. See, for example, "The Cost of Capital, Corporation Finance, and the Theory of Investment," *American Economic Review* (June 1958):655–669.
3. *Portfolio Selection: Efficient Diversification of Investments* (New York: John Wiley & Sons, 1971).
4. The first article is "A Simplified Model for Portfolio Analysis," *Management Science* (January 1963):277–293; the second article is "Capital Asset Prices: A Theory of Market Equilibrium under Conditions of Risk," *Journal of Finance* (September 1964):425–442.
5. For publications in the *FAJ* of specific people mentioned in this piece, see the *FAJ* Author Index at www.cfapubs.org/faj/home.html.

Letter from
L. Randolph Hood, CFA

Determinants of Portfolio Performance—20 Years Later

It might be one of the most quoted numbers in applied finance: 93.6 percent. Ironically, it is also often misquoted or taken out of context. Just where did this number come from, and what does it really imply for portfolio management? Also, importantly, what does it not imply?

In the early 1980s, Gary Brinson and I were wondering why our institutional pension clients spent so much time and effort in manager searches and so little time in reviewing their asset allocation policies. It was not as if all our clients had identical risk tolerances, liability streams, and funding policies. In discussions with the clients, we discovered that they had a firm belief that manager selection was important (and it is) because they could quantify the benefits of superior management. They could not, however, or perhaps did not wish to, quantify the contributory effects of their allocation policies on the returns to their funds. Explicit policies can be embarrassing because they facilitate measurement of the success or failure of liability funding and the implementation of investment programs. That is, poor outcomes resulting from asset allocation policies are difficult to blame on investment managers.

Our clients considered liability valuation the province of actuaries, and liabilities were far too complicated and esoteric to analyze or to use in making policy decisions. Nevertheless, we firmly believed that investment policy was the heart of the investment planning process. (And somewhat after the fact, the funding

"We would not have guessed that a six-page article would be the focal point of a 20-year discussion."

L. Randolph Hood, CFA, is the investment manager responsible for domestic employee retirement plans at Prudential Financial, Inc., Newark, New Jersey.

Editor's Note: The article being discussed is "Determinants of Portfolio Performance" by Gary P. Brinson, L. Randolph Hood, and Gilbert L. Beebower. First published in the July/August 1986 *Financial Analysts Journal*, this article was republished in the 50th Anniversary Issue (January/ February 1995) and is available online at www.cfapubs.org/faj/issues/v51n1/pdf/f0510133a.pdf. It is the most visited *FAJ* article online.

debacle of 2001–2003 illustrates allocation's importance. Over that period, plan sponsors lost billions of dollars for their shareholders—despite tremendous efforts devoted to manager selection. The culprit was asset allocation policies that were developed without adequate consideration of the *range* of possible outcomes or the behavior of the liabilities.) So, convinced as we were in the 1980s of the importance of allocation policy, and with the assistance of Gilbert Beebower at SEI Corporation, who had the relevant data, we set out to explore the effects of asset allocation policy on plan returns.

Our main finding was that, on average, 93.6 percent of the variation of actual quarterly total returns from 1974 to 1983 of a sample of 91 large corporate pension plans could be explained by using proxy return series. The proxy series were calculated by using each plan's average weight over the 40 quarters for equities, bonds, and cash equivalents and by applying passive index returns for those asset classes for each quarter. Simply put, we found that the broad types of asset classes a fund includes in a portfolio and the proportions they represent have a profound effect on the *variability* of returns. These decisions also directly affect the returns themselves, of course, although we did not choose to stress that aspect. We concluded that asset allocation policy is an important component of the management process and deserves careful consideration. We wanted plan sponsors to focus *first* on their liabilities and explicitly consider what they were trying to achieve with their plans. And with our research, we thought the point had been made.

But debates about the article's findings were surprisingly numerous. Criticisms as well as defenses of the approach—and perceptions of the lessons to be learned from the article—have abounded. So, on behalf of my co-authors and myself, I would like to address some of the most prevalent observations and reactions that have been discussed in the last 20 years.

I want to start with one that we believe has not been discussed much at all: Nothing in the original paper suggests that active asset management is not an important activity. It was not the point of our paper, and our goal was not to demonstrate otherwise.

Although by our calculations it is true that the average plan over the time period we studied lost money from security selection and from market timing as we defined the terms, some plans did quite well. In security selection, for example (see Table 6 of the published article), the average

FAJ Milestones (1985–1994)

1986		1988	
Gary Brinson, Randolph Hood, and Gilbert Beebower find that investment policy explains 93.6 percent of the variation in total plan returns.	Martin Leibowitz argues for balancing the duration of a fixed-income portfolio against the duration of the stream of liabilities it is funding.	André Perold and William Sharpe discuss establishing a system of explicit rules for rebalancing in response to changes in asset values.	Richard Roll analyzes the worldwide market crash of October 1987.

plan active return was –0.36 percent a year, but the range of active returns varied from a loss of –2.90 percent to a gain of +3.60 percent a year—a spread of 650 bps. We would suggest that any activity that can avoid the former or attain the latter is very important indeed. Most plan sponsors appear to agree and think that what might be a small expected loss (0.36 percent) is probably worth the cost of trying to outperform.

Other comments about the research have surfaced over time. Some of the early detractors dismissed the work as being applicable solely to our sample, which it was not, because the results have been repeated with other data. Other criticisms revolved around our use of policy portfolios. We believe policy portfolios are useful and, in many ways, necessary. However, we do not believe that they are never to be changed. Naturally, when the goals or circumstances surrounding the management of portfolios change, so should the investment policy. All we would urge is that the policy be specified in advance and be actionable. As we noted in our article, we had to infer policy targets because we did not have the necessary data. If we had possessed the data, however, our results would certainly have been stronger, not weaker: Unless sponsors and managers actively disregard their policies, the policy effects would have been stronger than we measured.

Another comment has been that perhaps analyzing plans as a group rather than individually across time is the important approach. However, we wanted specifically to challenge this concept. We had no reason to believe that a single asset allocation policy could possibly be right for all of our diverse clients or that the mean policy weights for a group of heterogeneous pension plans had much *ex ante* interest.

Some commentators disliked our use of the "other" term, although it was algebraically necessary in our formulation. One interpretation of the term is that it represents the effect of overweighting managers who then reliably outperform their respective benchmarks, and vice versa, which might be of interest today to those pursuing "portable alpha" approaches.

A further criticism involved our use of *variation of portfolio total returns,* not the returns themselves. We do not understand this point as a criticism. Understanding how something varies, in our context, leads to understanding where it will end up. Our policy portfolio return series all had regression coefficients near unity when explaining actual return series, which is not surprising given their construction, so we did not report the regression coefficients because of space constraints. In

1989		1990	1993
Martin Fridson becomes Book Review Editor.	Fischer Black presents a formula for deciding when and when not to hedge.	"What Practitioners Need to Know" series is introduced by Bob Hagin and Mark Kritzman.	Fischer Black argues that estimating expected return requires a theory to explain what factors are priced and why mispricing occurs. W. Van Harlow III becomes editor.

Table 6, we reported that the average annual return to the average actual portfolio was equal to its policy portfolio return less 110 bps. We thus did describe the total return, albeit indirectly because it was not our main point. At their best, the compound annual total returns of the plans we studied were not, in themselves, interesting. We thought what was interesting was how the returns turned out to be what they were—with policy, timing, and security selection each contributing with varying degrees of importance. An analogy would be driving directions: One can either give a compass heading and a distance, or more helpfully, one can describe the route. The heading and distance information is akin to total return itself (up 9.01 percent); the variance of total return is akin to the directions: Follow the policy portfolio return wherever it leads (remember, it is specified in advance), but subtract 110 bps each year; on average, you will be right, and you can also see how bumpy the ride is along the way!

Conversely, among the work's supporters, zealous marketing has apparently led some to take liberties with the research. For instance, our findings do not support the notion that "asset allocation" funds are somehow inherently superior to single-asset-class funds. The ability to forecast asset class returns is a far different matter from pointing out that the policy weights and returns will have a profound effect on the return variation—and results—of an investment strategy. Our point was solely that, in aggregate, individual asset class policies, with given weights and broad market representation for returns, appear to dominate portfolio return variations and, by extension, the returns themselves. Furthermore, this conclusion was meant to be descriptive, not prescriptive, of the process we observed.

Looking back, we would not have guessed that a six-page article would be the focal point of a 20-year discussion. The consensus, however, appears to have settled in to agree with us that investment policy will be very important in subsequent results and in describing those results. Of course, other factors (such as active management and cost control) also have roles, and important roles, to play. Our message today remains the same as before: Carefully consider what goal you are trying to achieve, how important it is to achieve it, and how much risk you are willing to tolerate in pursuing it. Then, create a policy portfolio that reflects that goal and your risk tolerance for the probable outcomes—because executing that policy will have a dominant effect on your success. And, then, get to work.

FAJ Milestones (1995–2004)

1996	1998	1999	
Rex Sinquefield argues that the same two factors, value and size, work in non-U.S. stock markets as well as the U.S. market.	H. Gifford Fong becomes editor.	The November/December issue is devoted to behavioral finance.	Andrew Lo describes how probabilities of extreme dollar losses, prices, and preferences interact to determine sensible risk profiles.

Letter from the
FAJ Book Review Editor, 1989–
Martin S. Fridson, CFA

FAJ Book Reviews: For Relevance, Value, and Scope

The *Financial Analysts Journal* invited me to become book review editor in 1989. Declining health had compelled my predecessor, a gracious gentleman named Robert Cummin, to give up the duty. Because I had derived a lot of satisfaction from a few previous opportunities to contribute reviews, I was glad to accept. The honor of serving on the *FAJ*'s distinguished editorial board was a wonderful bonus.

In the years since I took on the task, several enthusiastic volunteers have joined the effort. They have brought expertise in various areas in which my own knowledge is limited. The involvement of these dedicated volunteers has expanded the range of books that we can review in a well-informed manner.

I began my tenure as book review editor with no predetermined approach, aside from a commitment to upholding the *FAJ*'s high editorial standards. There were no guidelines concerning which books to review or how to review them. Over time, however, several commonsense principles have emerged.

"The book review section should be a resource for practitioners—whether they focus on fundamental analysis, quantitative methods, or asset allocation."

Martin S. Fridson, CFA, is CEO of FridsonVision LLC, New York City. Since he joined the FAJ *as editor of book reviews in 1989, he has not only written clear and erudite reviews but has also put together a team of reviewers that now number seven.*

2001	2002	2003	
FAJ is made available online.	Robert Arnott and Peter Bernstein demonstrate that today's long-term forward-looking risk premium is nowhere near the level of the past.	Clifford Asness and Robert Arnott argue that the low dividend payouts of recent times are a sign of weak earnings to come.	Robert D. Arnott becomes editor.

First, we concentrate on books that expand our readers' mastery of the CFA Institute Global Body of Knowledge (for a list, see www.cfainstitute.org). This rule excludes many titles that business-oriented publishers are eager to have reviewed. Among them are self-help treatises, works dealing with management (other than management of financial firms), and economic studies that do not bear directly on the investment process. In addition, we generally exclude "how-to" investment guides aimed at a nonprofessional audience. We strive to make room for worthy but specialized books that the mass-circulation newspapers and magazines will probably not review. The "big" books—for example, journalists' accounts of stock market scandals and biographies of celebrity chief executive officers—tend to come to the attention *FAJ* readers whether we review them or not.

Second, we strive for a serious critical response, as opposed to a "book report" that laboriously summarizes the contents. This criterion eliminates from consideration many textbooks that serve quite satisfactorily in colleges and business schools. Professors need to evaluate them for adoption on the basis of such criteria as comprehensiveness and didactic effectiveness, but they do not lend themselves to the intellectual engagement that befits review in the *FAJ*.

Third, we try to reflect the diversity of CFA charterholders. The book review section should be a resource for practitioners involved in stocks, bonds, or derivatives, whether they focus on fundamental analysis, quantitative methods, or asset allocation. We are also mindful that our readers participate in markets all over the world.

I am especially proud that in the past decade and a half, *FAJ* book reviews have exposed readers to a number of provocative new areas of investment analysis. It is difficult to gauge the staying power of a fresh approach, such as behavioral finance, neural networks, or chaos theory, at the outset. By providing a platform for innovative ideas, however, the reviews facilitate essential debate.

Finally, reviews can not only educate investment professionals but also spur publishers to raise the bar on quality. Writers of financial books labor largely for love of the work; they deserve to have their output edited well and carefully proofread. Above all, publishers should go to the expense of fact checking, instead of concerning themselves solely with the risk of being sued for libel. Too many books go to print with errors that could be corrected, thanks to Internet search engines, easily and inexpensively.

Serving as book review editor for the *Financial Analysts Journal* has been immensely rewarding for me. It has caused me to learn far more about the investment world than I ever would have otherwise. At the same time, it has been a privilege to advance the overall mission of CFA Institute in such a pleasurable way.

—MSF

Aristotle on Investment Decision Making

Abby Joseph Cohen, CFA

Most modern people acknowledge that Aristotle was a bright and insightful man, but most do not recognize that his wisdom can be applied to investment decision making. Aristotle is well known for saying:

> Our discussion will be adequate if it has as much clearness as the subject matter allows. Equal precision cannot be found in all discussions. Political science [and economics] investigates many things with much variety and volatility. It is the mark of an educated person to look for precision only as far as the nature of the subject allows.
>
> *Nicomachean Ethics*, 350 BCE

Ponder that statement for a moment, the last sentence in particular. And now think about all the power assigned to current computational techniques in the investment process. But as Aristotle's statement implies, if investors are not using the right model at the right time, they will get an answer that makes little sense. In addition, investors must take care that they are using reliable data and must formally recognize the inherent lack of precision in many of their observations and measurements.

In this article, I will apply Aristotle's wisdom found in this quote to some elements of investment decision making. I will clarify the lessons from Aristotle that can (and should) be applied to investment decision making and then look at these lessons in the specific context of economic data.

We have abundant economic and financial data, but analysts should be alert to the imprecision in much of this information.

Lessons from Aristotle

Investors today have wonderfully powerful models and access to thousands of data series. But quite often they are not as circumspect as they should be in terms of the quality of the inputs. I am sure most people are familiar with the idea of

Abby Joseph Cohen, CFA, is partner and chief U.S. investment strategist at Goldman, Sachs & Co., New York City.

Editor's Note: This article was developed from Ms. Cohen's presentations to the CFA Institute conferences *Equity Research and Valuation Techniques* (December 2004) and the *FAJ* 60th Anniversary conference titled *Reflections and Insights: Provocative Thinking on Investment Management* (February 2005).

"garbage in/garbage out." That concept has become magnified by the extraordinary power of computational techniques and the idea that investors have developed more disciplined approaches. They have to keep in mind, however, that discipline sometimes does not give the right answer. It just gives a formulaic answer and can intensify the consequences of an incorrect answer. Thus, investors must heed the lessons of Aristotle and "look for precision only as far as the nature of the subject allows."

Define the Market or Asset Clearly. Portfolio managers, investment strategists, and equity analysts—all talk about "the market." But one of the lessons learned from Aristotle is the need to clearly define the subject at hand. A model that works well for one part of the market may work poorly in others. Investors need to understand the asset. They need to know what sort of company they are evaluating. Is it private? Public? Is it young? Mature? Lesson number one is to define the market or asset clearly; even the U.S. equity market, the world's deepest and most liquid market, has multiple exchanges and indices. Know what is being modeled, and do not apply one approach to all, because one size does not fit all.

Consider Not Only Returns but Also Standard Deviations. Focus not only on return but also, as Aristotle said, on volatility. When observing nature, philosophers and scientists recognize that some things are easier to observe and measure than others. Investors have many sophisticated measures at their disposal. There are Sharpe ratios, measures of multicollinearity, covariance, and many others. But very often, investors, analysts, and media commentators neglect to mention these other meaningful statistics when describing "the market." For example, **Figure 1** depicts the volatility of the S&P 500 Index, which has moved notably lower since mid-2003. So, for all the current discussions in the investment industry about financial assets now entering a period of lower returns, the industry may also be in a period of lower volatility and risk. That lower volatility should be considered as well by portfolio managers and sponsors of pools, such as pension funds and endowments.

Figure 1. Rolling Six-Month Annualized S&P 500 Volatility, 1970–2004

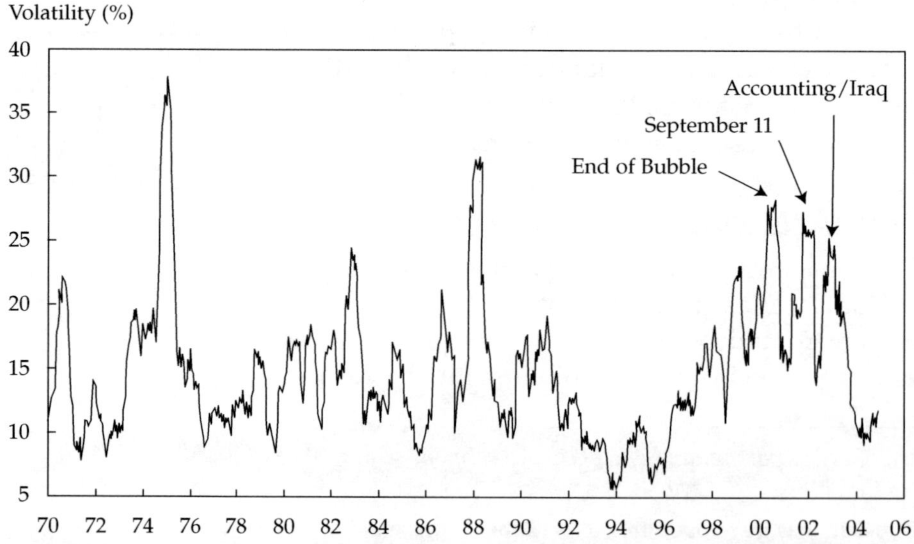

Note: Weekly data from 1 January 1970 through 19 November 2004.

Source: Based on data from the Goldman Sachs Equity Derivatives Research Group.

Define Earnings and Other Metrics of Company Performance Carefully. Of what other data considerations should investors be mindful? Investors must define what they are observing and the normal bounds of volatility; they must also carefully define the variables, both independent and dependent. They must know what they are trying to measure, and they must be aware of the problems that may be associated with accurately making those measurements.

For example, consider earnings data. Many participants in the investment business still rely almost exclusively on EPS, to the exclusion of important measures of corporate performance, such as revenues and cash flow, and what is worse, emphasize reported and pro forma EPS. Even when companies are reporting their data in as accurate a manner as possible, there may be dramatic disparities in the EPS calculations between industries and even among companies in a single industry. It is essential to recognize that the commonly used consensus data services are not especially helpful in this regard. There is usually little attempt made to ensure consistency within or among industries.

In our own earnings work at Goldman Sachs, we apply U.S. GAAP standards regardless of industry or sector and never rely on pro forma results. Instead, our proprietary EPS data series is based on filings made at the U.S. SEC. The consensus data services do not enforce a GAAP-like standard on the data. For each industry, the data tend to reflect the prevailing accounting approach preferred by the companies in the industry, including, in some cases, the heavy use of pro forma results. Pro forma data are typically available prior to the formal filings with the SEC, and investors often fail to review their analyses when more complete data are available. Furthermore, the lack of comparable standards across industries means that investors cannot readily compare the EPS numbers from one industry with another. Making the situation worse, some data services exclude the estimates coming from analysts who are using U.S. GAAP–consistent numbers because they are not using the same ill-conceived definition that others are applying.

Feeling discouraged? Here is another way to look at the situation that somewhat moderates the gloomy picture. The solid line in **Figure 2** shows reported EPS for the S&P 500. Notice that year-on-year changes in EPS are quite volatile. The dotted line in the same figure shows operating EPS. We developed those data by going through the SEC filings for each of the companies in the S&P 500 for each quarter and adjusting the data in a manner consistent with a standard definition for U.S. GAAP. We would encourage the Financial Accounting Standards Board (FASB) to move forward on its project to codify this type of approach in a timely fashion.

Please note that operating earnings show less volatility than reported earnings. In contrast, reported earnings accentuate good news as well as bad news. This effect is even more dramatic when the data are extended out from 2000 though the current period. This addition includes the period of enormous accounting cleanup associated with the post-bubble period and is numerically driven by the billions of dollars of impaired goodwill belatedly recognized by large U.S. companies. The extensive and disappointing merger and acquisition activities of a handful of industries—media, telecom services, and some technology—were responsible for about 85 percent of the dollar amount of accounting adjustments for the entire S&P 500.

Note that GAAP-consistent operating earnings themselves are still imperfect for several reasons. One factor is the lagged nature of some accounting: Adjustments taken in any given quarter may reflect previous overstatements, not necessarily problems in that particular quarter. In other words, originally reported S&P 500 earnings and book values were too high and were corrected only years later. Earnings and book values were overstated in 1998 through 2000, which led to dramatic declines in reported earnings when accounting adjustments were made between

Figure 2. Reported and Operating EPS: S&P 500, 1986–2006

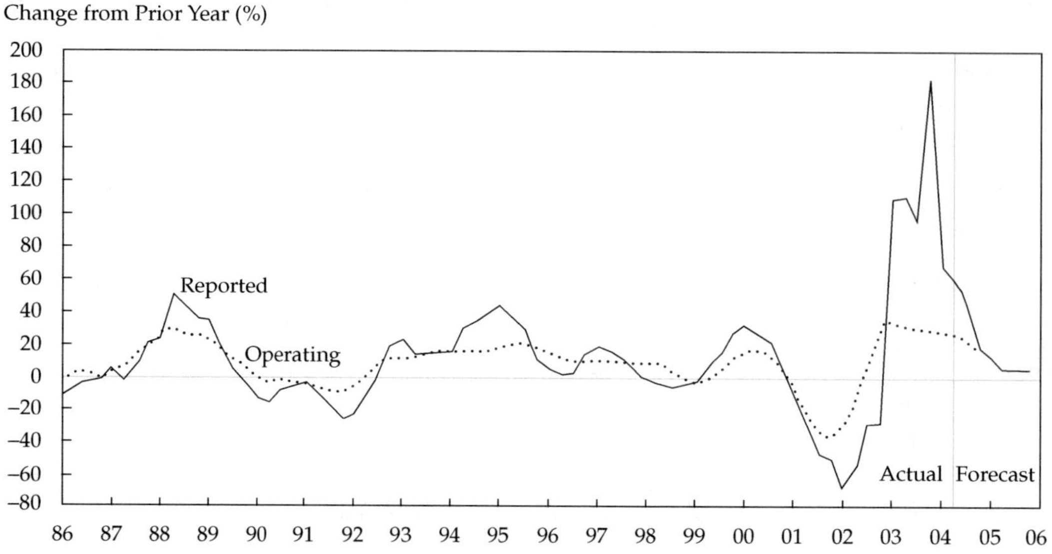

Note: Actual data from first quarter 1986 through second quarter 2004 (projected).

Sources: Based on data from Standard & Poor's and Goldman Sachs Portfolio Strategy.

late 2001 and year-end 2003. Those investors who based their valuation work on 2002 earnings, the year most afflicted by the adjustments, were making the same mistake (although in mirror image) as the mistake made in the late 1990s.

How does the situation stack up now? With regard to earnings information, the data quality is far better than before. The FASB and SEC have taken many dramatic steps over the past few years to improve the situation. Even more important, companies themselves have made many changes to improve the quality of their financial statements. The list of specific actions is lengthy, ranging from some provisions of the Sarbanes–Oxley Act of 2002 to changes in accounting standards for factors such as impaired goodwill and revenue recognition.

Even Assumed Constants Can Vary. Even some factors that investors regard as being fairly simple or straightforward, such as the dividend trend, can be easily misinterpreted. **Figure 3** reveals an uptrend in the dividend payments from U.S. corporations over the past few years. But some analysts are overanalyzing the data, responding to changes in quarterly data rather than the trend. Remember Aristotle's comment about volatility?

Dividend payments are among those items that exhibit strong seasonal patterns. Although investors typically remember to seasonally adjust economic data, they often forget to seasonally adjust some company data. Dividends are a great example. When a company's management decides to increase its dividend, the change most often occurs in the first half of the year, typically around the time of the annual meeting. Then, in the second half of the year, the company's excess cash tends to be used for other purposes, such as share repurchases or pension fund prepayments. Some investors have been extrapolating and annualizing volatile quarterly data on dividends, often reaching unfounded conclusions.

Figure 3. Number of U.S. Companies Instituting or Increasing Dividend Payments, 1991–2005

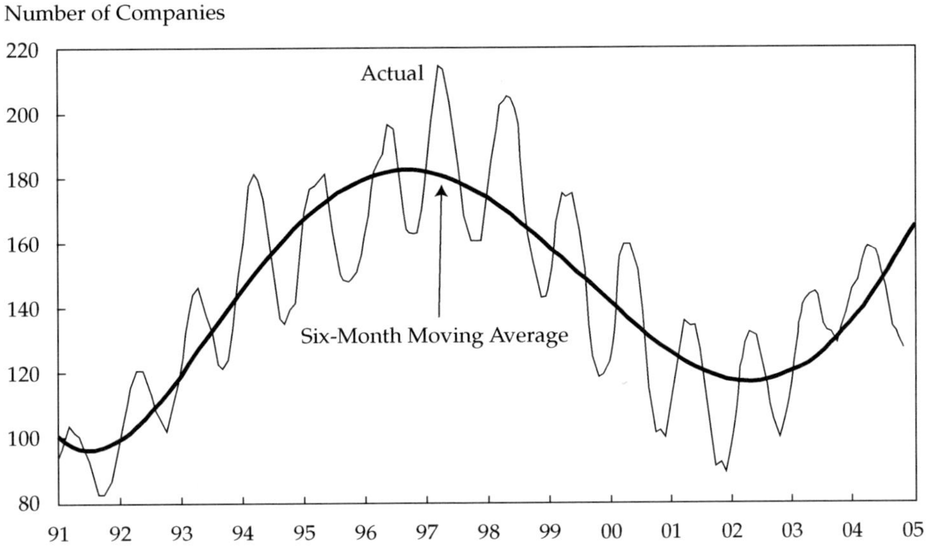

Note: Monthly data from January 1991 through October 2004.
Source: Based on data from Standard & Poor's.

The Long-Term Average Is the Arithmetic Mean, Not Necessarily Equilibrium. Another concern about the way investors view historical information relates to long-term averages. In many data series for the economy and market, the long-term average is the arithmetic mean, and the problem of focusing on this mean can be simply demonstrated by using the P/E multiple. Although I do not think a simple P/E multiple is the proper way to look at the market, especially across time periods, it is often used in this way. Over the past 75 years, the average price has been about 16–17 times earnings for the S&P 500. Many people simplistically assume that if the current P/E is above 17, then the market must be overpriced. Of course, this approach ignores other important factors, such as inflation, interest rates, long-term earnings growth, return on equity (ROE), and a host of other critical measures that have demonstrated effects on P/E multiples. For example, when inflation or interest rates are high, P/E multiples are low. When ROE and trend earnings growth are vigorous, P/E multiples are high. To ignore these other factors when considering market valuations is to rely on an incomplete and likely incorrect model. Indeed, most academics would agree that discounted cash flow (or discounted dividend) models, which incorporate these other variables, are among the most statistically robust valuation approaches for equities. Investor reliance on simple P/E approaches implies a willingness to assume that other factors—including inflation, interest rates, and earnings growth—never change. This certainly seems to be an unreasonable assumption.

Economic Data

In recent years, investors learned unhappy lessons about the poor quality of information coming from some companies and the need to dig deeper into its construction. But what about the quality of information coming from government agencies and the ease with which these data are misinterpreted?

The financial markets respond almost instantaneously to the public release of economic data. Yet, the quality of that data, especially prior to subsequent and standard revisions, may be poor. Enormous differences can exist from one source to another, with regard to both definitions and collection methodologies. This problem cuts across a whole host of economic data items where the quality can be questioned, even when there has been no intent to deceive. And the underlying definition matters a great deal yet receives little attention from many users.

Inflation statistics are a good first example. The U.S. Consumer Price Index, Producer Price Index, and GDP deflator can all lead to differing conclusions about the inflation rate because they are based on different methodologies and are sampling different parts of the economy. Another simple example is the monthly industrial production statistic, which many people view as clear-cut and accurate. Because of the frequency with which the data are collected, this metric is based on fairly small samples and is not particularly high in quality. Yet, investors respond to the monthly release almost immediately.

A third economic metric with similar issues of data sampling and sometimes dramatic post-release revisions is GDP. GDP data are typically not finalized for many quarters (three years is not an unusual length of time for all data to be collected and processed). Just as investors respond most notably to the pro forma earnings releases from companies, rather than the SEC filings that come later, they typically respond most vigorously to the first snapshot they have of economic data. Obviously, investors cannot wait for all the revisions before coming to a conclusion. But it is a problem if investors pay too much attention to the initial release while ignoring subsequent revisions. The misinterpretation can be compounded when users fail to recognize that many important economic metrics are derived from others. Consider that such critical factors as long-term productivity trends, which are essential to understanding the structural strengths of the economy, are calculated from measures that are subject to dramatic revision, such as GDP. In the 1990s, many economists looked at the then-reported GDP data and the then-reported industrial production data and concluded incorrectly that productivity growth was weak. When those data series, particularly the GDP data, were revised over the subsequent three years, the well-recognized conclusion was that labor productivity growth had indeed been outstanding during that period. Perhaps no single measure better describes the long-term prospects for economic growth and wealth creation than productivity, and yet it was woefully underestimated for several years.

Again, as investors, we need to respond on a short-term basis. But we also need to carefully regard the final version of the data to determine if our view of history should be changed, perhaps altering our views on future prospects.

A fourth confusing and sometimes misused statistic is the savings rate. There has been much hand-wringing about the low personal savings rate in the United States, and indeed it has declined in recent years. But try to understand what the standard savings rate is measuring. First, the commonly cited savings rate in the United States is the residual of GDP accounts. Think about that for a minute. The government adds up everything, and what is left over is the savings rate. That is not a high-quality way to collect information. Indeed, an alternative approach based on cumulative amounts moving into different financial vehicles, such as personal accounts, money market mutual funds, and so on, typically suggests a higher "savings" rate.

There is also a different point of view and definitional approach. Most Americans think of their savings during a time period as the increase in their wealth, which is a balance sheet approach to the issue. But the standard governmental approach is that of the income statement. Specifically, savings are not the increase in wealth but, rather, that portion of this period's income that has not been consumed. The difference can be intensified during periods of notable gains in assets, be they financial instruments or other family holdings, such as residential real estate. Specifically, when families see that their assets are increasing in value (and their balance sheet "savings" are rising), there is a tendency to save less out of current income, and the officially defined savings rate actually declines.

In fact, to further complicate the situation, there are circumstances in which a capital gain may further reduce the reported savings rate. Consider a simple example in which you own something that was initially worth $1,000 but is now valued at $2,000. You might look at that $1,000 increase in your balance sheet as an increase in savings. But the government accounting system does not count that $1,000 increase as a savings increase. The government does, however, account for the imputed tax on that capital gain that you will ultimately have to pay. So, in this hypothetical situation, you might think of your savings as having increased by $1,000, whereas the government would view your savings as having *declined* by $150 because of the imputed tax on the capital gain at a 15 percent rate. And you thought corporate accounting was odd!

Before leaving this subject, I would like to reiterate that the U.S. savings rate has indeed declined in recent years and is probably below an equilibrium level. However, any discussion of a specific estimate of what the rate is (or should be) must be held in the context of identifying the methodology most suited to the question.

Thus far, I have briefly discussed four examples of common problems with economic data. These are instances in which it is important to consider definitions of the data, the collection methodology, and ultimate revisions in the information. At this point, I will focus on a few statistics that are currently uppermost in investors' minds, not just those in the United States but those around the world, as they think about investing in U.S. assets: trade, employment and labor costs, the federal budget deficit, and global flows of capital.

Trade. Many investors have only a limited perspective on trade relationships. Yes, the United States has a very large trade deficit. Yes, the United States is the world's largest importer. But most months, the United States is also the world's largest exporting nation.

To understand this relationship, keep in mind that foreign trade is a fairly small part of the United States' overall GDP. Although it has roughly doubled from a few years ago, foreign trade is still less than 15 percent of U.S. GDP. But the U.S. GDP is the world's largest, and even a modest proportion represents a large dollar total.

Figure 4 shows the growth in the main components of GDP over time. GDP equals $C + I + G + (X - M)$, which is the summation of personal consumption, business investment, government expenditures, and net exports. Note that Figure 4 shows only exports rather than net exports (exports minus imports). Many people are surprised to see that during this time period, exports were the fastest growing sector of the U.S. economy. This is yet another example of why it is so important to look at data carefully and from different perspectives to fully understand the situation.

Although there is much discussion among investors, policymakers, and citizens about the trade deficit, there is also little recognition that the data are typically of poor quality. That is not just my view; it is the view of the U.S. Department of Commerce and other agencies, here and in other nations, that collect the data. Part of the problem is that import data are typically cleaner and timelier than export data, the reason being that the government collects duties and tariffs on imports. Because it does not collect duties or tariffs on exports, they are typically not counted as carefully. Furthermore, there is typically a time-lag between the collection of import data and the collection of export data.

Figure 4. Components of GDP, 1987–2004

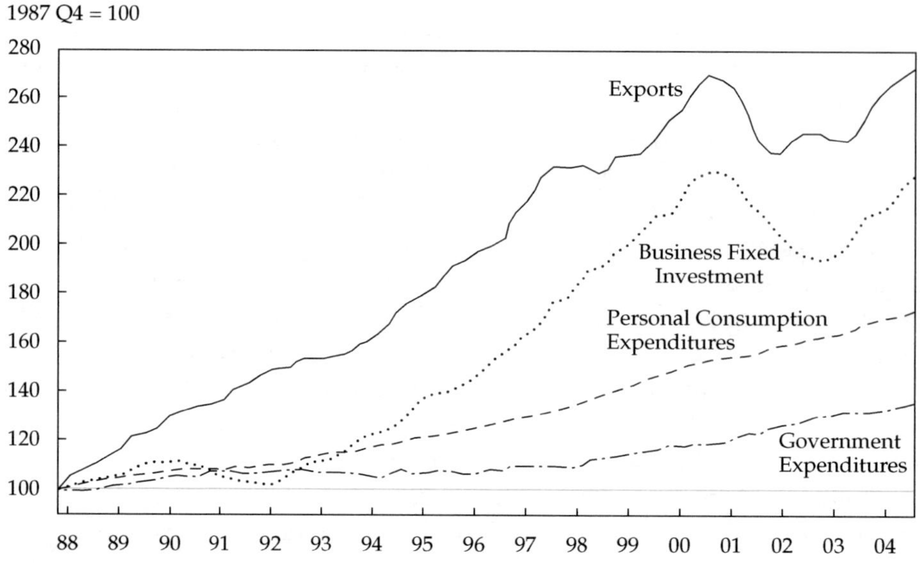

Note: Data from fourth quarter 1987 through third quarter 2004 (projected).

Source: Based on data from the Bureau of Economic Analysis.

According to some estimates, the United States could be undercounting aggregate exports by roughly 10 percent, with even larger discrepancies in some categories of goods. This suggests that the U.S. trade deficit is likely not as large as the standard published numbers suggest. The other major question, which is discussed later, involves the effect of the activities of multinational corporations. Specifically, much of what is imported into the United States is produced by U.S. companies with operations outside the country. Does our system of trade accounting properly reflect this factor—and the output of facilities in the United States owned by non-U.S. companies?

More information and insight can be found by considering the specific trade balances with particular countries and regions. **Table 1** compares U.S. exports and imports with various areas of the world. Notice that, by far, the United States' most important trade partners are its neighbors in North America. But, of course, the trade statistics with Canada and Mexico also reflect much of the movement across borders as goods are partially assembled in one country and re-exported to another.

Consider, for example, a situation in which a U.S. auto company manufactures some parts in Michigan, exports them to Canada for assembly, and then imports them back into the United States. The data reconciliation process is difficult, and although the U.S.–Canada trade data are the best, the data quality for relationships outside North America can be quite poor. Just imagine the complications for products where parts come from many nations, are assembled in others, and are ultimately sold somewhere else.

These technical data issues can be quite important given the focus of policymakers in many nations. There is much focus, for example, on U.S. trade relations with Asia. But in a surprise to many, Western Europe is by far the United States' largest trade customer outside North America.

Table 1. Share of U.S. Trade: October 2003 through September 2004

	U.S. Exports		U.S. Imports	
Country/Region	$ Billions	Share	$ Billions	Share
North America	$292.2	36.6%	$ 397.7	28.3%
Western Europe	178.9	22.4	289.8	20.6
Japan	49.3	6.2	126.8	9.0
Central/South America	53.9	6.8	92.1	6.5
China	32.1	4.0	183.7	13.1
South Korea	23.9	3.0	44.6	3.2
Total	$797.8	100.0%	$1,405.9	100.0%

Sources: Based on data from Goldman Sachs Portfolio Strategy and the U.S. Department of Commerce.

As can be seen from Table 1, the 12-month trade deficit with Western Europe was approximately $110 billion as of September 2004. Although it represents the United States' second largest trade deficit, the issue does not receive much attention, despite its great importance.

When there is discussion about currencies or the appropriate policies to be undertaken by the U.S. Federal Reserve or Treasury, care should be taken to ensure that there is a clear understanding of the trade picture, such as details regarding the nations with whom the United States has meaningful imbalances and the reasons for those trade imbalances, including the specific goods and services that are involved. As **Figure 5** illustrates, U.S. imports from Europe have grown at a rate that is roughly commensurate with the growth of the U.S. economy. As the U.S. economy has grown, aggregate domestic demand has increased, and consequently, imports have increased. The dramatic conclusion to be drawn from the data is that U.S. exports to Europe have not grown at all since the fourth quarter of 1997. Sluggish growth in continental Europe has meant little capital spending there; much of the prior growth in our exports there involved capital goods, aircraft, and avionics. Despite the current public focus on Japan and China, the trade situation with Europe requires careful review.

The largest U.S. trade imbalance is with China, a nation that is itself now running large trade deficits with other countries. Indeed, the large Chinese trade surplus with the United States is unusual because China has become a notable importer of many commodities, capital goods, and other items from other nations in Asia and elsewhere. As shown in **Figure 6**, U.S. imports from China have grown dramatically, again as U.S. aggregate demand has increased and as Chinese suppliers have increased their market share. Indeed, consider the following data problem. It is estimated that roughly 30 percent of U.S. imports from China are from facilities built or owned by U.S. companies for the primary purpose of bringing the goods back to the United States. The consequences of this situation must be considered in discussions about foreign exchange and trade policy. For example, when such a large percentage of U.S. imports from China is coming from U.S.-linked producers, changes in currency exchange rates will have limited impact on decisions about sourcing from these manufacturers.

In summary, the main point is that investors should be leery of simple analysis and simple conclusions because there is not one trade imbalance and the issues vary by country, currency, and the specific products involved. The classic trade model, based on simplistic bilateral relationships, doesn't properly capture more complex global trade patterns.

Figure 5. U.S. Trade with Europe, 1986–2003

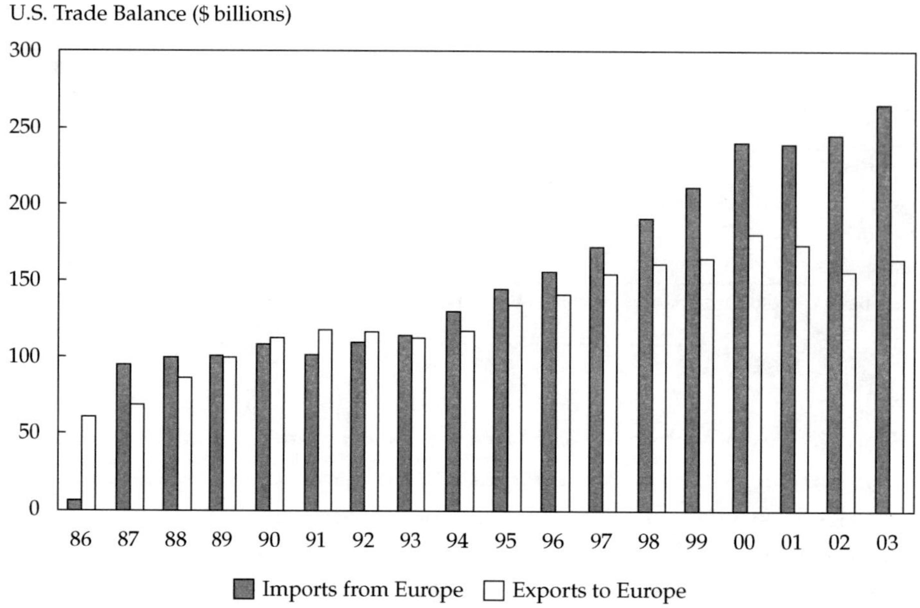

Sources: Based on data from Goldman Sachs Portfolio Strategy and the U.S. Department of Commerce.

Figure 6. U.S. Trade with China, 1986–2003

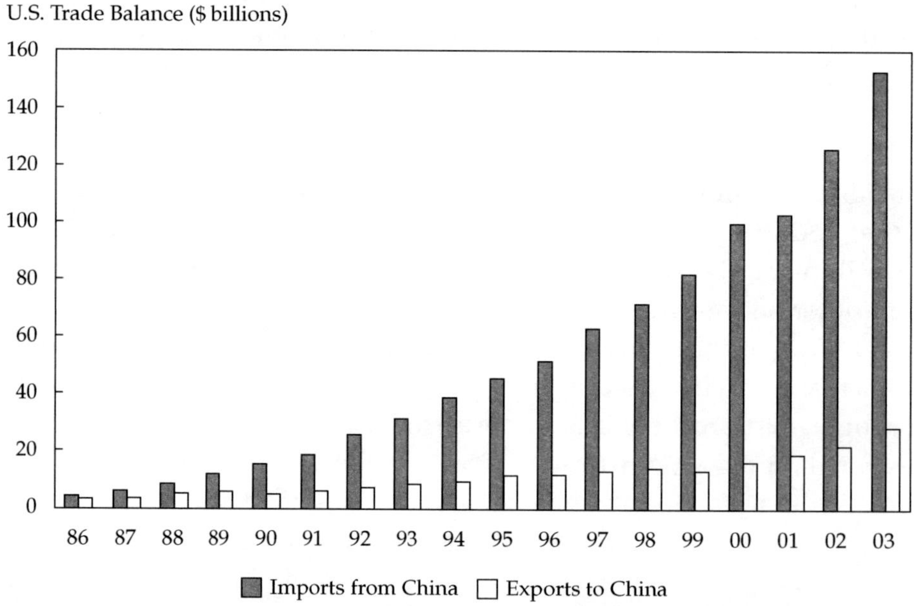

Sources: Based on data from Goldman Sachs Portfolio Strategy and the U.S. Department of Commerce.

Employment and Labor Costs. Another broad area in which investors would be well served to think more carefully about the quality and true implications of the data is employment and labor costs.

- *Employment*. The reported unemployment rate, currently 5.5 percent, is only slightly above the long-term average and is about half the unemployment rate in parts of Europe. So, why are many U.S. households, particularly middle- and lower-income households, not feeling all that comfortable about the employment situation? Answers can be found in exploring additional information beyond the headline unemployment rate.

For example, investors should take note of data on "discouraged" workers—that is, those unemployed workers who have stopped actively looking for jobs because they do not think they can find them. The current number of discouraged workers is among the highest ever seen. The standard Bureau of Labor Statistics definition of the unemployment rate excludes these individuals from the calculation of the labor force. In the commonly reported unemployment rate, U-3, the number of unemployed workers is divided by the labor force, but these discouraged workers are not counted in either the numerator or the denominator.

The median duration of unemployment is another valuable metric that receives little attention. During the last recession, it took a previously employed worker about 6 weeks to find a new job. It now takes almost 10 weeks, which helps explain why consumer confidence has not recovered to the levels generally seen when the unemployment rate is around the current 5.5 percent.

Also afflicting consumer confidence, but not notably impeding the U-3 unemployment rate, is the fact that many of the new jobs that have been created have been part-time, rather than full-time, jobs and temporary, rather than permanent. An alternative unemployment metric computed by the Bureau of Labor Statistics, U-6, tries to incorporate these other factors and now stands at about 9 percent. This number might be more consistent with the lackluster confidence data, especially for lower- and middle-income households. It is also important to note that about two-thirds of the jobs lost during the last recession were among these income categories.

- *Labor costs*. Labor costs are critically important to analysts in several ways; for example, labor costs are important to economists contemplating long-term economic growth and to investment analysts considering near-term profit margins. Employment costs in the United States are presently increasing at a 4.0–4.5 percent annualized rate before adjustment for productivity growth. Interestingly, salaries are growing relatively slower, at about 2.5 percent. But benefits are surging at about triple the rate of salaries, as shown in **Figure 7**. Much of this growth is concentrated in the cost of health care benefits and, to a lesser extent, pension costs. This trend may at least partly explain why much job creation has been for part-time and temporary positions. In most cases, part-time and temporary workers are not eligible for benefits.

One other factor must be considered when reviewing labor costs. Although compensation expenses are rising, in nearly every industry, unit labor costs, which are labor costs adjusted for productivity, are flat to down. This helps explain why profit margins have been at such high levels. Although productivity growth is now trending lower, as it does as every economy cycle progresses, the trend growth rate in productivity appears to exceed 2.5 percent. (Some economists believe that the rate exceeds 3 percent.) If maintained, companies can afford to pay their workers an increasing amount, yet the net increase in unit cost is small because the productivity gains are offsetting higher labor costs.

Figure 7. Benefits Costs vs. Wage and Salary Costs, 1982–2004

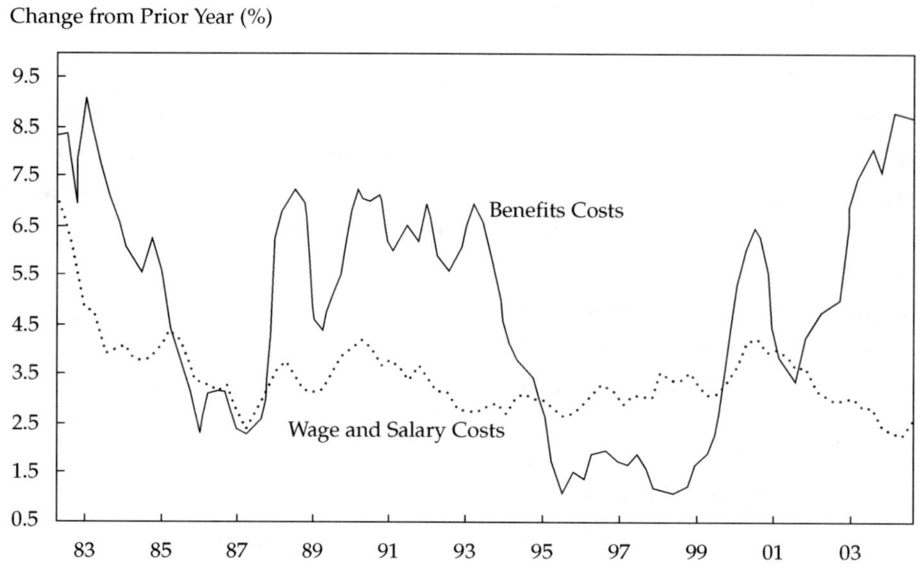

Note: Data from second quarter 1982 through third quarter 2004.
Source: Based on data from the Bureau of Labor Statistics.

Federal Budget Deficit. The federal budget deficit has noteworthy implications for many aspects of economic and investment decision making. Thus far, I have talked about some questionable accounting for companies and some awkward accounting for government data on economic performance. But the government itself has some odd accounting applied to its own accounts and the federal budget. For example, the federal budget contains many large off-balance-sheet items, including Social Security and Medicare. And on the other side of the balance sheet are dramatic questions about the proper accounting for government-owned assets.

Figure 8 shows the federal budget deficit. The bars show it in terms of dollars, and the solid line shows it as a percentage of GDP. Using data for FY 2004, the United States is currently running about a $410 billion deficit, which is about 3.5 percent of GDP. Based on financial market reactions, this deficit is not yet a problem.

There may be large changes in the coming years. Factors that could keep the deficit growing, both in terms of dollars and as a percentage of GDP, include the following: first, ongoing expenditures for military actions in Iraq and Afghanistan; second, President Bush's proposal to make the 2001–03 tax cuts permanent, although most had been introduced as needed stimulus following the recession and had specific "sunset" rules attached; and third, some versions of proposed Social Security reform, which could increase the budget deficit by $100 billion annually, although there are disagreements about the specific financing requirements. Budget analysts will attempt to distinguish between cyclical and structural deficits, the latter being more tenacious and more likely to disturb the financial markets.

What is the bottom line? The structural budget deficit can have a significant impact on cost of capital and can have a significant impact on the dollar. Suffice it to say, budget deficits are large numbers. Years ago, Senator Dirkson of Illinois reminded us that "a billion here and a billion

Figure 8. Federal Budget, 1967–2003

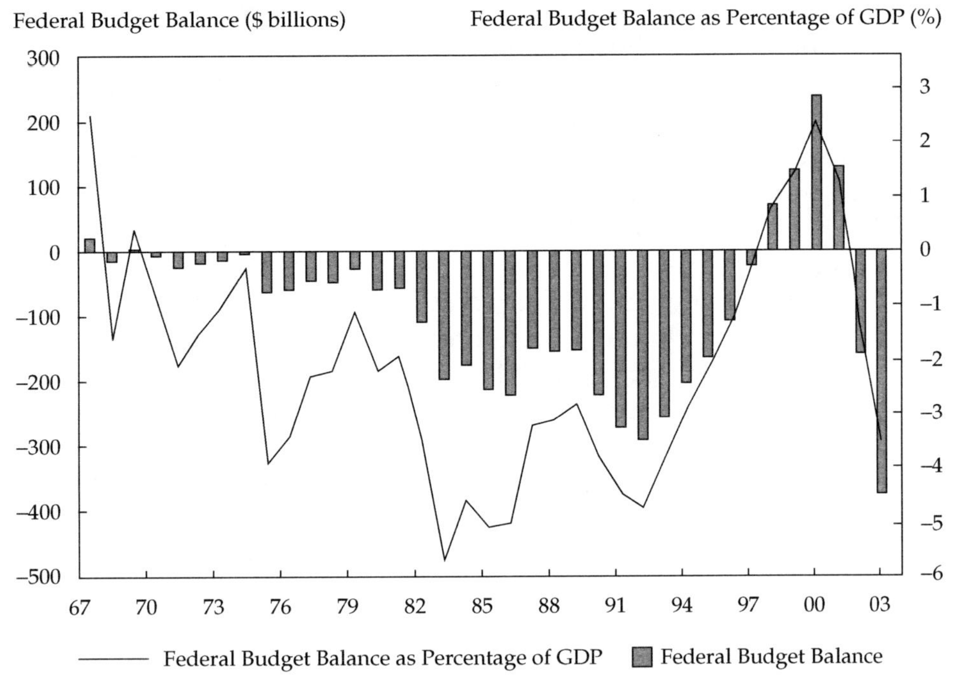

Sources: Based on data from the U.S. Department of the Treasury and Goldman Sachs Portfolio Strategy.

there . . . it adds up to real money." Moreover, deficits are notoriously difficult to forecast. This is not a political statement at all. A decade ago, the common forecast was that by the end of the 1990s the United States would have a budget deficit in excess of $500 billion. The United States had a surplus of $300 billion. The forecasters did not even get the sign right. Forecasting the federal budget is subject to the vagaries of economic forecasts, government accounting, and forecasting future policies.

Global Flows of Capital. Much current concern surrounds what foreign investors might do with regard to dollar-denominated assets. The United States is the world's largest importer but has also been the world's largest exporter. The United States is the world's largest debtor (in terms of dollars, if not as a percentage of national income), but it is also the world's largest investor. The conversation about the current account is subject to the same data concerns afflicting discussions about key components, such as the trade and budget balances. Assume that non-U.S. investors conclude that the dollar may decline in value and, therefore, have an unpleasant view on holding dollar-denominated assets. Where is the impact most likely to be seen? The usual, overly simplistic, conclusion is that all U.S. markets could be vulnerable and that all foreign participants would be aggressive sellers. But consider the markets separately and also look at particular holders.

Non-U.S. investors own about 10 percent of the U.S. stock market. Therefore, the direct effects of a currency decline are not likely to be large. Indeed, it is possible to argue that U.S. corporate profits would benefit from a declining dollar, providing some offset in the equity market.

Non-U.S. investors own about 24 percent of the U.S. corporate bond market and about 43 percent of the U.S. Treasury market. It would appear that fixed-income markets would be more vulnerable to a reduction in foreign buying interest.

Now, look at the markets, and their ownership, more closely. Specifically, which non-U.S. investors and which currencies are involved? As **Table 2** shows, the top three holders of U.S. Treasury securities are Japan, China, and the United Kingdom. But the motivations of the holders in these three nations are likely quite different. For example, most of the participation in U.S. capital markets from the United Kingdom relates to the activities of global portfolio managers and their asset allocation decisions. They are likely to respond to projected changes in currency, for example. In addition, U.K.-based holders of U.S. Treasury securities may be pension funds that are seeking to match long-term liabilities with long-duration assets. But for the other large holders of U.S. fixed-income securities, the decision to hold dollars is not a portfolio manager's decision. Instead, the major holders in these nations may be governmental entities that hold dollars for reasons involving foreign exchange reserves, large current surpluses, currency support, and the like. Simply stated, a nation with a large trade surplus with the United States is likely to be a large holder of dollars.

Recent flow data can be seen in **Table 3.** The largest foreign participant in the U.S. Treasury market has been Japan. Please note that, despite much recent attention, the Chinese have a much smaller role in the U.S. Treasury market.

Although much of this participation is from the Japanese government, some involves Japanese financial intermediaries, such as insurance companies that have sold fixed-income vehicles to their own customers. They have a choice: funding with U.S. Treasury securities yielding 4 percent or funding with Japanese government bonds at three-quarters of a percent. The data for 1999, 2000, and 2001 show that when many non-U.S. investors were selling U.S. securities, Japanese investors were not. This may have involved the Japanese financial companies that desired higher yields than were available in their domestic markets, and also currency intervention by the government.

Table 2. Foreign Holdings of U.S. Treasury Securities
($ billions)

Country	September 2004
Japan	$ 720.4
China (ex Hong Kong)	174.4
United Kingdom	134.6
Caribbean[a]	100.3
South Korea	66.6
Taiwan	57.4
Germany	51.0
Hong Kong	49.5
Switzerland	48.5
OPEC	43.1
Total foreign holdings	$1,854.8
Total government holdings	$1,117.5

[a]Caribbean includes Bahamas, Bermuda, Cayman Islands, Netherlands Antilles, and Panama.

Source: Based on data from the U.S. Department of the Treasury.

Table 3. Foreign Net Purchases of U.S. Treasuries ($ billions)

Country	1999	2000	2001	2002	2003
Europe	–$38.2	–$50.7	–$20.6	$ 43.7	$ 51.1
Netherlands	2.1	2.1	–6.7	–7.0	–0.2
United Kingdom	–20.2	–33.7	–7.3	61.6	36.0
Latin America—Caribbean	–7.5	–4.9	4.3	20.0	25.5
Asia	29.4	1.6	36.3	55.7	184.5
China	8.2	–4.0	19.1	24.1	30.5
Hong Kong	0.9	–0.3	7.2	–9.1	6.1
Japan	20.1	10.6	16.1	30.5	148.8
Australia	–0.4	2.5	1.1	–2.2	1.6
Total	–$10.0	–$54.0	$18.5	$119.9	$278.1

Source: Based on data from the U.S. Department of the Treasury.

One other point to make here relates to the flow of capital from the United States elsewhere. Foreign direct investment is often a good leading indicator. In 2003, U.S. net flows into foreign equity markets amounted to $71 billion, which was the single largest amount for the United States. Some of this flow is related to enthusiasm for the more volatile and higher-returning markets available in Asia last year, but some of it represents a return to diversification principles. Americans had notably undiversified portfolios over the past decade and are now returning to broader allocations with regard to both assets and country weightings. Data in recent months clearly suggest a renewed appetite for non-U.S. equities.

Conclusion

Recall that I started this presentation with Aristotle. I would like to end with a philosopher of our times, Peter Bernstein (1996):

> It is one thing to set up a mathematical model that appears to explain everything. . . . [But] the mathematically driven apparatus of modern . . . [investing] contains the seeds of a dehumanizing and self-destructive technology. . . . Our lives teem with numbers, but we sometimes forget that numbers are only tools. (pp. 6–7)

My message is twofold. First, there are many numbers available to investors, but many of them are not well understood. Many of them are misinterpreted, not just those related to corporate performance but also those related to the economy. Second, models work when they are appropriate for the particular circumstance, but some of the best investment judgments over time have come when people recognized that models derived in other periods were broken or not directly relevant.

Reference

Bernstein, Peter L. 1996. *Against the Gods: The Remarkable Story of Risk*. New York: John Wiley & Sons.

Value and Risk: Beyond Betas

Aswath Damodaran

Risk is narrowly defined in most financial analyses as systematic or nondiversifiable risk, and its effects on value are isolated to the discount rate. Generally, the costs of equity and capital are set higher for riskier companies and the resulting value is considered to be risk adjusted. In conjunction, risk management is considered to be primarily defensive—that is, firms protecting themselves against risks by using risk-hedging products, such as derivatives and insurance. I argue here for both a more expansive analysis of risk in valuation and a much broader definition of risk management. I believe that effective risk management can sometimes include aggressively seeking out and exploiting risk and that it can alter investment policy and affect expected cash flows.

Hedging company-specific risk can endanger firm value, but risk management can actually increase firm value.

Risk Management vs. Risk Reduction

The Chinese symbol for risk is a combination of two symbols—one for danger and one for opportunity. Although risk can have very negative consequences for those who are exposed to it, risk is also the reason for higher returns to those who use it to their advantage. Risk management as defined in practice misses this important duality and focuses on the negative consequences of risk. In fact, when risk management is discussed in corporate offices, consulting firms, and investments banks, what is being talked about is *risk reduction*, usually through the use of derivatives and insurance.

Risk reduction is a part of risk management, but it is only a part. Risk management has to be defined far more broadly to include actions that are taken by firms to *exploit uncertainty*. In fact, risk management may involve increasing, rather than decreasing, exposure to at least some types of risks when a firm

Aswath Damodaran is professor of finance and David Margolis Teaching Excellence Fellow at Stern School of Business, New York University, New York City.

believes that increasing the risk will give it an advantage over its competitors. To understand the difference between risk reduction and risk management, consider the following examples:

- Pfizer buys foreign currency options to protect itself against exchange rate risk; this action is risk *reduction*, and the payoff takes the form of smoother earnings and, perhaps, higher firm value. Pfizer restructures its research and development department to ensure that its product pipeline will remain full and balanced, with a mix of products at different stages in the U.S. Food and Drug Administration approval cycle. This action is risk *management* because it could well be the catalyst that allows Pfizer to dominate its competitors (e.g., Merck & Co. and Bristol-Myers Squibb Company) who have let their pipelines run dry or become unbalanced.
- A gold-mining company buys futures contracts to protect its earnings from a drop in gold prices; this action is clearly risk hedging. The same company revamps its mining facilities to speed up the production and delivery of gold, allowing it to ramp up production if gold prices go up; this action is risk management and could provide a competitive advantage in the long term.

These examples illustrate two clear differences between risk hedging and risk management. The first is that risk hedging is primarily about protecting against risk whereas risk management is about using risk to advantage. The second is that risk hedging is product based and financial (note the use of options, futures, and insurance products) whereas risk management is strategic.

Risk and Value: Conventional View

How does risk show up in conventional valuations? To answer this question, we will look at the two most common approaches to valuation. The first is intrinsic or discounted cash flow (DCF) valuation, in which the value of a firm or asset is estimated by discounting the expected cash flows back to the present. The second is relative valuation, in which the value of a firm is estimated by looking at how the market prices similar firms.

Risk and DCF Value. Much of what we know about risk in finance comes from the groundbreaking work done by Harry Markowitz and others studying portfolio theory in the 1950s and 1960s. In the process of considering how diversification affects portfolio risk, they considered the relationship between the expected returns on investments and the investments' risks. In keeping with this tradition, we still adjust the returns expected by equity investors in a stock (i.e., the cost of equity) for the risk of the stock and adjust the returns demanded by lenders to the firm (i.e., the cost of debt) for the default risk of the firm. In other words, the risk adjustment in valuation is entirely in the discount rate.

In equity valuation models, the cost of equity becomes the vehicle for risk adjustment, with riskier companies having higher costs of equity. In fact, if we use the capital asset pricing model to estimate the cost of equity, the beta used carries the entire burden of risk adjustment. In firm valuation models, more components are affected by risk (the cost of debt also tends to be higher for riskier firms, and these firms often cannot afford to borrow as much, which leads to lower debt ratios), but the bottom line is that the cost of capital is the only input in the valuation that we adjust for risk.[1] The cash flows in DCF models represent expected values, estimated either by making the most reasonable assumptions about revenues, growth, and margins for the future or by forecasting cash flows for a range of scenarios, attaching probabilities to each of the scenarios, and taking the expected values across the scenarios.

If the only input in a DCF model that is sensitive to risk is the discount rate and the only risk that matters when it comes to estimating discount rates is market risk (or risk that cannot be diversified away), the payoff to hedging risk in terms of higher value is likely to be limited and the payoff to risk management will be difficult to trace.

Relative Valuation Models. For better or worse, most valuations are relative valuations, in which a stock is valued on the basis of how similar companies are priced by the market. In practice, relative valuations take the form of a multiple applied to comparable firms; for example, a firm is viewed as cheap if it trades at 10 times earnings when comparable companies trade at 15 times earnings. Although the logic of this approach seems unassailable, problems arise in the definition of comparable firms and how analysts deal with the inevitable differences among these so-called comparable firms.

Although risk adjustment in DCF models is too narrow and focuses too much on the discount rate, risk adjustment in relative valuation can range from being nonexistent, at worst, to being haphazard and arbitrary, at best.

- When risk adjustment is nonexistent, analysts compare the pricing of firms in the same sector without adjusting for risk, thereby making the implicit assumption that risk exposure is the same for all firms in a business. For example, the P/Es of software firms may be compared with each other with no real thought given to risk because of the assumption that all software firms are equally risky.
- Relative valuations that claim to adjust for risk do so in arbitrary ways. Typically, analysts propose a risk measure (with little or no backing for its relationship to value) and then use the measure to compare companies. They then follow up by adjusting the values of companies that look risky according to this measure. If this description sounds harsh, consider a typical analyst who computes P/Es for software companies and then proceeds to argue that firms that have less volatile earnings or consistently meet analyst earnings estimates should trade at a premium to the sector because they have little risk. Unless this judgment is backed up by evidence that this measure of risk is indeed reasonable, it is an adjustment with no basis in fact.

If the assessment of risk in relative valuations is nonexistent or arbitrary, it should come as no surprise that firms that try to improve their relative value will adopt risk management practices that correspond to analyst measures of risk. For example, if earnings stability becomes the proxy measure for risk used by analysts and markets, firms will expend their resources smoothing out earnings streams by hedging against all kinds of risk.

Expanding the Analysis of Risk

The sanguine view that firm-specific risk is diversifiable and that it thus does not affect value is challenged by many managers. Many top corporate executives believe that conventional valuation models take too narrow a view of risk and do not fully factor in the consequences of significant risk exposure. In this section, we will consider ways in which we can expand the discussion of risk in valuation.

Simulations. In both DCF and relative valuation models, we use expected values for the inputs—earnings, cash flows, growth, and discount rates—and arrive at a base-case valuation. Even if our expectations are unbiased and reflect all available information, we are ignoring the reality that each of the expected values comes from a distribution that may reflect a great deal of uncertainty. Therefore, some analysts believe that valuations are enriched when we use all of the available information in the distribution to arrive at a range of values rather than one base-case number; thus, these analysts argue that simulations are an effective tool for risk analysis.

True?

Even if we accept this point of view, consider the inputs that we need for an effective simulation to be run. Assume for the moment that we are able to use either historical or cross-sectional data to make reasonable assumptions about the distributions of the input variables in a valuation. Because these distributions reflect both good and bad outcomes—revenues falling and rising, positive and negative margins—some analysts operate under the misconception that simulations represent risk adjustment. They do not. The final distribution of values that we get from the simulations will have an expected value and dispersion around that value. The expected value across thousands of simulations itself is not risk adjusted in any sense and will often be higher than the expected value from a conventional base-case valuation in which expected values for each input are used for the estimation.

Also note that the payoff to hedging risk is presented in simulations as a reduction in the dispersion of values around an expected value, but this representation is misleading. Reducing a firm's exposure to any risk can indeed reduce the standard deviation in the value of that firm as a stand-alone investment, but the real question is whether this change translates into an increase in firm value. In the terminology of risk and return models, the reduction of firm-specific risk may reduce dispersion in firm value in a simulation but may not increase the value of the firm.

I do not mean to suggest that simulations are not useful to us in understanding risk. Looking at the variance of the simulated values around the expected value provides a visual reminder that we are estimating value in an uncertain environment. Also, we may be able to use this variance as a decision tool in portfolio management for choosing between two stocks that are equally undervalued but have different value distributions. The stock with the less volatile value distribution may be considered the better investment. To use simulations as a tool in risk hedging, we have to introduce a constraint that, if violated, creates large costs for the firm and perhaps even causes its demise. A good example is regulatory capital ratios that banks have to maintain to stay in business. With the constraint in place, we can then evaluate the effectiveness of risk-hedging tools by examining the likelihood that the constraint will be violated with each one and weighing that probability off against the cost of the tool.

DCF Valuation. The value of a firm can generally be considered a function of four key inputs: (1) *cash flow from assets in place* or investments already made, (2) *expected growth rate in the cash flows* during what we can term a period of both high growth and excess returns (when the firm earns more than its cost of capital on its investments), (3) *length of time before the firm becomes a stable growth firm* earning no excess returns, and (4) the *discount rate* reflecting the risk of the operating assets of the firm and the financial leverage used to fund these assets. **Figure 1** summarizes the process and the inputs in a DCF model.

Figure 1. Determinants of Value

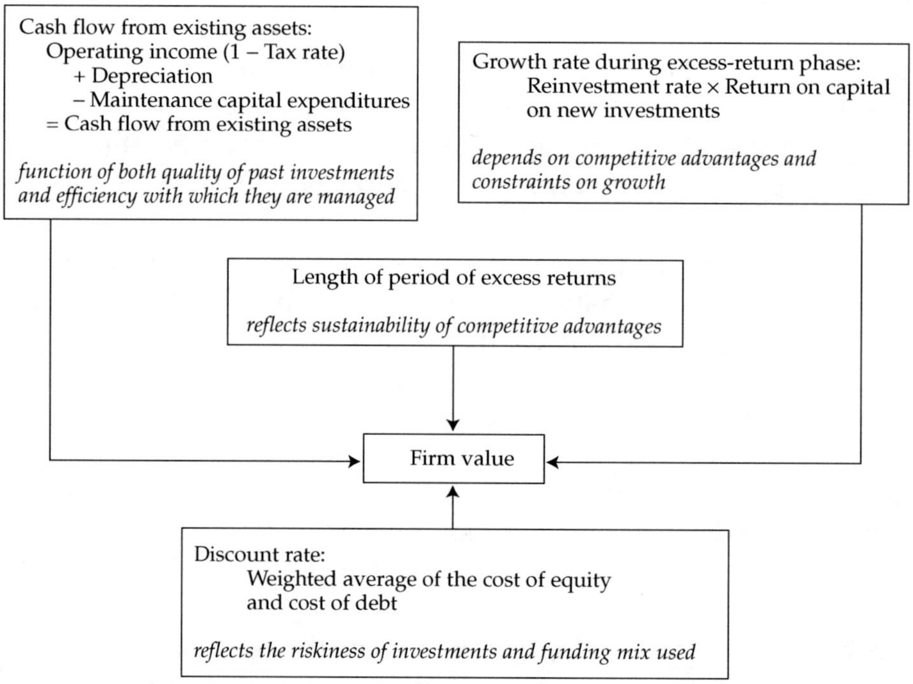

Clearly, for a firm to increase its value, it has to do one or more of the following: (1) generate more cash flows from existing assets, (2) grow faster or more efficiently during the high-growth phase, (3) lengthen the high-growth and excess-return phase, or (4) lower the cost of capital. To the extent that risk management can help in these endeavors, it can create value.

For a more complete sense of how risk affects value, we have to look at its impact not only on the discount rate but also on the other determinants of value. In other words, we have to consider the effects of risk on cash flows from existing assets, growth during the excess-return phase, and the length of the excess-return phase. **Exhibit 1** provides the possible effects of risk hedging and risk management on each of these inputs.

Relative Valuation. Although DCF models allow a great deal of flexibility when it comes to risk management, they also require information on the specific effects of risk hedging and risk management on the inputs to the models. One way to bypass this requirement is to look at whether the market rewards companies that hedge or manage risk and, if it does, to estimate how high a price it is willing to pay for either risk hedging or risk management.

A firm that hedges risk more effectively than its competitors should have more stable earnings and stock prices. If the market values these characteristics, as proponents of risk hedging argue, the market should attach a higher value to this firm than to a competitor that does not hedge risk. To examine whether this effect occurs, we could look at a group of comparable companies and either identify the companies that we know use risk-hedging products or come up with quantifiable measures of the effects of risk hedging; two obvious choices are earnings variability and stock price variability. We could then compare the market values of these companies with their book values,

Exhibit 1. Risk Hedging, Risk Management, and Value

Valuation Component	Effect of Risk Hedging	Effect of Risk Management
Costs of equity and capital	Reduces cost of equity for private and closely held firms. Reduces cost of debt for heavily levered firms with significant distress risk and may reduce cost of capital as a consequence.	May increase cost of equity and capital if firm increases exposure to risks where it believes it has a differential advantage.
Cash flow to the firm	Cost of risk hedging reduces earnings. Smoothing out earnings may reduce taxes paid over time.	Effective risk management can increase operating margins and cash flows.
Expected growth rate during high-growth period	Reducing risk exposure may make managers more comfortable taking risky (and good) investments. Increase in reinvestment rate increases growth.	Exploiting opportunities created by risk allows the firm to earn a higher return on capital on its new investments.
Length of high-growth period	No effect.	Strategic risk management can create a long-term competitive advantage and increase length of growth period.

revenues, or earnings and relate the levels of these multiples to the risk-hedging practices of the firms. If risk hedging pays off in higher value, firms that hedge risk and reduce earnings or price variability should trade at higher multiples than firms that do not.

Option-Pricing Models. A fourth way of looking at the value of risk hedging and risk management is to use option-pricing models. In this framework, risk hedging is essentially the equivalent of buying a put option against specific eventualities and risk management gives the firm the equivalent of a call option.

Risk hedging as a put option is illustrated in **Figure 2**. If we can estimate a standard deviation in firm value, we can value the put option and, by doing so, attach a value to risk hedging. Because this protection will come at a cost, we can then consider the trade-off. If the cost of adding the protection is less than the value created by the protection, risk hedging will increase the value of the firm:

Value of firm after risk hedging
= Value of firm without risk hedging
+ Value of put (risk hedging)
– Cost of risk hedging.

Figure 2. Payoff Diagram for Risk Hedging

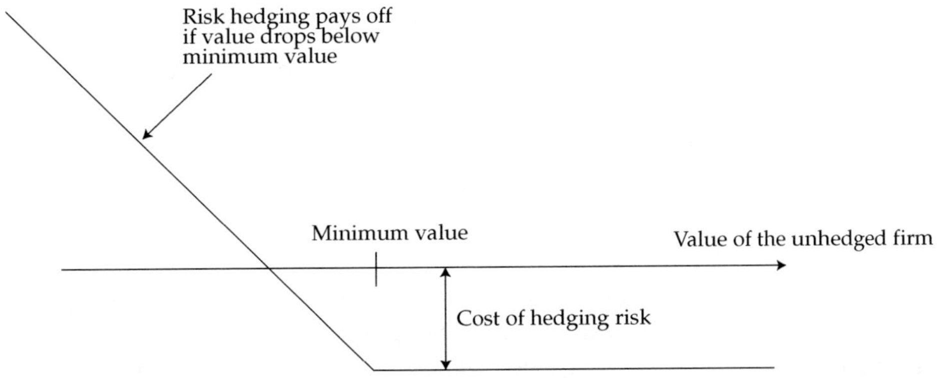

The value of hedging risk increases as the volatility in firm value increases and with the degree of protection against downside risk. The cost of hedging risk can be compared with these values to assess whether hedging the risk makes sense in the first place.

Although the value of risk management as a call option can also be shown in terms of payoff diagrams, defining the parameters and valuing the option is far more difficult. In fact, many of the practical problems we run into in valuing real options also show up if we try to value risk management as an option.

Final Assessment of Risk Management

Two extreme views dominate the risk management debate, and they are both rooted in risk hedging. One perspective, adopted by portfolio theorists and believers in efficient markets, is that risk hedging on the part of firms is almost always useless and will generally decrease the firm's value. Although proponents of this view concede that risk hedging potentially provides tax benefits (even though the benefits are likely to be small) and possibly produces a savings in distress cost, they argue that diversified investors can manage risk exposure in their portfolios much more effectively and with lower costs than managers in individual firms. At the other extreme are those who sell risk-hedging products and essentially argue that reducing risk reduces variability in earnings and price, which yields a payoff to the firm in the form of a higher stock price. Neither side makes a meaningful distinction between risk hedging and risk management.

I think there is an intermediate view on hedging risk that makes more sense. Risk hedging is most likely to generate value for small, closely held firms or firms with substantial debt and distress costs. It is also most likely to create value if it is focused on hedging risks for which investors cannot buy risk protection through market-traded securities.

As for risk management, all firms are exposed to risk and should, therefore, consider risk management an integral part of doing business. Effective risk management is about strategic rather than financial choices. Its effects for all firms will show up in increasing value as it creates higher and more sustainable excess returns. The benefits of risk management are likely to be greatest, however, in businesses with the following characteristics:

- *High volatility.* The greater the range of firm-specific risks a firm is exposed to, the greater the potential for risk management. After all, it is the uncertainty about the future that risk management exploits to advantage.
- *Strong barriers to entry.* Because the payoff to risk management shows up as higher returns, it is likely to create more value when new entrants can be kept out of the business, because of either infrastructure needs (e.g., in the aerospace and automobile industries) or legal constraints, such as patents or regulation (e.g., in pharmaceuticals and financial services).

Given that risk management can have such high payoffs, what lies behind the lack of emphasis on it by firms' financial managers? There are several reasons. First, the emphasis in risk management on strategic rather than financial considerations pushes it into the realm of corporate strategy. Second, tracing the payoff from risk management is far more difficult than tracing the payoff from risk hedging. Those who sell risk-hedging products can point to the benefits of less volatile earnings and even less downside risk in value, but those pushing for risk management have to talk in terms of excess returns in the future.

Conclusion

In this article, I spelled out the fundamental differences between risk hedging and risk management. The real work, however, will have to occur at the level of each firm because the right path to adopt will depend on each firm's competitive advantages and the sector it operates in.

Firms are paying too much attention to risk hedging and not enough to risk management. This unbalanced focus is troubling because the payoff to risk hedging is likely to be small even for firms for which it makes sense; for many large publicly traded firms with diversified investors, the payoff is often negative. The payoff to risk management can be substantial for a far larger number of firms.

Unlike risk hedging, which is the job of the chief financial officer, risk management should be on the agenda of everyone in the corporation. In today's world, the key to success lies not in avoiding risk but in taking advantage of the opportunities offered by risk. As businesses confront the reality of higher volatility, they have to get out of a defensive crouch when it comes to risk and think of ways they can exploit the risk to advantage in a global marketplace.

Note

1. Even this adjustment becomes moot for those who fall back on the Miller–Modigliani formulation in which the firm's value and cost of capital are unaffected by financial leverage.

From Theory to Practice

John J. Nagorniak, CFA

The investment profession has experienced major changes since 1970—primarily because of advances in technology—and change will continue to be a hallmark of our profession.

The investment profession has experienced major changes since my career began in 1970. Vast changes occurred over a relatively short period of time because of advances in technology. I was fortunate to be there and see it happen.

Theoretical work on various aspects of finance had been going on for quite some time. Indeed, as early as 1900, Louis Bachelier had written a thesis on the valuation of bond options. In his 1900 dissertation, *Theorie de la Spéculation*, and in his subsequent work, he anticipated much of what was to become standard fare in financial theory—for example, the random walk of financial market prices.[1] John Burr Williams wrote an economics thesis in the 1930s in which he talked of rigorous methods to be used for valuing securities and introduced what came to be known as the dividend discount model. Then, in 1952, Harry M. Markowitz followed up these early ideas in his dissertation examining the mathematics of portfolio risk.

The problem was that no one had a way to test these theories in the real world. Some of the work—Bachelier's, in particular—needed further theoretical insight. For all of the early work, however, researchers lacked the means to thoroughly test the theory, refine the theory, and then integrate it into financial market practices.

Computer Applications

Computers did not exist until World War II, and even in the 1950s, they were slow and costly. Computerized data were expensive and scarce. In the 1960s, calculations were performed by using punch cards. Firms had noisy, dusty rooms of card-sorting machines and printers (probably with hanging chads lying around!).

Markowitz's work in the 1950s on the mathematics of portfolio selection could not be applied commercially because a means of rapid, accurate, and economical computation was

John J. Nagorniak, CFA, is president of Foxstone Financial Inc., Walpole, Massachusetts.

lacking.[2] Computer-accessible data for the type of valuation work outlined by Williams and Markowitz did not exist until the 1960s. Bachelier's ideas were even more difficult to work with. The U.S. equity options market was informal and likely to be run out of back rooms and phone booths. A variation of Bachelier's work, or Markowitz's work, could be used in practice only for small portfolios. The work suffered from data limitations and computational drudgery.

Large advances in computer technology occurred during the 1960s and 1970s. These changes made testing practical and fostered a growth in the quantitative content of economics and finance. The day of the numerically challenged economist or finance professor was rapidly fading away.

In the 1960s and 1970s, the works of William F. Sharpe (e.g., 1963, 1964), Robert C. Merton (e.g., 1973), and Myron S. Scholes (1972) on asset pricing were published. By 1968, Scholes, Wells Fargo Bank, and others had made available an equity database that allowed testing of the capital asset pricing model with current data. Betas could be readily calculated through the use of added software. Compustat and the Center for Research in Security Prices at the University of Chicago also developed databases in the 1960s. Those who wanted computer time could usually obtain it either by having access to sufficient funding or by being a student or university researcher. Of course, computers were a slower and scarcer resource than they are today. Ambitious and curious young students had to get up and go to the computer center in the middle of the night.

Toward the end of the 1960s, Scholes ran a finance workshop for graduate degree candidates at the Sloan School of Management at MIT. Students studying finance missed these sessions at their peril.[3] There, students could mingle with the future stars of financial research and gain exposure to the newest ideas that were being developed. One of the ideas presented in the 1969–70 academic year was a formula for pricing stock options that became known as the Black–Scholes option-pricing model (see Black and Scholes 1973). It resembled the 1900 work of Bachelier, but it was based on a theoretical breakthrough (continuous risk-neutral hedging).[4] The Black–Scholes option-pricing methodology led to an explosion in the use of option-like instruments and strategies. New markets were born, and the model helped change the way we look at finance.

In the nonacademic world at this time, practice was often far removed from the textbooks. In the early 1970s, investors did not regularly calculate their performance. And the performance numbers they did compute were simple estimates. The Bank Administration Institute had devised performance guidelines, but they had not yet been widely adopted. For large pools of equities, only crude performance was calculated. Performance calculations were sporadic and haphazard. Today, performance is measured frequently and carefully.

Frequent calculation of performance does have a downside. Short-term feedback can lead to increased trading and an increased short-term focus. For example, some 401(k) and IRA participants may swap their funds around daily. Day trading of equities has become a more common occurrence. An increasing focus on short-term results is not a positive development because most of us are ill equipped for short-term trading.

In the 1970s, investments were usually not viewed as a portfolio. Instead, each investment was viewed on its own merit. Portfolios were built by using simple rules of thumb. Technology and time have slowly changed this situation. We can and do now view the aggregate characteristics of portfolios with relative ease.

As academically inspired investment models were developed, brokers made data and analytical tools available to institutional investors. They asked for commissions (soft dollars) in exchange. The falling cost of technology and the economies of scale it allows have extended the reach of these services. Individual investors also now have access to state-of-the-art investment tools.

Eventually, people realized the value of quantitative models. (On a cynical note, even if these new tools were not useful, they could still be a marketing plus. Many investment firms created quantitative units—some with only a vague mandate to "get something started.")

Quantitative work often became the focus of a generational power struggle in investment firms. Older staff who had not learned the new tools regarded the approaches as obscure and useless. Younger staff had an overconfident belief in the usefulness and applicability of the tools. In this environment, gaining legitimacy for new technology took a long time.

During the 1970s, practical applications of Markowitz's portfolio optimization work emerged. Barr Rosenberg, Andrew Rudd, and others built one of the first commercial portfolio optimizers. They initially ran their business from a multilocation nexus that was centered in a little house in Berkeley, California, with a pretty garden. It may have been one of the first "virtual" enterprises. The system developed by the business—originally, Barr Rosenberg & Associates and now, Barra—used fundamental and price data to build a model. Users' estimates of nonmarket returns (alpha) were combined with risk estimates to produce an "efficient" portfolio. In the early years, Barra had a modest number of users. Today, Barra has not only hundreds of users but also many competitors. Portfolio optimization can be implemented for individuals on their personal computers. The rise in popularity of these tools reflects the rise of a portfolio, rather than individual-security, point of view.

Market Theory and the New Analysis

The efficient market hypothesis (EMH) also emerged from the academic community in the 1960s (see Fama 1965) and caused angst and furor among professional investors. In an efficient market, prices reflect all known information and an investor's "good" performance is most likely the result of luck.[5] The implication of the strong form of the EMH is that indexing is the only way to win the investing game. Naturally, the idea was not terribly well received by traditionalists.

Using facts and forecasts to divine future investment performance is the essence of security analysis. Investors who emphasize fundamental valuation have thought about how to use data in valuing securities for a long time. They are interested in models that correctly measure value; buying the equities identified as "undervalued" by the model and selling those identified as "overvalued" is expected to produce investment success. In this approach, every asset has to reach its "fair" value eventually.

But the data analysts use need not measure aspects of value. They can also measure the behavior of security prices. Technical models fall into this camp.

The firm I founded in 1982, Franklin Portfolio Associates, was and is dedicated to succeeding in equity management by using modern techniques. From the beginning, we focused on finding ways to use investment information efficiently. One way was to combine data to predict future performance. But because expecting success from using public data was in conflict with efficient market theorists, we combined public data with "private" data (proprietary ways of looking at the data and specialized sources of data). There are two parts to using information efficiently. The first part is gathering relevant data and information. The information could be analysts' opinions. It could be value estimates. It could be past price data used to assess behavior and predict future behavior. Gathering and creating this information is the first part of the task.

The second part of using information efficiently is assembling the information that you have. To do this, you need to estimate the value of the information you have gathered. You also have to recognize that two pieces of information may be redundant. (Note that nothing I have said here about these tasks is *quantitative*. Indeed, both tasks can be handled with or without statistical models. Every investor gathers, evaluates, and combines information.)

The problems of combining investment information and using this information to build portfolios were dealt with in the 1970s by such authors as Jack Treynor, Fischer Black (the "Black" of the Black–Scholes model; see Treynor and Black 1973), Keith Ambachtsheer (e.g., 1972), and James Farrell (see Ambachtsheer and Farrell 1979). With the theory, the quantitative methods, and the data being accumulated, we could use quantitative approaches as additional tools to the ways investors had always evaluated their information and how pieces of information fit together. Quantitative methods would make the results more reliable than in the past because one could be sure that with the same inputs, outputs would be the same

A modeling approach can be inferior to a well-thought-out nonstatistical approach, for many reasons. Models may be based on incorrect assumptions. Models simplify. Simplification always removes factors from consideration. If these factors are important, the outcome will suffer. In addition, models are obtained through examining past data, but the availability of historical data in the form needed to build models is limited, and the data are not precise. Moreover, the past does not include all future possibilities. Consequently, models will suffer during panics or manias.

Nevertheless, models have many advantages. Data can be examined contemporaneously. Models allow the user to examine many potential investments. Models are consistent through time. They are not subject to popular manias or panic. Span of reach, lack of emotion, and consistency are major advantages of models. For the knowledgeable user, ease of use becomes another advantage of models.

The Constant of Change

In the past 35 years, the use of financial models has grown. For example, many investors use modeling approaches in their work with derivatives. Models are an accepted part of the financial landscape. The growth in quantitative modeling began with men and women with new ideas, and the application was enabled by cheap and fast information technology. Information technology is still improving, and the pace of change continues.

Another area that has seen tremendous change is the geographical composition of U.S. investors' portfolios. Initially, efforts were made to persuade the institutional marketplace of the merits of global investing on the basis of diversification benefits. Index funds based on the Morgan Stanley Capital International indices became available and slowly gained acceptance. Since the 1970s, favorable results for international investing have changed investor preferences and prejudices. Many of today's individual, as well as institutional, investors have global representation in their portfolios.

Other changes have occurred in the financial marketplace in the past 35 years. Markets have become more efficient; they adjust to news more quickly than in the past. Liquidity is easier to find in normal periods. Technology has made trading securities a more automated process, and the cost of trading has declined.

Defined-benefit plans have peaked in use. Individual-directed investments—particularly through defined-contribution plans and IRA plans—have been on the rise in recent years. For example, 401(k) plans have become a meaningful instrument for employers and employees. Mutual funds have grown in relative importance (see Bogle 2005). They have facilitated broad participation in the financial markets by individual investors.

New financial paradigms have not eliminated the challenges of investing. By definition, all investors, collectively, achieve average performance. Booms and busts still occur. Financial crises still occur. Indeed, the new investment technologies may have increased the potential that we will have *big* crises and have them develop more quickly; some pundits often cite program trading and portfolio insurance as having contributed to the market crisis of October 1987. With all these trends in place, investing remains a task that rewards merit and punishes the lack of merit.

The Future

Looking forward and projecting future markets and trends might be tempting, but the shape of things to come has not yet, of course, been determined.

We have a number of problems and quandaries—such as principal–agent issues and accounting clarity and consistency. Perhaps, thoughtful analysis and developments will alleviate such problems. But we know new, unforeseen problems will take their place.

New technology will arrive, and new technology always leads to change. Consider the ticker tape: As these machines disseminated news and price quotes more widely, interest and participation in the equity market broadened considerably. Leading the charge for change will always be the innovators. Just as the past had the Wizard of Menlo Park, the future will have its own Edisons.[6]

What trends will affect finance and investing? I can outline only what I hope:

- Capital markets will increase everyone's overall welfare to a greater degree than ever.
- Participation in the capital markets will be broad and thoughtful.
- The costs of investing will continue to fall.
- Information for all investors will be plentiful and of high quality.
- The average investing result of all investors, while remaining average, will be higher than ever before, and less risk will be involved in obtaining it.
- Access to capital markets will be fair, and ethical, high-quality advice will be available to all who need it.

Notes

1. And Bachelier did all this thinking before either Albert Einstein or the mathematical physicist Norbert Wiener! Bachelier's innovativeness was not appreciated, however, by his professors or contemporaries. The merits of his work were noted only long after his death.
2. Markowitz (2002); *Portfolio Selection: Efficient Diversification of Investments* was first published in 1959 by John Wiley & Sons as a Cowles Commission monograph (based on his 1952 doctoral thesis); it has been published since 1991 by Blackwell Publishers.

3. I was at the Sloan School from 1968 to 1970. At that time, MIT had an especially impressive list of professors in finance and economics, including Paul Cootner (see the 2000 edition of his book), Franco Modigliani (see Miller and Modigliani 1958), Scholes, and Paul A. Samuelson (for a summary of his work, see Samuelson and Puttaswamaiah 2002). These men had already achieved or would achieve a high degree of fame and recognition building on foundations laid by earlier pioneers.
4. Publication of the Black–Scholes model was delayed until 1973. Legend has it that this paper is the most cited paper ever published by the *Journal of Political Economy*.
5. EMH theorists fall into the weak-form believers (all past market prices and data are fully reflected in security prices), semistrong-form believers (all publicly available information is fully reflected in security prices), and strong-form believers (all information is fully reflected in security prices). The most upsetting form is the strong form, which implies that not only are technical analysis and fundamental analysis of no use but so also is inside information.
6. Thomas A. Edison was, incidentally, instrumental in the early development of stock ticker machines.

References

Ambachtsheer, Keith. 1972. "Portfolio Theory and Security Analysis." *Financial Analysts Journal*, vol. 28, no. 6 (November/December):53–57.

Ambachtsheer, Keith P., and James L. Farrell, Jr. 1979. "Can Active Management Add Value?" *Financial Analysts Journal*, vol. 35, no. 6 (November/December):39–47.

Black, Fischer, and Myron Scholes. 1973. "The Pricing of Options and Corporate Liabilities." *Journal of Political Economy*, vol. 81, no. 3 (May/June):637–659.

Bogle, John C. 2005. "The Mutual Fund Industry 60 Years Later: For Better or Worse?" *Financial Analysts Journal*, vol. 61, no. 1 (January/February):15–24.

Cootner, Paul. 2000. *Random Character of Stock Market Prices*. Cambridge, MA: MIT Press.

Fama, Eugene F. 1965. "Random Walks in Stock Market Prices." *Financial Analysts Journal*, vol. 21, no. 5 (September/October): 55–59; reprinted in vol. 51, no. 1 (January/February 1995 50th Anniversary Issue):75–80.

Levy, Robert A. 1967. "Relative Strength as a Criterion for Investment Selection." *Journal of Finance*, vol. 22, no. 4 (December):595–610.

Markowitz, Harry M. 2002. *Portfolio Selection: Efficient Diversification of Investments*. Oxford, U.K.: Blackwell Publishers.

Merton, Robert C. 1973. "The Theory of Rational Option Pricing." *Bell Journal of Economics and Management Science*, vol. 4, no. 1 (Spring):141–183.

Miller, Merton H., and Franco Modigliani. 1958. "The Cost of Capital, Corporation Finance, and the Theory of Investment." *American Economic Review*, vol. 48, no. 3 (June):655–669.

Rosenberg, Barr, and Andrew Rudd. 1982. "Factor-Related and Specific Returns of Common Stocks: Serial Correlation and Market Inefficiency." *Journal of Finance*, vol. 37, no. 2 (May):543–554.

Samuelson, Paul A., and K. Puttaswamaiah. Eds. 2002. *Paul Samuelson and the Foundations of Modern Economics*. New Brunswick, NJ: Transaction Publishers.

Scholes, Myron S. 1972. "The Market for Securities: Substitution versus Price Pressure and the Effects of Information on Share Prices." *Journal of Business*, vol. 45, no. 2 (April):179–211.

Sharpe, William F. 1963. "A Simplified Model for Portfolio Analysis." *Management Science*, vol. 9 (January):277–293.

———. 1964. "Capital Asset Prices: A Theory of Market Equilibrium under Conditions of Risk." *Journal of Finance*, vol. 19, no. 3 (September):425–442.

Treynor, Jack, and Fischer Black. 1973. "How to Use Security Analysis to Improve Portfolio Selection." *Journal of Business*, vol. 46, no. 1 (January): 66–88.

Williams, John Burr. 1997. *The Theory of Investment Value*. Burlington, VT: Fraser Publishing. Originally published 1938, Cambridge, MA: Harvard University Press.

The Present and Future of Empirical Finance

Clive W.J. Granger

Current topics of interest in empirical finance will remain in the forefront for years to come and perhaps be joined by questions that will shake the foundations of finance theory.

About 30 years ago, Oskar Morgenstern and I published a book on the forecastability of stock market prices (Granger and Morgenstern 1970) in which we generally used low-frequency data to test the random walk theory through autocorrelations and spectra. We did also consider, however, high-frequency transaction data plus dividends and earnings in macroeconomic relationships. Unsurprisingly, we found that returns are difficult to forecast, except in the very short run and the very long run.

In the third of a century since the book appeared, empirical finance has changed dramatically—from only a few active workers to hundreds, maybe thousands, of researchers. The number of finance journals has grown from one to dozens, and the techniques have become considerably more advanced. The availability of much more data and greatly increased computer power have produced impressive research publications.

One can argue, however, that many of these publications have relatively little practical usefulness. In fact, the purpose of much of the work is unclear. Papers keep appearing that reaffirm the random walk theory. Of course, if a researcher had discovered a method of *successfully* forecasting returns, she or he would not have published it but would have, instead, accumulated considerable wealth. So, it may well have happened and we simply do not know. Occasionally, papers are published suggesting how returns can be forecasted by using a simple statistical model, and presumably, these techniques are the basis of the decisions of some financial analysts. More likely, the results are fragile: Once you try to use them, they go away. Some recent viewpoints on this area can be found in Timmermann and Granger (forthcoming).

Several excellent textbooks on financial econometrics now exist, and they generally do a good job of surveying the safe features of the most popular procedures. I plan to take here a rather more realistic and forward-looking viewpoint on the available and forthcoming techniques. I will consider conditional means, conditional variances, conditional distributions, and finally, the future.

Clive W.J. Granger is professor emeritus of economics at the University of California at San Diego, La Jolla.

Conditional Means

Originally, much empirical financial research concentrated on mean returns conditional on previous returns, and possibly on other economic variables. Only quite recently have return and volume been modeled jointly, as would be suggested by a microeconomics text.

Most techniques are those developed in statistical and macro time-series analyses—that is, autoregressive models, vector autoregressive models, unit root models, cointegration, seasonality, and the usual bundle of nonlinear models, including chaos, neural network, and various other nonlinear autoregressive models.[1] Some of these models seem to be relevant and helpful; most do not.

Quite a lot of attention has been given to a property known as "long memory," in which empirical autocorrelations decline very slowly in comparison with the rate of decline in any simple autoregressive model. The autocorrelations of measures of volatility, such as $|r_t^d|$, where r_t is a return series and d is positive, have been observed to have the long-memory property. This behavior, which is widespread and occurs for many assets and markets, has produced a misinterpretation. Theoretical results show that the fractional integrated, $I(d)$, model has the long-memory property, so some researchers have concluded that any process with this property must be an $I(d)$ process. This conclusion is incorrect, however, as I have pointed out (Granger 2000 and elsewhere), because other processes can exhibit long-memory properties, particularly processes with breaks. If X_t is a positive process and, therefore, has positive mean and if it is $I(d)$, it must have a mean that is proportional to t^d, so it will have a distinct trend in mean. Because volatility has no such trend, it cannot be $I(d)$, especially since the "estimated" value of d is often found to be near 1/2. It follows that the $I(d)$ model is not appropriate for volatility, but a break model remains a plausible candidate to explain the observed long-memory property.

Several papers have pointed out that a stationary process with occasional level shifts will have the long-memory property. Examples are Granger and Hyung (2003), which was based on Hyung's 1999 PhD thesis, and Diebold and Inoue (2001). The breaks need to be rare but stochastic in magnitude. A break process considered by Hyung and Franses (2002) takes the form

$$\left.\begin{aligned} y_t &= m_t + \varepsilon_t \\ m_t &= m_{t-1} + q_t \eta_t \end{aligned}\right\},$$

where y_t is the observed variable, m_t is a hidden, unobserved driving force, and q_t and η_t generate the particular type of shocks to m, with ε_t and η_t being zero mean (white noise, with no serial or autocorrelation) and where q_t follows an identically and independently distributed (i.i.d.) binomial distribution so that $q_t = 1$ with probability p and $q_t = 0$ with probability $1-p$. The expected number of breaks is affected by p and the magnitude of variance σ_η^2. The break process produces stock prices that provide returns with a longer-tailed distribution but volatilities similar to those produced by absolute returns that do not suffer from the trending problem. These volatilities are found to fit as well as, if not better than (in other respects), an $I(d)$ model (Granger and Hyung).

Conditional Variance

If one wants to describe a distribution, knowing the mean only is inadequate; knowing the mean and variance is clearly better. For those of us interested in empirical studies, our immediate problem is that variance is not easily observed. One can form a sum of squared deviations of returns around a mean, but they take time to accumulate. The ARCH (autoregressive conditional heteroscedasticity) models partly circumvent this problem and provide quite up-to-date values for the variance.

The *purpose* of measuring variance as a measure of risk is somewhat less clear than the method of measuring it, particularly because returns have consistently been shown to have non-Gaussian distributions. The part of economics that discusses uncertainty, risk, and insurance has for many years emphasized that measures of volatility based on $E(|r|^d)$ for positive d are inappropriate measures of risk.[2] The problem is easy to illustrate. Suppose a small portfolio experiences a large negative shock to an asset; this event will be treated as an increase in risk because it increases the chance of selling the asset at a lower price than its purchase price. If an asset receives a large positive price shock, the event is considered an increase in uncertainty but not in risk. Both shocks produce an increase in variance, however, which takes equally into account movements in either tail of the distribution, although only those on one side are undesirable.

The typical investor's concept of risk coincides with the downside risk as defined by an economist, which is not measured by variance. Measurements of risk based on quantiles, such as the value-at-risk metric, avoid such problems, as does the semivariance metric suggested by Markowitz (1959) in his original book on portfolio theory.

Conditional Distributions

The next obvious step is to use predictive, or conditional, distributions. Major problems remain, however, particularly with parametric forms and in the multivariate case. For the center of the distribution, a mixture of Gaussians appears to work well, but they do not represent tail probabilities in a satisfactory fashion. If we consider a multivariate distribution written in terms of marginals and a rectangular copula, all tail properties will apparently come from the marginals.

A practical time-series approach to conditional distributions is to model quantiles, which can take autoregressive forms and have breaks, unit roots, and other driving variables. Modeling and estimation are not difficult, and in practice, the problem of estimated quantiles crossing appears to be not difficult to surmount (see Granger and Sin 2000). The long-memory properties observed in volatility should be observed in the quantiles because of breaks.[3]

Into the Future

The immediate future in any active academic field always involves endeavors that have already started. Conditional distributions will thus continue to be a major subject as finance learns how to convert more of its fundamental theories into distributional forms: arbitrage and portfolio theory, efficient market theory and its consequences, the Black–Scholes formula, and so forth. This period will be exciting; general results will appear, and new testing methods will be devised.

Also, structural breaks are likely in the present framework. Such breaks are, by nature, difficult to forecast, but two possibilities may already be visible. The first is a new approach to volatility, and the second is a reformulation of basic functional theory.

Most of the old literature on prices, returns, and volatility had, basically, a linear foundation. From studying the models suggested by these approaches, researchers have accumulated a number of "stylized facts"; they are empirical "facts" that have been observed to occur for many (possibly all) assets in most (possibly all) markets in most time periods and for most data frequencies. A list of these stylized facts would include the following:

- Returns are nearly white noise; that is, they have no serial or autocorrelation.
- The autocorrelations of r_t^2 and $|r_t|^d$ decline slowly with increasing lag (the long-memory effect), with the slowest decline for $d = 1$ (the Taylor effect).
- Autocorrelations of sign r_t are all small, insignificant.
- If one fits a GARCH(1,1) [that is, a generalized autoregressive conditional heteroscedasticity (1,1)] model to the series, then $\alpha + \beta \approx 1$, with the usual notation.

In a remarkable paper, Yoon (2003) showed, largely by simulation, that the simple stochastic unit root model

$$P_t = (1 + a_t)P_{t-1} + \varepsilon_t,$$

where P_t is log stock price and a_t and ε_t are independent white-noise series, produces return series that have all of the stylized facts observed in actual data. This outcome does not imply that actual log stock prices are generated by the model, but it does suggest that a simple model can capture many realistic properties. So, the model deserves further study. Yoon's model is an example of a "stochastic unit root process" as discussed by Granger and Swanson (1997) and by Leybourne, McCabe, and Mills (1996). Yoon considered a particularly simple case, one in which a_t is a zero-mean i.i.d. sequence and ε_t is zero-mean white noise.

Finally, I turn to an area in which I do not claim to have much special knowledge—namely, continuous-time finance theory. I have looked over a number of books in this area and found that much of the work starts with an assumption that a price or a return can be written in terms of a standard diffusion, which is based on a Gaussian distribution. This approach immediately raises warning signals because much of early econometrics used a similar Gaussian assumption, simply for mathematical convenience and without proper testing. Occasionally, someone asked whether a marginal distribution could pass a test with a null of Gaussianity, but I never saw a joint test of normality, which is what was truly needed for much of the theory to be operative. We have, effectively, no way to evaluate continuous-time theory by using empirical tests because we have no continuous-time data. Whether the theory continues to hold when it is brought over to discrete time is unclear. Bifurcation could occur in going from continuous to discrete time. Ito's lemma, which uses a Gaussian assumption, need no longer work in the discrete-time zone. In fact, the majority of the empirical work that I have seen appears to find that in the highest frequency data, the best models do not agree with continuous-time theory.

Some recent work by Aït-Sahalia (2002) suggests that the discrete-data results are more consistent with jump diffusions—that is, diffusions with breaks—than with standard diffusions. If further evidence for that result is accumulated, the majority of current financial theory will probably have to be rewritten with "jump diffusion" replacing "diffusion" and with some consequent changes in theorems and results. Because a great deal of human capital will be devalued by such a development, it will certainly be opposed by many editors and referees, as happens with all radical new ideas.

Notes

1. A *unit root* test is a statistical test for the proposition that in an autoregressive statistical model of a time series, the autoregressive parameter is 1. In the concept of $I(d)$, a variable is integrated of the order d if it is stationary only after differencing d times; two variables are *cointegrated* if they are both $I(1)$ but a particular linear combination of them is $I(0)$.
2. I mentioned this topic in Granger (2002).
3. I will not comment on the growing area of extreme-value theory applied to most events. The relevance of this theory to returns having heteroscedasticity and the apparently unsolvable problem of evaluation make this area opaque.

References

Aït-Sahalia, Y. 2002. "Maximum Likelihood Estimation of Discretely Sampled Diffusions: A Closed-Form Approximation Approach." *Econometrica*, vol. 70, no. 1 (January):223–262.

Diebold, F.X., and A. Inoue. 2001. "Long Memory and Regime Switching." *Journal of Econometrics*, vol. 105, no. 1 (November):131–159.

Granger, C.W.J. 2000. "Current Perspectives on Long Memory Processes." Chung-Hua Series of Lectures, No. 26, Institute of Economics, Academia Sinica, Taiwan.

———. 2002. "Some Comments on Risk." *Journal of Applied Econometrics*, vol. 17, no. 5 (September–October):447–456.

Granger, C.W.J., and N. Hyung. 2003. "Occasional Structural Breaks and Long Memory with an Application to the S&P 500 Absolute Stock Returns." *Journal of Empirical Finance*, vol. 11, no. 3 (June):399–421.

Granger, C.W.J., and O. Morgenstern. 1970. *Predictability of Stock Market Prices*. Lexington, MA: Heath Lexington Books.

Granger, C.W.J., and C.-Y. Sin. 2000. "Modelling the Absolute Returns of Different Stock Indices: Exploring the Forecastability of an Alternative Measure of Risk." *Journal of Forecasting*, vol. 19, no. 4 (July):277–298.

Granger, C.W.J., and N. Swanson 1997. "An Introduction to Stochastic Unit-Root Processes." *Journal of Econometrics*, vol. 80, no. 1 (September):35–61.

Hyung, N., and P.H. Franses. 2002. "Inflation Rates: Long-Memory, Level Shifts, or Both?" Report 2002-08, Econometric Institute, Erasmus University.

Leybourne, S., M. McCabe, and M. Mills. 1996. "Randomized Unit Root Processes for Modelling and Forecasting Financial Time Series: Theory and Applications." *Journal of Forecasting*, vol. 15, no. 3 (April):153–270.

Leybourne, S., M. McCabe, and J. Tremayne. 1996. "Can Economic Time Series Be Differenced to Stationarity?" *Journal of Business and Economic Statistics*, vol. 14, no. 4 (October):435–446.

Markowitz, Harry M. 1959. *Portfolio Selection: Efficient Diversification of Investments*. New York: John Wiley & Sons.

Timmermann, A., and C.W.J. Granger. Forthcoming. "Efficient Market Hypothesis and Forecasting." *Journal of Forecasting*.

Yoon, G. 2003. "A Simple Model That Generates Stylized Facts of Returns." Working paper, University of California, San Diego.

Retirement Income Guarantees Are Expensive

Don Ezra

Over the years, I have learned that retirement income guarantees are expensive. It is all too easy, and too tempting, to forget that fact in good times. Employee benefit plans, the U.S. Social Security system, and individual retirement arrangements—all confirm this lesson.

Employee Benefit Plans

Think back to the 1970s. Prompted by the collapse of the Studebaker-Packard Corporation pension, the Employee Retirement Income Security Act was passed in 1974. Stronger vesting and funding requirements came into effect for defined-benefit (DB) plans. The Pension Benefit Guarantee Corporation (PBGC) was born to provide a floor for benefits when the sponsor of an underfunded plan went out of business.

Did these legislative actions solve the problem? No. Today, with the legacy of labor arrangements in the older industries that have hit rocky times, the PBGC has taken on ever-increasing obligations, and the premiums it charges are still based on an inadequate risk framework.

Equity markets go up, and equity markets go down. So, too, does the funded position of a DB plan. But the U.S. Congress over the years has introduced an asymmetry in its rules for funding DB plans that is bound to produce an underfunding bias. When a plan is underfunded, it need not make good the deficiency for several years, which retards the journey of the plan up to 100 percent funding. When a plan is overfunded, the sponsor cannot contribute more to it, which accelerates any subsequent journey down to 100 percent. Even worse, when a DB plan is overfunded, the sponsor effectively cannot use the surplus, which creates an abhorrence of surpluses in sponsors' minds. No wonder underfunding occurs more often than overfunding.

Retirement funding security has proved to be elusive—and costly—whether sought through defined-benefit plans, the U.S. Social Security system, or defined-contribution plans.

Don Ezra is director of strategic advice at the Russell Investment Group.

Editor's Note: The views expressed in this article are entirely Mr. Ezra's and not in any way sanctioned by the Russell Investment Group.

Throughout the 1980s, economic symmetry was hardly foremost, however, in Congressional thinking. Instead, Congress was focused on reducing its huge budget deficit, and it passed the Consolidated Omnibus Budget Reconciliation Act of 1986 (and amendments) that restricted DB pension funding. These bills are what forced the contribution holidays in the 1990s and took away the cushions that might have prevented the devastation caused by the "perfect storm" of the early 2000s, when both equity prices and interest rates fell. Overfunding caused by rapid market appreciation is not an evil scheme dreamt up by sponsors to cheat the government out of well-earned tax revenue. The ability to create a cushion in good times is an essential part of the flexibility needed by an underwriter of defined benefits. And the ability to use that cushion, even to withdraw a part of it, is also an encouragement to sponsors if DB plans are to continue.

Guarantees involve risk, but the actuarial profession is only now coming to grips with this aspect of DB pension economics. Up to now, the actuaries have anticipated an equity risk premium when calculating pension funding requirements without allowing for the risk. This practice started innocently. In the early days of the actuarial profession, when these calculations were difficult and tedious, performing only one set of actuarial calculations was feasible. In those circumstances, the obvious single set of numbers to produce was the set that comes from the best estimate of future experience—namely, the risk premium being realized. Today, however, with computers making calculations easy, no serious obstacle stands in the way of producing a range of numbers corresponding to the range of future returns that might result.

This range of results would allow an actuary to establish two things. One is the value of the benefits. This value would be the value of the assets (typically bonds and the Treasury Inflation-Indexed Securities informally called "TIPS") that best match the projected benefit cash flows. The other is a "funding target" that would take into account the "mismatch risk," the expected rewards for taking that risk, and a contingency reserve to protect the benefits if the mismatch causes a loss and worsens the funded position. This approach, although feasible and sensible, is not yet done.

Today the funding target allows for the expected reward but includes no contingency reserve, and it is commonly confused with the value of the benefits. The first error makes defined benefits less secure. The second error leads to defined benefits being underpriced.

Both aspects need to be changed if DB plans are to live healthily. And their health is good for society. They enable individual risks to be shared by groups, making retirement incomes more secure. Sponsors, however, have gradually tired of all the complications and uncertainties associated with DB plans. Ever since the 1980s, companies have been replacing defined benefits and their uncertain contributions with defined contributions and their uncertain benefits. Today, corporate defined-contribution assets exceed corporate defined-benefit assets.

Guarantees are expensive. Sponsors need flexibility to underwrite them for employees. And employees need to recognize that the cost of guarantees is higher than commonly thought.

Social Security

In 1935, Congress passed social security legislation that was designed to provide a modest amount of social insurance against "the vicissitudes of life," including monthly income benefits to be paid from 1942 on to contributors who retired after age 65.[1] President Franklin D. Roosevelt insisted that the system be adequately funded, and he wanted contributors to feel they had earned the right to their benefits, "so no damn politician can ever scrap my Social Security program."[2]

The balanced approach to contributions and benefits, however, barely made it out of the starting gate. Because of the dire economic situation at the time, Congress moved benefit payments forward to 1940, raised benefits, added survivor benefits, and rolled back planned tax increases several times—overriding an FDR veto along the way. By the time Roosevelt died, it was no longer "his" Social Security program.

Ever since then, the program has depended mainly on a demographic balance between contributors and retirees rather than on prefunding à la employee benefit plans. This demographic balance has been moving toward unsustainability.

Part of the reason is increasing longevity. In 1940, the average male life expectancy (meaning the average age at which males died) was about 61; for females, it was about 66. These numbers have since increased to between 75 and 80. In any other context, such increased longevity would be good news. Only in the context of *paying* for longevity does it become a problem.

The other reason for unsustainability is declining birth rates. Birth rates immediately after World War II were unexpectedly high (creating the Baby Boomers), and the system thrived. Was a contingency reserve established in case the demographic balance turned? No. Instead, benefits were increased. When birth rates fell, the system's health gradually declined. The number of retirees per 100 contributors rose from an artificially low 2 in 1940 to a fairly stable 29 after 1975, but as the Baby Boomers reach retirement age, the number of retirees per 100 contributors is projected to rise rapidly—to 54 after 2010.

Many other countries with similar pay-as-you-go systems are even worse off than the United States—to name a few, Brazil, Japan, France, Germany, and Italy.

Two kinds of solutions are being discussed. One involves "parametric changes"; that is, the government changes the parameters of the system—such as the contribution rate or ceiling, the retirement benefit, or the retirement age. The other is to change the nature of the system itself by introducing a partial defined-contribution (DC) system. When I last counted, 27 countries (10 in Asia, 4 in Africa, 4 in Europe, 8 in Central and South America, and Australia) had introduced individual DC accounts. To the extent that these accounts are funded (rather than maintained notionally only on paper) and create new property rights, they introduce a new source of security. To the extent that defined contributions replace a portion of defined benefits, the level of the guarantee falls.

If we use the analogy of a building, we can say that a national pension system is more like the building's foundation, whereas an employment-based system is more like the portion of the structure above the ground. Guarantees are more naturally placed in the foundation because retirement income guarantees are more important to the lower-paid employees than the higher-paid employees.

In the Social Security system, benefits are defined but subject to political risk. They are not property rights. In fact, they have been reduced in the past—usually in subtle ways, such as raising the retirement age or taxing the benefits. DC benefits, in contrast, are subject to market risk. Guarantees—removing risks of either kind—are expensive. *Someone* has to pay for them, so an argument about numbers is less important than a philosophical discussion about the type of society we want, meaning what level of support to guarantee and who pays to hedge the risks. The numbers are important, but projections are simply estimates and will always change. If the national Social Security debate gets conducted in terms of philosophy, however, society may be able to decide on an approach to reform that is sustainable, even as the numerical details inevitably change over time.

Individual Retirement Arrangements

For some time, the trend has been to place risk bearing in retirement funding on the individual. Individuals have to consider two aspects of risk when that burden is placed on them. One is longevity; the other is market risk. Longevity raises the risk of outliving one's capital. Market risk affects how large that capital will be.

Experts understand market risk well. They talk routinely about uncertainty of return and characterize uncertainty in such terms as expected returns and standard deviation of returns. They understand these concepts and, having worked with them for a lifetime, intuitively understand the numbers for each asset class.

They do not discuss longevity risk in the same way. For example, experts will speak of "life expectancy," which is the equivalent of the concept of expected returns. But when was the last time you heard about the standard deviation of life expectancy? This concept, however, is what we need to understand if we are to cope with longevity risk.

If life expectancy is, say, 75 years for males, what is its standard deviation? One year? Three years? Five? Ten? I have no idea, and I'm an actuary. Consider a retired couple. What is the expected period until the survivor of the couple dies? What is the standard deviation of that expectancy? Until we know such numbers and understand them as intuitively as we do investment return distributions, we are taking into account only one of the two risks we need to consider in our planning.

How does one hedge longevity risk? Buying a life annuity is expensive; the seller is bound to overestimate longevity because an underwriter needs a cushion of safety. So, should one pay for the cost of an almost-worst-case scenario to hedge against simply outliving one's expectancy? If, instead of a life annuity, one underwrites the risk personally by establishing a series of programmed withdrawals designed to last, say, five years beyond one's life expectancy (assuming some constant return on one's assets), what is the probability that one will outlive that further five years? How much more uncertainty does asset volatility introduce? Is there a correlation between asset uncertainty and longevity?

We tend not to think in these terms. I know I want to change my own thinking because I am driven by the thought that risk is expensive, and the risk (and cost) may be bigger than my intuition tells me.

Many lay people believe they need to be investment experts to plan adequately for retirement. Lay people may not understand investments as well as experts, but Charley Ellis and others have noted that individuals do *not* have to be investment experts to make retirement planning decisions. They do, however, need to be able to characterize where they stand in the spectrum of choice between, on the one hand, wanting to eat well after retirement and, on the other hand, wanting to sleep well while they are saving. They need to take relatively greater risk if their goal is to eat well, and there is no guarantee that they will achieve the goal. They want more safety if their basic choice is to sleep well. If they can express their goals, they can hire investment experts to translate the goals into asset allocations, and they can then consider the likelihood of achieving their goals, the size of the risks, and so on. Then, they can make compromises if they so choose. Ellis's philosophical approach is the most practical way I have come across for helping individuals understand what risk means.

Investment risk takes on a more fearsome aspect for individuals when interest rates are low. For example, a 20-year annuity of $1,000 a month, without any expense loadings, requires a lump sum of $122,500 if one can lock in an interest rate of 8 percent a year. At 4 percent a year, the lump sum rises to $166,500—an increase of 36 percent. Forming a satisfactory plan becomes much more difficult in that case. Should one take on investment risk, or reduce one's hoped-for standard of living, or both?

Risk is not nice. But retirement income guarantees are expensive.

Notes

1. See the Social Security Administration website: www.ssa.gov/history/fdrstmts.html#signing.
2. This quotation is from *The Real Deal* by Sylvester J. Schieber and John B. Shoven (New Haven, CT: Yale University Press, 1999), p. 8.

The Structured Finance Market: An Investor's Perspective

Frank J. Fabozzi, CFA

The largest sector of the U.S. investment-grade fixed-income market is mortgage-backed securities and asset-backed securities. Investors who participate in this market sector are facing an array of issues, however, that they need to understand.

Traditionally, a corporation, municipality, or sovereign government seeking to borrow funds will issue bonds. With traditional secured bonds, the bondholder is dependent on the ability of the issuer, however, to generate sufficient cash flow to repay the debt. As an alternative to the issuance of bonds, an entity seeking debt funding can issue a security backed by a pool of loans or receivables. These securities are referred to as "asset-backed securities" (ABS).[1]

With an ABS, the burden of the source of repayment shifts from the cash flow of the issuer to the cash flow of the pool of loans or receivables and/or a third party that guarantees the debt payments if the pool of assets does not generate sufficient cash flow. To obtain the credit rating sought by the issuer for the ABS created in structured financing, both the value of the financial assets backing the issue and third-party credit support may be needed. The process of creating a pool of financial assets that will back securities is referred to as "asset securitization." The process of redistributing the cash flows and the risks of the pool of financial assets to create an ABS is called "structuring."

The largest type of asset that has been securitized is mortgage loans, both residential and commercial. Such mortgage-backed securities are a type of ABS, but in the United States, it is common to categorize MBS as a separate asset class. Collectively, ABS and MBS are called "structured products."

The Lehman Brothers U.S. Aggregate Bond Index, an index that includes only investment-grade products, allows us to see the importance of structured products. The index has six sectors: U.S. Treasury, agency, credit, mortgage pass-throughs, commercial MBS (CMBS), and ABS. The last three sectors are those that have structured products. The mortgage pass-through sector consists of pass-through securities backed by a pool of residential mortgage loans that are issued/guaranteed

Frank J. Fabozzi, CFA, is Frederick Frank Adjunct Professor of Finance at Yale University, New Haven, Connecticut.

by Ginnie Mae and two government-sponsored enterprises (GSEs), Fannie Mae and Freddie Mac.[2] The CMBS sector comprises securities backed by a pool of commercial mortgage loans, and the ABS sector consists of securities backed by auto loans, credit card receivables, home equity loans, manufactured housing loans, and stranded utility costs.[3] As of year-end 2004, the mortgage pass-through, CMBS, and ABS sectors constituted, respectively, 35.2 percent, 3.0 percent, and 1.4 percent (or a total of about 39.6 percent) of the Lehman index. From the standpoint of only spread sectors (i.e., sectors that offer a spread to U.S. Treasuries), structured products represent slightly more than half of the investment-grade index. Therefore, understanding structured products is critical in managing a portfolio relative to the Lehman or any other broad bond index. Moreover, structured products offer a range of securities from which to choose a good match for managing funds relative to liabilities.

This article focuses on the legal, market-structure, and analytical issues facing participants in this market sector today.[4] It closes with a discussion of the need to educate compliance staff and equity analysts about this sector.

Securitization as a Major Innovation

Financial innovations can be categorized in various ways, one of which is by specific functions—price risk–transferring innovations, credit risk–transferring innovations, and liquidity-generating innovations. Price risk–transferring innovations provide market participants with efficient means for dealing with price or exchange rate risk. Re-allocating the risk of default is the function of credit risk–transferring instruments. Liquidity-generating innovations do three things: (1) increase the liquidity of the market, (2) allow borrowers to draw on new sources of funds, and (3) allow market participants to circumvent capital constraints imposed by regulations and rating agencies.

Asset securitization provides all of these functions. The price risk of a pool of loans or receivables can be transferred from the originators of loans to a broad range of investors (not only banks or finance companies). Moreover, exposure to interest rate risk can be altered so as to create a range of securities with different liability-matching profiles. Finally, asset securitization permits the transfer of credit risk from the originators of loans to other parties and the redistribution of credit risk via credit tranching and/or third-party guarantees. Asset securitization results in

- securities whose liquidity is greater than that of an unsecuritized portfolio of loans or receivables,
- borrowing from ultimate investors who would not ordinarily want to hold a portfolio of loans or receivables, and
- reduction by depository institutions of their capital requirements by transferring assets off their balance sheets.

Asset securitization has changed and will continue to change financial markets. It involves the collection or pooling of loans/receivables and the sale of securities backed by those loans/receivables. This system differs radically from the traditional system for financing the acquisition of assets, which calls for a financial intermediary to originate a loan, retain the loan in its portfolio of assets (thereby accepting the credit risk associated with the loan), service the loan, and obtain funds from the public with which to finance its assets (except for the small amount representing the institution's equity).

Asset securitization provides various benefits for borrowers. Corporate issuers may find it more cost-effective to raise funds via asset securitization than to offer a typical corporate bond. Asset securitization can be used as a tool to manage risk-based capital requirements by regulated financial institutions, such as banks, thrifts, and insurance companies, throughout the world. With respect to the management of interest rate risk, asset securitization fulfills a dual role: A financial institution can securitize assets that expose the institution to higher interest rate risk and retain certain customized parts of the asset securitization transaction to attain an improved asset/liability position. In this respect, the financial institution serves as both issuer and investor.

Legal Issues

Legal or litigation risk is a major concern to investors in the structured products market. Two important legal risks arise from the "bankruptcy remote trust/true sale opinion" and from certain consumer lending legislation. The former represents by far the greatest potential threat to the growth of the structured finance market.

Bankruptcy Remote Trust/True Sale Opinion. The long-standing view has been that investors in a structured product are protected from the creditors of the seller of the collateral because of the bankruptcy remote trust/true sale opinion. That is, when the seller of the collateral transfers it to the trust (a special-purpose vehicle), the transfer represents a "true sale"; therefore, if the seller goes bankrupt, the bankruptcy court cannot penetrate the trust to recover the collateral or cash flow from the collateral. The bankruptcy remote trust/true sale opinion, however, has never been fully tested. The closest challenge was the bankruptcy of LTV Corporation. In the bankruptcy, LTV argued that its securitizations were not true sales and that it should thus be entitled to the cash flows that it transferred to the trust. Although the case was settled and the settlement included a summary finding that the LTV securitizations were a true sale, the court's decision to permit LTV to use the cash flows prior to the settlement is a major concern to investors.

Concerns were also raised in the case of Conseco Finance Corporation, which filed for bankruptcy in December 2002. Conseco had been the largest originator of manufactured housing loans, as well as an originator of other asset types (home equity mortgages, home improvement loans, and private-label credit cards). Measured in terms of assets, the Conseco filing was the third largest—after Enron and WorldCom—in the history of U.S. corporate bankruptcies.[5] In terms of potential impact on the structured products market, it was much more significant. At the time of filing, Conseco was servicing its prior securitizations for a fee of 50 bps. The bankruptcy court took the position that a 50 bp servicing fee was not adequate compensation and ordered that the fee be increased (to 115 bps). That increase was obtained by reducing the excess spread in the securitization transactions that Conseco was servicing. As a result of that reduction in the excess spread, the credit enhancement levels for the transactions being serviced were reduced and several of the subordinated tranches in those transactions were downgraded.

The Conseco bankruptcy set two noteworthy precedents that are of concern to investors. First, the servicing contracts between the bankrupt entity and the ABS trusts were "executory" contracts (i.e., contracts under which one of the parties must still do something to fulfill the contract). A bankrupt entity has the right to either reject or affirm executory contracts. If the bankrupt entity elects to reject an executory contract, renegotiation of the contract between the parties is required.

The rejection of an executory contract also creates an unsecured claim against the bankrupt entity for the estimated loss resulting from the new terms of the renegotiated contract. This procedure was not followed by the bankruptcy court in the Conseco case. Second, the court changed the cash flow waterfall of transactions being serviced by Conseco. Such a change is supposed to require consent of all the note holders on a trust-by-trust basis, but the bankruptcy court in the Conseco case did not obtain that consent. By unilaterally altering the servicing contract and the cash flow waterfall, the bankruptcy court effectively invalidated the documents and the legal protections that are assumed to apply to investors in an ABS.

Consumer Lending Legislation. Securitization has made credit available to nonstandard borrowers in the subprime loan market. This sector of the consumer credit market was previously underserved. But unfortunately, it is this sector that has attracted unscrupulous lenders seeking to extract from borrowers not only interest rates in excess of market rates but also loan provisions that would provide additional illegal compensation in the form of fees and penalties. Typically, these lenders pursue the illegal compensation by not disclosing to borrowers the adverse implications of the loan provisions. This practice is called "predatory lending."

To protect borrowers against predatory lending, in 1994, the U.S. government passed the Home Ownership and Equity Protection Act (HOEPA) as an amendment to the Truth in Lending Act. HOEPA assigns liability to the party who purchases or takes an interest in a loan (the "assignee") that is determined to be a "high cost" loan. By assigning liability to the assignee, HOEPA sought to motivate entities acquiring loans in the secondary market to ensure that those loans were originated in compliance with the law. For the structured products market, the implication is that an investor in, for example, a home equity loan securitization can be held liable if there are claims by the borrower against the mortgage originator.

Concern increased in the structured finance market as state and local governments also passed laws to protect against predatory lending. Unfortunately, these laws were not always clear as to what constituted predatory lending. Even within a state, conflicts had to be resolved by the courts. For example, a New York State court ruled that the New York City predatory lending law was preempted by federal and New York State laws.

This litigation risk is an issue that participants in the structured products industry must resolve to prevent investors from shying away from these transactions, as some have claimed to have done. Rating agencies have reacted by refusing to rate transactions in which a pool contains high-cost loans in certain states (e.g., Fitch Ratings did this with loans from New Mexico) or certain types of loans in some jurisdictions (e.g., Standard & Poor's Corporation indicated it would not rate loans for Los Angeles if a predatory lending law became effective).

Market Structure

The important market-structure issues involve the role of the GSEs, the survival of the "to be announced" (TBA) market, corporate issues masquerading as securitizations, the role of the servicer/trustee,[6] and the increased use of derivatives. These issues will have an impact on the valuation of structured securities and trading strategies.[7]

The Role of GSEs. Investors have concerns about various aspects of Fannie Mae and Freddie Mac (aside from the well-known privatization debate) in relation to market valuations and liquidity. Three specific concerns are (1) a slowdown in the growth of the mortgage portfolios of the GSEs, (2) the focus of the GSEs on acquiring for their mortgage portfolios higher-margin products (i.e., products with large spreads over funding costs), and (3) the expansion of GSEs on the "insurance" side of the business (i.e., generating revenue via guarantee fees).[8]

A strong driver of an expected reduced appetite for MBS by Freddie Mac and Fannie Mae has been the cheapening of the GSEs' debt and the subsequent increase in their funding costs. Another factor that will reduce demand on the part of Fannie Mae is the September 2004 agreement between it and its regulator, the Office of Federal Housing Enterprise Oversight, in which Fannie Mae agreed to "establish and maintain" a capital surplus of 30 percent over its minimum capital requirements. This agreement ties up funds that could otherwise be invested in the mortgage portfolio.

The level of demand by GSEs for their mortgage portfolios affects products that are not traditionally associated with the GSEs themselves. Included in these products are conforming-balance (i.e., conforming to GSE loan limits) adjustable-rate mortgages (ARMs), subprime loans, and second-lien loans. Moreover, even if the GSEs are not outright buyers of TBAs and pass-throughs, their activities could still affect the net float in conforming-balance securities. The GSEs have been buyers of conforming-balance Alt-A loans (moderately impaired loans with relatively high guarantee fees) in private-label form, and the expectation is that this demand will continue as they seek high-margin products.

Changes in the level of demand of the GSEs for conforming Alt-A loans will affect the supply of agency pools, even if the GSEs themselves are not buyers of pools. The reason is that a weakening of GSE demand will cause spreads for the senior bonds (which are GSE eligible) to increase in these deals, thereby reducing the marginal execution toward agency pools and away from private-label deals and thus increasing the production of agency pools. Basically, the GSEs will have an impact on supply/demand dynamics but in a less direct form than they have had in the past.

The profit-making activities of GSEs help stabilize the mortgage market; the system creates incentives for GSEs to buy when the market cheapens, ultimately dampening market volatility. (Basically, the incentives for the GSEs dovetail with the interests of the market as an entity.) With the decline in the growth of the GSEs' mortgage portfolios, market participants are concerned that during times of instability in the mortgage market, the GSEs may not be able to provide the level of support that they did in the past.

A good amount of the GSEs' portfolios are acquired through "cash windows" (i.e., buying loans directly from smaller originators). On the negative side, if GSE portfolio growth slows, the GSEs will be inclined to buy fewer loans, which will make it more difficult for smaller lenders to be competitive and presage renewed consolidation in the mortgage industry. On the positive side, if the portfolios of the GSEs shrink, demand for hedging instruments might fall, which would lower implied volatilities in the market. This outcome would have a positive impact on valuations in the MBS sector.

With regard to the insurance side of the GSE business, some market participants look for a continued push by GSEs to offer guarantees on products they do not currently back, such as lower-FICO ARMs.[9] Currently, some market observers believe that in the fixed-rate market, the GSEs will offer a guarantee fee on almost anything within the limits of their charters. In ARMs, however, the GSEs currently offer a guarantee fee only for certain products and attributes. Some market observers expect GSE participation in the ARM sector, as the GSEs seek to build the guarantee side of the business, to be comparable in the next few years to GSE participation in the fixed-rate sector.

TBA Market. One of the most important market innovations that has fostered the development of the fixed-rate agency pass-through security market is the practice of transacting on a to-be-announced basis. In a TBA trade, the parties agree to transact at a specified future date at a price determined today. Hence, a TBA is a forward contract. The two parties agree on the agency type, the agency program, the coupon rate, the face value, the price, and the settlement date. The actual pool numbers underlying the agency and the number of pools are not known, however, at the time of a TBA trade. (The information is provided by the seller to the buyer before delivery.)

The TBA market was developed to allow mortgage lenders to sell forward their originations via a securitization and thereby hedge their loan pipelines. This practice provided liquidity to the agency pass-through market. As noted by Davidson (2004):

> The TBA market is so successful that it has been able to withstand a number of attempts by the Chicago Board of Trade and others to create more liquid hedge instruments for the mortgage market. (p. 1)

The TBA market operates under the same economic principle as a futures market, where the seller can choose what particular security to deliver to satisfy the obligation. In both types of markets (forwards and futures), the seller has an incentive to deliver the cheapest security that meets the contract's requirements (hence, the "cheapest-to-deliver" nomenclature). Although in most markets the cheapest-to-deliver calculation is a straightforward function of a bond's coupon and maturity, in the TBA market (and for MBS and ABS in general), an additional variable is the expected prepayment performance of the pool. Briefly, changes in prepayment rates based on interest rate changes generally affect the performance of MBS and ABS negatively (especially those securities trading at a premium to par value). Recent advances in mortgage research have identified borrower and loan attributes (loan size, credit score, etc.) that make loans exhibit different prepayment performance and responsiveness to refinancing incentives. Thus, sellers will deliver pools with inferior characteristics or volatile historical prepayments into TBA trades and either hold the better-performing pools or attempt to sell them separately.

Trading based on the recognition of incremental value in mortgage securities (generally a result of expectations for more stable and predictable prepayment speeds) has long been expressed in the trading of individual or "specified" pools, where the pool number is known at the time the trade is executed. These trades are not executed in the TBA market, although their value is often quoted or benchmarked off TBA prices. At its inception, this type of activity represented the trading of pools after their issuance when their favorable attributes were either coincidental (e.g., a pool with many loans from a region with muted prepayments) or a function of the passage of time (referred to as "seasoning").

A fairly recent innovation is the creation of so-called "custom MBS," where originators proactively accumulate and pool loans with favorable attributes to create securities expected to experience favorable performance. These products are either traded as specified pools or in so-called "stips" or "stipped" (short for "stipulated") trades. A stipped trade may specify limits on certain attributes either of the pool (e.g., a weighted-average coupon within a certain range) or of the underlying loans (e.g., a maximum loan balance of $85,000).

The evolution of this activity has interesting implications for the market. Most custom pools can be delivered into TBAs, which implies that they should never trade at a discount to TBA values. Nondeliverable products, such as pools with prepayment penalties, are not deliverable into TBAs and will trade behind TBAs in certain market conditions. The deliverability can, therefore, be viewed as an option, which suggests that deliverable pools should trade closer to their intrinsic value than do nondeliverable products. In addition, the practice of originators segregating the "best" loans to sell into custom products (analogous to a dairy farmer skimming the cream off raw milk) suggests that the TBA market comprises pools backed by loans that have unfavorable characteristics and can be expected to exhibit inferior prepayment performance and returns. This condition is generically referred to as "adverse selection" and means that investors buying MBS through the TBA market can expect their securities to experience more prepayment volatility and responsiveness than the mortgage market as a whole.

The sellers in the TBA market are dominated by originators, agencies, and broker/dealers. These entities use details on borrowers by loan level and loan to identify and retain pools in their mortgage pipelines or portfolios that have the most favorable attributes with respect to prepayments. The pools that are thereby delivered to the seller in a TBA trade are likely to have prepayment protection inferior to that of the average pool. Recognizing this aspect, investors have, in certain periods, executed more trades on a specified pool basis or a stipped basis. This development threatens the liquidity of the TBA market because it reduces the ability of mortgage originators who seek to securitize a pool of loans to hedge pipeline risk. The result could be the demise of the TBA market.

Davidson raised the question of whether the TBA market should be saved and recommended actions that dealers and the GSEs could take to save it. If dealers were to standardize definitions of pool types, standard stipped pools could be created that could be traded like "mini-TBAs." In the futures markets, when a contract may have more than one deliverable acceptable to satisfy the contract, a conversion ratio to adjust the futures price is used. The conversion ratio makes delivery equitable to both parties. This mechanism for adjusting prices could be used for the mini-TBAs and would widen the range of loan types for transaction in the TBA market. The practical solution for the GSEs to enhance liquidity is to issue extremely large pools, which offer mortgage originators the opportunity to swap individual pools for a large monthly pool.

Expansion of Asset Categories and Disguised Corporate Bond Offerings. Some products are labeled ABS that are nothing more than corporate bonds disguised as ABS and should be evaluated by investors accordingly. To understand the difference between credit valuation for corporate bonds and credit valuation for ABS, an important aspect is how the cash flow that must be generated differs for the different transactions.

In a corporate bond issue, the company must carry out through its operations the activities that will produce revenues and must collect the revenues. In creating the necessary products and services, the company will incur costs—compensation, salaries, the cost of raw materials, and financial costs. Consequently, in evaluating the credit risk of a corporate bond issue, an analyst will examine the corporation's capacity to pay and the corporation's character.

In contrast, a securitization transaction involves assets (loans or receivables) that are to be collected and distributed to bondholders (i.e., investors in the ABS). No operating or business risks arising from a competitive environment exist, and no control systems are needed to assess the cash flow. What is important is the quality of the collateral in generating the cash flow needed to make interest and principal payments. The rating agencies will review the likelihood of the cash flow based on different scenarios of default and delinquency. The greater predictability of the cash flow that will be distributed to each bond class in a securitization transaction because of the absence of operational risks distinguishes it from a corporate bond issue.

In a "true securitization," the role of the servicer is simply to collect the cash flow. No active management with respect to the collateral need be considered. Standard & Poor's (1999) defined a true securitization as follows:

> In a true securitization, repayment is not dependent on the ability of the servicer to replenish the pool with new collateral or to perform more than routine administrative functions. (p. 2)

There are securitization transactions in which the role of the servicer is more than administrative. Standard & Poor's, for example, refers to such transactions as "hybrid transactions." According to Standard & Poor's:

> In a hybrid transaction, the role of the servicer is akin to that of a business manager. The hybrid servicer performs not only administrative duties, as in a true securitization, but also . . . other services that are needed to generate cash flow for debt service. (p. 3)

Moreover, Standard & Poor's notes that, unlike a true securitization, in which the servicer is a fungible entity replaceable with few, if any, consequences to the transaction,

> bondholders depend on the expertise of the hybrid servicer for repayment. . . . Not coincidentally, these are the same attributes that form the basis of a corporate rating of the hybrid servicer. They also explain the rating linkage between the securitization and its hybrid servicer. (p. 3)

Standard & Poor's provided an illustration of the distinction between a true ABS transaction and one requiring a more active role for the servicer. Consider a railcar company that has several hundred leases that are with a pool of diversified, highly rated companies. Suppose that each lease is for 10 years and the customers—not the railcar company—have the responsibility to perform the necessary maintenance on the leased railcars. If there is an ABS transaction backed by these leases and the term of the transaction is 10 years, the role of the servicer is minimal. Because the leases are for 10 years and the securities issued are for 10 years, the servicer is simply collecting the lease payments and distributing them to the holders of the securities. In such a transaction, this issue may obtain a high investment-grade rating as a true ABS transaction.

Suppose the assumptions change as follows. The securities issued are for 25 years, not 10 years. Also, the railcar company, not the customers, is responsible for railcar maintenance. Now, the role of the servicer changes. First, the servicer will be responsible for finding new companies to re-lease the railcars to when the original leases terminate in 10 years (because the securities issued have a maturity of 25 years but the original leases cover payments to security holders for only the first 10 years). Second, the servicer under this new set of assumptions must be capable of maintaining the railcars or have ongoing arrangements with other companies to perform such maintenance. This arrangement is a hybrid securitization.

Close Scrutiny of the Business, Servicer, and Trustee. Even in what may pass for a true securitization, investors have come to realize the importance of close scrutiny of the underlying business of the seller/originator, the strength of the servicer, and the economics that will produce the cash flows for the collateral. The alleged frauds of National Century Financial Enterprises, purchaser of health care receivables that were then securitized and serviced, and DVI, a securitizer of medical equipment leases, highlight for investors the importance of close scrutiny and the need for a trustee to be proactive if the performance of the servicer deteriorates.[10] The trustee's role goes beyond the traditional function of merely performing the ongoing tests on the collateral that are set forth in the deal documents.[11] In recent deals, in fact, trustees have been given the power, in certain circumstances, to take on an expanded role. The circumstance is referred to as a "trustee event trigger."

Increased Use of Derivatives. Participants in the fixed-income market are comfortable with the traditional hedging instruments for protecting against interest rate risk. Participants in the structured finance market have also used interest rate derivatives as part of offerings when a mismatch occurred between the coupon characteristic of the collateral and the obligations of the bond issues. Moreover, participants in the structured finance market have seen increased use of other derivative instruments: prepayment derivatives and credit default swaps.

- *Prepayment derivatives.* Although management of prepayment exposure is a central issue for MBS traders, until recently, no instruments provided a direct hedge. In June 2003, the interdealer broker ICAP began brokering prepayment derivatives for the direct hedging of assumed or modeled prepayment risk without the basis risk that one would face using existing hedging instruments (interest rate swaps, futures, and options).

A broad range of prepayment derivatives is available, including "plain vanilla" options, digital options, and forwards. Payoffs are based on the realized monthly conditional prepayment rate (CPR) of benchmark Fannie Mae 30-year MBS issued in a specific year. Options are priced and allocated through dutch auctions and are booked and settled as standard OTC options. (Goldman Sachs is clearing agent and principal for the auctions.) The first contracts had a maturity date of one month and then expanded to two months. The plan is to expand to three-month contracts in 2005 and then to six-month contracts. Furthermore, nonauction markets are evolving, and transactions outside the auctions have occurred.

Market participants are interested not only in hedging or taking short-term views of prepayments but also in hedges of from three months to one year. Here are just two examples of the potential use of these contracts and the need for short and long maturities.

First, with respect to TBA issues, MBS traders are faced with the variations in long- and short-term prepayment exposure. The "dollar roll" traders often buy the front-month MBS TBA and sell the back month.[12] Unmatched trades expose the dealer to prepayment risk resulting from variations between actual prepayments and the prepayments assumed in the purchase price. The one-month return earned by rolling the MBS is affected by, for example, faster prepayments, which result in more return of principal at par than at the forward price. Dollar roll traders are faced with another risk resulting from the variations in the balance to be delivered back to the seller when the dollar roll terminates. Such risk results in variations in the prepayment rate that is experienced over the term of the dollar roll. Prepayment derivatives are a good product (or, at the very least, a complementary tool) to use to hedge such an exposure.

The second example is the risk that interest-only (IO) traders are faced with stemming from changes in short-term prepayments, which can increase the cost of carrying IO inventory. These changes are challenging to hedge with existing hedging instruments without incurring basis risk. Prepayment derivatives provide an alternative/complementary option to manage the cost and the risks from an unexpected increase in prepayments. What is most important is that short-term variations in IO prepayment speeds can be indicative of future trends; for example, a faster-than-expected prepayment speed would forecast much-faster-than-expected prepayment speeds in future months, which would become priced into the IO market. That is, a number that is very far from expectations would probably move the IO markets substantially. Therefore, buying out-of-the-money options for prepayment speeds (in large size) would be a good hedge for a portfolio of IOs above and beyond the one-month roll consideration.

Prepayment derivatives have two challenges. First, current and future users of the product are requesting extended option tenures. So, the challenge is to extend the maturity while maintaining liquidity in the nearby months in a timely, measured way. Several market participants have developed models for valuing prepayment derivatives beyond the three-month product and up to one year. The second challenge is that, although traders appear to be supporting the product and the number of new participants is increasing, many in the market have been slow to adopt the product. It is expected, however, that over time, market participants will become comfortable with the product and it will be more widely accepted.

- *Credit default swaps*. The most commonly used credit derivative in structured finance transactions is the credit default swap (CDS). It is this product that permitted the creation of synthetic collateralized debt obligations (CDOs). Expectations are that the market for CDS will grow in the next several years, particularly because of their use in one of the larger sectors of the ABS market: home equity loans. CDS permit the issuer to remove the available funds cap risk in home equity loan deals.[13]

CDS in the ABS market will struggle with four issues. The first is the question, in the case of multiple obligors, of the correct default correlations to assume. The second is the ongoing issue of defining a credit event. The third is the need for the creation of valuation and settlement mechanisms. Finally, there is a need to find buyers of credit protection.

Analytical Issues and Challenges

The analytical issues and challenges in the valuation, risk measurement, and management of structured products relate to prepayment modeling, credit-risk modeling for ABS, valuation and the option-adjusted spread, and benchmarks.

Prepayment Modeling. Valuation and measurement of interest rate risk (duration, convexity, and key-rate duration) of MBS require the projection of the collateral's cash flow, and the cash flow itself depends on the prepayment forecast. Modeling perspectives have taken an empirical perspective or a behavioral perspective (see Sykes 2004). The empirical approach is based on the belief that history often repeats itself. In constructing a prepayment model, the empirical approach seeks to generate a forecast that produces as closely as possible the observed historical prepayment rate under the same conditions that prevailed at the past time. The behavioral approach focuses on modeling the borrower's decision-making process. By accurately modeling that behavior, the model can accommodate changing market fundamentals. In practice, modelers seek a balance between these two extreme perspectives.

Prepayment models fall into three general categories—econometric models, option-pricing models, and market-based models. Econometric models are the most common type in practice today. Various econometric techniques have been used to forecast the prepayment rate from a set of variables that are expected to affect prepayments. Because homeowners have an option to prepay, some researchers have proposed the use of option-pricing theory to model prepayments. This approach is difficult to implement in practice, however, and cannot explain why MBS prices exceed par value (i.e., the call value). Market-based prepayment models use the current price of an MBS to infer the prepayment rate that will make the present value of the cash flows equal to the current market price. These models are also referred to as "implied prepayment models" (see Cheyette 1996).

Early prepayment models were typically limited to the value of the prepayment option—determined chiefly by the gap between the mortgage coupon rate and the current mortgage rate and, to a lesser extent, by the impact of loan age or seasoning and by macroeconomic variables, such as GDP growth or the unemployment rate. Prepayment modelers knew, however, that prepayment models ideally should discriminate between a homeowner's decision to refinance an existing mortgage—whether to obtain a lower rate or to obtain cash—and the decision to sell the property. Modeling these decisions accurately requires much more data on borrower and loan attributes than does modeling the value of the prepayment option.

Imperfections in early prepayment models because of this inability to discriminate between refinancing and sale were not caused by the lack of creativity of modelers but by the limitations of the data released by the GSEs. These entities release only aggregate information, such as weighted-average coupon/weighted-average maturity by quartile and geographic concentrations at the state level, average loan age, and average loan size. Moreover, prepayments are not reported by type.

Issuers of private MBS have been much more forthcoming with data than issuers of nonagency MBS; private issuers generally release loan-level data for the collateral backing their deals. Based on these detailed pool data, Bendt, Ramsey, and Fabozzi (1995) found that for nonagency MBS, other than coupon and seasoning, the three major influences on prepayments (in order of importance) are (1) homeowner's equity, (2) transaction type (purchase versus refinance), and (3) level of documentation. The two major factors that homeowner's equity depends on are initial down payment and changes in housing prices. Together, these two factors determine the current loan-to-value ratio, defined as the current mortgage balance divided by the current market value. This finding suggests that changes in housing prices must be modeled into the analysis of prepayments.

In recent years, with the availability of data on borrower attributes for nonagency MBS and with loan attributes, prepayment models are more attribute sensitive and less generic. More variables are now used to compute prepayments attributable to refinancing and housing turnover. For example, in one dealer model, the refinancing components include, in addition to the usual refinancing incentive (weighted-average coupon versus prevailing mortgage rate) and burnout effect (the tendency of refinancing opportunities to dampen a pool's refinancing sensitivity), loan size, the "threshold-media" effect (so named because there will be a barrage of both general media reporting and mortgage banking advertisements when mortgage rates drop to historically low levels, making borrowers aware of the refinancing opportunities), the "cash-out" effect (change in loan-to-value ratio), the rate premium, and slope of the yield curve for hybrid alternatives; see Westhoff and Srinivasan (forthcoming 2005). The variables included in forecasting prepayments as a result of housing turnover include home price appreciation (change in loan-to-value ratio) and the lock-in effect (availability of alternative mortgages) in addition to the standard variable of seasoning.

The detailed (i.e., low-level) data on borrower and loan are not available in the agency market, so modeling for it has been done at the pool level. The major challenge has been in prepayment forecasting of a TBA security because of no collateral information. This forecasting can be done only for each TBA security by analyzing pool allocation data from a recent offering to assess what attributes are being delivered (see Westhoff and Srinivasan).

Credit-Risk Modeling for ABS. Projecting cash flows for ABS typically requires a projection of the default rate, the timing of defaults, and the recovery rate. In the past five years, a cottage industry has sprung up to perform credit-risk modeling for corporate bonds. The most commonly used approaches involve structural models (an option approach founded on the Black–Scholes–Merton option-pricing model) and reduced-form models.

Default modeling for ABS is in its infancy. Some believe that it is at the same developmental stage that prepayment models were a decade ago. Two reasons have been suggested for the slow development of default models. The first is that for most asset classes, credit enhancement is viewed as sufficient to insulate senior-class holders from credit exposure. The investors that traditionally care about default behavior are buyers of whole loans and buyers/holders of subordinated debt. This characteristic may change, however, as the structured finance market continues to evolve and new products come to market in which the potential buyers of senior classes seek additional assurance that credit enhancement levels will be adequate. The second reason for the slow development of these models is insufficient data to model defaults for many of the asset types that have been securitized. Moreover, a major concern is that some asset types have not gone through a full economic cycle yet so the data do not provide enough information for modeling. With all the innovations in structured finance, many sectors have never faced a full-fledged recession severe enough to challenge structures and loss assumptions.

An example of a product for which little information is available about performance under alternative economic environments is the IO hybrid ARM. By mid-2004, IO hybrid ARMs had garnered the largest share of the nonagency market and surpassed the share of fixed-rate nonagency products (see Goodman 2004). Obviously, a concern with any mortgage design that requires only interest payments is that housing prices may fall, resulting in defaults and low recovery rates because of the lack of amortization. Another concern is that because IO hybrid ARMs originate in the subprime market, their performance will depend on future economic conditions and housing prices. Yet, as of this writing, no data are available to allow a thorough analysis of the credit risk for the largest sector of the residential ABS market.

In addition, only in recent years have the rating agencies been sufficiently comfortable to publish rating-transition (rating-migration) tables for structured products. As with rating-transition tables for corporate bonds, these tables provide information about the likelihood of defaults and rating downgrades. They are also used in the evaluation of CDOs backed by structured products. Again, however, the information covers only limited economic periods.

The rating-transition tables that have recently been published undermine a long-held assumption of participants in the structured finance market that these products have lower historical default rates than equivalently rated corporate bonds. Lucas, Goodman, and Fabozzi (2004) explored the discrepancy between the default rates as reported in the tables calculated by the rating agencies and the rates proposed by market intuition. In their analysis, they discussed the methodological issues that must be considered in interpreting these tables for structured products and suggested the best way to use the tables. The implication of the discrepancy is important, not only for investors in ABS but also for investors in CDOs backed by these assets.

Valuation and the Option-Adjusted Spread. Prior to the introduction of MBS, market participants' exposure to fixed-income products with an embedded option was limited to callable bonds and bonds with optional sinking-fund provisions. The market seemed comfortable handling these products, but the uncertainty of the cash flows of an MBS from prepayments made the MBS investment and dealer communities uncomfortable.[14] The relative-value measure used early in the development of the market was the cash flow yield—the yield that equates the present value of the cash flow (based on some prepayment assumption) to the price. The yield spread was then computed as the difference between the cash flow yield and the yield of a duration-equivalent Treasury security.

The drawback in computing the yield spread for an MBS in this approach is that the yields for neither the MBS nor the Treasury security are properly calculated. The traditional yield calculation fails to take into consideration the term structure of interest rates for Treasuries. Moreover, the analysis is static because it does not recognize that changes in interest rates can change future prepayment rates and thereby change the expected cash flow. That is, the cash flow yield fails to take into account the expected volatility of interest rates.

It became clear to market participants that the yield spread should be viewed as compensation for an option granted to the pool of homeowners. Therefore, in the mid-1980s, proposals to use option-pricing theory to value the borrower's option appeared in the academic literature. Yet, the option in certain structured finance products, such as those backed by mortgage loans, is much more complex than a standard option. Every homeowner in the pool has his or her own strike rate for refinancing, and the option may not be executed efficiently. Consequently, standard option-pricing models are too limited to value the yield spread.

Waldman and Modzelewski (1985) proposed an alternative option-pricing framework for valuing Treasury-based adjustable-rate MBS. They proposed generating interest rate scenarios (paths). The yield spread (which they referred to as the "option-adjusted margin") was calculated as the spread that would make the average theoretical price (i.e., present value of the cash flow on each path) equal to the market price. Subsequently, this methodology was adopted for other MBS products, and this yield spread measure became popularly known as the "option-adjusted spread" (OAS). In a 1990 editorial in the *Financial Analysts Journal*, Toevs presented empirical evidence that this methodology had been accepted by the market to price MBS.

The OAS measures the average spread over interest rate paths generated in a Monte Carlo simulation. The interest rates that were first used were based on Treasury on-the-run securities—that is, the spread relative to a Treasury benchmark. In more recent years, other benchmarks have been used. Most commonly, the benchmark is LIBOR, which is more suitable than Treasuries for relative-value analysis for funded investors.

Using this methodology to obtain the value of an MBS or OAS has problems, however, that too many market participants fail to appreciate. First, the methodology is subject to considerable modeling risk. The inputs to the model include expected interest rate volatility, a prepayment model, the relationship between short-term and long-term rates, the interest rate process, and the speed of mean reversion of interest rates. In the case of nonagency MBS, a default rate and recovery rate must be used as well as a default term structure. These inputs are assumptions that can have material effects on the price or OAS computed, particularly for mortgage derivative products. Too many investors simply rely on the resulting values without examining the assumptions or asking dealers to provide sensitivity analyses. There is no industry standard for models that compute OAS. Consequently, OAS values differ from dealer firm to dealer firm.

Second, the typical OAS model does not incorporate changes in market liquidity. Therefore, these models performed poorly in the spring 1994 debacle in the MBS market. Two MBS with the same OAS may have significant differences in their liquidity that would not be identified by the model.

Third, users of Monte Carlo simulation are seeking information about the probability distribution for some decision variable. The average value is merely one piece of information. When used in MBS valuation, only the average value—the average theoretical price over all the interest rate paths—is used. Thus, information about the distribution of the theoretical values for the interest rate paths is ignored. Yet, this information is quite valuable. For example, consider a well-protected "planned amortization class" (PAC) bond.[15] The standard deviation of the theoretical value for the paths should be concentrated around the average theoretical value. In contrast, for a support bond (a security that absorbs the prepayment risk in a CMO structure that includes a PAC), the standard deviation of the theoretical value for the paths could be large. Ignoring information about the distribution of the theoretical values on the interest rate paths will prevent proper assessment of the tranche's potential OAS relative to the risk.

Finally, assuming a constant OAS over all interest rate paths introduces a theoretical problem. As Babbel and Zenios (1992) demonstrated, an MBS may exhibit different spreads on each interest rate path and may have a spread that varies with time (e.g., the spread will decline as the MBS approaches maturity). Therefore, one OAS number may be inappropriate on theoretical grounds.

In 1995, Kopprasch wrote:

> The rapid acceptance of OAS as an analytical tool is remarkable in light of its complexity. It provides a good example of how a sophisticated model can work its way into the mainstream where its limitations are not completely understood. (p. 637)

Unfortunately, the statement is probably just as valid today as it was a decade ago.

Managing Funds vs. the Agency Pass-Through Sector of a Bond Index. Portfolio managers whose mandate is to outperform a broad-based bond index face the problem of constructing a portfolio that has the desired tracking error vis-à-vis the agency pass-through sector of a bond index. To appreciate the difficulties of simply replicating this sector, portfolio managers need to understand the unique challenges in creating an index to represent it.

In the aggregate, more than half a million pools have been created by Ginnie Mae, Fannie Mae, and Freddie Mac, but the creators of bond indexes do not include all of these pools in the index. Instead, they create composites of these securities, what Lehman Brothers refers to as "index generics," which is consistent with the way agency mortgage pass-throughs trade in the market—that is, on a generic basis. To create index generics, Lehman Brothers, for example, does the following (see Dynkin, Hyman, Konstantinovsky, and Roth 1999). First, securities in the sector are categorized by three characteristics: (1) agency/program (e.g., 30-year Freddie Mac pass-throughs), (2) origination year (vintage) of the underlying mortgages (e.g., 1998), and (3) coupon (e.g., 7.0 percent). Each security is then mapped to an "index generic" according to these characteristics. So, one index generic in this example would be "1998 30-year Freddie Mac 7.0 percent." This process results in more than 3,000 annual aggregates. Based on other criteria, Lehman Brothers uses about 530 annual aggregates for its index generics. Consequently, replicating the agency pass-through sector, unlike replicating indexes in other sectors of a broad-based bond index, requires using traded securities to replicate nontraded aggregates.

Dynkin, Konstantinovsky, and Phelps (2001) of Lehman Brothers' Quantitative Group proposed a replication methodology for dealing with this problem. It involves creating a tradable proxy portfolio consisting of one or more traded MBS that track the index generic. Their empirical tests suggested that the tradable proxy portfolio increases the likelihood of tracking the performance of the mortgage sector. They concluded:

> We believe the results should convince investors with little mortgage market knowledge that they can replicate the MBS index without too much concern about pool selection. (p. 70)

A multifactor risk model has been proposed to control the risks associated with this mortgage sector (see Dynkin and Hyman 2002). In the Lehman Brothers multifactor risk model, for example, the three major risks associated with investing in the agency MBS sector are prepayment risk, sector risk, and convexity risk. Each of these risks is quantified, and the tracking error of the portfolio relative to the mortgage index is a function of the difference in the exposure to each of these risk factors. Using historical return data, an analyst can estimate the *ex ante* tracking error between a portfolio and the mortgage index and can attribute tracking error to each factor.

The tracking of an MBS portfolio for the mortgage sector is critical, so many more strategies should be forthcoming.

Importance of Education and Training

In the early 1980s, although bond trading was on the rise as a result of moves toward active trading and away from a buy-and-hold strategy (the bond market equivalent of passive investing at the time), universities in general viewed the fixed-income area as uninteresting. In investment management courses, the majority of course time was allocated to equity portfolio management and analysis.

Some professors simply skimmed the basic elements of fixed income in one class session: Bond prices move in a direction opposite to the change in interest rates, and non-Treasury bonds have credit risk that is gauged by credit ratings issued by nationally recognized statistical rating organizations. Not until 1987 or so did a few universities offer a course dedicated to fixed-income analysis and portfolio management. Even in these courses, however, the focus was more on technical issues, such as term-structure modeling, interest rate modeling, and pricing interest rate options, than it was on understanding structured products.

Consequently, when structured products were introduced in the bond market, portfolio managers and analysts, effectively, had to get on-the-job training. I would like to focus on two groups of investment professionals who badly need education and training in structured finance—compliance staff and equity analysts.

Compliance Staff. Typically at an asset management firm, the investment guidelines for a client's portfolio set forth the permissible security types that may be purchased and the compliance staff reviews the investments to make sure they fit the guidelines. In the fixed-income area, some of the restrictions can be easily understood. For example, the guidelines might state that the maturity of a security must not exceed a specified number of years or that the issuing company must not have a credit rating below a specified rating. If a bond's credit rating is downgraded to a level below the specified rating, the compliance staff can easily identify a security that may have to be sold.

But some guidelines are quite complex. Consider investment guidelines that forbid the portfolio from containing a CMO support bond, the bond class with the greatest prepayment risk in a structure. The problem the compliance staff faces is that a CMO support bond is not always labeled "support bond." It may be referred to as a "companion bond" (which even sounds like a nicer security than a regular bond!). Even if the language of the investment guidelines is broadened to say "support or companion bonds are not permissible," a bond that is a not a support bond can become a support bond in terms of its investment characteristics. A bond that is labeled a PAC bond may be a support bond in PAC bond clothing. For example, one type of bond is commonly referred to as a "PAC II bond" or a "scheduled bond." Although the word "support" is not in their names, these bonds are simply support bonds that have greater prepayment protection than other support bonds. Is this discussion confusing? That is my point.

Equity Analysts. Equity analysts performing fundamental company analyses must understand structured finance because one of the advantages of securitization is how it can accelerate earnings and, as a result, allow a company to manage earnings growth. The method, which is permitted under GAAP, is best explained with an illustration.

Suppose a company has $200 million in installment sales contracts for the purchase of equipment. For financial reporting purposes, installment sales contracts are not realized as revenue until the installment payments are received. Suppose that the agreement with the buyer of the equipment requires that the buyer pay 8 percent interest a year, and suppose further that the company can sell an ABS backed by the installment sales contracts at a cost of 5 percent (i.e., the average cost of all the ABS tranches is 5 percent) and the servicing fee is 1 percent. The 200 bp spread between the annual interest on the installment sales contract and the annual interest paid to the ABS bondholders is called the "net interest spread" and is a profit to the company that will be realized by the sale of the ABS. It can be booked as income immediately, with the income effectively in the form of an IO strip.

How much income will be realized by the company for financial reporting purposes? Or equivalently, what is the value of the IO strip? The answer is: First, the company must determine the dollar amount of the 200 bps for each year over the expected life of the ABS. Second, this amount must be reduced in each period by the expected losses from defaults and the interest lost from prepayments. Finally, the resulting cash flow must be discounted at an appropriate interest rate to reflect the risks associated with realizing the cash flow. The resulting value is the net income attributable to the securitization.

Obviously, the company has great leeway in determining the net income. If the expected losses and prepayments are underestimated, the net income will be inflated. If the risks associated with generating the cash flow are discounted at too low an interest rate, the net income will be inflated. An equity analyst who does not carefully examine these issues when valuing a financial institution that uses asset securitization can be burned.

In preparing this article, I greatly benefited from discussions with and comments by the following individuals: Mark Adelson, Anand Bhattacharya, Bill Berliner, Howard Chin, Andrew Davidson, Todd Fasnella, Patrick Fitzsimonds, Laurie Goodman, Dennis Kraft, Alexander Levin, John McElravey, Stefania Perrucci, Edward Reardon, Alex Roever, Andrew Samawi, and Tom Zimmerman.

Notes

1. A full discussion of ABS and the MBS (mortgage-backed securities) subset is available as supplemental material for this article in "Overview of Structured Financial Products" at www.cfapubs.org/faj/issues/v61n3/toc.html.
2. Ginnie Mae is the Government National Mortgage Association (GNMA), Fannie Mae is the Federal National Mortgage Association (FNMA), and Freddie Mac is the Federal Home Loan Mortgage Corporation (FHLMC).
3. Stranded costs are the transition costs that occur under deregulation when consumers are able to buy power from a supplier other than their local utility before the utility has had the opportunity to recover the costs it incurred to serve those consumers under traditional regulation.
4. For a primer on asset securitization, see Roever and Fabozzi (2003).
5. The Conseco amount is estimated at about $55 billion, compared with $102 billion for WorldCom and $64 billion for Enron.
6. Investor groups have argued that the initial offering and periodic reporting requirements for the securities are substandard. As a result, in December 2004, the U.S. SEC adopted sweeping changes to the disclosure requirements for ABS. In addition to defining an ABS, the more extensive disclosure included five years of "static pool" information (which reveals how delinquencies, losses, and prepayments develop over the period) and expanded narrative disclosures about the parties to the securitization transaction (i.e., sponsors, originators, servicers, trustees, and administrators).
7. In addition to the issues discussed in this section, the new Basel Accord will have an impact on the market, but it is generally believed that the impact will not be known for a few years.
8. For a more complete discussion, see "Countrywide Securities" (2004).
9. FICO stands for Fair Isaac & Company, an issuer of credit scores.
10. See www.forbes.com/2002/10/30/cz_ew_1030ncfe.html.
11. The trustee represents the interests of the bond classes by monitoring compliance with covenants and, in the event of default, enforcing remedies as specified in the governing documents. For a further discussion of the role of the trustee in a securitization, see Cook and Della Sala (1998).
12. Dollar roll trading is a simultaneous agreement to sell a security held in a portfolio with purchase of a substantially similar security at a future date at an agreed-upon price.
13. In a home equity loan securitization, there is often a mismatch between the floating rate on the underlying loans and the floating rate on the ABS issued. This mismatch results in basis risk, which is also referred to as "available funds cap risk."
14. To see how primitive modeling was in the 1970s, one need only be reminded of the first measure introduced for describing prepayments—the 12-year life assumption. This assumption was based on data from the Federal Housing Administration showing that, historically, on average, homeowners remained in their homes for 12 years. The assumption was that there would be no prepayments for the first 12 years and then all borrowers in the pool would prepay. This model was used even through the early 1980s.
15. A PAC security is structured to have a reasonable life expectancy provided the prepayment speeds stay within the defined ranges. The scheduled interest and principal payments tend to be more stable for these tranches relative to other tranches in a CMO deal.

References

Babbel, David F., and Stavros A. Zenios. 1992. "Pitfalls in the Analysis of Option-Adjusted Spreads." *Financial Analysts Journal*, vol. 48, no. 4 (July/August):65–69.

Bendt, Douglas L., Chuck Ramsey, and Frank J. Fabozzi. 1995. "Prepayment Analysis for Non-Agency Mortgage-Backed Securities." In *Whole Loan CMOs*. Edited by Frank J. Fabozzi, Chuck Ramsey, and Frank R. Ramirez. New Hope, PA: Frank J. Fabozzi Associates.

Cheyette, Oren. 1996. "Implied Prepayments." *Journal of Portfolio Management*, vol. 23, no. 1 (Fall):107–115.

Cook, Karen, and F. Jim Della Sala. 1998. "The Role of the Trustee in Asset-Backed Securities." In *Handbook of Structured Financial Products*. Hoboken, NJ: John Wiley & Sons.

"Countrywide Securities." 2004. *MBS Week* (October 4):7–8.

Davidson, Andrew. 2004. "Saving the TBA." *The Pipeline* (June):1–2.

Dynkin, Lev, and Jay Hyman. 2002. "Multi-Factor Fixed-Income Risk Models and Their Applications." In *The Theory and Practice of Investment Management*. Edited by Frank J. Fabozzi and Harry M. Markowitz. Hoboken, NJ: John Wiley & Sons.

Dynkin, Lev, Vadim Konstantinovsky, and Bruce Phelps. 2001. "Tradable Proxy Portfolios for an MBS Index." *Journal of Fixed Income*, vol. 11, no. 3 (December):70–87.

Dynkin, Lev, Jay Hyman, Vadim Konstantinovsky, and Nancy Roth. 1999. "MBS Index Returns: A Detailed Look." *Journal of Fixed Income*, vol. 8, no. 4 (March):9–23.

Goodman, Laurie. 2004. "Interest-Only ARMs—From Niche to Mainstream." *UBS Mortgage Strategies* (August 17):12–19.

Kopprasch, Robert W. 1995. "A Further Look at Option-Adjusted Spread Analysis." In *The Handbook of Mortgage-Backed Securities*. 4th ed. Edited by Frank J. Fabozzi. Chicago, IL: Probus Publishing.

Lucas, Douglas, Laurie Goodman, and Frank J. Fabozzi. 2004. "A Closer Look at Default Rates on Structured Finance Securities." *Journal of Fixed Income*, vol. 14, no. 2 (September):44–53.

Roever, W. Alexander, and Frank J. Fabozzi. 2003. "Primer on Securitization." *Journal of Structured and Project Finance*, vol. 9, no. 2 (Summer):5–19.

Standard & Poor's. 1999. "Rating Hybrid Securitizations." *Structured Finance* (October).

Sykes, David. 2004. "Assessing the Forecasting Accuracy of Competing Prepayment Models: A Case Study." *Durations*, vol. 1, no. 3 (Summer):2–3.

Toevs, Alden. 1990. "From the Board: Laser Brains Rejoice: Analytical Methods Can Help Shape Market Equilibrium Prices." *Financial Analysts Journal*, vol. 46, no. 6 (November/December):8–10.

Waldman, Michael, and Stephen Modzelewski. 1985. "A Framework for Evaluating Adjustable Rate Mortgages." In *Handbook of Mortgage-Backed Securities*. 1st ed. Edited by Frank J. Fabozzi. Chicago, IL: Probus Publishing.

Westhoff, Dale, and V.S. Srinivasan. Forthcoming 2005. "Agency Prepayment Model: Modeling Dynamics of Borrower Attributes." In *Handbook of Mortgage-Backed Securities*. 6th ed. Edited by Frank J. Fabozzi. New York: McGraw-Hill.

Selected CFA Institute Publications

The following list contains recent publications that relate to the topics discussed in this anthology. For more information on these books, see **www.cfapubs.org**. For information on CFA Institute, please visit the home page at **www.cfainstitute.org**.

RESEARCH FOUNDATION

Corporate Governance and Value Creation
Jean-Paul Page, CFA

Security Analyst Independence
Jennifer Francis, Qi Chen, Donna R. Philbrick, and Richard H. Willis

Conditional Performance Evaluation, Revisited
Wayne E. Ferson and Meijun Qian

Tax-Advantaged Savings Accounts and Tax-Efficient Wealth Accumulation
Stephen M. Horan, CFA

The Dynamics of the Hedge Fund Industry
Andrew W. Lo

CONFERENCE PROCEEDINGS

Dimensions in Private Equity

The New World of Pension Fund Management

The Transition to International Financial Reporting Standards

Challenges and Innovations in Hedge Fund Management

Fixed-Income Tools for Enhancing Returns and Meeting Client Objectives

Analyzing, Researching, and Valuing Equity Investments

CFA INSTITUTE TEXTBOOKS

Analysis of Derivatives for the CFA Program
Don M. Chance, CFA

Quantitative Methods for Investment Analysis
Richard A. DeFusco, CFA, Dennis W. McLeavey, CFA, Jerald E. Pinto, CFA, and David E. Runkle, CFA

Analysis of Equity Investments: Valuation
John D. Stowe, CFA, Thomas R. Robinson, CFA, Jerald E. Pinto, CFA, and Dennis W. McLeavey, CFA

CFA CENTRE FOR FINANCIAL MARKET INTEGRITY

Code of Ethics and Standards of Professional Conduct 2006 edition

Asset Manager Code of Professional Conduct

Global Investment Performance Standards (GIPS®) February 2005 edition